EDGAR F. HUSE
JAMES L. BOWDITCH
Boston College

BEHAVIOR IN ORGANIZATIONS: A SYSTEMS APPROACH TO MANAGING

ADDISON-WESLEY PUBLISHING COMPANY
Reading, Massachusetts
Menlo Park, California • London • Don Mills, Ontario

Cover photograph by Stephen J. Potter via Stock, Boston

ISBN 0-201-02981-2
DEFGHIJKL-MA-7987654

PREFACE

This book is written for those who need to know something about behavior in organizations. It is people—human beings—who make an organization succeed or fail, regardless of the type of organization. The X-ray machines, the lathes, the computers, the welfare programs, the checking accounts, the "signing on" procedures, the planning and organizing that go into making an organization work—all involve people.

Many books place a heavy emphasis on leadership problems and human relations. We discuss these problems, but take a much broader viewpoint. The book, therefore, has two major themes. The first is that an organization is an open behavioral system with a number of interdependent and interrelated subsystems. Each subsystem can be considered as either a system in its own right or a subsystem interacting with other subsystems and/or the total system. We use the systems approach throughout, dealing with the subject in verbal rather than quantitative terms.

The second major theme is the integration of the currently conflicting management theories. We do this by considering three different perspectives of the organization as a system. The first perspective is concerned with the way an organization is designed and builds on current research and practice to demonstrate that there is no one best way to design all organizations. Rather, optimal design depends on a number of factors, including the environment. The second perspective considers the organization as a series of horizontal flows through the organization and deals with the work of the management scientists, operations researchers, and computer-model theorists and practitioners.

The major emphasis in this book is placed on the third perspective—the human aspects of the organization as a system. We examine and discuss human behavior, including motivation, perception and communication, groups and group interaction, leadership and management styles, and change and organizational development.

Although we have placed primary emphasis on the human aspects of behavior in organizations, we feel that human behavior is highly influenced by the design of the organization and the nature and manner of the flows through the organization. As a result, we feel that optimal organizational effectiveness and efficiency cannot be achieved without simultaneously considering all three perspectives of the organization as a total system—structural, flow, and human factors. As a result, several chapters are devoted to the way in which the three different perspectives can be integrated into a total systems approach, including application in a case study. We also look into the future to make some predictions about what the successful organizations of tomorrow may be like, based on the data available today.

The purpose of the book is to provide the reader with both a systems and systematic way of understanding behavior in organizations. The major thrust of this book is to provide the reader with conceptual tools to help him identify, analyze, and reduce organizational problems. Managers and students are not impatient with "theory" as such, but they are impatient with the obvious, vague, and remote statements that are often made with regard to theory in social science. This is not a "how to" book in the sense of providing "off the shelf" answers to specific problems. Rather, we have attempted to provide relevant theory rather than specific techniques. What relevant theory can do is to show how to analyze an organization or a specific organizational problem so that the individual can then make judicious selections of specific techniques. There do exist appropriate techniques for solving specific problems, but the most important problem is to define the goals and the source of the difficulty. Here, relevant theory is essential. Throughout the book, we have attempted to provide concrete illustrations and examples of problems in organizations so that the reader can become more analytic in defining problems and selecting better techniques to solve problems. In addition, the cases, exercises, and the questions at the end of the chapters are designed to help the reader apply what he has learned to real life or to classroom simulations of real life.

Chestnut Hill, Massachusetts E. F. H.
January 1973 J. L. B.

ACKNOWLEDGMENTS

Writing, reviewing, editing, and producing a book is a complex process. Although only two names appear as authors, a number of people made significant contributions to the publication of this book. Since it is impossible to identify all of them by name, we will mention only a few who helped to make this book possible.

A number of reviewers made valuable comments, recommendations, and suggestions about the content, structure, and style of the book. Specifically, we would like to thank the following: Jon H. Barrett (The University of Texas at Austin), Wilmar F. Bernthal (University of Colorado), Frederic Finch (University of Massachusetts), Bernard L. Hinton (Indiana University), Thomas A. Kayser, David A. Kolb (Massachusetts Institute of Technology), Gerald C. Leader (Tulane University), Leon C. Megginson (Louisiana State University), John W. Newstrom (Arizona State University), Walter Nord (Washington University), Benson Rosen (University of North Carolina), Peter B. Vaill, University of Connecticut), and Arthur Walker (Northeastern University).

We would like to thank the following people at Boston College for their helpful comments and suggestions during the prepublication tryouts of the text: Monetta Newman, Donald Goss, Dennis Belisle, Francis Rich, Jr., John Neuhauser, and Alan Thayer. We would like to extend our particular thanks to John W. Lewis III and Dalmar Fisher for contributing to the chapters on organizational development and cases, respectively; to Pearl Alberts, reference librarian, who can find even the most obscure references; to Pamela Redding and Linda Surette, whose cooperation, typing, filing, and other activities were of great help; to Thomas Anderson, our graduate assistant; and to Deans Albert J. Kelley and Christopher J. Flynn, Jr., whose cooperation was of material assistance.

We would also like to express our appreciation to the staff at Addison-Wesley for their help and encouragement in our undertaking. Last, but certainly not least, we extend our thanks and appreciation to our wives, Mary Louise Huse and Felicity Bowditch, whose patience, understanding, encouragement, and occasional harassment made this book possible.

CONTENTS

viii
Contents

9   Selection and Training

**PART IV   A SYSTEMS APPROACH TO ORGANIZATIONAL
IMPROVEMENT**

10   Organizational Improvement—Perspective I

11   Organizational Improvement—Perspective II

12   Organizational Development—Perspective III

Appendixes: Case Studies

INTRODUCTION

For those who like this kind of a book,
This is the kind of a book they will like.

ABRAHAM LINCOLN

This is a book about organizations and the people in them. Examining an organization from three different perspectives, or viewpoints (explained in more detail in Chapter 2), we look at the interaction of individuals, groups, managers, and the organization as a whole. We consider social organizations in contact with their environment, including the impact of new technologies and knowledge on organizations and the way they operate. For example, in the future, hospitals, as organizations, will be run much differently from the way they are today. Similarly, the appearance and activities of tomorrow's business organization may well be quite different from what they are at present.

Thus, this book is not only about organizations and the people in them, but also about the impact of rapidly accelerating change—on individuals, organizations, and the culture within which both exist—and how to deal effectively with change. Our purpose is to help you become more effective as an individual in coping with organization life—both today and in the future. Why is this important? It is important simply because so much of our waking time is spent in contact with various organizations. Most of us were born in an organization— a hospital. As students, we have contact with educational organizations. As citizens, we are affected by municipal and state governments. As participants, we belong to such formal or informal organizations as the Little League, Boy Scouts, Sierra Club, local bowling club, high school "group," college fraternity, and bridge or poker clubs. As adults, we hold jobs in organizations—law firms, dental clinics, travel bureaus, universities, or industrial companies. Generally, at least eight hours a day will be spent in such formal organizations. After work we may spend a great deal of time in clubs, political activities, or social events. Even when we watch television or drive down a street, we are involved with, or affected by, organizations, e.g., stopping for a traffic light is a consequence of an organizational decision. In other words, organizations are ubiquitous and cannot be avoided. Therefore, an understanding of organizations, behavior in organizations, and change and its consequences is helpful to everyone.

Our *point* is that in this culture, we are continuously in contact and interaction with organizations. Our *emphasis and thrust* is primarily on work organizations, and it is our *belief* that organizations in the future will change even more rapidly than they have in the past. Our *concern* is that you understand such change and become adept at dealing with and controlling change, especially on the job.

The book is divided into five parts. Part I is concerned principally with two issues. First, how did we get to where we are today? (Exhibit 1 shows one example of how far we have already come.) Second, how do we deal with the complexities and interrelationships of modern organizational life? We are so accustomed to thinking about events in simple cause-and-effect terms that

Rules To Employees
CARSON, PIRIE, SCOTT Co., CHICAGO ∼ 1856

1. Store must be open from 6 a.m. to 9 p.m.

2. Store must be swept, counters and base shelves dusted, lamps trimmed filled and chimneys cleaned, a pail of water, also a bucket of coal brought in before breakfast, and attend to customers who will call.

3. Store must not be open on the Sabbath Day unless necessary and then only for a few minutes.

4. The employee, who is in the habit of smoking Spanish cigars, being shaved at the barber shop, going to dances and other places of amusement, will surely give his employer reason to be suspicious of his honesty and integrity.

5. Each employee must not pay less than $5 per year to the church and must attend Sunday School regularly.

6. Men employees are given one evening a week for courting and two if they go to prayer meeting.

7. After 14 hours of work in the store, the leisure time should be spent mostly in reading.

Signed: THE MANAGEMENT

Exhibit 1. *Work rules at Carson Pirie Scott & Co., 1882.*

frequently we do not explore the complexities of situations. By using a systems approach, however, and examining the variety of factors that make a situation or organization complex, we can see a host of variables that influence or "cause" a given effect. For example, we frequently see a simple "cause" to an automobile accident without stopping to consider that we need to have cars, roads, and drivers before an accident can even occur, not to mention such additional factors as speed, road conditions, and the road-worthiness of the car.

In Part II we discuss the things which affect the individual, the group and more specifically, the manager and other leaders in the organization. Most of us, without thinking about it too much, would probably say that money motivates people in a working situation. But of course there are other influences as well, and we look at the conditions under which these other factors also motivate people. Here, we consider the psychology of perception—particularly social perception—which is critical to our behavior and communication patterns. The section on leadership is divided into two parts. First, we describe the research in the area of leadership and influence. We then examine the role of the manager —not just what he "should" be doing, but also what he actually spends his time doing.

All too frequently, people assume that the goals and control systems of an organization have already been defined and put into effect. In Part III we make explicit the various methods for establishing organizational goals and appraising work performance. The other two issues which we cover are personnel selection and individual training, including selection through psychological testing and the psychological research in learning. We also outline techniques by which the effectiveness of both selection and training can be evaluated, for with the emergence of such concerns as minority hiring, women's liberation, and early retirement, the issue of how people are picked to join an organization is becoming more and more important.

In Part IV we present three models for improving an organization. To attain optimal effectiveness in an organization, one needs to be aware of organizational structure, information and material flow, and the human component. We look at the organization from each of these perspectives, ending with a discussion of the integration of these three factors and a recent case study of this integrative approach to organizational improvement.

In Part V we speculate on the organization of the future and summarize the major concepts presented in the book. You may find it helpful to quickly read this part first so that you will have a better understanding of where this book will take you.

Before going on we would like to share with you some of our thoughts about the term "theory," since we will be dealing with theories throughout the book. Building a theory occurs in much the same way as did the early settlement of this country. A small clearing was hacked out of the forest by a pioneer. Other pioneers made their own clearings and built their separate cabins. Later, when cabins were closer together, footpaths began to emerge and eventually became roads.

The evolution of management thought has occurred in much the same fashion. In one part of the "forest" someone developed a "clearing" (theory), while someone else was developing another theory, quite independently. Now, the theories are interconnected by conceptual pathways and roads. Yet theories of organizational behavior and administrative science are continually being revised and modified, just as the Apollo missions have caused us to revise our theories of the moon, based on landings (clearings) scattered across the face of the moon. Throughout the text, we will show how these new developments are occurring, together with their links to the past.

PART I
HISTORY
AND
SYSTEMS
APPROACH
TO
MANAGEMENT

1
HISTORY
AND
OVERVIEW
OF
PERSPECTIVES
IN
MANAGEMENT

History is bunk.

HENRY FORD

I. INTRODUCTION

Ever since man first divided the functions of labor so that certain people tended the fields while others hunted, there have been management problems. Work organization, the basic thrust of this book, has been a problem for centuries. As an orientation, we shall briefly review the history of various schools of management—how they emerged and developed and in what context they were practiced. Since each perspective of management grew out of a hospitable cultural context, we must keep in mind that what may now appear to be a naive procedure may at another time have been a useful solution to a perceived problem.

The first perspective discussed is the structural-design perspective. The theories and schools of management in this category are concerned with such issues as how organizations should be internally structured, what functions should be grouped together, who should boss whom, and what style of management should be used. As you might expect, much of this thinking is deductively prescribed by "experts" and is authoritarian. Thus, it is no surprise that the principles derived from this perspective originated in the management of the military and the Roman Catholic church.

Perspective II deals with information processing and flow, operations research, and computer simulation—how information gets to the various depart-

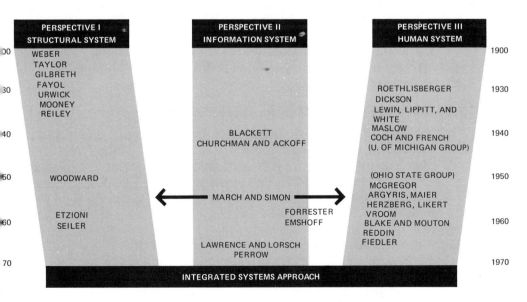

Figure 1.1. *Key names in management theory.*

ments of organizations so that intelligent decisions about production, marketing, types of servicing, and financing can be made. We examine the origins of this approach, namely, attempts to improve both the Royal Air Force's "hit" rate on German submarines in World War II and the usage of antiaircraft weapons together with radar. The principles and concepts of this perspective stem from research in real management problems and hypothetical computer problems.

The data and theories of the human perspective, Perspective III, have come about through research dealing with human and social concerns. This sociological and/or psychological view of management and the organization resulted from research in the late 1920s which indicated that the work group is an important variable in the process of effective management.

Figure 1.1 shows some of the key names in management thought in relation to the various historical trends. Much of the Perspective I work was completed by the 1930s, some as far back as 1910. Perspective II research gained momentum in the 1940s. Perspective III studies were first conducted before the 1930 depression, but it was only after World War II that this approach became a serious concern within management circles.

II. PERSPECTIVE I—THE STRUCTURAL-DESIGN VIEW OF MANAGEMENT

Within this perspective there are three different historical views of management, each of which has its slightly modified counterpart today. These three views do not exhaust the Perspective I schools; instead, they are simply representative of the kind of thinking which made up the school. These three schools are the universal principles of management school, the structuralist school, and the scientific management school.

A. Universal Principles of Management School

The principles of management regarded as the foundation of this perspective (listed in Table 1.1) were seen as common to state, church, military, and industrial organizations. Mooney and Reiley depict the efficiency of the Roman Catholic church and the military and their management of people.[1] They trace the history of management from the government of ancient Greece to recent industrial organizations. More than half the book gives the historical background and principles upon which they believe all management depends. Taking an authoritarian, one-best-way approach to all problems, these theorists treat workers as extensions of machines and derive their principles from a logical approach. However, this one-best-way (authoritarian) approach has been modified to conform with the data collected from more recent studies showing the value of participative management under certain conditions.

Table 1.1 A brief outline of Fayol's principles of management

1. Division of work—the specialization of workers, including management, to improve efficiency and increase output.
2. Authority and responsibility—"the right to give orders, and power to exact obedience" (p.21). Responsibility occurs as a direct result of authority.
3. Discipline—in essence, "obedience, application, energy, behavior"(p.22) given to the organization, and it depends on the worthiness of the leaders.
4. Unity of command—the principle that no one should have more than one boss.
5. Unity of direction—specifies that in addition to having only one boss, there should be only one plan for accomplishing goals (related to 4).
6. Subordination of individual interest to general interest—the organization's concerns should be placed ahead of individual concerns.
7. Remuneration (pay) of personnel—specifies fair pay arrangements, satisfactory to all, whereby competence is rewarded, but not overrewarded.
8. Centralization—consolidation of the management function should be done according to the circumstances surrounding the organization.
9. Scalar chain—the chain of command which can sometimes have several tracks. Persons at parallel levels down the tracks may be authorized to solve problems with the superior's knowledge.
10. Order—the principle that everyone has a position and should operate from only that position; similarly, all materials should have, and be in, a certain place.
11. Equity—loyalty should be encouraged by kindliness and justice, but does not exclude sternness and forcefulness when needed.
12. Stability of tenure of personnel—high turnover of personnel both causes and is the result of inefficiency; better organizations have stable managerial personnel.
13. Initiative—the necessity for "thinking out a plan and ensuring its success" (p.39). Fayol sees this as a strength for businesses, particularly during hard times.
14. Esprit de corps—morale and team feeling are enhanced by keeping teams together and having good face-to-face communication.

Adapted from H. Fayol, *General and Industrial Management,* trans. C. Storrs (London: Sir Isaac Pitman and Sons, 1949).

B. Structuralist School

The German sociologist Max Weber, one of the founders of the structuralist school, distinguishes between illegitimate and legitimate power.[2] According to Weber, the exercise of raw, illegitimate power alienates the worker; the exercise of legitimate power, on the other hand, conforms with worker norms, and as a result the worker internalizes the rules.

To many, bureaucracy is synonymous with long, slow-moving lines. (Photograph courtesy Stock, Boston)

In the Weber framework, this use of legitimate power is called authority. Weber distinguishes between traditional authority, which is based on past ways of doing things, and bureaucratic (rational-legal) authority, which is based on rules considered legitimate by those coming in contact with it. Weber's final classification is charismatic authority, which results from the superior's magnetic personality.

Weber characterized bureaucratic structure as:

1. an organization with continuity which operates according to rules

2. an area, or domain, of competence in which the persons involved share the work toward specified goals under predetermined leaders

3. an organization with scalar (hierarchical) principles

4. an organization with rules which are either norms or technical rules

5. an organization in which administrative staff is separated from ownership of production devices or administration, and private belongings and the organization's equipment are separated

6. an organization whose resources are free of outside control, and in which no administrator can monopolize personnel positions

7. an organization in which any administrative acts, rules, policies, etc., must be stated in writing.

Weber also said that worker loyalty could be ensured by having the organization, rather than its clients, pay their wages. Promotions and organizational career planning would also help to increase loyalty. Finally, Weber saw the need for continued protection of the bureaucratic organization.

As Weber points out, the head of a bureaucratic organization is not necessarily appointed to his position. Rather, he might have been elected or have inherited the job.

In examining Weber's model, Etzioni notes that many organizations have mixed modes of authority—partly traditional, charismatic, and bureaucratic.[3] In short, a pure bureaucracy is hard to find; moreover, it may not remain "pure" for long.

The important feature to remember about Max Weber is that he gives a description of what *is*, not what *should* be. From this standpoint, then, the comparative analysis of organizations (to look for common characteristics) is primarily what distinguishes the structuralists from other early groups of prescriptive theorists, even though both arrived at many of the same conclusions.

C. Scientific Management School

The scientific management school emphasizes the measurement of work rather than the nature of the organization or its principles of organization. Nevertheless, this school had a major effect on the ways in which tasks were combined into jobs and organizations were put together. As in the other two schools of thought, the scientific management theorists assumed that man is machine-like —that his feelings, personality, and work group are relatively unimportant. This seems quite naive today, but at the time, operating under these assumptions was effective, given the largely immigrant labor force and the large number of tasks requiring only unskilled labor.

Frederick W. Taylor was the founder of this school.[4] His best-known work was done in determining how much pig iron a laborer should be able to carry between two points. By studying workers' bodily motions and the time required to complete them, Taylor concluded that a laborer could carry 47.5 rather than

Mass production in an automobile assembly plant about 1913. (Photograph courtesy Ford Motor Company)

12-15 long tons per day if he took lighter loads each time and had scheduled rest periods. Taylor also developed different shovels to provide a 21-pound load for any given kind of material, the optimal amount for long-term work. Formerly, steel workers had been using the same shovel for rice coal and the heavier iron ore. It is important to stress that although Taylor was interested in the application of science and the search for the one best way, he also assumed a commonality of interest between workers and management. This latter concern, however, was largely ignored by the "efficiency experts" of the 1930s and later.

One of Taylor's associates, Frank Gilbreth, continued to develop time-and-motion studies for industry showing the most efficient physical motions for accomplishing particular tasks. Again, the emphasis was on man as an extension of a machine. Another of Taylor's associates, Henry L. Gantt, devised an industrial control system, the Gantt chart, which is still used in the United States and elsewhere. Time-and-motion studies continue to this day, as inputs into job design.

Since it focuses on the components of task performance rather than on broad principles of management theory, scientific management is more inductive and data-based than the universals of management school and therefore does not fit entirely within the Perspective I category. Nor does it explicitly identify a systems approach to work as does Perspective II.

Recent Additions to Perspective I

Since the late 1940s there have been studies which, though structural in nature, indirectly make some assumptions about humans at work, namely, that they do not have to be watched at all times. An example of this is Worthy's span-of-control study, which indicated that a supervisor could in fact oversee many more workers than had previously been thought possible.[5] Therefore, the number of management levels and workers in an organization could be reduced, producing a "flatter" organization with fewer gradations of management and workers. Worthy's findings were later challenged by Porter and Lawler as not being very rigorous research.[6]

One curious feature about the more recent research is that although it is still concerned with the structure of an organization, it takes a Weberian approach, attempting to discover what actual organizations are like as opposed to what they should be like. Nevertheless, much of the recent research still implies that there is *one best way* to organize. Likert's "linking-pin theory," for example, which structurally specifies that the leader of a subordinate work group is a linking pin with a superior group in organizational level, illustrates the structural, one-best-way theory.[7]

A second interesting feature about the more recent research is that much of it approaches organizational structure comparatively. Woodward, for example, notes that organizational structure varies with the nature of the industry.[8] Thus, industries with continuous-process production (e.g., detergents, oil refining) have vertical structures (many levels of management and workers), whereas industries with unit-production (e.g., locomotives) have horizontal structures (few levels of management and workers).

Some of the most recent research, by Lawrence and Lorsch, for example, is even more concerned with organizational structure.[9] However, it does not ignore the human component, and it admits the possibility that perhaps organizational structure should be *situationally* determined, depending on such variables as the rate of technological advance in the given industry. Their research is of further interest because in order to arrive at their principles, they had to empirically examine successful and unsuccessful organizations in different industries to determine the most successful structure for a given industry.

Perrow has taken the work of such researchers as Woodward, Lawrence and Lorsch, and others and considerably expanded upon it in stressing the need for a proper "fit" between the organization and the environment.[10] Perrow believes that the proper design and management of organizational structure is the key to changing both human behavior within the organization and organizational competency. He developed an elaborate, fourfold typology of organizations— craft, nonroutine, engineering, and routine—and concluded that each type of organization needs to be designed differently. He points out that it is essential to carefully analyze technology and structure in light of the organizational environment—that a style of management which is successful in one situation may well be dysfunctional in another situation unless it is considerably modified.

III. PERSPECTIVE II—WORK FLOW

The management theories in this category are concerned primarily with information flow, which has been synonymous with "mathematically quantifiable" because of its close association with computer usage and simulation. Perspective II theories developed from operations research during World War II, but as new approaches to management emerged from these beginnings, the boundaries of Perspective II theories have become blurred, just as they did with Perspective I theories.

A. Operations Research

As was true for most of the other schools of management thought, operations research (OR) came into being to fulfill specific organizational needs. Initially, OR was considered an integration of the behavioral, social, and physical sciences. However, since mathematicians predominate in the area, OR has not lived up to its original idea. As Churchman notes, the earliest use of OR, the "*systems* or *overall* approach to problems," was to bring about an organized approach to military strategy.[11] In her chapter on the history of OR, Trefethen indicates that its roots may be found as far back as the third century B.C., when the King of Syracuse asked the mathematician-philosopher Archimedes to create a way for him to break the Roman siege of his city.[12]

In World War I there were attempts at mathematical analysis of military operations, and by World War II there were organizations with the title "operational research" in Great Britain. OR was slower to take hold in the United

Highly sophisticated computers rapidly process vast quantities of information. (Photograph courtesy IBM)

States, but by the early 1950s it had become established, and since then it has been increasingly influential.

One of the early problems solved by OR specialists during World War II was to determine how to allocate reconnaisance aircraft to detect enemy ship convoys. By figuring out the patterns and speeds of enemy ships and the ability of aircraft to cover a given amount of space in a certain time, Allied commanders were able to significantly reduce the number of reconnaisance aircraft and to increase the effectiveness of their surveillance of enemy sea routes.

One of the distinguishing chararcteristics of OR is its use of a mathematical model to systematize the particular problem, thus allowing for an optimum solution to any given situation. Another unique characteristic is that individual differences in *performance* between men or groups in various situations are usually excluded from the model, although their *capabilities* are taken into account.

Churchman takes a systems approach within a framework of easily quantifiable factors to describe the phases of OR:

1. formulating the problem
2. constructing a mathematical model to represent the system under study
3. deriving a solution from the model
4. testing the model and the solution derived from it
5. establishing controls over the solution
6. putting the solution to work—implementation.[13]

The overall approach is to take account of as many variables as possible, so that the result should be reasonable, workable alternative courses of action. The basic form of the model is that the effectiveness of the system (E) is a function of those variables (x) which are subject to control and those variables (y) which are not subject to control. The solution which is derived may be either deductive (analytic) or inductive (numerical). Since no model is anything more than a "representation of reality," controls or guidelines to the solution must be set before the model can be tried out. If any of the variables vary beyond certain prescribed limits, a new model or new relationship will have to be determined. Finally, the solution is attempted. Should some significant new and different variables appear, a new solution must be found.

Newer Considerations. A more recent mathematical model, closely linked to operations research, is Forrester's "system dynamics," an attempt to describe the interaction of an organization's behavior and the external environment.[14] Forrester develops methods for organizational improvement by taking account of six "quantifiable" subsystems in his model: (1) orders (from buyers), (2) materials (raw and premanufactured), (3) money, (4) personnel, (5) capital equipment, all of which are interconnected by (6) information flow. This relatively small number of variables is considered by some to be an oversimplified view of reality. In addition, the large amounts of data that are "plugged" in to the model require large computing facilities, thus making it difficult to use.

Another, more recent contributor to this area is Emshoff, who in a very lucid fashion distinguishes between behavioral (human) and mechanistic (nonhuman) problems.[15] Emshoff differentiates between an *output* and an *input* model representing reality. The output model uses empirical data which do not include causal and other antecedent factors in behavior. One example of output data for humans might be that the elderly tend to die before the young. This is a mechanistic factor requiring little understanding of human life. On the other hand, if some effort were made to determine whether blacks, whites, or orientals die earlier, it would help to have input data such as diet, sanitation, work habits, etc., or *antecedent* variables perhaps causally related to death. Emshoff states in effect that input-oriented rather than output-oriented research is needed for behavioral systems.

A final approach which has been gaining use recently is the management information systems approach which, with the help of computers, speeds information across the organization so that orders can be filled rapidly, production can be scheduled, purchasing requirements can be forecasted, customers can be billed, etc. Diebold notes that in order for this system to be effective, the traditional departments in organizations must be less compartmentalized within the organization.[16]

Clearly, the newer Perspective II theorists are aware of the importance of the human component. The fact that both Emshoff and Forrester are concerned with the human variable is an indication of its recognition by the quantitatively oriented theorists.

IV. PERSPECTIVE III—THE HUMAN PERSPECTIVE

This section is concerned with management theories which are oriented toward the work group and human perspective. Forerunners of this viewpoint were Alfred Binet, who in his early work attempted to test for individual differences in intelligence, and Hugo Munsterberg, who set up training programs for persons running trolley cars. Yet there was another factor which had even more impact, namely, the effect of the work group on organizational goals. Only then was the importance of the worker's needs, desires, and feelings recognized.

A. Human Relations School

The human relations school in management resulted from looking at the effects of light intensity on production efficiency. In 1924 the Western Electric Company in connection with the National Research Council of the National Academy of Sciences set out to examine this relationship. When no consistent relationship was found between light intensity and work efficiency, a group of behavioral scientists, including Elton Mayo and Fritz Roethlisberger of the Harvard Business School, started their work at the Hawthorne plant of Western Electric Company.[17] As part of the overall package of studies, a group of female relay assemblers was set apart from the others and observed very closely. The illumination in their work area was varied from moderate intensity to that similar to bright sunlight and then darker, to the level of a full moon. Each time the intensity was changed, the production rate went up until it was physically impossible to see. The workers knew that the researchers were interested in their performance, but did not really think about the implications of the differing levels of illumination. They were in a "goldfish bowl" and performed accordingly. This highly reactive measurement produced the *Hawthorne effect,* which describes the increased performance resulting from the workers' knowledge that they were being observed with interest, treated as important, and that their inputs were being taken into consideration.

At this point worker attitudes, morale, and group effects became interesting to researchers. This led to interest in supervisory styles and a reaction away from classical, prescriptive management thought. (This interest in supervisory styles and the relationship between morale and productivity will be taken up in more detail later.) The post-World War II studies done at the University of Michigan and Ohio State University indicated that "people oriented" leadership was more effective than "production oriented" leadership.[18] From this school emanated human relations training, which was designed to make "nice guys" out of foremen who heretofore had been trained to be authoritarian and strict. Inasmuch as the reinforcement structure of the work situation was not changed, however, foremen coming back from human relations training, or "charm school," were ridiculed to such an extent that it did not take long for them to fall back into their old behavioral patterns and leadership styles. In some circles human relations has been described as "warm feeling" training and consists primarily of company picnics, getting the wives together, and company-sponsored athletics. But this is a distortion of the research findings provided by the original human-relations studies.

Closely related to the human relations school, but with one very important difference, is work which has attempted to integrate interpersonal and intergroup relationships with systems theory. In their book *Organizations,* written in the late 1950s, March and Simon put the available human research into systems terms.[19] The interesting feature about this work is that its essentially Perspective III data are put into a Perspective II methodological framework.

B. Organizational Development School

The origin of the organizational development school of theorists is difficult to pinpoint, since it is really an extension of the human relations school. Perhaps as much as anyone, Kurt Lewin and his associates, and Coch and French are regarded as the founding fathers of the organizational development school. In a post-World War II study entitled "Overcoming Resistance to Change," Coch and French show that when the workers in a pajama factory helped plan production changes, the "lag time" for production to return to a normal rate was far less than when the changes were imposed on the workers by an authoritarian management style.[20]

Just prior to World War II, Lippitt and White (1939) found that the leadership style in children's clubs affects the group process and output.[21] Children in groups with authoritarian leaders produced more articles but of lower quality than did the groups led by democratic leaders. In addition, the authoritarian groups fell apart when the leader left the room, whereas the democratic groups continued to produce. As might be expected, satisfaction was higher in the democratic groups. The third style of group leadership, *laissez-faire* ("to leave alone"), was less successful on all counts than was either of the other two kinds of groups. This group of studies is relevant here because it focuses on problems with which the researchers have continued to be concerned—effectiveness within groups.

In 1946 Lewin and his associates met to develop action frameworks in social psychology. Out of this came the forerunner of sensitivity training, or T-groups. Many T-groups are agendaless meetings lasting one day to two weeks or longer and are designed to make the participants more aware of their personal strengths and weaknesses, how they communicate to others, and how to change their behavior (Chapter 12). At this point, we can say that this technique and its variations have become a standard tool of organizational development practitioners.

Since the early stages of organizational development, many other techniques have come to the forefront as methods and devices specifically designed or adapted for use in organizations. These will be considered in detail in Chapter 12, "Organizational Development—Perspective III."

C. The Multidimensional Theorists

Although several of the issues inherent in the human aspect of organizations started off as a single dimension, theorists began to think of concepts and practices in multidimensional terms as time and research continued. Perhaps the first to do this was Herzberg, who conceived of motivation as comprising two dimensions.[22] Prior to Herzberg, motivation had been considered as a stepped continuum; Maslow, for example, felt that people will not try to satisfy higher needs until lower-order, more basic needs have been fulfilled.[23] What made Herzberg's formulation interesting was that the two dimensions of motivation were not highly connected. Herzberg found that when some contextual aspects of jobs, such as working conditions and supervision, are favorable, there will be neither satisfaction nor dissatisfaction. Similarly, when some content aspects of jobs, such as amount of responsibility and the nature of the work itself, are favorable, there will be satisfaction.

Another of the multidimensional theorists is Robert Blake.[24] Instead of being directly concerned with motivation, he is more interested in a style of management which leads to an optimally efficient organization. The two dimensions he uses are (management's) concern for people, and concern for production. Basing his theory in part on some of the Ohio State leadership studies, he and his associates felt that no organization will be optimally efficient unless it is totally concerned with *both* people and production. Thus, although he is a multidimensional theorist, he also implies that there is one best way to solve problems.

A third multidimensional theorist is Fred Fiedler. His leadership-style theory, based on over 20 studies, identifies three dimensions—position power of the leader (strong or weak), leader-member relationships (favorable or unfavorable), and the definition of the job (clearly or vaguely defined).[25] Fiedler suggests that in very favorable or unfavorable work situations, the leader should adopt an authoritarian style of leadership; in intermediate work situations (neither very favorable or unfavorable), the leader should adopt a democratic style of leadership.

Finally, there are Lawrence and Lorsch, who suggest that one look at the structural differentiation and structural integration of an organization in its particular environment.[26] Certain organizational functions, e.g., marketing, production, research and development, should be more or less closely tied in with one another. However, the relative independence of these operations should vary, depending on the nature of the industry and the environment.

Multidimensional approaches are here to stay. Coupled with a situational approach to organizational design, leadership style and organizational development appear to be the current direction for the study of organizations. In contrast to the one-best-way approach, examining each situation to determine the most appropriate direction allows much more flexibility in the study and development of organizations.

SUMMARY

In this chapter, we have not attempted to give a complete history of the various schools of management. Rather, we focused on distinctions which will continue through the book. The universals of management theorists, the scientific management proponents, and the structuralists all fall into the Perspective I group. The operations researchers and management scientists represent the beginnings of Perspective II. Finally, the human relations group and the organizational development theorists are within the framework and concern of Perspective III. Although in later chapters we will attempt to bridge these distinct systems, at present it will be helpful to maintain these distinctions and their antecedents.

REVIEW

1. What are the differences and similarities between the universal principles of management school and the structuralist school? How appropriate are these schools currently?

2. Operations research attempts to solve a problem by putting all dimensions of an organizational situation into quantifiable terms. How does this differ from the approaches used by those allied with Perspective III?

3. What influence does the "Hawthorne effect" have on Perspective I management approaches?

4. "Those who do not understand history are doomed to repeat it." What does this mean in the context of the evolution of management thought?

Critical Concepts

Perspective I
Perspective II
Perspective III
Universal principles of management school
Structuralists
Scientific management
Bureaucracy
Time-and-motion study
Operations research
Human relations school
Organizational development school
Styles of leadership:
    authoritarian
    democratic
    laissez-faire
T-group
Hawthorne effect

REFERENCES

1 J. D. Mooney and A. C. Reiley, *The Principles of Organization,* rev. ed. (New York: Harper and Brothers, 1947).

2 M. Weber, *The Theory of Social and Economic Organization,* trans. A. M. Henderson and T. Parsons, ed. T. Parsons (New York: Oxford University Press, 1947).

3 A. Etzioni, *Modern Organizations* (Englewood Cliffs, N.J.: Prentice-Hall, 1964).

4 F. W. Taylor, *Scientific Management* (New York: Harper & Row, 1911).

5 J. V. Worthy, "Organizational Structure and Employee Morale," *American Sociological Review,* 15, 2, (April 1950): 169–179.

6 L. W. Porter and E. E. Lawlor, "Properties of Organization Structure in Relation to Job Attitudes and Job Behavior," *Psychological Bulletin,* 64, 1, (1965): 21–51.

7 R. Likert, *New Patterns of Management* (New York: McGraw-Hill, 1961).

8 J. Woodward, *Management and Technology* (London: Her Majesty's Printing Office, 1958).

9 P. Lawrence and J. W. Lorsch, *Organization and Environment: Managing Differentiation and Integration* (Boston: Harvard University Graduate School of Business Administration, Division of Research, 1967).

10 C. Perrow, *Organizational Analysis: A Sociological View* (Belmont, Cal.: Wadsworth, 1970).

11 C. W. Churchman, R. L. Ackoff, and E. L. Arnoff, *Introduction to Operations Research* (New York: John Wiley, 1957).

12 F. N. Trefethen, "A History of Operations Research," in *Operations Research for Management,* ed. J. F. McCloskey and F. N. Trefethan (Baltimore: Johns Hopkins Press, 1954).

13 C. W. Churchman, R. L. Ackoff, and E. L. Arnoff, *op. cit.,* p. 13.

14 J. W. Forrester, "Counterintuitive Behavior of Social Systems," *Technology Review,* 73, 3, (Jan. 1971) Alumni Association of the Massachusetts Institute of Technology, pp. 52–68.

15 J. R. Emshoff, *Analysis of Behavioral Systems* (New York: Macmillan, 1971).

16 J. Diebold, "ADP—the Still-sleeping Giant," *Harvard Business Review,* 42, 5, (Sept.–Oct. 1964): 60–65.

17 F. J. Roethlisberger and W. J. Dickson, *Management and the Worker—an Account of a Research Program Conducted by the Western Electric Co., Hawthorne Works, Chicago* (Cambridge, Mass.: Harvard University Press, 1939).

18 E. A. Fleishman, E. F. Harris, and R. D. Burtt, "Leadership and Supervision in Industry," *Ohio State Business Education Reserve Monograph,* 33, (1955).

19 J. G. March and H. A. Simon, *Organizations* (New York: John Wiley, 1958).

20 L. Coch and J. R. P. French, "Overcoming Resistance to Change," *Human Relations,* I (1948):512–532.

21 R. Lippitt and R. K. White, "An Experimental Study of Leadership and Group Life," in *Readings in Social Psychology,* ed. T. M. Newcomb and E. L. Hartley (New York: Holt, Rinehart and Winston, 1947).

22 F. P. Herzberg, B. Mausner, and B. Snyderman, *The Motivation to Work,* 2d ed. (New York: John Wiley, 1959).

23 A. H. Maslow, *Motivation and Personality* (New York: Harper and Brothers, 1954).

24 R. R. Blake and J. S. Mouton, *The Managerial Grid* (Houston, Texas: Gulf, 1964).

25 F. Fiedler, *A Theory of Leadership Effectiveness* (New York: McGraw-Hill, 1967).

26 P. R. Lawrence and J. W. Lorsch, *op. cit.*

2
THE
ORGANIZATION
AS
A
SYSTEM

For want of a nail the shoe is lost,
For want of a shoe the horse is lost,
For want of a horse the rider is lost.

GEORGE HERBERT

A car ("total system") will not operate properly unless all of its subsystems are in good working order. (Photograph by Edgar F. Huse)

I. INTRODUCTION

If you step on my toe, you hurt *me*. If the battery is dead, the car won't start. If the electric power goes off, the furnace doesn't operate. If the planes are grounded in Airport X, the passenger may not make his scheduled flight from Airport Y. When a circuit breaker malfunctioned on Apollo 13, an oxygen tank blew up, and the entire mission was aborted, barely making it back home.

All of these examples show the interrelationships among the parts in a system. The concept of a "system"—the interstate highway system or the educational system—is one with which we are all familiar. In this chapter, we describe the modern social organization in systems terms. Bakke defines an organization as a continuing system which is able to differentiate and integrate human activities which utilize, transform, and weld together a set of human, material, and other resources into a problem-solving whole.[1] The function of the organization is to satisfy particular human needs in interaction with other subsystems of human activities and resources in its particular environment.

We then consider the organization as a social "system" with interdependent and interrelated parts. Such a system is continually changing, dynamic, but yet usually manages to achieve an internal "balance" as it interacts with itself as well as with its environment. Finally, we present three different perspectives of social organizations to help you gain a better understanding of how organizations can be improved and made more effective while, at the same time, allowing the individuals within the organization to better reach their own personal goals and objectives.

II. TYPES OF SYSTEMS

Although sociologists have long been familiar with the term "systems," it has become really fashionable only since the advent of the computer. The basic concept was well described in the 1930s by Henderson, who pointed out that "the interdependence of the variables in a system is one of the widest inductions (inferences) from experience that we possess; or we may alternatively regard it as the definition of a system."[2] At this stage, we can define a system as a series of interrelated and interdependent parts, such that the interaction or interplay of any of the subsystems (parts) affects the whole. In fact, if we use the systems approach, the interactions and interdependencies among the subsystems are at least as important as the individual components. For example, the automobile is a total system, consisting of a number of subsystems—ignition, fuel, steering, engine, and drive-train. If all the subsystems are working well, so does the car. But if one of the subsystems malfunctions, it affects the performance of the entire system, the car.

Boulding has pointed out that there are at least nine different levels of systems, ranging from static structures (the simplest) to cybernetic structures (such as a thermostat) to human and social systems (the most complex). Each succeeding level is more complex and more difficult to conceptualize (Table 2.1). These nine levels of systems are arranged in ascending order of both complexity and openness to change and modification from the outside. The higher the level, the more likely the system is to be influenced and affected by events or phenomena outside the system.

Boulding believes that these nine levels serve a useful function by indicating where there are serious gaps in our knowledge. He believes that our knowledge is generally inadequate to build mathematical or other models beyond the level of the dynamic structure (level 2). However, strides are being made at the upper levels, especially with the cybernetic system and the self-maintaining system, though we still know very little about the process of self-maintenance. Boulding also believes that we have not yet discovered the rudiments of theoret-

Table 2.1   Levels of systems

1. Static structure—the ordering of planets in the solar system
2. Simple, dynamic system—most machines and most of Newtonian physics
3. Cybernetics system—control mechanisms, such as the thermostat
4. Open system—the self-perpetuating structure, such as the single cell
5. Genetic-societal system—division of labor, including subsystems, such as a plant
6. Animal system—includes self-awareness and mobility, as well as specialized subsystems for receiving and processing information from the outside world
7. Human system—includes the capacity for self-consciousness, self-awareness, and the use of symbolism to communicate ideas
8. Social organizations—humans as subsystems within the larger organization, or system
9. Transcendental systems—alternatives and unknowables which are yet to be discovered

Adapted from J. Boulding, "General Systems Theory: The Skeleton of Science," *Management Science*, 2, 3 (April 1956): 197–208.

ical models beyond the fourth level. For example, he points out that economic theorists still use concepts drawn primarily from levels 2 and 3, although the material and subject matter being studied is at level 8.

As a practical matter, he warns that although a great deal of work has been done at levels 7 and 8, our ability to build actual theoretical, systematic models is far in the future and that we still have a tremendous amount to learn before we can capture and identify the variables sufficiently to build an adequate model.

III. CHARACTERISTICS OF HUMAN ORGANIZATIONS

Our primary concern in this book is with systems levels 7 and 8, and we consider systems from several points of view. For example, level 7, the human system, can be viewed from the biological perspective, according to which a human being comprises a number of subsystems—nervous, circulatory, digestive, reproductive, etc.—each of which can be considered as a system in its own right. Each of these individual systems is a subsystem of the total system, and all of them are interrelated and interdependent, i.e., a change in one of the systems affects the other systems. If an individual becomes excited, for example, his glandular system pumps more adrenalin into the blood stream, his circulatory system speeds up, the stomach lining turns red as excess acid is poured into the stomach (which may produce ulcers), and under extreme stress, the functioning of the nervous system may be impaired.

One can also look at the human system from a psychological perspective. Here, the important variables are one's attitudes, motives, feelings, values, and norms of behavior, and they all interact with and are affected by the others. Throughout the text, we use the psychological perspective to study the human being as a complete system and also as a subsystem of the social organization (level 8 of Boulding's classification system) and society as a whole.

Although the use of the concept "systems" is not new, researchers are now examining social organizations—schools and other educational systems, governmental bodies, business, industry, etc.—from a systems point of view. Although our knowledge is still inadequate for building mathematical models, it is possible to discuss what appear to be some common characteristics of social organizations in systems terms. Thus, we can describe social organizations (systems) by their complexity, degree of interdependence of their subsystems, openness, balance, and multiplicity of purposes, functions, and objectives.

A. Complexity and Interdependence of Social Systems

Any social system, or human organization, consists of a number of individuals, groups, or departments, each of which is a subsystem within the total system. For example, the subsystems of a university include the different colleges, the various departments within the colleges, and such support functions as purchasing, security, and janitorial service. A manufacturing company's subsystems include the purchasing, finance, accounting, and marketing functions. A bank may have such subsystems as commercial deposits, loan, and investment departments.

The existence of subsystems causes the social organization to be complex. But even more important to management theory is the interdependence among the subsystems. Sayles and Chandler provide a dramatic illustration of the interdependence of subsystems. In the NASA biosatellite program, researchers found that an artificial bladder designed to handle the waste products of the monkey passenger was incapable of doing so. "A '2 bladder' replacement system cost half a million dollars and created enormous design problems."[3]

Figure 2.1(a) is an oversimplified diagram of a hypothetical organization of three members, A, B, and C. The square around A, B, and C represents the closed boundary of the organization, and the elastic bonds of the interdependence of

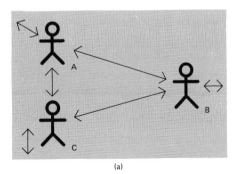

(a)

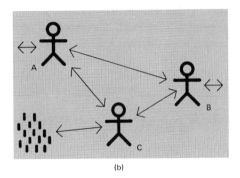

(b)

Figure 2.1. *A closed system.*

A, B, and C to one another and to the organization are shown by the various two-way arrows. The system is in "static" equilibrium—a steady state, or balance. If organization member C moves to a new position, as shown in Fig. 2.1(b), all three members of the organization will be affected, and the original state of static equilibrium, or balance, will be dynamically altered to reflect the change that has occurred, thus establishing a new state of equilibrium.

In real organizations, the introduction of a computer causes stresses, strains, and changes throughout the entire organization. Because this subsystem causes changes and modifications which, in many cases, are resisted by the intended "beneficiaries," the computer is rarely fully effective and used to full potential in modern organizations.

B. The Social System as an Open System

Although Fig. 2.1 depicts a self-contained organization, most systems are open —they are continually interacting with the outside environment. A human organization is open in that it exists in a wider environment of many other larger or smaller organizations, or systems. Thus, since any particular system (human organization) is itself a subsystem in interaction with other subsystems in the environment, we cannot understand the functioning of an organization without taking into consideration the influence of other subsystems and the environment. For example, the behavior of a business organization cannot be fully understood without knowing something about its market, suppliers, the public, and the governmental rules and regulations which affect it.

Figure 2.2 shows typical patterns of interpersonal interaction. The system created by interaction at a party, for example, is also in dynamic interaction with the environment, e.g., governmental officials (represented by the mailman in the foreground) and other systems (shown by the painter).

OTHER SYSTEMS
(ORGANIZATIONS)

Figure 2.2. *An open system.*

One of the important concepts of an open system is "input," or something that enters the system from the environment. For example, the input for a computer subsystem is data, without which this subsystem cannot operate. In the human system, the input of information from the outside world comes from the five senses.

Obviously, the complexity and variety of the input increase with the complexity of the system. The input for a social system, or organization, is highly complex—information, people, energy, materials. Similarly, each type of input is also highly complex and varied.

Once an input enters the system, it undergoes "transformation," or "operation." A manufacturing company, for example, has elaborate mechanisms for transforming incoming raw materials into finished goods. Once these inputs have been transformed, they represent "output" and are ready to leave the system as finished goods. In other words, "output" which the system exports is the result of the operation, or transformation, process. An automobile manufacturer, for example, "exports" finished goods (cars) to dealers who in turn "export" cars to customers. Or, a bank "imports" dollars (deposits), "transforms" them (record keeping), and "exports" the money to customers (mortgage loans, bond purchases, etc.).

The term "feedback" originated from studies on cybernetics conducted by Norbert Wiener to better understand the processes of control and communication. For Wiener, the key explanatory mechanism for communication and control is the feedback loop, which carries a continuous flow of information between the system, its parts, and the environment. In other words, a portion of a system's or subsystem's output is fed back to the inputs in order to affect succeeding inputs. Since open systems are never completely closed off from the outside world, they are affected by the environment and, in turn, have an effect on the environment through output information which, in turn, is fed back into the system as an input to guide and control the operation of the system. Figure 2.3 illustrates that feedback comes from not only the environment, but also the various subsystems of a social organization.

Figure 2.3. *The feedback concept.*

-13-

fashion, the specific materials imported are more complex
and varied and vary considerably from organization to
organization. As a simplified example, a bank may import
dollars through the teller window, and insurance company may
import insurance applications; hospitals import patients and
a steel manufacturing company may import iron ore.

Once an input enters the system, it undergoes

The term "transformation" or "operation" means that
something is done to the inputs. At the level of the thermostat,
switches are activated to turn the furnace off or on. The human
system somehow filters, modifies or changes the input. We shall
discuss this particular process in our sections on perception
and motivation. At the level of the social system, the transformation is even more complex. A manufacturing company, *for example,* *has*
~~have~~ elaborate mechanisms *for transforming* ~~to change~~ incoming raw materials into
finished goods. *Once these inputs have been* ~~For example, an automobile manufacturing company~~
transformed, they represent "output"
~~inputs a tremendous variety of materials to manufacture~~
and are ready to leave the system as
~~(transform) the incoming materials into a finished automobile.~~
finished goods.

The term "output" means that the system exports some of the
results of the operation or transformation. Our automobile
manufacturing company exports finished automobiles to the dealers
and the dealers, in turn, export the automobiles to the customer.
Our bank imports dollars in the form of deposits, transforms
the dollars in some form of record-keeping and outputs may be
in the form of mortgage loans, bond purchases and the like.

Leave in

An author receives feedback in the form of his editor's markings on the manuscript; the editor, in turn, gets feedback from the author, e.g., "leave in."

Several examples may help here. At the lowest cybernetic level, the input from the outside environment causes a thermostat to turn the furnace on; as it gets feedback about the house temperature, it turns the furnace off at the appropriate point. A simple experiment illustrates feedback at the physiological level. Place a coin or pencil on your desk. Then close your eyes and pick it up. This is quite easy to do, because the nerves in your hand send "feedback" information which enables you to pick up the object. Finally, the information about sales relayed back to a company by a salesman (feedback) may be used as new input by the organization in determining its future production activities.

Another concept of an open system is that of "boundaries." In real life, there are few truly closed systems with impenetrable, impermeable physical boundaries. Rather, almost all systems require, as a minimum, energy from the outside to maintain the system. It is difficult, however, to define the boundaries of social systems, since there is a continuous inflow and outflow of energy through the boundaries of the system.

A boundary exists when there is less interchange of inputs across the line than within the system. However, this definition of the boundary is somewhat arbitrary, since a social system has multiple subsystems, and the boundary line for one subsystem may not coincide with that for a different subsystem. Nonetheless, we may need to assign arbitrary boundaries to a social organization, depending on the variables we wish to stress. The boundaries used for studying or analyzing leadership, for example, may be quite different from those used for assessing marketing strategy.

In addition, the permeability of boundaries varies considerably in social organizations. For example, the boundaries of a community's police force are probably far more rigid and sharply defined than those of the political parties in the same community.

C. Balance and Social System

In any social system there are two conflicting forces—one directed toward maintaining the "status quo"; the other directed toward change and growth. Although such terms as "equilibrium," "entropy," and "homeostasis" have been used to describe the relationship between these forces, we prefer to use the term "balance." "Balance" does not imply a static, unchanging organization, because the organization can reach and maintain a balance at different places along a continuum—the balance point may change.

In discussing balance, one must distinguish between "fixed-point" balance and "steady-state" balance. For example, man's body temperature is usually a fixed point (98.6°F), and the body will resist attempts to raise or lower this temperature. The term "steady state" describes a balance which is not dependent on such a fixed point, or level. Although many managers strive for a "fixed-point" balance in the hope that things will "settle down," their efforts are meaningless, because social organizations are highly dynamic. Although many of the forces within a social system—the individual, the subsystems of which he is a part, the managerial hierarchy, and inputs from the outside environment—seek a balance within the organization, many of them also continually disturb the "steady state" of the organization. To see these opposing forces at work, one need only attend the meetings of a university academic senate comprising students, faculty, and administrators.

The terms "positive" and "negative" feedback do not connote good or bad, but rather forces for and against change. "Negative feedback," which describes the forces working against change, is used to collect and transmit information to keep the system directed toward a preset goal or objective. In an industrial organization, for example, negative feedback is used to ensure that production plans and schedules are being met. "Positive feedback," on the other hand, is used to change the course or direction of the organization—it upsets the existing balance of the organization. Examples of positive feedback are a salesman in the field reporting that sales of a particular product are not going well and insisting on a change, or a market research group recommending that a new product be developed and put on the market.

D. Multiplicity of Purposes, Functions, and Objectives

Most social organizations have a multiplicity of subsystems, each of which is in dynamic interaction with the others. However, we do not always need to look at the entire system—we can select out specific parts, or subsystems, for study and enlarge our analysis from the micro to the macro level. For example, an individual is a subsystem in his own right, with certain needs, goals, and expectations. Since not all of his goals and objectives will coincide with those of the organization, we could therefore expand our study to examine the stresses and strains resulting from the discrepancy between individual and company goals.

At another level of complexity, we may consider the individual as a member of a group which, in turn, has its own set of goals and expectations. For example, a group may establish work norms inconsistent with those of top management.

At the highest level of complexity is the system in interaction with other systems in the outside environment. Here, we can consider a particular organization as either a system in its own right or a subsystem within a supersystem. As in lower levels, the supersystem may have goals and expectations which differ considerably from the social organization under consideration. The current emphasis on ecology—including air, water, and thermal pollution—is one example of such diversity of goals. A particular industrial organization, striving for survival, may regard enforcement of pollution laws as threatening the survival of the organization.

In short, the complexity of internal and external forces acting on the social organization makes it difficult for the organization to either arrive at a steady-state balance or have only one objective. This multiplicity of forces also makes it impossible to maintain what Seiler calls "the single cause habit of thinking" —the assumption that events have a simple, single cause. For example, we have already mentioned the fallacy of attributing an automobile accident to any single "cause" such as "driver carelessness." Since the variables are so highly interrelated and interdependent, we must recognize a multiplicity of causes for any particular event. Nonetheless, one can still "isolate" the number and range of phenomena to be studied, thus dealing with one level of complexity at a time.

Seiler makes an important point when he discusses the tendency of the system to seek equilibrium, or balance. He makes a strong distinction between the tendency to seek equilibrium and the need for a more optimal equilibrium.

The tendency toward equilibrium is a fact. The tendency toward optimal balance is not. The administrator's challenge is to find ways, through his understanding and imagination, to uncork more effective balances between systems. It is not humanistic values but a considerable body of clinical observation and methodical research which leads us to the conclusion that the work group hostile to management is not experiencing the only viable balance between itself and other systems. While conflict between systems is inevitable by the definitional difference between systems, there is no evidence to support the idea that conflict is inevitably nonproductive. [4]

Summary

1. An organization (firm, company) is composed of a number of subsystems, all of which are interdependent and interrelated.

2. An organization (system) is open and dynamic, having inputs, outputs, operations, feedback, and boundaries.

3. An organization (system) strives for balance through both positive and negative feedback.

4. An organization (system) has a multiplicity of purposes, functions, and objectives, some of which are in conflict. The purpose of the administrator is to strive for an optimal balance among the subsystems.

IV. DIFFERING PERSPECTIVES OF ORGANIZATIONS AS SOCIAL SYSTEMS

There are several different perspectives, or viewpoints, from which we can look at organizations as total, open systems. First, we must differentiate between formal and informal systems within organizations. The formal organization, run according to prescribed rules, policies, and procedures, is best depicted by the organization chart, the officially prescribed structure, or framework, of the organization as a formal system. Koontz and O'Donnell point out that the structure of an organization involves not only the departmental framework, but also the procedures for assigning formal activities to these departmental units.[5]

The informal organization, or system, evolves from the ways in which the employees (at all levels) within an organization interact and work with one another. Many of these activities and interactions are not prescribed by the organization and are much more informal in nature.

Bakke stresses the importance of both formal and informal systems "as factors influencing human behavior, the formal and informal systems are not separable . . . The social system to which participants in an organization reach and which is an effective determinant of their behavior, is a synthesis of both formal and informal elements."[6] Or as Katz puts it, "The organization that depends solely upon its blueprints of prescribed behavior is a very fragile social system."[7]

Figure 2.4 shows a typical organization chart. The solid lines represent the lines of authority, and the boxes show who reports to whom. The shaded areas represent areas of interaction which are not prescribed by the formal organiza-

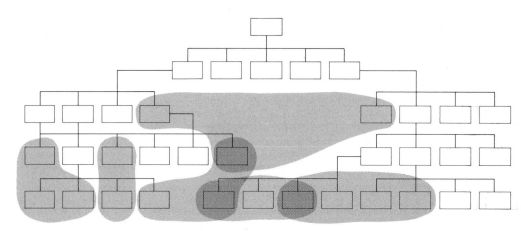

Figure 2.4. *The interaction between formal and informal systems.*

tion and which cut across organizational lines. We are all familiar with the difference between the two—there is always somebody in an organization who can circumvent the "red tape" and get something done quickly. If you know the mechanic at the local gasoline station, you may get work done faster than someone else. The student whose girlfriend works in the registrar's office may get information about his grades long before the official grade notification is sent out.

The concept of the formal/informal structure is implicit in all of the three perspectives of organizational systems outlined in the previous chapter: the formal, structural design perspective; the work-flow perspective; and the human perspective. In other words, both formal and informal structures exist simultaneously in organizations within each perspective, and each perspective represents a different way of looking at the organization as a system.

A. The Structural-Design Perspective

The most usual way of looking at organizations is from a somewhat depersonalized point of view. This perspective of the organization as a total system emphasizes formal structure and predetermined lines of authority and responsibility. For example, if we look at an industrial organization from this perspective, its most salient characteristics are the formal subdivisions, or subsystems, formed on the principles of specialization and the division of work tasks. This view of the organization as a system is essentially vertical.

1. Marketing Department. The function of this subsystem is to carry out market research, advertising, and other activities required to sell the outputs of the total system.

2. Manufacturing Department. This subsystem is concerned primarily with "operation," or the transformation of goods from raw materials to finished goods, or output, to be handled by the marketing department.

3. Finance and Accounting Department. This subsystem is concerned primarily with inputs (in the form of money) and operation (in the form of internal feedback through accounting records, etc.).

4. The Organization as a Whole. Here, we can view the organization as a total, formal, departmentalized system consisting, minimally, of the three subsystems just mentioned, as well as such others as personnel and research and development.

B. The Work-Flow Perspective

This perspective of subsystems within the total organization is essentially horizontal, as it focuses on the ways by which work flows through an organization. As organizations continue to increase in size and complexity, as the boundaries between organizations and their outside environment become more vague and diffuse, as organizations increase the diversity of their products, and as the importance of computers and management information systems becomes greater, we must give greater attention to the way in which work flows through an organization. For example, Jasinski stresses the importance of increasing organizational effectiveness through more direct consideration of work flow, pointing out that the normal, vertical (Perspective I) approach causes problems by not giving adequate consideration to this factor and stating that techniques must be developed to ensure that greater time and attention are given to this concept.[8] He comments that he knows of companies which studied the work-flow process in anticipation of installing data processing equipment. However, when they realized that merely studying the process could save them money, they decided they didn't need the equipment after all. The increasing use in both management practice and the literature of such terms as "project manager," "program manager," and "integrator" are indications of the need for greater attention to the way in which work flows through an organization.

As J. W. Forrester points out, there are at least five interacting subsystems, which are interconnected primarily by information flows and a decision-making network, which need to be considered in the work-flow process:[9]

1. Information Flow. This is the flow of ideas and information from the environment in to and out of an organization. This information-feedback approach influences present and future decisions.

2. Material Flow. This process deals with the input of raw materials from outside the organization, the transformation of these raw materials into finished goods, and the output, or exportation, of finished goods to the environment. The process of material flow includes such areas of the Perspective I organization as purchasing, manufacturing, accounting and finance, and marketing.

3. Money Flow. This subsystem, concerned with the flow of money throughout the entire system, involves the same departments involved with the flow of materials.

4. Order Flow. Any complex system requires extensive paperwork to follow the flow of orders into the organization (one type of input) through the final stage when shipping orders and bills of lading are made out (one type of output).

Incoming natural gas from various sources is processed through automation for distribution to many plants. (Photograph courtesy W. R. Grace & Co.)

5. Capital Equipment Generation and Usage. Forrester views this subsystem as a process to determine whether capital equipment is needed, the ordering and purchasing of such equipment, and determining the proper usage of such equipment.

A number of other authors have also discussed the importance of the work-flow concept. For example, Sayles points out that the manager's primary role is not to deal with his subordinates, but rather "to maintain the regularity or the sequential pattern of one or more of the (work) flow processes."[10] Diebold indicates that one reason for the inefficient use of the computer is that there is no place for it in the traditional business structure. "The new technology makes it imperative that we build information systems which break through the compartmentalized structure of the traditional business organization."[11]

If an organization were to be run according to the horizontal work-flow concepts of Perspective II, there would be a manager of information flow, another manager of materials flow, etc. In such an organization, the roles and responsibilities of the various managers are vastly different from those of managers in Perspective I organizations. Although at present few organizations fall into the Perspective II category, the increased use of the computer and the emphasis on integrated management information systems (information flow) make work-flow concepts and practices ever more important.

C. The Human Perspective

The primary concern in Perspective III is human beings and the ways in which they interact in the total organization.

1. The Individual. The individual, as a system in his own right, can also be considered as a subsystem within the organization. As such, he has motives, needs, and desires. He also belongs to groups (larger subsystems) within the total system and has an impact not only on the groups to which he belongs, but also on the organization as a whole.

2. The Group. Since groups (subsystems) are composed of individuals, a group is obviously at a higher level of complexity than the individual. In addition, a group facilitates several types of interaction (either formal or informal): among individuals, an individual on the group, or vice versa. Finally, the group has an impact on the total organization.

3. The Organization. Finally, we can look at the organization as a total human system composed of subsystems of individuals and groups, each of which affects the others and the organization. In other words, the various subsystems and the total, human organization are interdependent.

V. THE NEED FOR A MORE INTEGRATED APPROACH

Although the structural-design, Perspective I system will probably always exist, recent advances in knowledge of human beings and group dynamics, the advent of the computer, the attempts at integrated management information systems, and the espousal of such concepts as program management are forcing us to rethink and reconsider our ideas about organizations as large, complex systems. We can understand an organization better and help it to be more effective if we consider the concepts of all three perspectives, and this task is made easier by clearly delineating the differences among the three approaches.

The study and understanding of an organization's interrelated, interdependent subsystems are just beginning. In the past this lack of understanding caused many problems. For example, in many manufacturing organizations there is often conflict between the manufacturing department, which is charged with making and assembling goods, and the quality control department, which is charged with inspection. Manufacturing believes that quality control is out to "trap" them; quality control feels that the shop is out to "put something over" on them.

In the same vein, the finance department, concerned with cash flow, tends to keep the inventory low. Manufacturing, on the other hand, likes to maintain a high inventory of parts. Marketing likes to have many different products with a high inventory so that they will never be out of stock and lose a sale.

These conflicts, which are not "caused" by people, are built into the organization, because organizations have not really been designed to maximize the concept that the various subsystems are interrelated and interdependent. Thus, differing segments of the same organization may well have quite different overall goals and objectives.

In the past, this was not too important, since products changed slowly and organizations were relatively stable. Further, the built-in conflict was not too damaging, since formal departments could function semi-independently of one another. Now, however, the amount, degree, and rate of change are increasing so rapidly that organizations need to remain flexible.

For example, Huse studied one company's two-year attempt to install a computer-based, complete management information system. The project finally failed after several million dollars had been spent. The computer programs were well written. But,

with the advent of mechanized programs, work groups that in the past have been quite independent become much more interdependent. The walls between groups, units, and sections begin to crumble as the programs and information flow out, across and through them. Currently, the possibility of losing "control" of one's own operation and being dependent on other areas is quite threatening, especially to the manager of what has been an autonomous area. [12]

Another example of a Perspective I organization's difficulty in keeping up with the change process has been the development, especially since World War II, of the "project," or "matrix," organization.

A project is [defined as] *an organization unit dedicated to the attainment of a goal— generally, the successful completion of a developmental product on time, within the budget, and in conformance with predetermined performance specifications.* [13]

Gaddis notes that many projects have a manager whose task is to coordinate the project across the traditional, departmental lines. The need for the project approach arises primarily in the more modern, advanced technology industries where change is the norm. Further, it is in these industries—electronics, astronautics, nucleonics—that complex products are designed, developed, and

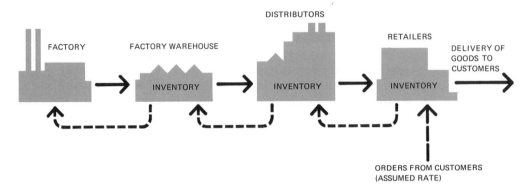

Figure 2.5. *Organization of production-distribution systems. (Adapted from J. W. Forrester,* Industrial Dynamics, *Cambridge, Mass.: M.I.T. Press, 1961, p. 22.)*

manufactured according to predetermined performance specifications and due-dates. Implicit in the use of the project-manager approach in such industries is the admission that traditional managerial and organizational concepts have not worked. The project approach has been, in essence, "grafted on" to the existing, and largely obsolete, concepts of traditional organizations.

Forrester has dramatically pointed out the tremendous impact on the organization of poorly designed information flow. In one of his models, for example, he shows how relatively small changes in retail sales can lead to large swings in factory production and how a factory manager may find it impossible to fill his orders even though he is always able to produce more goods or materials than are being sold to consumers (Fig. 2.5).[14] Similarly, Lawrence and Lorsch have shown that the organization must be designed to fit its particular environment and that proper design of the organizational structure (Perspective I) can make major impacts on the profitability of the organization.[15]

VI. SUMMARY

As an open system, the organization affects and is affected by its environment; the interdependencies among the subsystems are as important as, if not more so than, the individual subsystem. Although organizations strive to achieve a balance among the subparts, this balance is continually changing with the need to adapt to a nonstable environment and the interdependence of the parts of the social organization.

Social organizations may be seen from several different perspectives: as formal organizations, as flow systems, and as interacting humans. However, it is not enough to study organizations from just one perspective; for a complete understanding it is necessary to use an integrated approach.

Later in the book, we point out dramatic improvements in profitability, commitment, and worker motivation that resulted from an integrated approach. Therefore, although we use the systems approach to organizations in this text, our primary emphasis is on the human system.

REVIEW

1. How do you distinguish between the "formal" and "informal" organization? Discuss.

2. Are there times when resistance to change may be valuable for an organization? Discuss.

3. What impact does the installation of a computer have on an organization? Short-term? Long-term?

4. From your own past experience in organizations, describe instances in which the "informal" organization has been (a) helpful in assisting the formal organization and (b) harmful to the formal organization. What were the reasons underlying these results?

5. The next time you go to a cafeteria, note what the employees and customers are doing. How would you describe a cafeteria as a system?

6. What basic relationships must exist to make a concept of systems workable?

Critical Concepts

Input

Transformation

Output

System:
    complexity
    interdependence
    open system
    closed system
    balance

Perspective I
Perspective II
Perspective III
Integrated approach to systems
Negative feedback
Positive feedback

REFERENCES

1   E. Bakke, "Concept of the Social Organization," in *Modern Organizational Theory*, ed. M. Haire (New York: John Wiley, 1959).

2   L. Henderson, *Pareto's General Sociology* (Cambridge, Mass.: Harvard University Press, 1936), p. 80.

3   L. Sayles and M. Chandler, *Managing Large Systems—Organizations for the Future* (New York: Harper & Row, 1971) p. 10.

4   J. Seiler, *Systems Analysis in Organizational Behavior* (Homewood, Ill.: Richard D. Irwin and Dorsey Press, 1967), p. 15. Reprinted by permission.

5   H. Koontz and C. O'Donnell, *Principles of Management: An Analysis of Managerial Functions*, 4th ed. (New York: McGraw-Hill, 1968).

6   E. Bakke, *Bonds of Organization* (New York: Harper & Row, 1957), p. 191.

7   D. Katz, "The Motivational Basis of Organizational Behavior," *Behavioral Science*, 9 (1964):132.

8   F. J. Jasinski, "Adapting Organizations to New Technology," *Harvard Business Review*, 37, 1 (Jan.–Feb. 1959):79–86.

9   J. Forrester, *Industrial Dynamics* (Cambridge, Mass.: M.I.T. Press, 1968).

10   L. Sayles, *Managerial Behavior* (New York: McGraw-Hill, 1964).

11   J. Diebold, "ADP—the Still-sleeping Giant," *Harvard Business Review*, 42, 5 (Sept.–Oct. 1964):60–65.

12   E. Huse, "The Impact of Computerized Programs on Managers and Organizations: A Case Study in an Integrated Manufacturing Company," in *The Impact of Computers on Management*, ed. C. Myers (Cambridge, Mass.: M.I.T. Press, 1967), pp. 290–291. Reprinted by permission.

13   P. Gaddis, "The Project Manager," *Harvard Business Review*, 37, 3 (May–June 1959): 89.

14   J. Forrester, *op. cit.*

15   P. Lawrence and J. Lorsch, *Organization and Environment: Managing Integration and Differentiation* (Boston: Harvard University Graduate School of Business Administration, Division of Research, 1967).

PART II
SOCIAL BEHAVIOR, PERCEPTION, AND COMMUNICATION

INTRODUCTION

In the preceding chapter on the organization as a system, we discussed the systems approach and the three perspectives from which a system can be viewed —the formal, structural-design perspective; the flow perspective; and the human perspective. Part II is devoted to a consideration of Perspective III, the human perspective. In the next few chapters, we look at specific parts of subsystems and expand our analysis from the micro to the macro level.

THE INDIVIDUAL IN THE ORGANIZATION (CHAPTER 3)

Chapter 3 focuses on the individual as a subsystem in his own right. After a detailed analysis of motivation, we move on to study the individual subsystem in interaction with the larger system. Here, the focus is on the process of social exchange, or the "psychological contract," whereby the individual contracts to give something of himself in exchange for something from the organization. An important issue here is the way in which individual needs and motivations do or do not get satisfied on the job. The individual will "give" to the organization only to the degree and extent that he perceives the exchange as relatively equitable. Should he see the exchange as being unequal (for example, if he is giving more to the organization than he is receiving), he must decide whether to leave the organization for one where he thinks he will get a better break or to remain within the organization and adjust his level of work output to what he thinks is a proper balance, or exchange.

PERCEPTION AND COMMUNICATION (CHAPTER 4)

In the first part of this chapter, the focus is still on the individual, but the emphasis is on the ways in which the individual sees, or "perceives," the world, a factor that is highly affected by the individual's internal motivational state. The perceptual process, truly internal to the individual, is highly important, because it gives a clue to the reasons for a person's behavior. In addition to explaining and describing the perceptual process, we explain how perception can be improved.

Closely linked to the perceptual process is the problem of communication —the clear, accurate transmitting and receiving of information. Thus, we move from the individual as a subsystem and look at individuals in contact with one another in describing what occurs in the communication process and providing you with some insights and ideas for improving communications.

THE GROUP IN THE ORGANIZATION (CHAPTER 5)

At a higher level of complexity is the individual as a group member. In Chapter 5 we examine the individual's influence on the group and the influence of the group on him. We discuss the process of group formation and examine the interaction and influence of the group as a subsystem within the more complex system, the total organization. Because groups have such profound influence on their members and on the organization as a whole, we describe various observational tools and techniques you can use to better understand and diagnose group effectiveness. We also suggest some methods for increasing not only your own effectiveness within a group, but also the effectiveness of the group as a whole.

INFLUENCE, POWER, AND LEADERSHIP (CHAPTER 6)

When we think about leadership, we usually think about formal leadership, that is, a boss with formal authority and responsibility. However, when we consider the organization as a complex system of interdependent and interrelated subsystems, the issue of influence, power, and leadership becomes much broader. Chapter 6 deals with several types of both formal and informal social power and influence. Influence, for example, is a complex, two-way process which does not necessarily reflect the formal, vertical structure of the organization. After considering the issues of power and influence, we describe several current theories of formal leadership and give you some insight into the effectiveness of differing leadership styles on human performance.

THE MANAGER IN THE ORGANIZATION (CHAPTER 7)

Here, the emphasis is on the manager as a complex subsystem within the larger system. The manager is heavily involved with other subsystems and groups, primarily at the lateral, or flow, level of work (Perspective II), and his function within the organization is much broader than just a formal leader of subordinates. Since organizations have changed greatly in recent years, the manager's duties and functions and some of the concepts about the managerial function must be reexamined. For example, today's effective manager spends more time in the lateral, work-flow process (Perspective II) than does the less effective manager, who spends more time dealing directly with subordinates in the vertical relationships of Perspective I organizations. We conclude our examination of the manager's job by describing it as a highly important, shifting set of relationships requiring the continual making and renegotiating of decisions. To be successful, the manager must be able to interact with a large number of people at a variety of levels, both inside and outside the organization.

To summarize, Part II of this text begins at the level of the individual in the organization; examines the problems of motivation, perception, and communication; discusses the problems of group formation and effectiveness; distinguishes among different types of power and influence; examines the nature and functions of leadership; and finally, provides a new insight into the manager's job in today's complex organization.

3

THE
INDIVIDUAL
IN
THE
ORGANIZATION

All the world's a stage,
And all the men and women merely players:
They have their exits and their entrances;
And one man in his time plays many parts.

SHAKESPEARE

I. INTRODUCTION

Our primary concern in this chapter is why people work and behave as they do in formal work organizations. Most people spend one-third of their adult years on jobs. There are several compelling, common-sense reasons for working. First, people need jobs in order to earn a living—to survive. In the early days of our society, John Smith coined the phrase, "He who does not work does not eat." In all races and all cultures, people work. In primitive cultures, of course, survival is perhaps the most important reason for work.

Another major reason why we work is that society expects it of us. Ours is a work-oriented society, and even those whose survival does not depend on their earning a living usually hold some sort of job. By complying with society's expectations, we acknowledge that the opinions of "others" are important to us. Wealthy Texas oilmen and Greek shipping magnates are two examples of such cases. However, society may be gradually shifting to a less work-oriented ethic.

In addition to being necessary for survival and expected of us, work can also be fun, challenging, and exciting. Although Webster defines work as "bodily or mental effort exerted to do or make something; purposeful activity; labor; toil," such efforts can also be pleasurable, and frequently that is sufficient reason for working. Small children build a snowman; the amateur artist paints a picture; the skier goes down the mountain; the machinist makes a highly complex part; the advertising executive develops a new campaign for his client—all of these people are probably enjoying their work. But even enjoyable work has its troublesome moments: children have to repair the snowman; the artist cannot get the colors right; the skier makes a *sitzmark*; and the client rejects the proposed advertising campaign.

Many people have the impression that "work" is a hardship that must be endured until they get home from the job and can begin their leisure-time "play." But this is a false distinction, for to a great extent, play is work and work is play. To be sure, many people have jobs they do not enjoy, and many jobs are only minimally rewarding. Yet, there is a great deal of potential satisfaction and enjoyment that can be obtained from work—whether it be on or off the job.

II. MOTIVATION AND PERFORMANCE

In this section, we look at man as a system and examine variables that affect the quantity and quality of his work performance. After defining the concepts of motivation and attitudes, we analyze their influence on behavior.

Earlier, we said that social systems are characterized by their complexity, openness, striving for balance, and their multiplicity of purposes and objectives. The individual also fits this definition: he is complex, consisting of a multitude

"Work is play, play is work." These men *enjoy the challenge of the annual 26-mile Boston Marathon race. (Photograph courtesy Christian Science Monitor)*

of subsystems; he is open, acting on inputs received from the outside world; he seeks a balance between his desire for consistency and stability and his need for growth and change; and he has a multiplicity of objectives, some of which conflict with one another. For example, a man may find that his desire to spend time with his family conflicts with his need to put in long hours on the job in order to be successful. Or, the need of a college student to take his girl to a dance may conflict directly with his need to study for an examination being held the next morning.

As Vinacke has shown, there are a number of variables that affect the quantity or quality of an individual's work performance: intelligence, ability, muscular coordination, past experience, practice in the task, and motivation.[1] Figure 3.1 shows the relationship of these variables to the individual's output —his performance.

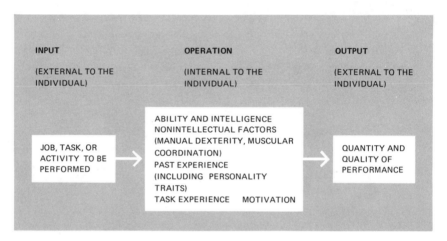

INPUT

(EXTERNAL TO THE INDIVIDUAL)

OPERATION

(INTERNAL TO THE INDIVIDUAL)

OUTPUT

(EXTERNAL TO THE INDIVIDUAL)

ABILITY AND INTELLIGENCE
NONINTELLECTUAL FACTORS
(MANUAL DEXTERITY, MUSCULAR
COORDINATION)
PAST EXPERIENCE
(INCLUDING PERSONALITY
TRAITS)
TASK EXPERIENCE   MOTIVATION

JOB, TASK, OR
ACTIVITY TO BE
PERFORMED

QUANTITY AND
QUALITY OF
PERFORMANCE

Figure 3.1. *Variables influencing performance.*

Motivation can be defined as "the conditions responsible for variation in the intensity, quality, and direction of ongoing behavior."[2] The "conditions" are both extrinsic and intrinsic to the individual. Most, if not all, behavior is caused by the individual's attempts to satisfy his needs. Similarly, the individual avoids activities that do not provide him with rewards or reinforcement or that would result in punishment, a negative kind of need satisfaction.

The human motivational system is highly complex, and the individual may have a number of highly interrelated and sometimes contradictory motives. Therefore, the motivation system requires a steering function. Such guidance may be in the form of the individual's values, sentiments, habits, and defense mechanisms, all of which are included in the term "attitude" used by Vinacke. As he points out, attitudes are developed over time, are relatively permanent, and are cognitive structures which determine, or "steer," the individual's behavior.

Because there are both positive and negative consequences to behavior, any specific behavior is a complex interrelation of the individual's perceptions of both the goal and his own performance, the outside situation, and the task— its importance, the extent to which it will satisfy motivations and needs, and its difficulty. The individual may be highly motivated to achieve, but if the task seems too difficult or unrewarding, he may not even try.

Figure 3.2 shows that behavior is a direct function of both the perceived task or activity, including the possible rewards or reinforcement for task accomplishment, and the current motivational state and attitudes of the individual. In other words, he is always asking "What's in it for me?" The particular behavior which occurs in a given situation is a direct result of his answer to that question.

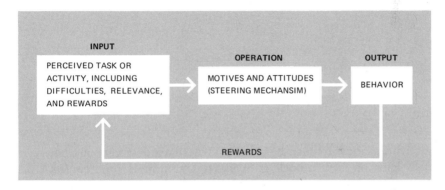

Figure 3.2. *Human motivational system.*

III. MODELS OF MOTIVATIONAL SYSTEMS

A "model" is a representation of reality. However, since "reality" differs for each person, more than one model is required. First, it is impossible to know what really makes another individual "tick." Sometimes he does not know exactly why he does what he does. The second reason for using several models is that as research expands the field of motivational theory, new models are needed to reflect the new findings.

Throughout history, there have been a number of different assumptions, or "models," which have attempted to explain why people work and behave as they do. Today, none of these models appears in a completely pure state. Rather, these models form a continuum along which workers' behavior and the ideas guiding the actions of supervisors can be placed.

Three major points, or models, along this continuum are shown in Fig. 3.3. The use of only three models is a vast oversimplification of the complex area

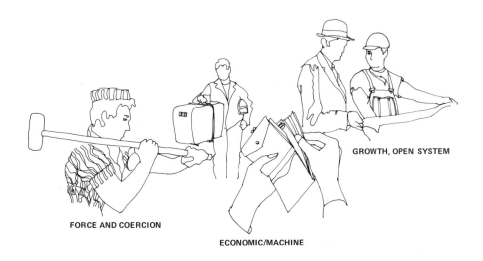

Figure 3.3. *Motivational models of man.*

of motivation, but it illustrates the lack of sharp demarcations between the models. Each of these models is in use today, although the emphasis in the literature has shifted heavily toward the right-hand side of the continuum. Prisons, for example, are run on force-and-coercion principles of motivation. Business organizations rely heavily on economic factors to motivate their members. Although educational systems strive to promote "growth," their emphasis on grades sometimes overshadows their efforts to promote learning as an end in itself.

A. Force and Coercion Model

Many of the early models of man depended on coercion and force as "motivators." Perhaps one of the earliest recorded descriptions of such an "incentive system" is given in the Book of Exodus. Since the Pharoah felt that the Israelites were not being worked hard enough, he gave orders that their task (making bricks) be made more difficult. No longer would they be given the straw with which to make the bricks; rather, they would also have to collect the straw, while still maintaining their previous quota of bricks. When the quota was not met, "the children of Israel were scourged" as an incentive to meet the quota.

Prior to the French Revolution, the institution of serfdom was a form of coercive motivation, as was slavery in the United States. Indeed, coercive authority was widely used in England in industrial organizations immediately after the Industrial Revolution. However, there is evidence that slavery and feudalism were not economically viable. For example, in order to avoid the corrupting influence of wealth, the Cistercian order of monks during the Middle Ages deliberately built their abbeys in wastelands far from towns and were not allowed to have serfs. They did the work themselves and were embarrassed to find that this method of operation was far more profitable, since the "old-fashioned great estate, cultivated by servile labor, was not a very profitable property for its owner."[3]

Reliance on coercion has caused other problems as well. Coercion used by the Nazis during World War II resulted in high sabotage rates in war plants. In the post-Stalin era, Soviet leaders have failed to maintain a coercive state and their more "enlightened" methods of motivation have caused a considerable relaxing of state rules and regulations, with an accompanying "decentralization" of decision making. Today, the Chinese Communists are being faced with the necessity of either becoming even more coercive or of following the lead of Russia in relaxing some of the measures previously thought necessary to maintain high production levels.

In summary, the basic assumption behind this model is that man works best when he is forced into a situation in which he must produce or be punished. The problem with this assumption is that coercion at best produces alienation and withdrawal—either actual or psychological—from the task. When physical withdrawal is not possible, sabotage, uprisings, and other forms of rebellion may occur.

B. Economic/Machine Model

The two branches of this model are conceptually related, but may also be considered separately (Fig. 3.4). The first branch is the economic model, which stresses economic rewards. The second branch uses methods of "conditioning" to achieve the desired behavior.

1. Economic Model. The so-called economic theory of motivation replaced the coercive model of human behavior long before Adam Smith formulated his assumptions about economic man in 1776. The coercive and economic models were used conjointly for a long time, perhaps most clearly in the world's navies at about the time of the Revolutionary War. Sailors were often flogged (coerced), and prize money was used as an economic motivation.

It was Adam Smith who did the best job of conceptualizing the model of economic man. The basic assumption of this model is that man works primarily for money. He is like a machine in that he is unconcerned about social feelings, does not need other rewards such as feelings of accomplishment and achieve-

FORCE AND COERCION   ECONOMIC/MACHINE   GROWTH, OPEN SYSTEM

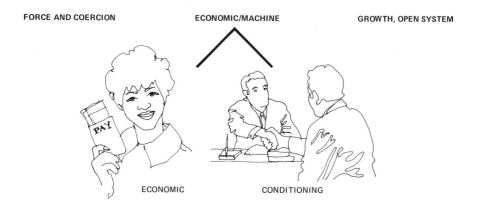

ECONOMIC   CONDITIONING

Figure 3.4. *Motivational models of man.*

ment, and is motivated to do only that which provides him with the greatest immediate economic reward.

The concept of rational-economic man was popularized by Taylor and more particularly, by the "efficiency experts" who followed his lead in the 1920s and 1930s. This model makes many of the same assumptions about the nature of man as does the coercive model—man is motivated primarily by money; he is inherently shiftless and lazy; he will respond only when he is "bribed" by financial rewards; work needs to be planned out for him in great detail; and the manager needs to tightly supervise and control the worker's activities if work is to be performed properly.

In Chapter 1 we described how Taylor used scientific methods to increase the amount of pig iron carried by a laborer between two points. Taylor describes the set of formal instructions that he gave to Schmidt, his experimental worker. First, Taylor asked Schmidt whether he was a high-priced man which, in Taylor's terms, was the difference between $1.15 and $1.85 per day. When Schmidt admitted that he was a high-priced man, Taylor stressed the importance of Schmidt's following instructions without ever questioning the correctness of the instructions. As Taylor put it, "Now, a high-priced man does just what he's told to do, and no back talk."[4]

According to Weber, the ideal human organization is highly standardized, and everyone knows his duties and follows them to the letter. The individual's needs and wants are subordinated to the requirements of the institution, and the individual gets the formal economic rewards that he deserves for his perfor-

By permission of John Hart and Field Enterprises, Inc.

mance.[5] Obviously, then, the primary incentive in the economic model is financial reward, usually based on the rate of the worker's output.

The importance of pay as a motivator has been discussed widely. In general, managers and economists have tended to considerably overrate the importance of pay, whereas psychologists and sociologists have tended to underemphasize the importance of economic rewards. All too often, theorists regard pay as *either* "financial" *or* "psychological" income. In fact, however, pay serves both functions; some sort of an income is necessary to satisfy both physiological and security needs.

In addition, money serves as a tangible sign of recognition and achievement, thereby satisfying the individual's social, ego, and other higher-level needs. Although a large portion of a top executive's pay increase may be lost through higher taxes, he may still get a great deal of inner satisfaction from this increase.

Because money is precise and easily measurable, it is an excellent yardstick for measuring comparative success, recognition, accomplishment, and achievement. In this context, it has been amply demonstrated that the *relative* amount of pay is far more important than the *absolute* amount of pay. In other words, many people are not bothered by knowing that they could leave their place of work and go somewhere else for more money. However, they are troubled by knowing that someone else in their office is making more money than they are. On the other hand, money can act as a bribe to keep people in jobs they dislike.

Another symbolic measure of success is the *method* of payment, i.e., wage or salary. At least three companies—IBM, Gillette, and Canon Electric—have put all of their workers on straight salary, and all three companies report positive results. For example, both Gillette and Canon Electric reported a drop in absenteeism and turnover after the change. It is likely that straight salary gives an employee a greater sense of security and increases his sense of personal worth and responsibility. At the same time, such measures represent a shift from the economic model toward the growth model.

2. Operant Conditioning Model. The second branch of the economic/machine model is best described by Skinner, who believes that human behavior depends on operant conditioning and is, therefore, shaped largely by the environment.[6] Operant conditioning theory postulates that man responds to rewards; behavior which is reinforced by rewards will continue, whereas behavior which is not reinforced by rewards will cease. All that is necessary for an "operant response" (behavior) is that the behavior be "reinforced" by some type of reward. As Nord states, "If the outcome is pleasing to the individual, the probability of his repeating his response is apt to be increased."[7] Of course, the converse is also true.

In his tightly reasoned article, Nord makes the strong point that although Skinner's operant conditioning is applicable to a wide variety of situations, it has not been given enough consideration by theorists interested in human motivation. He points out that one of the most crucial factors in operant conditioning is the pattern of frequency by which a particular behavior is rewarded. One pattern is the continuous schedule, in which the reinforcement, or reward, follows the response every time the response occurs. He also describes several patterns of "partial reinforcement" and shows that a schedule of variable or random reinforcement leads to more durable, long-lasting response patterns than do schedules which are either fixed or continuous. For example, sport fishing is an excellent example of a variable-reinforcement schedule; the fisherman never knows when he is going to "get a strike," or catch a fish. Skinner has

By permission of John Hart and Field Enterprises, Inc.

trained pigeons to peck thousands of times at a target without reinforcement—
the pigeon never knows when it will get a food pellet.

Perrow describes two cases in which operant conditioning was used to train
pigeons to inspect drug capsules and small electronic parts called diodes. In both
cases, the pigeons' accuracy of inspection surpassed that of human inspectors.
In the diode inspection case, one pigeon had a one percent error rate while
inspecting 1000 pieces per hour for extremely minute defects. When two pigeons inspected the same pieces, the error rate was infinitesimal. However, top
management killed the project, primarily because of cultural reasons and the
possible adverse reaction of organized labor. As the chairman of the board of
the drug company said, "Who would trust medicine inspected by pigeons?"[8]

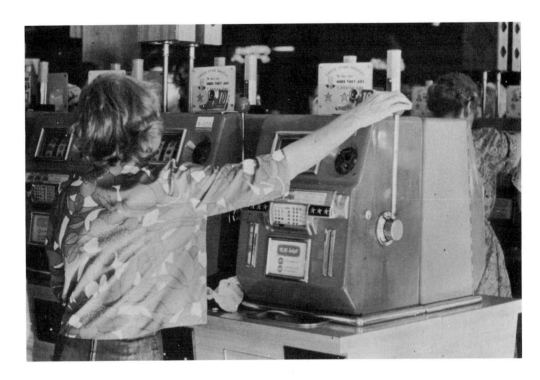

Operant conditioning is one of the major attractions of slot machines. The gambler never knows when he will "make a killing." (Photograph by Felicity S. Bowditch)

C. Growth-Open System Model

Both the coercion and economic-machine models assume that man is controlled by his environment. The growth-open system model, however, regards man as:

1. A decision-maker in his own right
2. Purposive and having individualized goals
3. Following only those orders that are compatible with his own needs and values
4. Having motives that are far more complex and interrelated than those in either of the other two models
5. Striving for growth, responsibility, and achievement when conditions for growth are present.

FORCE AND COERCION   ECONOMIC/MACHINE   GROWTH, OPEN SYSTEM

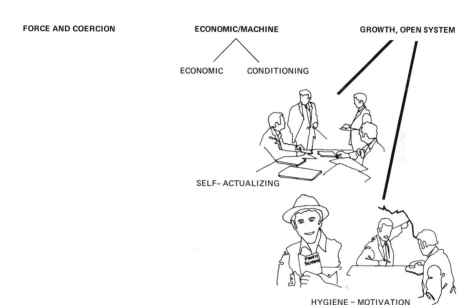

ECONOMIC   CONDITIONING

SELF–ACTUALIZING

HYGIENE – MOTIVATION

Figure 3.5. *Motivational models of man.*

Theorists have used these assumptions to go in two, interrelated directions
—the self-actualizing man theories of Maslow and the motivation/hygiene
theories of Herzberg and his associates (Fig. 3.5). Although both models are
currently popular, they have yet to be proved viable.

1. Self-actualizing Man Model. The economic model of man was discredited
by the Hawthorne studies (discussed in Chapter 1, p. 19), which showed that
physiological factors are less important than psychological factors on the job and
that social pressures from peers have a greater impact on productivity than do
purely economic incentives. The enthusiasm and cooperation of the group of
workers being studied was highly related to the interest the supervisors and
researchers showed in the work group, the lack of coercion on the group, and
the participation which allowed the workers to become involved in changes
which would affect them.

As a result of the valid questions about the economic-man model, research-ers began placing more emphasis on the study of groups and group behavior. These studies laid the foundation for a rather uncritical acceptance of Maslow's theory of self-actualizing man. According to Maslow:

1. Motives in the adult are highly complex, and no single motive affects behavior. Rather a number of motives may be in operation at the same time.

2. There exists a hierarchy of needs so that, in general, lower-level needs must be at least partially satisfied before a higher-level need is satisfied.

3. A satisfied need is not a motivator. In other words, when a need is satisfied, another emerges to take its place so that in a sense, man always remains a wanting being.

4. The higher-level needs can be satisfied in many more different ways than can the lower-level needs.[9]

Maslow also identified five levels of needs: the physiological, safety, social, ego, and self-actualization, or developmental, needs (Fig. 3.6). Currently, Mas-low's hierarchy of needs is one of most highly appealing and popular theories in the literature.

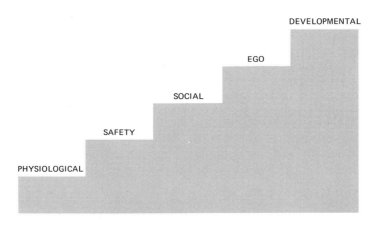

Figure 3.6. *Hierarchy of needs.*

1. The lowest level of the need hierarchy comprises the universal physio-logical needs for food, clothing, and shelter. Man generally tends to concentrate on meeting these needs before concerning himself with higher-level needs. When an individual has at least partially satisfied this level of need, other needs emerge.

2. The second level of need is for safety and security. Although "safety" originally meant freedom from physical harm, more recent writers include freedom from job layoff, loss of income, etc.

In the United States these first two levels of needs are generally well satisfied. The importance of these needs can be seen in the widespread emphasis on some form of job tenure and protection, various types of insurance, and savings accounts. However, when these needs are threatened, behavior changes, e.g., people may trample one another in trying to escape from a fire.

3. At the third—social, or belonging—level in Maslow's hierarchy, man is concerned about his social relationships. He wants to belong, to be loved, and to be accepted by others. This begins with the primary human group, the family, and expands to include his social and work groups as the individual grows older. Some groups are, of course, far more important to the individual than others. The importance of social groups is perhaps most striking in the adolescent, whose peer group may become far more important to him than his family.

4. At the fourth level are esteem, or ego, needs. Man needs to have a firm, stable, and usually high evaluation of himself. It is not enough to merely belong to a group; he also needs and wants the respect and esteem of those group members. In other words, the ego level has both internal and external aspects. The internal aspect is represented by the individual's self-perceptions; the external aspect is his desire to appear competent to his peers, to be accepted, and to be recognized as capable in his job, family, and social life. He needs *deserved* respect from others.

This ego level of need differs from the social level, in which man wants only to be accepted for himself as a person; at the ego level, he wants to be seen as competent and capable. At this higher level, man is concerned about promotion, achievement, accomplishment, prestige, and status which are *earned.* Failure to satisfy these needs can lead to feelings of inferiority, helplessness, and weakness which in turn may give rise to either compensatory or neurotic trends or to feelings of discouragement, passivity, and apathy.

5. The highest-level needs—for development and self-actualization—are satisfied only after needs at the four lower levels have been met. At this fifth level, the individual is concerned with the development of his full potential. This requires that he be psychologically healthy. The person at this stage, which many people never reach, has a better perception of reality, accepts himself and others, is more creative, and is, in a sense, better able to become completely human in the realization and development of his full potential.

The model of the self-developing and self-actualizing man is based on the assumption that man has innate needs to grow and mature and that he feels a sense of meaning and accomplishment in life and his work. As his lower-level needs are satisfied, the higher-level needs are activated.

McClelland provides some evidence of the need for self-actualization in his discussion of the drive for achievement.[10] McClelland asked his subjects to write a story about a set of pictures which were then scored for evidences of achievement; the pictures in this "projective technique" are relatively ambiguous, and the subject is forced to "project" himself in writing about the pictures. McClelland found that stories written by middle-level executives contained more references to the need for achievement than did stories by other executives either lower or higher in the organizational hierarchy. He postulates that the need for achievement propels a man upward into middle management; in large companies, a top-level executive has already satisfied this need.

McClelland also believes that one can determine the overall nature of the "achieving society" by examining children's reading books from various cultures. The more achievement-oriented the society, the greater the number of achievement-centered stories. He further believes that individuals can be trained to be higher achievers and that training for achievement can affect the growth of nations.

Since Maslow's hierarchy covers a wide span and several levels may be in operation at any one time, e.g., security, social, and ego needs, not all motives may be satisfied at one place and at one time. Some aspects of the job may be more satisfying than others; some motives may be involved only in job behavior, whereas others are reserved for behavior away from the job.

Lyman Porter, in applying Maslow's need hierarchy to management personnel, investigated perceived need fulfillment deficiencies of nearly 2000 managers in numerous companies.[11] The questionnaire he constructed was divided into five need categories: security, social, esteem, autonomy, and self-actualization. Responses were grouped according to managerial levels: presidential, vicepresidential, upper-middle, lower-middle, and lower.

Porter found that managers at all levels had similar security and social needs. However, satisfaction of the three higher-level needs varied greatly with managerial rank; the lower the manager's level, the less likely it was that these needs would be satisfied. Nonetheless, satisfaction of esteem, autonomy, and self-actualization needs seemed to be critically deficient at all levels of management, with the possible exception of the top managerial level, as McClelland would have predicted. Porter concluded that top management may have to be as concerned with the satisfactions and motivations of their lower-level managers as they are with the motivations of their blue-collar workers.

Vroom provides a review of similar studies that have been conducted by other researchers.[12] However, the studies conducted by Porter and others can be criticized for being cross-sectional rather than longitudinal. In other words, situational, selection, or cultural factors, rather than growth factors, may have determined the results. To test this hypothesis, several researchers conducted longitudinal studies of Maslow's need hierarchy. Lawlor and Suttle, for example, collected longitudinal data in questionnaire form from 187 managers in two different organizations in order to test the validity of Maslow's concept of the need hierarchy.[13] One group completed the questionnaire twice in six months; data for the other group were collected over a period of one year. There was little evidence to support Maslow's theory that human needs exist in a hierarchy of levels.

The authors suggest a two-level theory, with the basic biological needs at one level and all of the other needs at the second level. Needs at the higher level would emerge only after those at the lower level had been satisfied. On the basis of the results, Lawlor and Suttle could make no prediction as to which of the higher-level needs would emerge at any given time. For some people, it might be social needs; for others, self-actualization needs.

In another longitudinal study of Maslow's need hierarchy, Hall and Nougaim interviewed a group of managers over a period of five years.[14] They did not find strong evidence for the hierarchy; rather, they found that as managers advance, their needs for safety tend to decrease, with a corresponding increase in their needs for affiliation, achievement, esteem, and self-actualization. Hall and Nougaim argue that these changes result from sequential career stages rather than from lower-order need gratification.

Building on the Hall-Nougaim study, Alderfer, like Lawlor and Suttle, has proposed modifying Maslow's need hierarchy by a reduction in the number of categories.[15] As shown in Fig. 3.7, Alderfer has combined the Maslow categories into three groups of core needs: maintenance of material existence, maintenance of interpersonal relationships with people who are significant to the individual, and the need to find opportunities for growth and personal development.

Alderfer's first level of needs—*existence*—includes Maslow's physiological (survival) and safety categories, including pay, fringe benefits, and working conditions. Alderfer's second level—*relatedness*—encompasses Maslow's social and esteem levels and includes such significant persons as family members, coworkers, subordinates, superiors, enemies, and friends. Alderfer indicates that the basic ingredient of this need is sharing, or mutuality. He believes that relatedness needs are distinguished from existence needs in that "the process of satisfaction for existence needs prohibits mutuality." According to Schein, this model of "social man" provides evidence which "lends support to the assumptions that man is essentially socially motivated in his organizational life."[16]

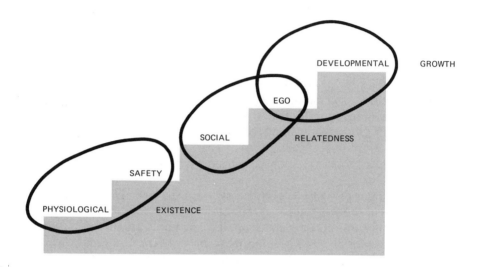

Figure 3.7.   *Alderfer's modification of Maslow's hierarchy of needs.*

As Fig. 3.7 shows, there is an overlap between Maslow's ego category and Alderfer's relatedness and *growth* categories. Whereas Maslow combined the external and internal aspects of ego needs, Alderfer has separated these two factors. To Alderfer, growth includes the individual's desire to be self-confident, creative, and productive—to engage in problems or tasks which require him not only to utilize his capacities fully, but also to develop additional capabilities or skills.

In modifying Maslow's approach Alderfer does not assume that lower-level needs must be satisfied before higher-order needs can emerge. He also feels that his modification conforms to a later distinction Maslow made between deficit and growth movitators.[17]

2. Motivation-Hygiene Model. This second branch of the growth-open system model is closely related to Maslow's need hierarchy model with its subsequent alterations. The motivation-hygiene theory emerged from two studies published in the 1950s which had a profound impact on motivational research. These studies, by Brayfield and Crockett[18] and Herzberg and others,[19] demonstrated that there is little or no relationship between productivity and morale. The results of these two studies came as a great shock to other researchers and practitioners in the field who had always assumed that these two factors are closely linked. Subsequently, there has been more research on motivation and morale.

To study the relationship between productivity and morale more closely, Herzberg and his associates used semistructured interviews to elicit from accountants and engineers the occurrences which made them like or dislike their work.[20] The five areas of critical incidents cited most frequently by those who liked their work were: achievement, recognition, nature of the work, responsibility, and advancement—all of which pertain to job *content* and are growth, or motivating, factors. Workers who were dissatisfied with their jobs, on the other hand, cited critical incidents related to the job *context*. The most important of these dissatisfiers, or hygiene factors, was company policy and administration (ineffective, deleterious, or unfair). Other dimensions were supervisors' lack of competence in carrying out their functions (poor technical qualifications or poor interpersonal relations) and poor working conditions (Fig. 3.8).

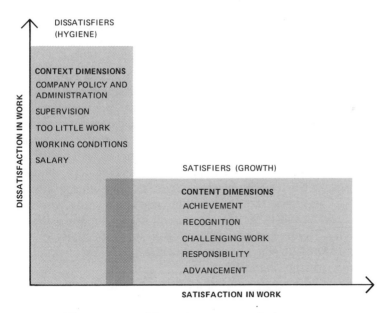

Figure 3.8. *Hygiene versus growth factors.*

To briefly summarize the findings, Herzberg would call the content dimensions to the right of the overlap area growth, or motivating, factors. The context dimensions to the left of the overlap area are dissatisfiers, or "hygiene" factors. In effect, he is saying that improvement of the hygiene factors is a little like vaccination—it can keep a person from getting sick, but it doesn't make him well.

One of the unique aspects of the Herzberg study is the finding that different dimensions account for satisfaction and dissatisfaction. Herzberg and his associates believe that earlier studies could find no consistent link between morale and productivity because investigators were tapping attitudes found in both the satisfier and the dissatisfier dimensions.

According to the Herzberg findings, at least half of the long-range dissatisfier incidents resulted in physical or psychological withdrawal from the job. Half of the satisfier incidents reported improved the individual's attitude toward the company, whereas only one-fourth of the dissatisfier incidents resulted in more negative attitudes. One-fourth of the dissatisfiers adversely affected mental health, but only one-eighth of the satisfiers improved mental health (sleeping better, better frame of mind, etc.). One-fourth of all satisfier and dissatisfier incidents affected home life, but satisfied persons were more likely to say home life would affect their job attitudes.

One of the early criticisms of the Herzberg study was that since only engineers and accountants were interviewed, the results may not be applicable to other occupational groups. A later, and potentially more serious, criticism was that Herzberg allowed his methodology to determine his results. Since people usually attribute good results to their own efforts and blame others for bad results, it is possible that this human tendency predetermined Herzberg's findings. After reviewing more than 20 studies, Hinton concluded that "in general, the more the methodology varies from the methodology used in the 1959 Herzberg study, the more likely are the conclusions to vary also."[21]

One of the "follow-on" studies stemming from Herzberg's pioneering work was conducted by Myers, who used Herzberg's dimensions with various types of workers—supervisors, technicians, and female assembly workers.[22] Myers found that the variables affecting motivation may have quite different effects on productivity. Factors having a positive effect on productivity, growth factors, challenge and stimulate employees to work effectively. Factors that reduce productivity are "hygiene" factors.

However, as Myers points out, the motivating and dissatisfying factors vary with the individual's personality and his type of job. For example, people who seek motivation, or "growth seekers," look for opportunities for achievement and responsibility, have positive feelings toward work and life in general, and derive a great deal of satisfaction from work accomplishment. Since these people strive for quality and are motivated primarily by the nature of the task itself and the desire to get the job done right, they are relatively unconcerned about poor environmental factors and, indeed, have a high tolerance for them.

"Maintenance seekers," on the other hand, tend to avoid looking for motivational opportunities, are more passive and cynical about their jobs, and distrust the positive values of work and life in general. Their dissatisfaction is expressed in their concern with the maintenance factors surrounding the job—pay, fringe benefits, job security, supervision, working conditions, fellow employees, and company policy and administration. These people seem to be more dependent on external conditions and are less inner-directed and self-sufficient than are growth seekers.

When "growth" seekers are treated as "maintenance" seekers, however, they tend to behave like maintenance seekers; in the absence of growth opportunities, they become more concerned with the environmental factors. Similarly, when maintenance seekers are treated as growth seekers, they tend to adopt the latter role and to acquire the behavior and value patterns of motivation seekers.

The controversy over Herzberg's original work continues to rage. Two recent studies add new light to the implications of the theory, although Herzberg's original methodology was used in neither study. Using job-attitude questionnaires on a sample of 141 female office workers in 32 administrative and service sections of a state university, Bobbitt and Behling found no real support for any of the alternative theories.[23] They justified their results on the grounds that "intrinsic variables are generally more potent than extrinsic variables and overall satisfaction is more predictable than overall dissatisfaction."

Waters and Waters, using questionnaire responses on critical incidents, could not support the hypothesis that defense mechanisms operate to attribute unfavorable outcomes of situations to others (extrinsic) and favorable outcomes to oneself (intrinsic).[24] The sample was composed of supervisors from an insurance company, nursing supervisors in a pediatric hospital, and station managers from an oil company.

Clearly, the research generated by Herzberg's findings has been inconclusive. As a result, Herzberg's "two-factor" theory has been neither completely validated nor discredited.

D. Review of the Theories

Although the various theories of motivation differ and the research does not solidly support any one theory, there are areas of common agreement, and the various models and theories are interrelated. If we use Alderfer's basic core needs of existence, relatedness, and growth, perhaps we can put the state of the current motivational art into better perspective. This is shown in Fig. 3.9.

Existence includes the coercive model of man, since man does strive for existence and survival, as well as parts of the machine/economic model, since money and economic rewards are necessary for survival. Existence also incorporates many of Herzberg's dissatisfiers; if such aspects of the surrounding envi-

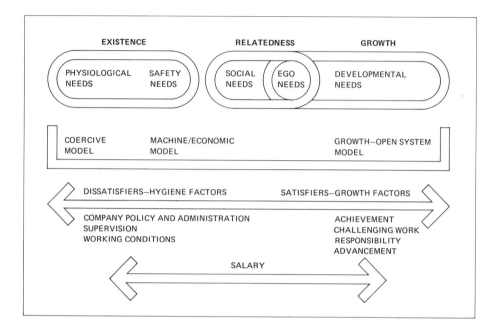

Figure 3.9. *Interrelationships of the models and theories of motivation.*

ronment as working conditions, company policy and administration, and salary are unsatisfactory, workers will be less motivated.

The core need for *relatedness* is consistent with Maslow's social and ego categories and can also include Herzberg's supervision and recognition factors as being either satisfiers or dissatisfiers. Finally, the core need for *growth* fits the growth-open systems model, since it includes both Maslow's developmental category and Herzberg's satisfier factors of achievement, challenging work, responsibility, and advancement.

Nord feels that all three core needs can be satisfied through operant conditioning. He discusses the need for exchange of both economic and social reinforcers and points out that the process of social exchange depends on the set of rewards which follow behavior, stressing that "the operant approach focuses attention on these exchange processes."[25]

The motivation to work is not a simple process. Rather, it is a complex interrelationship of such variables as:

1. expectations, the nature and strength of which vary with the individual's needs and aspirations over time

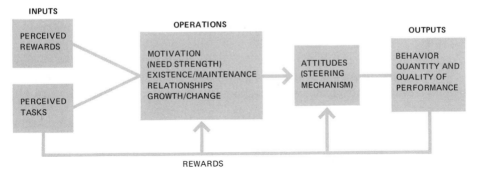

Figure 3.10. *A systems model of motivation and behavior.*

2. rewards, the individual's perception of potential satisfiers in the situation

3. relationships, the individual's perception of possible rewards for his output.

Figure 3.10 depicts the process of motivation in systems terms. An individual's activities are a function of inputs, the perceived task or tasks, and the perceived rewards. He then evaluates these inputs according to his current motivation and need strength, which results in an attitude, or steering mechanism. This attitude determines his behavior (output) and the quantity and quality of his performance.

IV. THE INDIVIDUAL IN INTERACTION WITH THE ORGANIZATION

Now that we have discussed several theories of motivation, we will consider the individual as a subsystem interacting with the larger system, the social organization. Earlier, we said that behavior is caused; people work to satisfy needs, and in this sense, people are *always* motivated. Thus, the individual comes to the organization with a set of needs; if the organization provides a climate conducive to the satisfaction of his needs, he will work. If, however, the larger system does not provide these opportunities for need satisfaction, he will subordinate the organization's goals to the satisfaction of his own needs. For example, there is the well-known story of the man who bought a new car which rattled. After he had taken the car back to the dealer several times, a thorough search was conducted to locate the source of the rattle. Finally, the mechanic found a bottle suspended from a piece of string inside the right front door. The note attached to the bottle was, "Noisy, ain't it?" The "saboteur" had clearly been motivated, but in a form obviously contrary to the goals of the manufacturer. This example illustrates the fact that it is easier to change the situation to allow the individual to satisfy his needs on the job rather than to try to change the individual.

As the individual interacts with the organization, two key elements emerge.

1. Interaction is always a two-way process of exchange. Unless both parties benefit from the exchange, the interaction will be reduced or halted by the one dissatisfied. As Homans states:

Social behavior is an exchange of goods, material goods, but also non-material ones, such as the symbols of approval or prestige. Persons that give much to others try to get much from them, and persons that get much from others are under pressure to give much to them. This process of influence tends to work out at equilibrium to a balance in the exchanges. For a person engaged in exchange what he gives may be a cost to him, just as what he gets may be a reward . . . Not only does he seek a maximum for himself, but he tries to see to it that no one in his group makes more profits than he does. The cost and value of what he gives and what he gets vary with the quantity of what he gives and what he gets.[26]

Thus, motivation is a balance—motivation equals reward minus cost ($M=R-C$). There are personal costs to remaining in an organization—the individual may have to give up some of his autonomy and independence in order to have a steady, secure job. He therefore expects something from the organization in return for putting in his time on the job.

In a laboratory study, Adams and Rosenbaum found that an individual's productivity is considerably greater when he believes his pay is too high.[27] However, some doubt was cast on this *wage inequity theory* by Valenzi, who found that differential effects on productivity may be caused by the worker's attempt to protect his self-esteem rather than by his perception of pay inequity.[28] Whatever the interpretation of the research, however, it is clear that interaction is an exchange, whether it be money for productivity or self-esteem for productivity.

2. Interaction always involves a sense of mutual obligation. If either person in an interaction fails the other, the relationship will probably be discontinued. In an organization, of course, this process of mutual obligation, or interdependence, is of critical importance in maintaining the stability of the organization.

We define "psychological contract" as the mutual exchange and reciprocation between the individual and the organization. This includes the influence process for mediating conflict between the goals of the organization (larger system) and those of the employee (subsystem). This psychological contract stipulates that material wages and "psychological income" be given to the individual in exchange for his commitment to work toward the goals of the organization. In other words, the psychological contract constitutes the sum total of the expectancies perceived by both the individual and the organization about their relationship. The organization expects the employee to be at work, to work hard, and to obey its authority and uses its authority to enforce these expectations. The employee expects payment for his work and fair and just treatment from the organization. If the organization fails to live up to the individual's expectations, he is likely to withhold his involvement or to become alienated and apathetic.

Etzioni has developed a typology for classifying different types of organizations according to the types of power exercised by the organization and the types of involvement and expectations of the employee.[29]

1. If the organization exercises primarily coercive power and authority, as do jails, penal institutions, concentration camps, and slave labor camps, the worker is likely to become *alienated* and to withdraw psychologically from the organization of which he is coerced to remain a member.

2. The second type of organization exerts primarily rational/legal authority and uses economic rewards in exchange for membership and performance. The reaction of the member is primarily *calculative*—he perceives his contract as a "fair day's work for a fair day's pay."

3. Hospitals, colleges and universities, professional associations, and religious institutions exemplify organizations which stress *normative* rewards; membership in the organization or the opportunity to perform a task or function has intrinsic value. The member of this type of organization regards involvement with the organization as having intrinsic value rewards; he performs his function primarily because he values it. In addition, he is frequently willing to accept the lower economic rewards provided by this type of organization.

Table 3.1 shows the nine types of organization relationships which Etzioni's typology produces. Etzioni stresses that the type of "psychological contract" depends heavily on the kind of power or authority used by the organization. Schein states that the types of organizations which fall along the diagonal seem to have workable and "just" psychological contracts. The kind of involvement obtained is consonant with the kinds of rewards given by the organization and the kind of authority exercised.[30] If a manufacturing concern uses primarily "scientific management," economic rewards, and rational/legal authority, it should expect a calculative type of involvement from its members. If it expects its members to be "loyal," to enjoy their work, and to be morally involved, it may be asking its workers to give more than they are receiving in return.

Table 3.1   Types of involvement versus types of power: the psychological contract

Type of involvement	Type of power		
	Coercive	Utilitarian	Normative
Alienative	X		
Calculative		X	
Moral			X

Adapted from A. Etzioni, *A Comparative Analysis of Complex Organizations* (Glencoe, Ill.: Free Press, 1961).

The importance and influence of the psychological contract on members of the organization cannot be overestimated. In his review of the literature on labor turnover among life insurance salesmen, industrial employees, nurses, and supermarket employees, Scott found a number of studies which clearly showed that new employees often quit their jobs because they had no opportunity to "achieve what they expected when they were hired."[31] Scott strongly recommends that prospective employees be given a much clearer picture of their jobs and the organization's expectations of them so that they can make a better choice. In one industrial firm, "30% of prospective employees decided not to sign up after a tour of the plant."

Perrow reports the change in attitudes and behavior of workers in a juvenile correctional institution, which was basically an alienative organization.[32] Applicants for low-level supervisory positions in the organization were asked to complete a questionnaire about their opinions on delinquency and differences between delinquents and nondelinquents. The responses indicated that the applicants were enlightened and permissive. After the applicants had been employed by the institution and had gained experience, the questionnaire was readministered to them and to all of the other personnel of the institution. The opinions of the new supervisors had changed radically to conform with the attitudes of the other personnel in the correctional institution; they had become much less permissive and were taking a punitive approach. In other words, the new supervisors had adjusted to the implicit "psychological contract" prevailing in the institution and had changed their opinions and attitudes to conform to the behavior that was expected of them.

In an article about the assembly line, which is perhaps the best example of Etzioni's utilitarian (economic/machine) model, Serrin quotes a supervisor describing the assembly-line worker, "You don't think ... You're just an automated puppet." A worker said, "That's all I'm working for—my paycheck and retirement." The article also describes the case of an employee who began shooting "at everybody in white shirts" with an M-1 carbine. In several minutes three men were dead. At the trial, the worker was found innocent because of temporary insanity resulting from the worker's early life in the South as a sharecropper and the impact of factory life. As one juror was heard to remark, "Working there would drive anyone crazy."[33]

In recent years the trend has been to slowly change the nature of the psychological contract from coercive/utilitarian to utilitarian/normative, and this has been particularly apparent in R & D organizations. As organizations increasingly expect their members to become committed to organizational goals and to value their work, management must change its part of the psychological contract to give workers more opportunity for personal involvement, decision-making, and growth. For example, Volvo and Saab-Scania have begun to use a team-production method whereby semiautonomous groups of four to seven workers assemble truck and auto components.[34] Female assembly workers at Volvo spend one day every two weeks performing office jobs. The Swedish automakers report other experiments and indicate that they are getting improved production quality and lower absenteeism. (In the United States, by contrast, the auto industry absenteeism rate rose from 2.8% in 1960 to 5.3% in 1970.)

V. SUMMARY

In this chapter we have looked at some commonly held beliefs about why people work. We have traced the history of motivational theory from the early concept of coercion and slavery through the concept of the economic/machine model and the currently more popular idea of man belonging in a growth/open system model.

We have examined some of the important research to make several points more vivid, concentrating most heavily on the research generated by Maslow's theory of the need hierarchy and the subsequent modifications of this theory, as well as on Herzberg's hygiene/growth theory. We concluded that the needs for existence, relatedness, and growth seem to fit the differing theories more closely than do other concepts we could use.

We pointed out that behavior is a process of social exchange wherein the individual acts in ways that satisfy his own personal unique needs. A closely related concept is the psychological contract. According to Etzioni, social exchange within the organization is based on the notion that organizations must provide their workers with opportunities for need satisfaction—by changing job situation, if necessary.

The manner in which an employer or leader "motivates" others depends largely on: (1) his own motivation; (2) the accuracy of his perceptions of his workers' needs; (3) the psychological contract he has with his subordinates; and (4) the effectiveness of the communication process. As Kolb says, "We do not see people as they are, we see them for what they mean to us."[35] Therefore, the extent to which a leader understands his own motivational structure and applies this understanding in his relationships with his subordinates is one determinant of his success. Although he can never be totally objective in perceiving another individual or situation, the successful manager must have the sensitivity and ability to diagnose, sense, and appreciate the differences among his subordinates in order to take appropriate action.[36] Logically, then, if the leader or manager initiates a proper psychological contract, he will be that much better able to properly "motivate" his subordinates. In order to do this, he must calculate his expectations of his subordinates in relation to their abilities and motives.

Another important motivational tool available to the manager is effective communication, which will be accepted more willingly and used more constructively by subordinates "when it is presented in a manner that [the worker] regards as objective, that is, without personal bias."[37] The sensitive and diagnostic manager will, therefore, have to understand his own assets and limitations in communicating to others.

The letter which follows is a humorous, if all too typical, example of what can occur when the processes of need fulfillment, motivation, and communication go awry.

Dear Boss,

I hereby give notice of my formal resignation, effective two weeks from today.

I've been a designer with the Gargantuan Grimble Group, Incorporated (G Cubed) ever since I finished college. My work here has been very educational, although I do confess to occasional bewilderment regarding big business management. This example should illustrate what I mean: Once at a gripe session the director of manufacturing responded to a question of mine by telling a story about the "mushroom" theory of management. He said that you should always keep your employees in the dark, feed them lots of horse manure, and, when they grow up, cut them off at the ankles and can them. Everybody thought it was a funny story; but by the time the meeting was over I still didn't have an answer to my question.

However, I'm not writing this letter to complain. I'd like to take this opportunity to thank you and the company for all you have done for me.

That $100 bonus I got last Christmas in exchange for patent rights on my 14th invention was a welcome addition to my son's college fund. And I get a real kick out of seeing the production department turning out thousands of my gadgets every day, even if my name isn't on the label. I only regret that I had to spend two years and write three fat proposals persuading you and the division manager that it was a good product in the first place.

In case you think that my decision to leave has anything to do with the layoff of Larry Longtimer last week, I want to put your mind at ease. I had been wondering why Larry was still on the payroll. His enthusiasm and drive really went to hell after he was promoted to vice president of historical planning. I just didn't feel he was doing the company any good in that new position. Confidentially, though, something has been puzzling me. Why did the top brass transfer him out of the Stockholder's Delight Division he started 12 years ago, especially right after it racked up its tenth straight record year? The new manager, Mr. Presidentson, isn't doing nearly as well.

At Larry's farewell luncheon last Friday, I was really moved by the company's generosity in giving him a solid-gold 25-year service pin with a real diamond in it. It's too bad Larry couldn't hold out until he was eligible for retirement next year, though. I guess it couldn't be helped, what with the big losses this year in the Stockholder's Delight Division. Anyway, that check for two weeks' severance pay should tide him over until he qualifies for unemployment compensation. I understand you can get as much as $75 per week nowadays.

I'd also like to say that my resignation is in no way related to my having to terminate those summer-hire students last year just two weeks after they started working. I guess the company's sudden realization that it was in a cash bind and required immediate layoffs couldn't be helped. I sure had a tough time explaining to those students, though. They went away grumbling some terrible things about their first introduction to big business.

Boss, I remember your explaining that the last 6 percent raise you gave me was the largest in the whole department, that I'm the youngest guy in the company's history to have the responsibilities I hold, and that my salary is the highest in the company for my job classification. I also recall that to be eligible for my next promotion to novice manager, I have to put in at least two more years with the company.

Boss, you've gotta understand! Each month, I get a copy of the *Alumni Review* from my alma mater. My wife reads me the class news at bedtime every evening after that damn thing comes in the mail. You wouldn't believe the jerks I used to have for classmates and lab partners who have started businesses of their own and are making out pretty well. One has launched a successful magazine with international circulation; another has his own real estate development corporation. Still another has a computer peripheral company with 500 people on the payroll that grossed $10 million last year, and our "most likely to fail" classmate is a bona fide magnate in the alfalfa exporting business. Phil Anthrope, my former class president, just made a $100,000 Alumni Fund donation to establish a perpetual scholarship bearing his name. With competition like this, you can understand why I was too ashamed of my career progress to go to last year's reunion. I know I'm at least as good as most of these guys, and I've got to prove it to my wife, my friends, and most of all, to myself. G Cubed timetables just don't hack it!

By now, I'll bet you're wondering what my plans are. I want you to know that I am not going to work for a competitor. You remember that new electromechanator Willie Whizbanger recently finished an 18-month development program on? You know, the one you circulated a memo about, saying the company was going to abandon it because there was no market for it? (You even let Willie buy the sole patent rights for $1.) Guess what? The vice president of corporate development at Upward Spiral Industries read Willie's recent *IEEE Transactions* article about it and called our Marketing Department to see if he could buy some electromechanators from G Cubed. When he learned we weren't going to make any here, the Upward Spiral man asked if they might buy the patent rights. That's when Marketing referred the call to Willie.

Later that evening Willie telephoned me at home to say that if I wanted to start a company with him to make electromechanators, Upward Spiral had indicated they would be our first customer. Willie said that the man at Upward Spiral even told him that he could help us get some venture capital if we would prepare a business proposal. He mentioned the possibility of our being a subsidiary or some such thing, but Willie and I are going to get more details after we finish working on our business plan. Incidentally, we will probably be calling our new company Nimble Whizbanger Laboratories. I'll be president and Willie will be vice president of engineering.

The main reason Willie and I feel so confident about our prospects for success is the way Fred Faithless and his group made out when they spun off to start Levitation Laboratories two years ago. They were just acquired last month by Colossal Conglomerate in a stock swap deal, and we understand that Fred has now retired to a cattle ranch in the Canadian Rockies at the tender age of 37.

Of the seven or eight companies started by former G Cubed staff members, the only one we know of that has failed was started by Stanley Spleen and Gilbert Gall. As near as we can reckon, their difficulties were basically due to walnut paneling, palace revolts, and their 35-hour work week.

Willie and I have built a new prototype of our electromechanator at my uncle's auto repair shop, using parts we bought at the Spleen and Gall bankruptcy sale. We have also gone to one of these new seminars on how to get started. Willie and I have talked to our wives about this, and last night we came to our final decision. Boss, it has been a pleasure working for you, and if you decide you might like to join us in about six months, we'd be glad to talk it over.

Sincerely,
Jack B. Nimble[38]

REVIEW

1. Interview a worker and a manager about the unwritten expectations (psychological contract) they have of the organization and the organization has of them. What influence does this seem to have on their behavior?

2. Why were the authors motivated to write this book? What needs might have been satisfied?

3. Discuss the implications of the psychological contract. Describe from your own experience what effect the psychological contract has had in either the classroom or a job you have held or are now holding.

4. Discuss the implications of the statement "I can't influence you unless I allow you to influence me."

5. Discuss the reasons why there seems to be little consistent measured relationship between morale and productivity. How important is the presence of "good morale"?

6. Interview several different people—a manager, a worker, a labor leader—to get their ideas on why people work. Do their concepts agree? How do their ideas tie in to the text?

7. Discuss the statement "You cannot motivate someone else." What does it mean? Do you agree with it? What are the implications of the statement?

8. What is the psychological contract in this class *as you perceive it?* What are some of the ways it can be changed? Modified? Improved?

9. Compare Maslow's need hierarchy model with Herzberg's motivator-hygiene model. What are the similarities? Differences?

Critical Concepts

Motivation:

    force and coercion model

    economic-machine model

    growth-open system model

Maslow's need hierarchy

Achievement needs

Existence needs

Relatedness needs

Growth needs

Motivation-hygiene theory

Psychological contract

Etzioni's typology of power and involvement in organizations

REFERENCES

1 W. E. Vinake, "Motivation as a Complex Problem," in *Nebraska Symposium on Motivation,* ed. M. R. Jones (Lincoln, Nebraska: University of Nebraska Press, 1962), pp. 1-49.

2 *Ibid.,* p. 3.

3 J. R. Strayer, H. Mumo, and C. Dana, *The Middle Ages, 359-1500,* 4th ed. (New York: Appleton-Century-Crofts, 1969), p. 248.

4 F. W. Taylor, *Scientific Management* (New York: Harper & Row, 1911), p. 46.

5 M. Weber, *Essays in Sociology*, trans. H. Gerth and C. W. Mills (New York: Oxford University Press, 1946).

6 B. F. Skinner, *Science and Human Behavior* (New York: Macmillan, 1954).

7 W. R. Nord, "Beyond the Teaching Machine: The Neglected Area of Operant Conditioning in the Theory and Practice of Management," *Organizational Behavior and Human Performance*, 4, 4 (Nov. 1969):375-401.

8 C. Perrow, *Organizational Analysis: A Sociological View* (Belmont, Cal.: Wadsworth, 1970), pp. 118-120.

9 A. Maslow, *Motivation and Personality* (New York: Harper and Brothers, 1954), p. 13.

10 D. McClelland, "Business Drive and National Achievement," *Harvard Business Review*, 40, 4 (July-Aug. 1962):99-112.

11 L. M. Porter, "Job Attitudes in Management: I. Perceived Deficiencies in Need Fulfillment as a Function of Job Level," *Journal of Applied Psychology*, 46, 6 (1962): 375-387.

12 V. Vroom, *Work and Motivation* (New York: John Wiley, 1964).

13 E. Lawlor III and J. Suttle, "A Causal Correlational Test of the Need-Hierarchy Concept," *Organizational Behavior and Human Performance*, 7, 2 (April 1972):265-287.

14 D. T. Hall and K. Nougaim, "An Examination of Maslow's Need Hierarchy in an Organizational Setting," *Organizational Behavior and Human Performance*, 3, 1 (Feb. 1968):12-35.

15 C. P. Alderfer, "An Empirical Test of a New Theory of Human Needs," *Organizational Behavior and Human Performance*, 4, 2 (May 1969):142-175.

16 E. Schein, *Organizational Psychology*, 2d ed. (Englewood Cliffs, N.J.: Prentice-Hall, 1970), p. 58 ff.

17 A. Maslow, *Toward a Psychology of Being* (Princeton, N.J.: Van-Nostrand, 1962).

18 A. Brayfield and W. Crockett, "Employee Attitudes and Employee Performance," *Psychological Bulletin*, 52, 5 (1955):396-424.

19 F. Herzberg, B. Mausner, R. Peterson, and D. Capwell, *Job Attitudes: Review of Research and Opinion* (Pittsburgh: Psychological Services of Pittsburgh, 1957).

20 F. Herzberg, B. Mausner, and B. Snyderman, *The Motivation to Work* (New York: John Wiley, 1959).

21 B. L. Hinton, "An Empirical Investigation of the Herzberg Methodology and Two-Factor Theory," *Organizational Behavior and Human Performance*, 3, 3 (August 1968): 286-309.

22 M. S. Myers, "Who Are Your Motivated Workers," *Harvard Business Review*, 42, 1 (Jan.-Feb. 1964):73-88.

23 H. R. Bobbitt and O. Behling, "Defense Mechanisms as an Alternate Explanation of Herzberg's Motivator-Hygiene Results," *Journal of Applied Psychology*, 56, 1 (1972):24-27.

24 L. Waters and C. Waters, "An Empirical Test of Five Versions of the Two-Factor Theory of Job Satisfaction," *Organizational Behavior and Human Performance*, 7, 1 (Feb. 1972):18-24.

25 W. R. Nord, *op. cit.*

26 G. Homans, "Social Behavior as Exchange," *American Journal of Sociology*, 63, 6 (May 1958):597-606. Reprinted by permission.

27 J. S. Adams and W. E. Rosenbaum, "The Relationship of Worker Productivity to Cognitive Dissonance about Wage Inequities," *Journal of Applied Psychology*, 46, 3 (1962):161-164.

28 E. R. Valenzi and I. R. Andrews, "Effect of Hourly Overpay and Underpay Inequity when Tested with a New Induction Procedure," *Journal of Applied Psychology*, 55, 1 (1971):22-27.

29 A. Etzioni, *A Comparative Analysis of Complex Organizations* (Glencoe, Ill.: Free Press, 1961).

30 E. Schein, *op. cit.*

31 R. Scott, "Job Expectancy—An Important Factor in Labor Turnover," *Personnel Journal*, 51, 5 (May 1972):360-363.

32 C. Perrow, "Reality Adjustment: A Young Institution Settles for Humane Care," *Social Problems*, 14, 1 (Summer 1966):69-79.

33 W. Serrin, "The Assembly Line, *Atlantic Monthly*, 227, 10 (Oct. 1971): 62-68.

34 "Disassembling the Line," *Time Magazine* (Jan. 17, 1972).

35 D. A. Kolb, I. M. Rubin, and J. McIntyre, *Organizational Psychology, an Experiential Approach* (Englewood Cliffs, N.J.: Prentice-Hall, 1971), p. 204.

36 E. Schein, *op. cit.*

37 R. N. Anthony, *Management Accounting, Text and Cases* (Homewood, Ill.: Richard D. Irwin, 1970), p. 418.

38 D. Dible, "Dear Boss: Why I'm Quitting . . .," *IEEE Spectrum*, 9, 5 (May 1972):63-64. This material has been adapted and exerpted from *Up Your OWN Organization! A Handbook for the Employed, the Unemployed, and the Self-Employed on How to Start and Finance a New Business*, Donald M. Dible (Santa Clara, Cal.: The Entrepreneur Press, 1971). Reprinted by permission.

4
INTERPERSONAL PERCEPTION AND COMMUNICATION

O wad some power the giftie gie us
To see ourselves as ithers see us!

ROBERT BURNS

I. INTRODUCTION

The processes of perception and communication form a system: communication depends on perception, and perception, in turn, depends on two classes of antecedents—internal states and external, or environmental, states. Most of the internal states depend on learning and include values, goals, beliefs, perceptions, (perceived) relations between actions and their outcomes, and the expected consequences of these actions.[1] The external states are totally environmental and include such things as upbringing, reading habits, and hobbies or other leisure-time activities. Obviously, the two states are closely related.

These two states determine our perceptual biases—the "rose-colored glasses" through which we see the world. Because of these two antecedents, we cannot be truly objective about anything. At best, we can only know what some of our prejudices are. The *perceptual set,* or outcome of the internal and external conditioning, determines what we communicate to others, our perception of what other persons hear, as well as what we hear from others (Fig. 4.1).

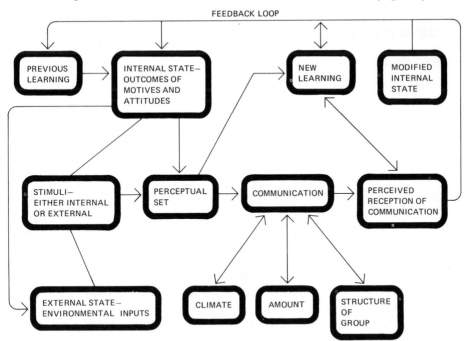

Figure 4.1. *Systems model of perception and communication. (Adapted from diagram in J. G. March and H. A. Simon,* Organizations, *New York: John Wiley, 1958, p. 11.)*

Perception and communication are the foundations upon which interpersonal behavior rest and have important implications for the three types of models discussed in Chapter 3. For example, a supervisor acting primarily according to assumptions of the economic/machine model is less likely to treat his subordinates as "humanely" as he would if he were following the relatedness model. Similarly, if he believes that money is the sole motivator, he is unlikely to provide his subordinates with opportunities for intellectual growth and achievement.

After discussing perception, we examine some of the reasons for both perceptual variation and the use of perceptual manipulating devices.

In the section on communications, we look at several factors that affect the communication process—the nature and amount of information received; how it is processed, condensed, and used; group factors in communication; and the "climate" of the situation. Finally, we review some specific techniques for improving the communication process.

II. PERCEPTION

A. Introduction

Such phrases as "that's not what I meant" or "that isn't what it means to me" are familiar expressions indicating that people see the world somewhat differently. Thus, although two people may receive the same visual and aural stimuli, they may perceive these stimuli differently. In other words, *sensations* are the inputs to the sensory system, and *perception* is the process whereby these incoming data are organized.

The organization of sensations through the perceptual processes serves a very useful and essential function. For example, in hearing, it enables us to "screen out" the myriad sound waves continuously hitting our ear drums and thereby pay attention to only certain, selected sounds. This organizing process, or perception, is learned over time. A good example of this is that one of the major difficulties a hard-of-hearing person has when he begins to wear a hearing aid is that at first, it is virtually impossible for him to "screen out" all the sounds that the hearing aid picks up. He must learn to readjust, and until he does, the hearing aid will be more of a distraction than a help.

Not only does the perceptual process help us screen out unwanted stimuli, but it also is of great value in helping us organize what we see and hear into something that is meaningful to us. This enables us to view the outside world as something consistent, something with which we can cope. We can use a minimum of cues to help us understand what is going on in the world around

The perceptual process enables us to "straighten out" this distorted view of the UN building caused by rain falling against a window. (Photograph courtesy Christian Science Monitor)

Figure 4.2. *Perception—expectancy.*

us. We can make almost instant order out of what would otherwise be chaos. We can predict how people will behave, and we can understand situations better.

For example, look at the seven dots in Fig. 4.2. According to Gestalt psychologists, most people "see" a triangle and a rectangle. The perceptual process by which such ambiguous sensations are organized into patterns meaningful to the individual is called *expectancy*. In other words, we tend to see what we expect or wish to see. For example, we *know* from past experience that most rooms have walls and ceilings that meet at right angles. As a result, when we look at a room, we *see* the walls and ceiling in terms of right angles, even though optically, they are actually at odd angles to us from our position in the room.

Given the same set of data, managers with different backgrounds will see different problems. A large inventory welcomed by an auto salesman may be decried by the production manager. Similarly, if different managers are given the same case to study or are asked to give their opinions about a company crisis, the manufacturing manager is more likely to see the problem as a need for more efficient production, and the financial manager is more likely to see the problem as the need to maintain a good financial picture for the company.

In the same way, management consultants with different backgrounds are quite likely to see quite different solutions to the same problem. The consultant with a Perspective I orientation may tend to see corporate inefficiency as resulting from poorly defined job descriptions, lack of centralized authority, too loose cost controls, poor industrial engineering, etc. The Perspective II consultant is more likely to see the problem as underutilization or misuse of the computer or the lack of appropriate mathematical models. The Perspective III consultant may well see the problem as a "people" problem and therefore recommend better motivational techniques and pushing decision-making to lower levels.

In summary, the manner in which we organize incoming sensations has two aspects.

1. Aspects of sensations that we have in common with others are called facts. An automobile accident witnessed by several persons is a fact, although they may not agree on the cause or details of the accident.

2. Sensations are organized in ways that are unique to us. This aspect of the perceptual process depends on biological mechanisms, past experience, and present assumptions, all of which stem from our own needs, experiences, values, and sentiments.

B. Internal and External Reasons for Perceptual Variation

Perceptual variation comes about from the fact that each person is different, with a different personality, background, and set of experiences. Therefore, several factors influence the development of the individual's perceptions.

1. Physiology. A person's perceptions of the world are affected by his physiological condition. A glorious sunset, for example, may just look like so many shades of gray to someone who is color blind. Or, a loud passage from Stravinsky's *Firebird Suite* may not be very impressive to a person who is hard of hearing or tone deaf.

2. Family. The strongest influence on a child is his family. Since the parents have already developed characteristic ways of seeing the world, many of their attitudes and perceptions are passed on to the children. It is no accident that most Catholics come from Catholic families and Lutherans from Lutheran families. A child whose father is a strong believer in trade unions is much more likely to grow up with similar attitudes and values. The attitudes and values provided by the family are, therefore, of primary importance.

3. Culture. The culture and society in which one lives has a strong effect on his attitudes, values, and the way in which he perceives the world. In 1947 Bruner and Goodman conducted a social psychological study in which they asked poor children and wealthy children to draw a quarter.[2] As might be expected, the poor children drew quarters which were significantly larger than those drawn by the wealthy children. Obviously, a quarter was more significant to a poor child than to a wealthy child. For example, people in some parts of the world consider dogs, cats, ants, snakes, and sheep's eyes to be delicious. The average American does not regard eating pork in the same way as does a devout Muslim. Similarly, he finds it difficult to understand why many Indians regard cows as sacred. In addition, any culture has subcultures, which may have greater influence on members than does the larger culture. Rock music and long hair, for example, are essential to one subculture but repugnant to members of other subcultures.

C. Devices for Manipulating Perceptual Data

An individual uses several devices to: reduce the amount of data he must work with, keep himself immune from data which might otherwise tend to lower his self-esteem, and try and keep combinations of events conceptually simple. The use of these devices, sometimes called a perceptual set, usually produces a tendency to behave in particular, predictable ways. Such devices are: stereotyping, halo effect, projection, expectancy, selective perception, and perceptual defense.

1. Stereotyping. This phrase, originally coined by Walter Lippmann, refers to generalizations used to classify groups of people. "Blondes have more fun," and "Germans are methodical but unimaginative" are examples of such stereotypes. Although stereotyping is frequently useful, it can also lead to highly inaccurate results. In 1950 Haire and Grunes examined what happened when people were confronted with information which did not fit a cultural stereotype, i.e., they were asked to justify the word "intelligent" in conjunction with the words "works in a factory."[3] Some subjects denied the incongruity. Others rendered the word "intelligent" meaningless by saying, "He was intelligent in the way he screwed the nut onto the bolt." Still others, recognizing the difficulty, used the discrepant information to make a real change in their previous stereotype.

We have used this exercise with our own students, using two lists—one containing the word "intelligent" and the other with the word left out. Our findings were essentially the same as those reported in the original study. Students using the list with "intelligent" left out always came up with much more uniform descriptions of the individual than did the groups of students using the list containing the term "intelligent."

2. The Halo Effect. This is the process of using one particularly favorable or unfavorable trait to color everything else we know about a person. For example, we generally assume that an ambitious person is also energetic, aggressive, and punctual (because he is so ambitious, he always seems to be around). If an "intelligent" man makes a mistake, our reaction might well be, "Anbody can make a mistake." On the other hand, if a "stupid" man who is a poor worker makes the same mistake as the "intelligent" man, our reaction is quite likely to be "What else would you expect from him?"

3. Projection. Here, we attribute our own feelings or characteristics to someone else. Murray studied this phenomenon in 1933 by dividing children into two groups, one of which played a game called "Murder."[4] Both groups were then asked to judge some photographs. The children who had played the game "saw" much more malice and violence in the photographs than the control group did.

A similar reaction occurs in labor relations; each group—the union and management—attributes its own malice and distrust to the other.

4. Expectancy. In addition to visual perceptual expectancy, there are other types as well. Sometimes called the *self-fulfilling prophecy,* expectancy is the process whereby the person makes happen what he wishes to have happen. In his classic 1964 experiment, Rosenthal, for example, told some students that he had bred one group of laboratory rats for their intelligence and another for their stupidity.[5] He then asked the students to perform an experiment to see whether the rats could be differentiated according to their ability to learn a particular task. Sure enough, the smart rats did better than the stupid rats. However, Rosenthal had not been truthful with the students; in fact, there was *no* consistent difference between the two groups of rats. The students had seen what they expected to see.

Rosenthal conducted a similar study with teachers and children.[6] After intelligence tests had been administered to the students, the teachers were told that some of their pupils were much more intelligent than others. In actuality, however, the researcher had randomized the group so that both groups represented the same level of intelligence. Nevertheless, those children that the teachers *thought* were more intelligent received considerably better grades than those whom the teachers *thought* were less intelligent.

5. Selective Perception. Another manipulative device is for the perceiver to draw unwarranted conclusions from an ambiguous situation. For example, a stockholder looking at a financial report may be so alarmed at noting that the company will not pay dividends this year that he completely overlooks the information that four highly salable new products will be introduced. In their 1965 study of selective perception, Dornbusch *et al.* noted that when children at a summer camp were asked to describe other children, the messages about *different* children from the *same* perceiver were more similar than descriptions of one child written by several others.[7]

6. Perceptual Defense. Once we have established characteristic ways of seeing the world, we tend to hang on to these characteristics—we have difficulty "letting go." Perceptions are useful in that they help us classify and organize the world in ways that make sense to us. However, these perceptions can also reduce our ability to fully understand another person in a given situation, i.e., he may sometimes seem to act "out of character." Perceptual defense may also include such other perceptual devices as stereotyping, denial, and projection.

These are only some of the processes which affect behavior. However, our purpose here is not to give a complete catalog of perceptual processes or devices,

"What makes you think I'm upset?"

but rather to give examples of the types of processes which operate in *any* perceptual situation.

D. Organizational Research Studies

In the "real world," of course, perceptual processes and devices do not occur in isolation. Rather, as the following studies show, they usually occur in combinations.

As Table 4.1 shows, there is considerable disagreement among workers, foremen, and general foremen about why people work. For example, managers believe that wages are much more important to subordinates than subordinates do. Getting along with people is perceived as far more important by subordinates than by their managers. The same is true with the opportunity to do interesting work.

Table 4.2 shows Mann's findings that higher-level supervisors and their subordinates have widely divergent views about the subordinates' "freedom" to discuss important things about the job. Although 85% of the supervisors believe their subordinates feel free to talk about the job with the boss, only half of the subordinates share this belief. More than 90% of the foremen and 100% of the

Table 4.1 Perceptual differences about reasons for work

	Workers' self-ratings	Foremen's ratings for workers	Foremen's self-ratings	General foremen's ratings for foremen	General foremen's self-ratings
High wages	28%	61%	17%	58%	11%
Getting along well with people I work with	36%	17%	39%	22%	43%
Good chance to do interesting work	22%	12%	38%	14%	43%

Adapted from R. Likert, *New Patterns of Management* (New York: Mc-Graw Hill, 1961), p. 50.

Table 4.2 Perceptual agreement and disagreement between supervisors and subordinates about their communications

	Workers see themselves	Foremen say about the workers	Foremen see themselves	Top management say about foremen
1. Feel very free to discuss important things about the job with the boss	51%	85%	67%	90%
2. Always or nearly always tell subordinates about changes affecting them or their work	47%	92%	63%	100%
3. Always or almost always get subordinates' ideas	16%	73%	52%	70%
4. Very often get a "pat on the back" for good work	13%	82%		

Data summarized and adapted from R. Likert, *New Patterns of Management* (New York: McGraw-Hill, 1961), pp. 47-53. Much of these data are from unpublished studies by F. C. Mann.

top management feel that they always or nearly always tell subordinates about changes affecting them or their work. Only about half of the subordinates feel the same way. Item 4 shows one of the major discrepancies—82% of the foremen say they frequently give the man a pat on the back for good work, but only 13% of the men agree. There have been many studies like these, and the findings are always similar—there are major perceptual differences between bosses and their subordinates.

In summary, each individual is an open system. He receives information inputs, transforms these inputs from sensations to perceptions, which then become modified outputs. These outputs may be modified still further as a result of the feedback loop. This perceptual process is shown in Fig. 4.3.

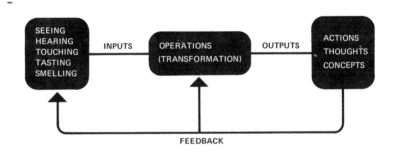

Figure 4.3. *The perceptual process.*

The complexity of the operations, or transformation, process is highly dependent on the situation. If, for example, one touches a hot stove, little perceptual bias or distortion occurs and through the feedback process, he recognizes what is happening and pulls his hand away almost instantly. In a highly complex social situation, however, many more factors are involved, including stereotyping and the halo effect. In general, perceptual biases and distortions are more likely to occur as (1) the information input becomes more central and more important to the individual and (2) the input diverges from deeply held beliefs. For example, a truly suspicious or paranoid person may perceive very innocent acts of other people as being extremely threatening. Here, the feedback process may be entirely internal in that the paranoid's suspicions may not be translated into direct action.

E. Summary

At the end of the last chapter we said that social behavior is an exchange—there is mutual interdependence and sense of obligation between people, and we behave in order to get something from the situation, the "psychological contract." However, because of the way in which we see the world, our attempts to influence others may be highly inaccurate because our perceptions are inaccurate. We need to improve the accuracy of the perceptual process before we can increase the accuracy of our communications. This means that we must continuously check our perceptions and assumptions and get feedback.

In addition to checking ourselves, we must also check the other person. In short, every individual behaves in ways that make sense to him. Each of us *always* acts in ways that are meaningful to us in terms of our perceptions of the world. Therefore, in order to better understand both how someone else feels about the world (communications) and his logic, we have to better understand both ourselves and others.

III. COMMUNICATIONS

A. Introduction

Communication is the process of sending and receiving messages, and accurate communications do not take place unless the sender sends properly and the receiver receives the message in an undistorted form. However, there are a number of possible blocks, or filters, in the communications channel. Figure 4.4 shows that communication requires encoding and decoding. The sender encodes a message into what he considers a suitable form. He transmits the message, and the receiver decodes it. However, there are a number of perceptual sets and/or "noise" in the line which reduce the clarity and accuracy of the information. For example, perceptual variation by both the sender and receiver is one of the biggest blocks to effective communications. Or, the sender's message may lack clarity, use the wrong transmission channels (perhaps a face-to-face meeting would be better than sending a memorandum), or be too complex. The receiver, for his part, may be preoccupied with other things, hear only what he expects to hear, and ignore conflicting information, e.g., material that conflicts with what he already knows or feels about the person.

B. Three Personal Factors in Communications

Although "open communication" is generally regarded as a positive goal, we have seen that perceptual factors greatly affect what is communicated. In this

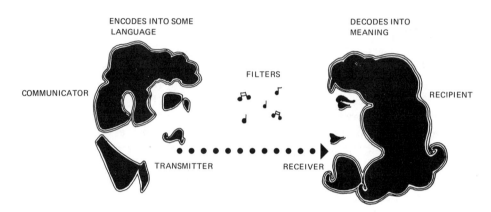

Figure 4.4. *The communications process.*

Ambiguous messages block effective communications. (Photograph by Edgar F. Huse)

section we examine some other variables relating to the communication process: the nature of the information to be communicated, the effect of group structure on the flow of information, and the effect of "climate" on communications.

1. Nature of the Information. We have seen that the process of communication is affected by such factors as who we are, our motivations, our upbringing, and our personal biases. In turn, the nature of the incoming information is affected by the quantity in which it is received, the manner in which it is presented and perceived, and the feedback process.

a) Overload. One of the factors directly related to the nature of the incoming information is "overload." According to Miller, there are seven types of reactions to information overload.[8] First, the individual may simply fail to take account of information. This type of reaction is likely to occur when he gets too busy with too many activities, has too many appointments on his calendar, etc. As a result, he starts missing regularly scheduled meetings or forgets what he was supposed to get at the supermarket.

A second type of reaction to overload is making errors. Here, the individual is likely to show up for a meeting the day after it has occurred or to incur his wife's wrath by bringing home the wrong brand of detergent. Making errors is perhaps the most common reaction to overload.

A third reaction is delaying, or queuing. We all do this at times. During the rush period of exam time or during the heavy production season, we adopt the motto "Put off until tomorrow anything not due today, and put off forever anything possible."

Miller's fourth category is a filtering process, whereby some of the information is omitted, sharpened, or ignored. Here, the individual sets priorities among things intended to have equal importance. If, for example, he must go to stores X, Y, and Z, his desire, and hence his decision, to go to store Y first would reflect this filtering process.

Another reaction to overload is for the individual to generalize categories of information. An example of this type of behavior is the tendency of committee secretaries to say merely that the committee voted to take up a certain problem, without noting how the members voted.

A sixth reaction is to designate another person or organization to handle the overload. Thus, for example, a boss may have his secretary go through his mail and sort out those things requiring his immediate attention. Or, a corps of junior executives may take over some of the tasks formerly handled by one overworked, senior official.

The final reaction to overload described by Miller is the deliberate avoidance of the information—the head-in-sand approach. Thus, a student who has studied diligently for three exams, for example, might decide that there is no point in even taking the fourth exam, since he will probably fail it. Miller, however, does not differentiate between the perceived and actual overload in his discussion of this type of reaction.

b) Comprehension. The nature of incoming information is also affected by the recipient's understanding of the message. In other words, communications may, as Bennis indicates, have multiple meanings.[9] Strictly verbal messages rarely have multiple meanings. However, interpreters of diplomatic correspondence between two countries look closely for shades of meaning and nuances, which sometimes "tell" much more than the written words. Very often what is *not* said is just as important as what is said. During the recent national debate about school busing to achieve racial balance, the President indicated that desegregation is a desirable goal. But as he did not specifically call for busing to achieve this goal, one might assume that he is against busing (even though this was not said at the time). At a more personel level, a girl's "no" to her boyfriend's amorous intentions could be interpreted literally or could simply indicate that the proposition was open for negotiation.

Similarly, the interaction of verbal and nonverbal communication may provide a host of multiple meanings. A girl who responds to her boyfriend with a quick, "Now you quit it!" but smiles like a 200-watt bulb gives a mixed message with multiple meanings. Bennis notes that in accenting certain words, raising eyebrows, or gesturing in certain ways, we are communicating nonverbally. Frequently, the strict verbal message is altered because of the nonverbal element. Bennis points to the truism that frequently the receiver of the information may not hear everything that has been said (overload?). Or, he may have heard part of what has been said, but it may not be what the sender intended to be heard. Taking a remark out of context is one common way in which this happens. Political campaigns are rife with this sort of thing. A candidate's remark will be either misinterpreted or altered to mean something which was not intended. The candidate will then deny having made the statement, assert that he was quoted out of context (frequently true), or that his remark has been misunderstood.

Nonverbal factors, then, obviously play a critical role in communications. For example, in 1952 Birdwhistell developed a system for recording gestures.[10] When he analyzed the body movements of an adolescent group's leader (who was not very articulate), he found that the leader's body movements were quite "mature," with little foot shuffling. The leader's body movements indicated that he was receptive and that he was a good listener.[11]

Nonverbal "body language" may communicate a message far more effectively than spoken words. (Photograph courtesy Christian Science Monitor)

Additionally, we know that there are common nonverbal "phrases" which are used in everyday life. For instance, a long exhalation may indicate satisfaction, whereas a short one may indicate a certain boredom. Still other common nonverbal communications are hand gestures, open arms, a greeting gesture, to indicate a certain warmth. However, some gestures are characteristic of particular ethnic groups. For example, Fast reports that Jews in Nazi Germany were frequently identified by certain gestures not used by non-Jews.[12] Although people were apparently able to change their living arrangements, occupations, and appearance, they could not change their gestures, which were a complete giveaway.

c) Feedback. In considering the meaning of what is said, we must examine what was intended, as well as how it was interpreted. The concept of feedback, described in greater detail in the chapter on the nature of systems, is one way of testing how well a communication is understood. Feedback, or "reality testing," is the process of reporting what was said or intended to the sender to "test" it for validity.

In an early study demonstrating the effects of feedback, Leavitt and Mueller note that while feedback improves the accuracy of task performance, it slows the process down.[13] A class of students was asked to draw a series of rectangles in various relationships to one another. In one experiment, no feedback was allowed, i.e., the instructor was not told when the students were having difficulty following instructions. In another experiment, free feedback was allowed —students could ask questions. The results confirmed the obvious. The "no feedback" condition was faster, because the instructor did not know how well the students had understood his directions. However, the "feedback" condition led to much greater accuracy, and the situation was perceived as such even prior to knowledge of the results.

The practical implications of this study are clear. Feedback can have either positive or negative results, depending on whether the goal is accuracy or speed. However, emphasis on speed (no feedback) can result in frustration for both the sender and receiver of the message. Providing for feedback, on the other hand, alleviates these frustrations. Therefore, although "efficiency" may be a goal of the Perspective I, formal, structuralist-design outlook, this goal may be thwarted without a consideration of worker morale, as occurs in Perspective III. In the long run, it may be unwise for an organization to stress "efficiency" at the expense of morale.

2. Influences of Group Structure on Communication. Table 4.3 shows the various ways in which information processing may be affected by group struc-

Table 4.3 Group structure and information processing

Speed	Slow	Fast	Fast
Accuracy	Poor	Good	Good
Organization	No stable form of organization	Slowly emerging but stable organization	Almost immediate and stable organization
Emergence of leader	None	Marked	Very pronounced
Morale	Very good	Poor	Very poor

A. Bavelas and D. Barrett, "An Experimental Approach to Organizational Communication," *Personnel*, 27, 5 (1951): 366-371. Reprinted by permission.

ture. The diagrams in the table show hypothetical situations, of course, since groups seldom have such clearly defined structures. However, they do help to explain some of the communication phenomena in groups. Some patterns of communication are linear, or unidimensional, flowing between a leader and each of his subordinates; others are circular—communication occurs only between adjacent positions on the circle; and others form a star-like pattern superimposed on a circle—characteristic of all-channel communication patterns. In a circular type of communication network, typified by a carefully defined gossip pattern, the speed of information processing is slow, and the accuracy is poor. The gossip simply proceeds from one person to the next, until it gets back to the originator. Obviously, there is a wide margin for error or distortion in this type of pattern, since at no point is there cross-checking or validation of the "facts." In organizations that adhere to this pattern of information flow, there is no clearly defined leader, or central processing agent, for the information. As a result, the organization is unstable, but morale tends to be very high. By contrast, in a unidimensional type of communication, characterized by a strong leader, the speed of information flow is fast, the accuracy is high, and because there is a key person, the organization is stable. Curiously, however, the morale is poor.

The practical implications of this research are that if one is interested in group consensus on a project, one might strive for a leaderless group situation in which everything is discussed by everyone. On the other hand, if efficiency is of paramount importance, there should be a leader and a well-defined and controlled number of communication channels. However, research such as this is artificially structured. Seldom do groups operate in these ways, for these models do not take into account informal groups, which in fact cut across all parts of an organization.

One study which does consider "real-life" communication patterns in organizations was conducted by Davis, who found that although the prescribed norm was communication down the chain of command, a great deal of communication took place across departmental lines, along the "grapevine," informal communication that is passed along very quickly.[14] In the industrial organization Davis studied, a company picnic was being planned for half of the executives (roughly 60 persons). Only two members who were *not* to be invited knew about it beforehand; all the invitees knew about it before they actually received their invitations.

This type of informal network, in addition to processing information quickly, also tends to remain "relevant," that is, it is rarely carried over to the home or "off-campus" club. A third characteristic is that its relationship to the formal communication network is highly correlated; when there is an increase in formal communication, there is also an increase in informal communications. Thus, one can use this close relationship to create a more open communication network simply by tying in some parts of the informal network with the formal network.

Davis suggests that one must increase the number of liaison persons between key organization members if communications are to improve. A communication network should depend much more on staff executives than on line executives for the spreading of information. In addition, the organization should develop a horizontal type of communication network across departments in conjunction with the vertical "chain-of-command" type of communication network and develop methods for bringing the more isolated groups into the communication network. This, in effect, may capitalize on the informal group by formalizing communication links across equivalent levels of the organization.

3. Effects of "Climate" on Communications. In addition to informal group and horizontal communication links, both organizational climate and personal receptiveness affect how well communications are heard or received. If an organization insists on using the chain of command for all communications and if the climate is repressive or coercive, certain important communications may not be received. Gibb has outlined two basic types of climate: one which threatens the receiver or puts him on the defensive, and one which is supportive.[15] Each threatening communication, however, can be made supportive, or at least non-judgmental. For instance, the statement "The cafeteria provides horrible food" is threatening to someone connected with the cafeteria, whereas a descriptive remark such as "Last week, three out of the five dinner menus at the cafeteria featured some form of chicken" is factual and nonevaluative. Similarly, a question of control can be made less threatening by shifting the emphasis to a problem-orientation. The recipient may feel threatened by his perception of "strategy" or artificial neutrality (or "clinical detachment," as Gibb says). The supportive equivalents to these types of perceived communications are spontaneity (no particular strategy) and empathy (an open concern for the receiver). A superior air is threatening, and equality is supportive: the former tends to either shut off communication or make it argumentative, thereby shutting off effective communication; equality implies "no judgment" and openness.

Gibb's two final types of communication are "certainty" versus "provisionalism," the former creating a threatening, closed climate, and the latter creating a supportive climate. To illustrate the difference between these two types of communication, suppose that an observer said to the individual running a meeting, "You have a real problem because you continually interrupt others." This exemplifies "certainty." However, the observer could have created a nonthreatening, supportive climate by saying, "It is interesting to note that in the first hour of the meeting, only one other person was able to 'hold the floor' for as long as 24 seconds."

Carl Rogers, the nondirective psychotherapist, also helps to pinpoint these issues in different terms.[16] Like Gibb, he notes that one of the strong barriers to effective communication is a person's tendency to evaluate someone else's communication. Sometimes two or more people will get into an argument, and such statements as "You're wrong!" or "That's a bunch of bull!" or "How silly can you be?" will be made (or screamed). Such statements add only heat, not light, to the subject. People arguing from different perceptual sets tend to make highly evaluative, judgmental remarks, a situation which Rogers regards as a major stumbling block to effective interpersonal communication.

Another obstacle to listening, he reports, is heightened emotions. We all know this. If we feel very strongly about a particular viewpoint, we find it very difficult to listen. A third obstacle may be the size of the group, because most people become defensive in large gatherings. A large group may inhibit communication by intimidating the person from asking questions or stating a position, particularly if he is uncertain how the group will react or is certain that the group will respond with some sort of disapproval.

The solution to these problems, says Rogers, is to listen with interest, which is much easier said than done. Listening with interest permits persuasion to occur; however, if one's mind is made up, he merely evaluates and does not listen. Rogers notes that listening with understanding and interest takes courage, for it requires an open mind. Listening with understanding can be fostered by having an influential person listen empathically, trying to understand both the content of and frame of reference for what is being said. When the tone is thus set, listening will be much easier.

C. Techniques for Improving Communication

One technique useful in group problem-solving situations is brainstorming. These sessions are usually of short duration and are frequently tape recorded. The group leader begins by defining the problem and then encourages the group members to "flights of fancy." Persons are expected to contribute ideas, and all ideas are accepted; the unique feature of this technique is that there is no evaluation of the ideas. After the session has been concluded, the tape is played back to glean whatever ideas are worth pursuing.

A second technique for improving the communication process is role-playing, in which two or more people "act out" a conflict situation in order to gain a better understanding of why someone else feels a certain way. An effective variation of this technique is reverse role-playing, in which a husband and wife adopt each other's role, for example. Their problem might be to decide whether to spend $1000 to redecorate the kitchen or buy a new(er) car. By acting out reverse roles, each "actor" comes to a better understanding of his partner's point of view.

A third technique is observer feedback. Here, a neutral outsider observes a discussion and at regular intervals reports back what has transpired in the group. Taking particular care not to evaluate what has gone on, he reports perceived misunderstandings between group members. Inasmuch as a person caught up in a group discussion does not recall events from a neutral frame of reference, the technique of observer feedback can pinpoint misunderstandings overlooked by the group members.

Davis has outlined several procedures which individual managers can follow to enhance communication between workers and management.[17] First, the manager can adopt an open-door policy. As Davis notes, however, this policy may be difficult to implement if the manager is unreceptive, shy, or otherwise awkward about communicating with workers. Davis also suggests that social gatherings at which the families of workers and managers are present can aid communications. At such times the worker and his boss see each other in a different, more relaxed setting, and this more "human" atmosphere can be translated into more effective communication on the job. Finally, the manager can encourage use of the "suggestion box." This technique, however, requires extensive feedback in order to be successful. Unless changes resulting from such suggestions are well publicized, the suggestion box is likely to remain empty.

In one organization studied by Beer and Huse, communications improved greatly from a "coffee with the boss" program whereby the manager of an organization held weekly meetings with randomized samples of production and clerical employees.[18] This approach has also been used successfully in other organizations.

Foltz points out that increasing outside social pressures and inside humanistic pressures are forcing managers to operate much less by fiat and much more by persuasion.[19] Therefore, they have to improve their behavioral science and communications skills in order to work better with their peers and subordinates. One of the problems with improving communication skills is the sheer number of meanings inherent in any communication; he notes that the dictionary lists 14,000 meanings for the 500 most used words, an average of 28 meanings per word! Or, as Mark Twain said, "The difference between the right word and the almost right word is the difference between lightning and a lightning bug."

IV. CONCLUSION

In this chapter we have stressed the importance of two-way interaction with others. Much of behavior is a process of social exchange, and perception and communication are the two variables that most strongly influence social interchange. Perception, however, is affected by various personal factors, the result of which is that each person sees the world differently and behaves in ways that make sense to him as he sees the world.

Since perceptions affect communications, many obstacles to effective social exchange can arise unless steps are taken to improve the processes of both communication and perception. Thus, feedback is critical to improved understanding and accuracy in communications. For example, although a great deal of perceptual variation exists between supervisors and their subordinates, mutual feedback can help improve one group's understanding of the other's motivational needs.

The concept of feedback will be central in the chapters that follow, especially in the discussion of the interaction of managers with their peers and subordinates. Improving the processes of feedback, perception, and communication can help improve not only communication within the organization, but also the effectiveness of the organization itself as a system for social interchange and exchange.

REVIEW

1. Ask a number of different people how they interpret a particular controversial statement in a newspaper or magazine. How often and in what ways do these interpretations differ from the "sender's" intended meaning?

2. What are some attitudes or beliefs you hold which have never been exposed to a conflicting point of view in an argument? Explain how this can occur.

3. In a class discussion or elsewhere, try an experiment by establishing the rule that each person must repeat the words or intent of the previous speaker before he can begin speaking. Do this for 20 minutes. What effect does this have on communication? How do you feel about discussions handled in this manner?

4. Table 4.2 showed significant perceptual discrepancies between supervisors and subordinates about their communication patterns with each other. What is the impact of such perceptual differences on the people involved? How can such discrepancies be minimized?

5. With two or three others, observe people talking in a closed telephone booth. Without attempting to listen in on the conversation, draw your own conclusions about the content of the conversation from the speaker's body movements and gesticulations. Share your perceptions with the others in your group. Did everyone see the same things? Did everyone draw the same inferences from what was observed?

6. Describe what you perceive to be an individual's perceptual defense. When might such a perceptual defense be useful? Discuss.

7. Find an example of a "mixed message" and describe the situation.

Critical Concepts
Sensations
Perceptual set
Stereotyping
Halo effect
Projection
Expectancy
Selective perception
Perceptual defense
Overload
Communication filtering
Feedback

Grapevine

Communication climate

Mixed message

REFERENCES

1 J. G. March and H. A. Simon, *Organizations* (New York: John Wiley, 1958).

2 J. S. Bruner and C. C. Goodman, "Value and Need as Organizing Factors in Perception," *Journal of Abnormal and Social Psychology,* 42 (1947): 33–44.

3 M. Haire and W. F. Grunes, "Perceptual Defenses: Processes Protecting an Organized Perception of Another Personality," *Human Relations,* 3 (1950): 403–412.

4 H. A. Murray, "The Effect of Fear Upon Estimates of the Maliciousness of Other Personalities," *Journal of Social Psychology,* 4 (1933): 310–329.

5 R. Rosenthal and R. Lawson, "A Longitudinal Study of the Effects of Experimenter Bias on the Operant Learning of Laboratory Rats," *Journal of Psychiatric Research,* 2 (1964):61-72.

6 R. Rosenthal, *Experimenter Effects in Behavioral Research* (New York: Appleton-Century-Crofts, 1966).

7 S. M. Dornbusch, A. H. Hastorf, S. A. Richardson, R. E. Muzzy, and R. S. Vreeland, "The Perceiver and the Perceived: Their Relative Influence on the Categories of Interpersonal Cognition," *Journal of Personality and Social Psychology,* 1 (1965):434-440.

8 G. Miller, "The Magical Number 7, Plus or Minus Two: Some Limits on our Capacity for Processing Information," *Psychological Review,* 63 (1956):81-97.

9 W. G. Bennis, "Interpersonal Communication," in *The Planning of Change: Readings in the Applied Behavioral Sciences,* ed. W. G. Bennis, V. D. Beane, and R. Chin (New York: Holt, Rinehart and Winston, 1961).

10 R. Birdwhistell, *Introduction to Kinesics: An Annotation System for Analysis of Body Motion and Gesture* (Washington, D.C.: Foreign Service Institute, Department of State, 1952).

11 R. Birdwhistell, "Kinesics and Communication," in *Explorations in Communication,* ed. E. Carpenter and M. McLuhan (Boston: Beacon Press, 1960), pp. 54-66.

12 J. Fast, *Body Language* (Philadelphia: Lippincott, M. Evans, 1970).

13 H. J. Leavitt and R. A. H. Mueller, "Some Effects of Feedback on Communication," *Human Relations,* 4 (1951):401-410.

14 K. Davis, "Management Communication and the Grapevine," *Harvard Business Review,* 31, (Sept.-Oct. 1953):44-49.

15 J. R. Gibb, "Defensive Communication," *Journal of Communication,* 11, 3, (1961): 141-148.

16 C. R. Rogers, "Barriers and Gateways to Communication," *Harvard Business Review,* 30, 4 (July-Aug. 1953):44-49.

17 K. Davis, *The Dynamics of Organizational Behavior* (New York: McGraw-Hill, 1967).

18 M. Beer and E. Huse, "A Systems Approach to Organizational Development," *Journal of Applied Behavior,* 8, 1 (Jan.-Feb. 1972):79-100.

19 R. Foltz, "Communication: Not an Art, a Necessity," *Personnel,* 49, 3 (May-June 1972):60-64.

5

THE
GROUP
IN
THE
SOCIAL
ORGANIZATION

We few, we happy few, we band of brothers.

SHAKESPEARE

I. INTRODUCTION

In Chapter 3, we first considered the individual as a system in his own right concentrating heavily on motivation and behavior in work settings. We also examined the individual as a subsystem in interaction with other subsystems (individuals perceiving and communicating with other individuals). Now we turn to groups, which are central to all concepts of organizational behavior. With a knowledge of group dynamics, groups and committees can become more productive.

Cartwright and Lippitt have stressed that groups do exist, they are omnipresent, group forces have extremely important effects on the individual, and the consequences of group behavior (from an organizational point of view) can be either good or bad.[1] Therefore, proper knowledge and understanding of group dynamics can be used to consciously improve the consequences of group actions.

It is obvious that knowledge about group dynamics, especially group behavior, is tremendously important to the manager who wants to run an effective enterprise. The effective manager knows when to make decisions by himself and when to use groups, including meetings and committees. For example, there is the story of a new manager in a textile plant. He found the chief union executive and in no uncertain terms told him that when he ran a plant, he *ran it*, whereupon the union representative waved his hand. Recognizing this signal, the workers stopped work, and immediately the looms were shut down. The union representative's comment to the new manager was, "O.K., now go ahead and run it."

For a long time, management literature did not discuss, understand, or recognize groups that were not "subordinate," i.e., did not report to a single manager. Although good managers have always been far ahead of the management literature, it was not until the Hawthorne studies in the late 1920s and early 1930s that management writers began to recognize that behavior is affected not only by formally defined relationships, but also by more informal relationships. Subsequent research and observation have made it abundantly clear that within the formal structure there exists a pattern of *social* relationships, or informal groups, which do not appear on the organization chart and may not be formally or even informally recognized by the organization. However, there is ample evidence to prove that these patterns of informal social relationships have a great deal of influence on behavior. As we have noted elsewhere, informal groups can either restrict or enhance productivity. Similarly, the informal group can speed up information flow. Likert postulates that unless an organization is created and sustained through participative groups, the informal organization is likely to be at odds with, or at least not fully supportive of, the goals of the formal organization.[2] When the organization is created and supported by participative groups, the formal and informal organization will be undifferentiated.

In this chapter we examine the role of the group as a subsystem within the larger system, the social organization. We also look at the group as a social system, the reasons and methods for group formation, the internal structure of groups, groups in interaction with one another, and techniques for observing and diagnosing meetings.

II. THE GROUP AS A SOCIAL SYSTEM

It seems self-evident that a random collection of people—in a restaurant or on a bus—is not a group. However, if something happens to change this pattern so that they have a common purpose, the collection of people will have become a group. If, for example, people standing in a line band together to keep someone from crashing the line, they will have been transformed from a collection of people to a group with a common purpose.

Davis defines a group as "a set of persons among whom (by definition or observation) there exists a definable or observable set of relations."[3] Therefore, the term "group" need not refer to a stable set of relationships, but rather to the location of the interaction or the interaction of relationships. In systems terminology, a group is a "set of mutually interdependent behavioral systems that not only affect one another, but also respond to exterior influences."

One way of looking at a group is as a social system within a larger system —the organization. Earlier, we characterized a system as: complex, with interdependent parts; open, consisting of inputs, transformations, outputs, feedback, and boundaries; in balance, resulting from positive and negative feedback; and having a multiplicity of purposes and objectives.

As Davis points out, group performance and behavior are affected by three classes of variables: such personal factors as motives, perceptions, abilities, and personality traits; the environment (spatial and social) in which the group action takes place; and variables related to the group's immediate tasks or goals.

Figure 5.1 shows a social group from a systems point of view. As a social system, a group has: inputs, including expectations from within and outside the boundaries of the system; operations, or transformations, including group structure, interactions, and leadership; and outputs, including productivity (whether helpful or harmful to the organization) and satisfaction. In addition, it has both positive and negative feedback, by which it attempts to achieve changes and maintain balance, respectively.

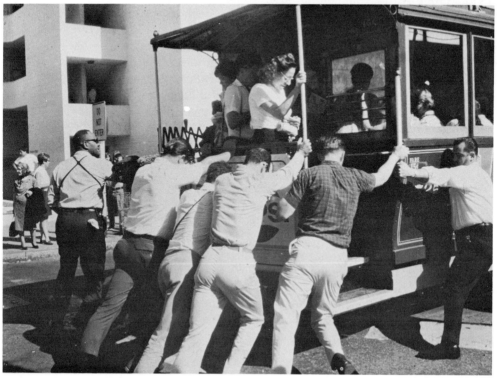

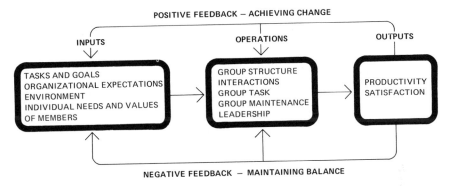

Figure 5.1. *The social group in systems terms.*

However, by adding systems terminology to the description of a group as a social system, we get a slightly different, more psychologically-oriented definition of a group. A group, in the psychological sense, is any number of people who: (1) have a common purpose or objective, (2) interact with one another to accomplish these objectives, (3) are aware of one another, and (4) perceive themselves to be part of a group. As a system, this group may be either closed (with only internal interaction) or open (processing much information coming from the outside).

The purpose of a particular group may or may not be well defined. The purpose of the group may be primarily social, highly work-oriented, or not even well understood. For example, teenagers who band together to "protect" themselves from their parents may be unaware of this fact. The interaction may be face to face, conducted by mail, or carried on over the telephone. The interaction may be either permanent or transitory, thus determining the length of the group's duration.

However, it is psychological awareness that differentiates a "group" from an "aggregation of people." Unless people are aware of one another and the fact that they are a group, they remain a collection, or aggregate, of people, rather than a group in our definition. They must perceive themselves to be a group in order to interact with one another to accomplish their common objectives. For example, the various tenants in a large apartment building constitute an aggre-

This pit crew exemplifies a formal, cohesive work group. (Photograph courtesy Stock, Boston)

A random collection of people banded together in an informal group to help turn around a San Francisco cable car. (Photograph by Edgar F. Huse)

gation of people, even though they have similar complaints about their landlord
If, however, they band together and "speak with one voice" to the landlord, they
become a "group." They have a common purpose (getting the landlord to make
repairs); they interact (organize) in order to accomplish this objective; are aware
of one another (the result of their interaction); and most important, these tenant
consider themselves to be part of a cohesive group (and so does the landlord)

III. WHY AND HOW GROUPS ARE FORMED

A group formed through and by the formal organizational structure is called a
formal group; one formed to accomplish tasks on the job is a *work,* or *task,* group
one formed within the structure, but without official sanction, of the organization is an *informal* group; and a group formed for purely social reasons is a *social*
group. In addition, there are such other types of groups as *family* and *interest*
groups. Of course, there may be a great deal of overlap; a task group (group of
managers) may also be a social group (golf foursome). A work group may be
either formal or informal, depending on whether it is officially recognized and/
or supported by the formal organization. For example, it is reported by several
knowledgeable people that top management in a large computer manufacturer
gave an order to stop work on a particular product which did not seem to be
worth the time and effort. A group of engineers from different units continued
to work on the project under "bootleg" conditions, and in a few months they
developed random-access memory, which is the core of the modern, third-
generation computer which operates "on-line in real-time."

The type of group formed and the reason for its formation in work settings
depends in large measure on the perspective in which it exists. Thus, groups
formed from a structural design (Perspective I) viewpoint will differ from those
emerging from an "information flow" (Perspective II) viewpoint. And groups
formed on the basis of "human" needs (Perspective III) will differ from those
found in either of the other two types of perspectives.

A. Groups from the Perspective I Viewpoint

The formal group, found primarily in Perspective I, exists to achieve organizational goals and is therefore established, maintained, and supported by the
organization. The tasks or objectives of the formal group are usually well defined, and members are assigned to the group with little regard for either their
personal wishes or ability to work together. In short, the formal group exists
because of the *demands* of the organization.

A formal group consisting of a manager and his subordinates may be relatively permanent, even though the group's membership may change. If, on the

other hand, the formal group is established to attain a specific objective, it will probably be disbanded once its objective has been met. The use of such "temporary" groups is increasing rapidly, giving rise to such common terms as project manager or program director.

B. Groups from the Perspective II Viewpoint

Informal groups tend to form spontaneously as the result of people interacting at work. Indeed, it was only after the Hawthorne studies that the existence of informal groups was discussed in management literature, and only in the past 20 years have we begun to study and understand the operation of informal groupings within the formal social organization.

Informal groups, which are not sponsored, recognized, or perhaps even approved by the formal organization, exist primarily to expedite and improve the flow processes of information and communication. People whose work is interdependent and interrelated develop informal groups in order to get the job done better and more quickly. In addition, workers may find informal groups more rewarding than formal groups.

Whyte questions the wisdom of making a dichotomization between the formal and informal organizational structure; he feels that except at the opposite ends of a continuum (e.g., a supervisor giving a subordinate a direct order or a group of employees discussing a sports event during a coffee break), the two are inextricably mixed.[4] We will consider this intermingling of the formal and informal system in much more detail in Chapter 7, in which we show that a manager spends the majority of his time in the lateral work-flow processes of trading, interacting, and negotiating.

Nevertheless, if we look at the organization as a work-flow process, interaction in an informal group is most likely to occur among persons whose work is interdependent and interrelated. In most organizations there exists an informal network of people who "get the job done" by avoiding the "red tape" of formal communication channels. In their study of lateral work-flow relationships, for example, Walton et al. found that cooperative and harmonious relationships between departments were accompanied by informal exchanges that were more frequent and positive and that resulted in greater payoffs; departments with less harmonious relationships were characterized by greater adherence to formal rules and more formal interaction with fewer people.[5]

Farris confirms the Walton findings by noting that the informal organization "ticking along under the surface" can help an organization become much more effective and innovative.[6] He believes that the proper approach is to find the key people in the informal organization and facilitate their interactions in the informal organization, even if they will thereby spend less time in their formal positions or jobs. This approach, he contends, is even more necessary in research and development groups, which need to be creative, than it is in other areas of an organization.

As we mentioned at the beginning of this chapter, however, the consequences of group behavior (from an organizational point of view) can be either good or bad. It is clear that informal groups sometimes work actively against the advancement of organizational goals. Roy has proved conclusively that the informal group can work against the stated goals and objectives of the enterprise through informal quotas or quota restrictions.[7] The workers in his studies developed informal groups that were highly distrustful of management and which served to protect their members against what they perceived as hostility on the part of the formal organization.[8]

C. Groups from the Perspective III Viewpoint

In addition to being formed because of organizational demands or the requirements of the work-flow process, groups may arise because they meet certain personal needs, such as those described in Chapter 3. Since many of these needs cannot be satisfied by the individual himself, they must be satisfied by others, usually in groups.

Man is a social being, and belonging to groups satisfies needs which he cannot satisfy in isolation. According to Homan's exchange theory, therefore, every social activity or group represents a reward by meeting specific needs of the individual.[9] For example, one of the chief causes of casualties among troops in a battle is "bunching up." Men who are in danger need to be physically close to one another, even though they know that this increases their collective danger. As Stouffer's studies indicate, a soldier's need for contact with his buddies is considerably more important in determining his behavior than the orders of his military supervisors.[10]

We can use Maslow's hierarchy of needs to identify some of the specific needs that groups can satisfy.

1. Security Needs. Membership in groups can provide protection, because there is power and security in groups. Union membership, for example, helps an individual satisfy this need.

2. Social Needs. Since most people have strong affiliation needs, groups can help meet this need. Indeed, America has been called a country of "joiners." Group membership gives one a sense of belonging.

3. Ego Needs.   Membership in groups helps satisfy ego needs by providing the individual with feelings of accomplishment, recognition, an "identity," and competency; helping him solve work problems; and providing him with opportunities for building his self-confidence. Ego needs are also used to provide a guide for acceptable work behavior and checking judgments, e.g., "Hey, Jim, what do you think of this?" One of the authors once had a boss whose behavior varied tremendously. As a result, the first man to see him in the morning was asked by the others, "What is he like today?" With that information, the rest of the group could modify their behavior accordingly.

4. Self-Actualization Needs.   Most people are unable to satisfy needs at this highest level, for they are trying to meet their social and ego needs. However, membership in groups can provide the individual with better insight into his own behavior; feedback from group members can help him realize his own potential to a fuller extent.

In other words, man's social and ego needs are both satisfied and reinforced by his participation in groups. Certain needs can be satisfied only by the group; therefore, man turns to the group in order to satisfy his needs. Furthermore, by providing feedback, the group can help the individual meet his highest, self-actualization needs.

The need satisfaction obtained from group membership is highly complex; no single group can satisfy all of our needs. Any or all of our needs may contribute to our reasons for belonging to a particular group at a particular period of time. As our needs change, our group affiliations, both on and off the job, are likely to change. We remain members of a particular group only so long as the needs being satisfied by that group are more important than the work or expenditure of effort necessary to remain within the group. When the group no longer satisfied our needs or when the energy level required becomes higher than the rewards obtained by the group, we drop out of that particular group.

As we have looked at groups in social organizations, one common theme in the "how" of group formation is the concept of interaction. Anything that causes people to interact with one another, whether at work or at home, increases the odds that they will form a group. It is a truism to say that if people do not know one another and have never met, they cannot comprise a group as we have defined it.

The simple matter of geography, then, has much to do with the formation of groups. One is much more likely to form a social group with his immediate neighbors than with people in the next block. For example, one of the authors has lived for four years in a house which has a high fence and a lot of shrubbery along the back end of the lot. The author does not know the names of the two "neighbors" on the other side of the fence. Similarly, individuals living near the main entrance of an apartment house are much more likely to know the other tenants than if they live on the top floor to the rear of the building. The same is true for people attending the same church, the same school, or working in the same company. Within an organization, people working in the same building or geographical area are much more likely to form groups than with people working in a different building.

Although interaction can facilitate the development of a group, it is not the only factor in group formation. As we have seen, unless a group can satisfy the needs of its members, it will either cease to exist or individual members will drop out, although the group itself may remain as an entity. Common values or shared interests are thus a powerful factor in determining why groups form. People with shared interests, whether task related or hobbies such as stamp collecting, golf, sailing, or photography, are more likely to gather together in groups than are those with different work interests or hobbies.

IV. THE INTERNAL OPERATION OF GROUPS

Groups have a clearly distinguishable internal structure which emerges over time. The extent to which this internal structure is effective determines, in large measure, the degree to which the operating group is successful in meeting its purpose, in reaching its objectives and, just as importantly, in satisfying the needs of its members. To understand the internal operation of groups, we need to explore such concepts as group functions and activities, leadership, group norms and standards of behavior, group cohesion and solidarity, and group decision-making.

A. Group Activities

The basic function of a group is to accomplish its objectives. However, in addition to the overall and sometimes expressly stated objectives of a group, each member of the group also has his own objectives, i.e., satisfying his own personal, idiosyncratic needs. As a result, any group has a multiplicity of objectives: explicit, implicit, recognized and discussed, only recognized, or not even recognized.

Benne and Sheats have identified at least three different activities taking place within a group as a result of these different objectives: group task activities, group-building activities, and self-serving activities.[11]

1. Group Task Activities. Activities such as initiating, clarifying, coordinating, and orienting the group to its goals, giving and seeking information, and establishing contact with the "outside world" all help the group attain its primary goals and objectives. Examples of group task roles are: orientation ("It's getting late, and we need to move along"); information-seeking ("John, don't you have some information that may be of help here?"); clarifying ("Isn't Jim trying to say that . . ."); and information-giving ("The latest report shows that . . ."). All of these are attempts by a member of the group to help move it toward the accomplishment of its goals and objectives.

2. Group-building Activities. These activities allow the group to build and maintain itself by helping to satisfy members' needs and fostering trust and cooperation among group members. Any group can be made more effective by the application of such principles as harmonizing ("You two really aren't as far apart as you think"); use of humor to reduce tensions ("That reminds me of the story about . . ."); and encouraging people to participate and compromise ("Sam, we know this is the first time you have attended our group's meetings, but we feel you have a great deal to contribute" or "Let's see if we can work out something that is agreeable to both sides"). All of these activities are attempts to build better relationships within the group so that the group can maintain itself.

3. Self-serving Activities. Since each member of a group has his own set of unique needs, values, and goals, he will carry out such self-serving activities as attention-getting, dominating, aggression, and withdrawal. Although such activities may satisfy the individual's particular needs, they contribute little to the overall success of the group in attaining its formal or primary objectives. Examples of self-serving roles are: "I don't care how you explain it, you're dead wrong" (aggression); "We're not getting anywhere, why don't we each work on the problem by ourselves?" (withdrawal); "I know more about the subject than anyone else, and *I* think . . ." (dominance). When an individual engages in these kinds of activities, he may be more interested in serving his own interests than in performing either group task or group-maintenance roles.

B. Group Leadership

The term "leader" usually connotes someone with formal authority, the "boss" of a formal task group. But since the "official" leader may be only a figurehead, we cannot use the term "leader" synonymously with "boss" or "manager." Rather, a leader is anyone who takes on group task, group-building, or self-

lēad′er *n.* a person who makes an important decision,

then sits back,

and answers stupid questions for the rest of his life.

By permission of John Hart and Field Enterprises, Inc.

serving roles. Therefore, a group may have, over time, many different leaders, some more effective than others. In other words, leadership is not a function or trait of a single individual, but is distributed throughout the entire group, and any group member may be a leader at any point in time.

This is not to deny that one or more individuals may be more influential than others in the group (e.g., the "boss" may well have more power and influence in a work group than any other single member). It is, however, essential to point out that leadership, in terms of power and influence, is distributed at various times in the lifetime of the group. In fact, groups frequently have at least two commonly recognized leaders—one who most frequently takes on the job of moving the group along toward task accomplishment, and another who most frequently takes on the group-maintenance role. A person who frequently adopts a self-serving role may serve as a disruptive "leader," i.e., he may be very influential in impeding the group from reaching its objective. (Leadership is discussed more fully in the next chapter.)

A group deviant may be ostracized or even expelled from the group. (Photograph courtesy Christian Science Monitor)

C. Group Norms and Behavior

Over time, a group tends to develop a life, history, and culture of its own. Concurrently, the group members tend to either develop roughly the same attitudes and values or leave the group. This similarity in attitudes and values is called a norm, or standard, against which the appropriateness of the members' behavior can be judged. As Davis points out, some norms apply only to overt, perceived behavior; some are formal, i.e., written; and others are informal, i.e., they emerge from the interaction of the group members.[12]

Norms also influence a person's decision whether or not to join a particular group. For example, Republicans in a local community tend to associate, at least in their political activities, with other Republicans. Union members tend to associate with other union members. Teenagers tend to associate with other teenagers. The tendency to associate with, pay attention to, and listen to other group members further enhances the commonality of group attitudes and norms.

Group norms can be translated into specific types of behavior resulting from the interrelationships and interdependence of group members. The existence of group norms exerts a pressure on group members to conform to these norms. For example, a college student's behavior may vary greatly, depending on whether he is with his parents, with fellow students at the local bar, or in class. Each of these groups has norms and standards of behavior to which this student is expected to conform.

Members whose attitudes and values differ widely from group norms must decide whether to try to change these values, learn to accept them, or to drop out of the group. However, as Davis points out, overt deviation from established norms is generally met with sanctions by the group, and in extreme cases the member may be expelled from the group.[13] For example, in 1971 the chairman of the board of IBM, Thomas Watson, wrote a memorandum ordering all IBM employees to wear white rather than colored shirts. The memo made it clear that anyone disobeying this dictum could expect to be fired.

Unwritten norms may be just as important as formal, written ones. Dalton describes a widespread, unwritten norm that violated established rules in a chain of drug stores.[14] According to the unwritten norm, employees, especially managers, could take free food and confections from the soda fountain, and fountain managers could take food items home. The result of this common practice was that the chain's soda fountains consistently showed only a small profit. In one store, however, the fountain manager adhered rigidly to the published rules, and her profits, of course, were consistently higher. The questioning by higher management, the resentment of other fountain managers, and the unhappiness of the employees in that particular drug store put the store manager under a great deal of pressure. As a result, he continually rechecked her records and withheld the praise she felt she deserved for having the highest profit margin. After two years of increasing frustration and resentment, she quit the firm. Since this particular unwritten norm was in direct violation of established company rules, the store manager was never able to tell her why he was unhappy with her.

D. Group Cohesion

The term "cohesion" simply means "solidarity." The more cohesive the group, the more likely it is to have common values, attitudes, and standards of behavior. As we will see later, this has profound implications in industrial settings. The degree of a work group's cohesiveness affects the degree to which that group is helpful or harmful to the organization as a total system.

A group can be highly cohesive only if it has been successful in accomplishing its group-building and task activities and minimizing the self-serving activities of its members. In addition, there are other factors which affect group solidarity. Generally, the greater the *status* of a group, the greater its cohesion. In a high school or college, for example, there are always one or two high-status groups to which many people want to belong.

The *size* of a group affects its cohesion. If a group is too small, e.g., two or three people, there may not be enough skill within the group to perform the group-building and task activities. Conversely, if the group is too large, communications within the group may break down, and group members may not find enough opportunity to satisfy their own needs. Frequently, groups larger than eight or ten members tend to divide up into smaller subgroups.

Solidarity is also affected by the *homogeneity* of the group. If the group's members have widely differing values or statuses, they will find it difficult to become a cohesive unit. For example, it may be very difficult to have a cohesive group which includes both the president and the janitor of the organization.

The more a group is *isolated* from other groups, the more it tends to be cohesive. Similarly, members of an isolated group are more likely to share common values and standards of behavior. Thus, a small work group isolated from the rest of the organization may become highly cohesive and demand a great deal of conformity from its members.

Reacting to *outside pressure* is one of the fastest ways a group can develop strong solidarity. In industrial work groups, outside pressure may take many forms: union-management conflict, competition between groups, mistrust between line and staff personnel, or reaction against a dictatorial supervisor.

Generally, the more *successful* the group is, the more likely it is to become highly cohesive. Conversely, if the group fails to achieve a particular goal, its solidarity may, but not always, decrease.

E. The Importance of Group Cohesion and Solidarity

Cohesiveness has direct bearing on a group's behavior; the more cohesive the group, the greater the likelihood that its members will have similar attitudes, values, and behavior patterns. The fact that a group is highly cohesive also increases the chance that members can influence other members to *change* their behavior. If, for example, influence is exerted for conformity to group norms, changes thereby accomplished should in turn increase the group's cohesiveness. In other words, the more cohesive a group is, the greater the number of members who conform to its norms.

Thus, group cohesiveness and conformity to norms are mutually reinforcing factors. The fact that there is cohesiveness means that a member can change the norms to which other members conform. One member's desire to bring about change within the group is of value, particularly if others find his feelings and attitudes worthwhile, thus reinforcing his feelings. This leads to a relatively stable situation, which Homans identifies as a basic sort of equilibrium, i.e., the basic variables of group operation (the rate of interaction, who speaks to whom, etc.) remain stable over time. This stability, Homans argues, is reflected in the paradigm: profit = reward – cost, and can be described as "distributive justice."[15] For example, a bright student may feel even more superior (profit) if he takes the time (cost) to tutor poor students, an activity he enjoys (reward). In short, by using the reinforcement paradigm, one can predict and account for much of a group's behavior. Homans has helped focus on reinforcement as the basis for group operation. Taking an extreme position, it is virtually certain that if there were no reinforcement for staying in a group, members' needs could not be met, and the group would dissolve.

As we have said previously, membership in a group provides a number of rewards. However, in order to receive the rewards, the member must accept the group's behavioral demands. Individuals remain or drop out of a group to the extent that they accept these behavioral demands and perceive the rewards to be greater than the "cost" of the demands.

However, when group membership is not highly relevant for achieving the individual's goals, group pressure can still have a profound effect on individual judgment. For example, Asch conducted a series of experiments in which all but one of the members of a group were "stooges" who had been instructed to publicly state wrong judgments when asked to compare the length of a given line with one of three unequal lines.[16] In a large majority of the cases, the naive (uninstructed) subject conformed to the group judgment of the line length, even when he knew that the consensus was wrong. In other words, he denied the evidence of his senses in order to conform to the group's judgment. However, it must be pointed out that this occurred when he was the last to state his estimate of line length.

Given that the members of a cohesive group have similar attitudes and behaviors, behavior in work situations is greatly affected by the dynamics of work groups. However, it is important to realize that a cohesive work group is, as far as the organization is concerned, essentially neutral. Conformity to group norms is neither good nor bad; it is merely a fact.

Although there is a pressure toward conformity in a work group, this tells us little about the content of these norms, since they may vary from creativity, originality, and high productivity in one group to rigidity, qualification, and restricted output in another group. In order to deal with the effects of group cohesion and solidarity, therefore, we need to distinguish between group norms or objectives that are helpful to the organization and group norms or objectives that are harmful to the organization.

There is abundant research evidence that many work groups have established norms, objectives, and standards of behavior that are harmful to the organization (see, for example, Roy).[7,8] There are few industrial managers who are unaware of such group activities as restricted production, strikes, and slowdowns, all of which are contrary to the aims and goals of the enterprise. Conversely, almost every manager of an organization can cite examples of ways in which informal groups have contributed materially to the aims and goals of the organization by helping to solve production problems, increase productivity, etc.

V. GROUPS IN INTERACTION

Especially in social organizations, groups can be considered as subsystems in continuous contact with other subsystems throughout the entire system. There are a number of different ways in which groups come into contact and interact with one another: the manager of one group may attend a committee or staff meeting with the managers or representatives of other groups; or he may meet formally or informally with other managers or representatives of other groups. As we shall see in Chapter 7, it is not uncommon for a manager to maintain contact and negotiate with as many as 30 different groups! Individual members of groups may interact with individual members of other groups on either a formal or informal basis. Finally, entire groups may meet with other entire groups. Such meetings are relatively free of conflict: a meeting occurs, decisions get made, and people get back to work. This is an example of intergroup cooperation to achieve common goals. However, since groups also have their own unique goals, intergroup cooperation may be lessened by the intergroup competition based on conflicting goals and competition for resources (budgets). As a result, there exists a range, or continuum, between complete cooperation and complete competition and conflict. It is frequently possible to have several groups cooperating on one issue and simultaneously competing with one another on another issue.

The primary causes for intergroup cooperation stem from a mutual desire to get the job done or to band together against a common enemy. The main causes of intergroup conflict, on the other hand, stem from the attempt to reach mutually exclusive goals or competition for limited resources, status, and power. For example, the various university departments may compete for the better students as "majors," more tenured positions, or more staff.

This section focuses on groups in conflict because the results of group conflict generally tend to be more dysfunctional than the results of group cooperation. Furthermore, group conflict occurs far more frequently than complete cooperation.

A. Groups in Conflict

Conflict between two or more groups occurs so frequently as to make it appear almost inevitable. Conflict occurs not only between groups, but also between classes of people and between nations. Obviously, conflict does not have to be accompanied by violence; indeed, most of the time it does not. Conflict of some kind appears to be almost inevitable in the modern social organization, even if only because of conflicting goals. For example, the people in the marketing and sales department want a variety of products to sell and a continually shifting product mix. People in manufacturing, however, would prefer to build fewer products in larger quantity, since this simplifies *their* life. A common tendency is for the inspection foreman to firmly believe that the manufacturing people are trying to put something over on him; that they are "trying to slip bad parts through." Conversely, the manufacturing foreman firmly believes that the inspectors, aided and abetted by their foreman, are out to catch him and that they will reject even good parts just to prove that they are on the job. Indeed, in conversation with an inspector in a large manufacturing plant, one of the authors asked him, "What would happen if a day or a week went past and you didn't reject any parts?" The inspector's response was, "Oh, I couldn't do that. My boss would think I wasn't doing my job."

Group conflict frequently occurs between policemen and demonstrators. (Photograph courtesy Christian Science Monitor)

When groups are in conflict, they begin to distrust the other. Such distrust is evident in black-white relations. The black distrusts "whitey" and in effect tells him to "stay out."

Second, each group begins to distort its viewpoint and to build two kinds of stereotypes. The other group is no longer seen as neutral; rather, it becomes a "bad guy." Concurrently, each group tends to see only the best of itself, denying that it has any faults or that the other group has any virtues. For example, in World War I, many Americans were ready to believe that German soldiers actually ate babies. Similarly, the inspection and manufacturing foremen each began to believe that the other's group was trying to put him in a bad light and keep him from doing his job properly.

Third, as conflict increases, each group becomes more cohesive and tightly knit, allowing less deviation from group norms. For example, can you imagine what would happen if an Army cadet cheered for the Navy during the annual Army/Navy game? Consequently, the group will accept much more authoritarian, rigid, and dogmatic leadership than under more normal conditions, as can be seen in the extraordinary powers given to the President or the leader of a democratic nation during war. The various developmental stages of intergroup conflict are illustrated in a classic study conducted by Sherif and Sherif.[17] In this field study, boys from similar backgrounds were brought together at a summer camp and divided into two groups. *Intra*group solidarity and spirit were promoted to the extent that *inter*group hostility developed in the form of raids on the other group's camp. Additionally, each group developed negative stereotypes, made unflattering remarks, and expressed the desire for complete segregation from the other group. Harmony was later restored by having the two groups perform common tasks promoting interdependence, such as raising funds to go to a movie, and fixing the water tank which supplied the whole camp.

B. Effects of Intergroup Competition

Some people feel that conflict between groups is generally good, i.e., it "keeps the men on their toes." However, the question of the utility of group conflict cannot be answered with a simple yes or no; rather, it depends primarily on the situation. For example, conflict is good and does serve to keep people on their toes in sporting events: competition impels a runner to run faster and a team to do better. In a "win/lose" situation, therefore, competition probably does enhance the motivation, involvement, and performance of the participants. Similarly, competition between two plants for a safety record or between different marketing divisions for increased sales is usually helpful to the organization.

However, win/lose situations are not usually helpful to the organization, especially if considered as an interrelated and interdependent system. In other words, for intergroup conflict to be "good," the groups must be *independent* of each other so that a "loss" by one group does not adversely affect the other group. When these two criteria (a win/lose situation and independence) are not met, competition between two opposing groups may indeed be bad.

The opportunity for productive conflict occurs when two groups are dependent on each other. A conflict is productive when there is open discussion and confrontation concerning ideas about tasks and projects. In this case conflict is regarded as a problem to be worked through using problem-solving methods. Here, a win-lose situation is avoided, and ideas are freely discussed and pooled in order to come up with a better solution than could be arrived at by a single group.

When two conflicting groups began to perceive each other as "the enemy," cooperation between the groups drops off markedly, as does communication. As a result, the two groups cannot work together to solve common problems, and neither group gets accurate feedback from the other. Instead, the communication is likely to be hostile, be received defensively, and be marked by distorted perceptions. In such a situation, neither group really believes what the other has to say and the norm is rejection rather than acceptance of the communication. When this occurs within an organization, and it frequently does, effort is spent not in problem-solving, but in fault-finding, buck-passing, and in attempts to place the blame on others. This is a modified win/lose situation—everybody loses in the long run. The organization, in particular, loses because time and effort are not spent in productive problem-solving.

To conclude, therefore, we can say that conflict between groups can be helpful when a win/lose situation is desired and when the two groups are truly independent of each other. Cooperation, on the other hand, is needed when a win/lose situation is not wanted and when the two groups are dependent on each other.

C. Reducing Intergroup Conflict and Competition

There are a number of ways of reducing conflict between groups, some of which are impossible without first redesigning the organization, and these will be discussed later. However, methods do exist for minimizing conflict within the existing organizational framework.

1. Ensure that Data for Problem-Solving are Generated in Common. Although much of the time problems involve more than one of the subsystems or groups in an organization, only one group will find a solution to the problem. Because the other group may have additional data (thus making the first group look bad), it may reject the solution. For example, Huse studied groups in conflict: defensiveness between the groups was high, and numerous efforts to improve the quality of a particular product had been unsuccessful.[18] However, when representatives of the different groups were brought together to study each rejected lot and to develop *joint* solutions, the quality of the product was improved by more than 60%.

This illustrates the use by more modern and advanced organizations of "task forces" to solve problems that cut across groups and the organization. To be successful, the task force generally has to have representatives of all the groups involved, as well as outside experts. Huse and Beer, for example, report on the success of having a task force consisting of representatives from R & D, purchasing, marketing, and production departments meet to integrate the work of the various units and departments as new products moved through the various developmental and manufacturing stages.[19] At each step of the way, the task force met to identify and solve problems.

2. Rotate People Among the Different Groups. This solution is more difficult to accomplish than to set up a task force, since many groups in social organizations are highly specialized and management does not find it practical to transfer people from one group to another. However, there are many, many groups in which this can and indeed should, be done. Too often, however, this solution is not even considered or recognized as a possibility.

3. Recognize the Interdependence of the Groups and Establish Methods to Bring Them into Closer Contact. As the old army major said, "What I'm not up on, I'm down on." Frequently, the defensiveness and conflict between groups can be reduced by bringing them together for mutual problem-solving meetings or by sending representatives to work with the other group on a temporary basis. One successful technique is to bring the two opposing groups together to share their perceptions of each other, to clear up misunderstandings, and to ensure that each group has a better understanding of the role, purpose, and objectives of the other group. One such meeting can do much to "clear the air" and may followed by additional meetings to iron out persistent differences between the groups. Blake, Shepherd, and Mouton have shown, in excellent detail, how union-management conflict can be considerably reduced through a more formalized, but highly effective, use of this basic technique.[20] They have the opposing groups write down their perceptions of themselves and of the other group and then discuss these perceptions. This technique will be discussed more fully in a later chapter on organizational improvement.

4. Locate a Common Enemy. A recurrent theme in science fiction is an invasion from outer space. In such a situation, the opposing great powers of Earth quickly resolve their differences, pool their technologies, and work together to repel the invader. In the same fashion, groups in conflict can quickly resolve their differences to join forces against a common enemy—a competing company, a governmental agency, or a third group in the organization. For example, one of the authors was sitting in on a meeting at which two managers, each the head of an opposing group, were having a rather heated discussion. A third manager came in and interrupted in such a fashion that the two other managers closed ranks against him in a defensive action. After the "intruder" had left, the two managers resumed their conflict. The author, acting as an observer, pointed out that only a moment before, they had closed ranks against the intruder. The discussion of why this had happened and its significance marked a real turning point for both managers, and in the next several weeks, cooperation between the two managers and their respective groups improved markedly.

5. Develop a Common Set of Goals and Objectives. In a sense, this is the more positive side of "locating a common enemy." Much of the conflict between groups in any social organization arises because the subsystems have different goals. Currently, most managers are rewarded (pay increases, promotions, etc.) to the extent that they accomplish the goals and objectives of their particular subsystem. This almost automatically breeds conflict, since each subsystem is concerned about making itself look good and is less concerned about working with other subsystems toward common goals and objectives. Beckhard has developed an approach called the "organizational confrontation meeting" to encourage organizational subsystems to work toward establishing and striving for common goals.[21]

In a variation of this approach, Huse, in an unpublished study, was able to reduce manufacturing costs in one plant by more than 45% in less than six months. The plant was shut down for an afternoon and every member of the organization, including hourly, clerical, technical, and professional people, was assigned to a cross-functional group. Each group, called a problem-identification group, was encouraged to come up with a list of problems facing the organization. At the end of the afternoon, the groups reported back their findings and conclusions to the entire organization. There was, of course, some overlap in the problems identified by the different groups. Two weeks later, the plant was shut down for another afternoon. By this time, the problems had been sorted into lists, and new cross-functional teams were established to work on a specific set of problems identified in the first set of meetings. During the next two months the plant shut down every Friday afternoon to allow the groups to work on their list of problems. As a result of this "team approach," manufacturing costs dropped by 45%, morale and productivity rose, and absenteeism dropped considerably.

VI. OBSERVING AND DIAGNOSING A COMMITTEE MEETING

One of the most widely used forms of group interaction is the formal committee. Tillman surveyed 1200 *Harvard Business Review* subscribers and found that 94% of organizations with more than 10,000 employees had formal committees.[22] In another study, Kriesberg found that executives spend an average of 10 hours a week in formal committee conferences.[23] Since these studies were made a number of years ago, it is likely that the amount of time spent in formal conferences and meetings has vastly increased in the intervening years.

A committee is usually composed of representatives of different groups and has a specific purpose or task. There is usually a chairman, but most "formal" committees are not run according to *Robert's Rules of Order.*

Keeping in mind that you are an observer rather than a participant, one of the first things you should observe upon entering the meeting room is the physical layout of the room, for this is related to the *structure* of the group, i.e.,

By permission of John Hart and Field Enterprises, Inc.

authoritarian or egalitarian. If the chairs are arranged in a circle or around a table, you will probably be correct in assuming that participation is encouraged. If the chairs are arranged as in a classroom, however, it may indicate that the chairman or leader does not really want participation but rather, wants to emphasize his status and push hard for the acceptance of his ideas, since this arrangement tends to decrease participation and interaction among the members.

Once the meeting starts, there are two types of observation you need to make: the *content* of the meeting, i.e., what is being said, and the *process* of the discussion, i.e., how well the members are working together, who talks to whom, the emotional responses of the members (pleased, disinterested, irritated, bored), who is leading the group and how, the extent and degree of participation of the members.

We have already said that in order for any group to be productive, it must give attention to both the task-building and task-maintenance roles. In other words, the group must coordinate and merge the efforts of the committee members so that all are working toward goals for which the committee was established. At the same time, the emotional and personal welfare needs of the members cannot be sacrificed without reducing the likelihood of accomplishing the committee's goals and possibly endangering the survival of the group.

Behavioral scientists are now in almost complete agreement (and the literature in the field has been stressing this more and more) that man is not only a rational, cognitive being, but also an emotional one. Formerly, it had been assumed that in committee meetings, the most important thing was the task at hand and that somehow, man could separate his problem-solving, rational self from his emotional self. This neglect of group-maintenance roles is probably the most important factor in reducing the effectiveness of committee meetings. In actuality, attempts to ignore the personal, emotional, and affective components of committee meetings impede the progress of the meeting. For example, one of the authors analyzed tapes of a three-hour staff meeting which had been called to reply to a letter from the corporate office. Early in the meeting, one member of the group brought up an idea which was quickly rejected by the chairman. Several times in the next two hours, he again brought up this idea, and each time it was quickly rejected by the chairman. Only toward the end of the meeting was his idea thoroughly discussed by the group. When the idea was once more rejected, the group had done so for what appeared to be good reasons. This time, the individual accepted the rejection of his idea, recognizing the logic behind it, and then became one of the most creative members of the group, submitting a number of other ideas which were accepted by the group. If the chairman had not been such an obstructionist and had allowed the idea to be discussed earlier, much time could have been saved, and the individual would have become a much more positive contributor earlier in the meeting.

Bales' system of categories may be useful in observing and analyzing meetings (Fig. 5.2). As you can see, group-building and maintenance functions are in the first three categories. The next six categories deal with the task, and the last three categories deal with self-serving activities which inhibit the progress of the group.

In order to observe a meeting properly, you must be aware of both the "overt agenda" and the "hidden agenda." Items on the overt agenda are discussed and openly expressed; the hidden agenda is important for what is *not* expressed openly. For example, in a formal committee of department heads, each member (manager) represents his own constituency and cannot be a "traitor to his own group." In addition, he may have strong personal feelings and values

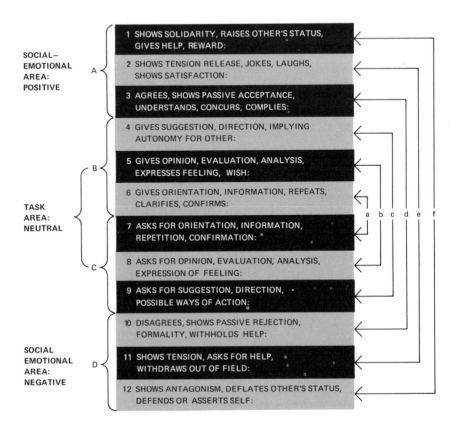

Figure 5.2. *Bales' system of categories used in observation and their relations. (Reprinted by permission from R. F. Bales,* Interaction Process Analysis, *Reading, Mass.: Addison-Wesley, 1950, p. 9. Revised in R. F. Bales,* Personality and Interpersonal Behavior, *New York: Holt, Rinehart and Winston, 1970.)*

about himself and others which he is reluctant to share. Thus, if it is "common knowledge" that one of the committee members is an incompetent manager, certain critical issues or problems may be skirted or avoided altogether. Such a hidden agenda may therefore limit the productiveness of the meeting.

In addition to observing the *group* process, you must also be able to analyze the group's *decision-making* process. Generally, for simple tasks or problems for which one person knows the solution, the use of a committee or group approach is ill advised. If, on the other hand, the task is complex, no one person has the answer, or if a number of groups must be coordinated, the use of a committee is much more appropriate. As Davis notes:

If we were to summarize the comparison of group and individual products, the gross conclusion would be that on most criteria, groups are generally superior to individuals but that the existence and degree of superiority depend upon a number of situational and task factors . . . If the emphasis is on achieving a correct *or* good *or* early *answer, then a group has a higher probability of achieving this aim (other things being equal) than does the single individual.*[24]

In addition, there is evidence that the decisions made by groups are more risky than those made by individuals in isolation. Whether this is a function of the anonymity of the group or of some other function is as yet uncertain. For example:

Mr. D. is the captain of College X's football team. College X is playing its traditional rival, College Y, in the final game of the season. The game is in its final seconds, and Mr. D's team, College X, is behind in the score. College X has time to run one more play. Mr. D, Captain, must decide whether it would be best to settle for a tie score with a play which would be almost certain to work or, on the other hand, should he try a more complicated and risky play which would bring victory if it succeeded, but defeat if not.[25]

Imagine that you are advising Mr. D. The following are several probabilities, or odds, that the risky play will work. Check the *lowest* probability you would consider acceptable for the risky play to be attempted.

— Place a check here if you think Mr. D should not attempt the risky play, no matter what the probabilities.
— The chances are 9 in 10 that the risky play will work.
— The chances are 7 in 10 that the risky play will work.
— The chances are 5 in 10 that the risky play will work.
— The chances are 1 in 10 that the risky play will work.

Davis also points out that when individuals request group confirmation of a decision, the group decisions tend to become riskier. This is known as the "risky shift." Stoner points to the same phenomenon, noting that under certain conditions, groups make more risky decisions than do individuals.[26]

In summary, your task as an observer is to watch how the group goes about its task. Using the categories developed by Bales, you can watch for the way in which the committee handles the task, the group-building roles, and negative, self-seeking roles. You can observe whether or not the meeting is productive and begin to diagnose why the meeting is productive or identify some of the factors that reduce the effectiveness of the meeting. For example, if the chairman says, "Let's get back on the track," you can look for the basic causes for the group's going off on a tangent. If someone else says, "Let's leave emotions out of this and stick to the facts," this is a clear sign that group-maintenance roles are being ignored. You can observe the extent and degree of the members' involvement and whether or not ideas are really listened to. How many times are people "cut off?" How is leadership shared, or is it really shared? Does the chairman try to impose his own viewpoint, or is he really looking for new, constructive ideas?

VII. CONCLUSION

In this section we have looked at groups in operation. We have described the group as a social system, or as a subsystem operating within the larger social organization. We have examined some of the reasons and methods of group formation, including their use in the service of the three perspectives of the structural, flow, and human systems. We have discussed the internal structure of groups: group activities, leadership, norms and standards of behavior, and group solidarity. We then examined groups in interaction and pointed out some of the ways in which group competition can be reduced or made more productive. Finally, we have suggested various tools for more accurate observation and diagnosis of group dynamics.

Throughout this chapter, we have stressed that in addition to accomplishing their objectives or tasks, groups must also satisfy their members' needs. In return, a group makes certain demands of its members: it asks for a certain amount of loyalty and conformance to group norms and standards of behavior. Although interpersonal behavior is always a social exchange, an individual need not lose his individuality in a group. In some groups, the norm is for a high degree of individuality and creativity.

In discussing the impact of groups on the organization as a total system, we noted that a group's productivity may be either high or low, depending on what the group wants it to be. As we shall see later, there are ways of helping a group simultaneously meet both its own goals and needs and those of the organization.

REVIEW

1. Groups tend to make more risky decisions than do individuals acting alone. What effect does this have in decisions made by juries rather than by judges, for open, group meetings, and for other similar decision-making processes?

2. Attend a meeting (school committee, city council, fraternity), preferably one at which *Roberts' Rules of Order* is not used, and observe the interaction, using the interaction analysis categories as your basic tool. What kinds of interaction do you observe? What inferences can you draw?

3. Find two groups that are interdependent. Describe the relationship between them, and give recommendations for improving the working arrangements between the two groups.

4. We have described a number of different types of groups. Give an example of each from your personal experience.

5. How does the behavior of a group affect the way management treats the group?

6. Analyze and describe the impact of an "informal" group on the "formal" organization.

7. Think about a group that you have belonged to. How effective was the group? What are some of the factors that were involved in its effectiveness or ineffectiveness?

8. Assume that you have just watched a sports event in which there was a decisive victory. What are the group characteristics of the winning team? The losing team?

Critical Concepts

Properties of groups

Types of groups

Group task activities

Self-serving activities in groups

Group norm

Group deviant

Group development

Group homogeneity-heterogeneity

Properties of groups in conflict-competition

Properties of winning groups

Properties of losing groups

Methods of reducing intergroup conflict

Critical dimensions in observing groups operate

REFERENCES

1   D. Cartwright and D. Lippitt, "Group Dynamics and the Individual," in *Organizational Psychology: A Book of Readings,* ed. D. A. Kolb, I. M. Rubin, and J. McIntryre (Englewood Cliffs, N.J.: Prentice-Hall, 1971).

2   R. Likert, *The Human Organization: Its Management and Value* (New York: McGraw-Hill, 1967).

3   J. H. Davis, *Group Performance* (Reading, Mass.: Addison-Wesley, 1969), p. 4.

4   W. F. Whyte, *Organization and Behavior* (Homewood, Ill.: Richard D. Irwin and The Dorsey Press, 1969).

5   R. E. Walton, J. M. Dutton, and H. G. Fitch, "A Study of Conflict in the Process, Structure and Attitudes of Lateral Relationships," in *Some Theories of Organization,* rev. ed., ed. A. W. Rubenstein and C. G. Haberstroh (Homewood, Ill.: Richard D. Irwin and The Dorsey Press, 1966).

6   G. Farris, "Organizing your Informal Organization," *Innovation,* 25 (Oct. 1971):2–11.

7   D. Roy, "Quota Restriction and Goldbricking in a Machine Shop," *American Journal of Sociology,* 57 (March 1952):425–442.

8   D. Roy, "Efficiency and 'The Fix': Informal Intergroup Relations in a Piecework Machine Shop," in *Sociology: The Progress of a Decade,* ed. S. M. Lipset and N. J. Smelser (Englewood Cliffs, N.J.: Prentice-Hall, 1961), pp. 378–390.

9   G. C. Homans, "Social Behavior as Exchange," *American Journal of Sociology,* 63 (1958):597–606.

10 S. A. Stouffer, *et al., The American Soldier: Combat and its Aftermath* (Princeton, N.J.: Princeton University Press, 1949).

11 K. D. Benne and P. Sheats, "Functional Roles of Group Members," *Journal of Social Issues,* 4, 2 (Spring 1948):41–49.

12 J. H. Davis, *op. cit.*

13 *Ibid.*

14 M. Dalton, *Men Who Manage* (New York: John Wiley, 1959).

15 G. C. Homans, *Social Behavior: Its Elementary Forms* (New York: Harcourt, Brace & World, 1961).

16 S. E. Asch, *Social Psychology* (Englewood Cliffs, N.J.: Prentice-Hall, 1952).

17 M. Sherif and C. Sherif, *Groups in Harmony and Tension: An Integration of Studies on Intergroup Relations* (New York: Harper and Brothers, 1953).

18 E. F. Huse, "The Behavioral Scientist in the Shop," *Personnel,* 42 (May–June 1965): 50–57.

19 E. F. Huse and M. Beer, "Eclectic Approach to Organizational Development," *Harvard Business Review,* 49, 5 (Sept.–Oct. 1971):103–112.

20 R. R. Blake, H. A. Shepard, and J. S. Mouton, *Managing Intergroup Conflict in Industry* (Houston, Texas: Gulf, 1964).

21 R. Beckhard, *Organization Development: Strategies and Models* (Reading, Mass.: Addison-Wesley, 1969).

22 R. Tillman, Jr., "Problems in Review: Committees on Trial," *Harvard Business Review,* 47, 3 (May–June 1960):162–172.

23 M. Kriesberg, "Executives Evaluate Administrative Conferences," *Advanced Management,* 15, 3 (1950):15–17.

24 J. H. Davis, *op. cit.,* p. 43. Reprinted by permission.

25 N. Kogan and M. A. Wallach, "Risk Taking as a Function of the Situation, the Person and the Group," in *New Directions in Psychology III,* ed. G. Mandler, P. Missen, N. Kogan, and M. Wallach (New York: Holt, Rinehart and Winston, 1967), pp. 134–135. Reprinted by permission.

26 J. A. F. Stoner, "Risky and Cautious Shifts in Group Decisions: The Influence of Widely Held Values" (M.I.T Sloan School of management working paper, October 1967).

6
INFLUENCE, POWER, AND LEADERSHIP

Power tends to corrupt
And absolute power corrupts absolutely.

LORD ACTON

I. INTRODUCTION

If the chairman of the board of a major oil company in the United States persuades the president of the United States that a certain governmental policy toward Middle Eastern nations is desired by oil interests and the president agrees to implement it, is this power or influence? In this chapter, we discuss the nature of influence, the bases, or sources, of power, and the types of leadership styles. Additionally, we examine research which specifies the conditions under which one particular leadership style is more effective than another.

If we were not using the systems approach, there would be no need to separate the concepts of influence, power, and leadership from that of management. However, since influence, power, and leadership may be derived from many sources inside and/or outside the formal or informal organization, the use of this approach enables us to examine all three concepts as systems variables and to determine their origin and proper place in the organization. For example, Ralph Nader's book *Unsafe at any Speed,* which describes certain defects in the Corvair, is an example of an outside influence which helped bring about the demise of this car.[1] Here, Ralph Nader was an outside "input" to the General Motors "system."

II. INFLUENCE AND POWER

In their thought-provoking monograph, French and Raven identify five different bases of power and influence that one person can use to influence another: legitimate power, expert power, reference power, reward power, and coercive power.[2]

A. Legitimate Power

Legitimate, or position, power derives from either the culture or the organization, but only if the organization is accepted as legitimate. This is especially true in organizations having a hierarchy of authority; those at lower levels in the hierarchy accept the power and influence of those higher in the organization. For example, a judge has the "right" to levy fines; the Congress has the "right" to pass laws; the president of an organization has the "right" to make certain management decisions. In a formal organization, legitimate power is exerted primarily between positions or "offices" rather than between individuals.

However, legitimate power depends on the individual's acceptance of the organization or culture and the person exerting the influence. For example, during Prohibition there was widespread violation of the laws because people did not accent the laws as legitimate. Today, many people disregard the laws

Many individuals are unwilling to accept the state's legitimate power, as personified by the police force. (Photograph courtesy EPI)

about the use of drugs for similar reasons. The result of widespread rejection of "legitimate power" is to severely reduce the power potential of the authority figure.

B. Expert Power

Expert power, based on the authority of knowledge, is particularly important in the flow process (Perspective II). Physicians and lawyers, for example, have a great deal of expert power. Within an organization, people with expert power can wield a great deal of influence; in a meeting with his peers and those higher in the hierarchy, the computer expert may in fact have the greatest amount of power simply because he is the only one with sufficient knowledge of the

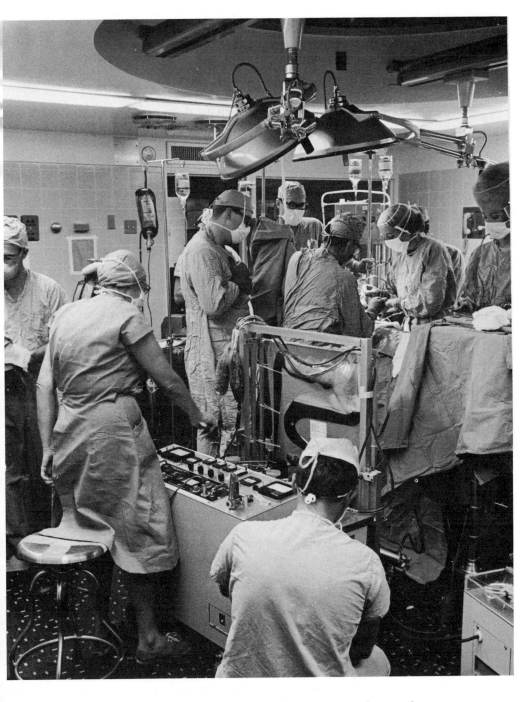

An operating-room team represents a high degree of expert power. (Photograph courtesy Black Star)

computer's operation and potential. Similarly, because of his expert knowledge, the market research analyst carries a great deal of influence in determining the future direction of the organization.

C. Referent Power

Reference power, which can be described as the power of "identification," or "charismatic" power, is based on the attractiveness of a particular person or group to others. Mahatma Ghandi and Martin Luther King had little legitimate power, but to their many followers they did have a high degree of referent power. Any currently popular musical group may, at any given moment, exercise a tremendous amount of referent power over many people in this country. Someone meeting with his peers in a business enterprise may be able to exercise much more influence than someone else, simply because people want to believe in him and his ideas.

D. Reward Power

This type of power is based on the leader's ability to reward a follower and in some situations may be closely linked to referent power. In an industrial organization, reward power is closely linked to the manager's legitimate power in awarding pay increases or promotions. In a peer group it may be the leader's power to admit a new member. The nature of work-flow relationships is such that an individual manager may have a great deal of reward power simply by his place in the work flow, e.g., a purchasing agent can "reward" a cooperative manager by expediting his orders, or a maintenance manager may "reward" another manager by giving his requests higher priority.

E. Coercive Power

Coercive power, the opposite of reward power, is the power to punish, whether by firing a man for insubordination or arresting someone for violating a law. Yet coercive power is not necessarily absolute—the individual may choose to quit or enter a new profession or plead his case before a higher court.

These five types of power are interrelated and indeed may rest with the same person. Since this interrelationship does exist, the use (or misuse) of one kind of power affects the exercise of the other types of power. For example, a manager's use of coercive power may reduce his referent power. Conversely, his extensive use of reward power will, over time, increase his referent power.

III. LEADERSHIP

Leadership is the effort to influence or change the behavior of others in order to accomplish organizational, individual, or personal goals. Indeed, the individual who leads a "wildcat" strike is a true leader, but he is working at cross-purposes to the stated, formal goals of the organization. It is clear, therefore, that there is both an overlap and a distinction between a *manager* (formal leader) and a *leader* (who may be either a formal or informal leader).

We also need to distinguish among attempted, successful, and unsuccessful leadership. Attempted leadership, as the term implies, refers to an individual's efforts to influence the behavior of another person or group, and his leadership is successful to the extent that the individual or group responds to this attempt. However, there is a difference between successful leadership and effective leadership. If the individual responds because the leader controls rewards and punishments, the leader has been successful. But if the individual is unable to reach his own goals, the leader has not been effective. However, if the individual responds because he both wants to and perceives that he will gain something, the leadership has been both successful and effective.

It is clear that the more influence and power a leader has, the greater the potential for his leadership attempts to be successful. It is also clear that the more a leader's power is based on all five areas, the greater his potential for successful leadership. The ideal leader would be highly charismatic, occupy a position of legitimate authority, and have expert knowledge, as well as a great deal of reward and coercive power. In real life, however, the manager may lack charismatic and expert power, although his status as a leader is ensured by his position in the hierarchy and his powers to reward and punish his subordinates.

Even though a manager has at his command all five types of power and therefore has high leadership potential, he may still be unable to bring about change. For as Leavitt notes, the ultimate control in the influence and change process rests with the changee, no matter how much power a leader may possess.[3] It is therefore perhaps even more important for the follower rather than the leader to understand the problem and the reasons for the proposed change. If we accept the notion that it is the follower who has the ultimate control, he must be able to make a well-reasoned decision about the leader's desire for change. In other words, the "follower" must understand the problem in his "own" perceptual terms, although these may be quite different from those of the "leader." For leadership to be truly successful, the follower must see "something in it for him." In short, both leader and follower must be adept at the process of social exchange.

Just as the process of social exchange is shared, so must the responsibility for change be shared. Or, this responsibility may be taken over completely by the follower. A teacher can promote more effective learning in a student by assisting him to *want* to learn in order to satisfy his own needs. The leader (teacher) thus changes the situation by giving the follower (student) responsibility for change (learning). In most educational and other organizations, however, pressures and concepts about authority and leadership tend to make the "leaders" feel the primary responsibility for influence and change, thereby encouraging the "follower" to take the easy, passive course of action. (At this point, it might be helpful to refer again to the concept of the psychological contract, which was discussed in Chapter 3.)

A. Leadership Styles

The whole area of leadership style became an important topic for research and thought shortly after World War II. A number of different theories of leadership have evolved, some of which are complementary, whereas others are contradictory. In this section we give a brief historical overview of several of the major studies that have contributed to current ideas and theories about the manager as a leader before presenting the actual theories.

Kahn and Katz provide a comprehensive review of an important group of studies conducted at the University of Michigan.[4] One of the key findings of these surveys of a large insurance company, a tractor factory, and section gangs on a railroad was that supervisors of sections with good production records appeared to emphasize the interpersonal functions of their leadership role, i.e., they were employee-oriented. Supervisors of low-producing sections, by contrast, tended to spend more time on their actual task or on the paper-work portion of the job, i.e., they were more production-oriented.

Another dimension that appeared to be related to productivity was closeness of supervision. In all three Michigan studies, *general* supervision was more clearly related to high productivity than was *close* supervision. (A later series of studies, however, indicated that general supervision is effective primarily when the supervisor has a fair amount of influence with his own boss.) Since close supervision is likely to go hand in hand with the use of coercive power, it is no surprise that supervisors of low-producing sections of railroad gangs tended to use coercive power, whereas foremen of high-producing sections in the tractor factory appeared to take a great deal of interest in their workers and to use reward rather than coercive power.

Similar studies were conducted at Ohio State University. Fleishman, Harris, and Burtt, who conducted the primary study, developed a "leadership description questionnaire" which was then factor-analyzed (a statistical method for categorizing the individual responses).[5] The factor analysis resulted in two major categories: (1) initiating structure, that is, the degree of structure the supervisor initiated in performing his leadership role, and (2) interpersonal effectiveness. Using grievance rate as a criterion for measuring the supervisor's interpersonal consideration, the researchers found that increasing consideration was highly correlated with a lower grievance rate. Similarly, the higher the initiating structure, the higher the grievance rate.

In a later study, Fleishman and Harris found that the grievance rate was lowest when there was both high structure and high consideration; when low consideration was coupled with low structure, the grievance rate was high.[6] With medium consideration, a high grievance rate was found in conjunction with high structure, and a low grievance rate was found with low structure. Turnover rate showed the same trend.

In comparing the Michigan and Ohio studies, one might conclude that general supervision is beneficial and that initiating structure is dysfunctional. However, when Woodward classified 100 firms in England according to production techniques used, she was able to distinguish three different types of production: unit, or one-of a kind production (special-purpose electronic equipment or custom-tailored suits); large batch-and-mass production (standard gasoline engines); and continuous-process production (chemical production or gasoline refining).[7] Woodward found that in continuous-process production there are more levels of authority than in mass production and even more than in unit production and a smaller span of control and hence closer supervision for continuous-process production than for the other two types of production.

With these findings in mind, a reexamination of the Michigan and Ohio State studies is warranted, since both studies involved either unit or mass-production techniques. When Fleishman and Peters collected similar data on a detergent factory, a continuous-production industry, they could find no relationship between the leaders' attitudes and effectiveness and no combination of initiating structure and consideration predictive of management effectiveness.[8] These findings, together with the Woodward conclusions, suggest that general supervision is not appropriate in continuous-process production. In more recent research, Lawrence and Lorsch placed successful and unsuccessful organizations on a continuum ranging from highly stable environments (e.g., the container industry) to highly unstable, changing environments (e.g., the plastics industry) and found that the type, nature, and span of successful supervision must vary with the organization and its environment.[9]

One of the factors affecting organizational environment is the subordinate's perceptions of his supervisor's leadership style. Graen *et al.* studied "initiation

The manufacture of peanut butter exemplifies continuous-process production. (Photograph courtesy Christian Science Monitor)

of structure" and "consideration" in a large organization in a basic industry by asking 600 managers and supervisors (ranging from first-line supervisors to the president and his immediate staff) to complete a lengthy questionnaire.[10] The researchers found that the leader's "structuring" behavior greatly influenced the relationship between his "consideration" behavior and the performance of his subordinates. This was caused in large part by the subordinates' interpretations of the leader's evaluation of them and the amount and degree of feedback they received. Subordinates' understanding of their bosses' evaluations was much more accurate if the leader was at either end of the "structuring" continuum than if he had an intermediate position. In other words, the more consistent (either high or low) the leader was in performing his *bureaucratic* role of structuring, the more accurately the subordinate could describe his boss's behavior in his *interpersonal* role of consideration. The researchers conclude that leadership style is important in organizations, but that the difference "may not be so much in terms of what the leader does but may be in terms of how it is *interpreted* by his members."

These landmark studies have stressed the importance of a leader's effectiveness by the type of industry he is in, as well as his personal style of leadership.[11] In other words, these studies form the basis for a contingency theory of leadership and organizational design; one cannot be studied without taking into account the other, a failing in most of the early studies on leadership.

B. Major Theorists

Certain researchers and theorists have been instrumental in shaping the currently popular theories about supervision and effective leadership styles. Although each stresses somewhat different variables, their combined influence is at the root of the current theories and concepts of managerial behavior and organizational development and improvement.

1. Douglas McGregor. One of the most influential behavioral scientists is Douglas McGregor, who classifies managers according to two basic leadership styles: (1) an authoritarian style, which he calls *"Theory X,"* and (2) a more egalitarian style, which he calls *"Theory Y."*[12]

According to McGregor, the Theory X style of management, which originated in the Roman Catholic Church and military institutions, is based on the coercive and economic models of man. The typical Theory X manager believes that man is inherently lazy, dislikes work, and will, therefore, avoid work whenever possible. As a result, the Theory X leader must use strong measures to control the behavior of subordinates to ensure that they work toward organizational goals. He controls his subordinates through the use of coercion and the threat of punishment should they not put forth adequate effort. The use of these external controls is necessitated by the fact that most human beings are incapable of self-direction and control; they prefer to respond to direct orders rather than to accept responsibility for their own actions. Implicit in this assumption, of course, is the notion that there are two basic classes of people— those who want to lead and to take responsibility (the manager or leader) and those who want to be directed and who will duck responsibility whenever possible. According to Theory X, the manager's watchword is "you gotta watch them all the time."

The assumptions of a Theory Y leader, by contrast, are based on Maslow's concept of self-actualization, i.e., work can be enjoyable, and people will work hard and assume responsibility if they have the opportunity to satisfy their personal needs while at the same time achieving organizational goals. Thus, there is no sharp division between elites (leaders) and the masses (followers). Rather, the Theory X leader underutilizes his people; they have a great deal more ability and potential for imagination and creativity than he gives them credit for. Given the proper conditions, individuals really do want to do a good job and will work hard to do so; their performance will be based on internal rather than external controls.

In his discussion of these two contrasting theories of management, McGregor points out that assumptions about human nature and behavior color and influence every managerial decision or action; the leader will act and behave according to his own basic assumptions and beliefs. He stresses that many managers really do assume that people are inherently lazy and must be coerced in order to work. But these Theory X assumptions are outdated, he declares. Today, Western man lives in democratic societies with a rising standard of living and an increasing level of education. In fact, by trying to motivate modern man with outdated methods based on false assumptions, organizations adhering to Theory X assumptions are not motivating their employees toward fulfillment of either organizational or their individual goals. (It should be noted, however, that these assumptions are not ncesssarily valid for non-Western cultures.)

Managers who believe in Theory Y assumptions about people, on the other hand, structure the work situation so that subordinates can assume self-control and responsibility for the outcome of their efforts, thus helping them to satisfy their needs for relatedness (affiliation), and growth (esteem and self-actualization). The goal of the Theory Y approach is to make the work inherently satisfying to the employee. This means that the manager must work toward fostering an environment which is conducive to the growth of both the organization and the subordinates. Otherwise, people will look elsewhere for satisfaction, e.g., sabotage or other acts harmful to the organization.[13]

2. Rensis Likert. Likert's approach to the problem of leadership differs somewhat from McGregor's, although the two theories do overlap. Likert feels that managing the human component of the organization is the manager's most important task, because everything else depends on how well this task is accomplished.[14]

Unlike McGregor, Likert focuses on the group and organization within which the manager works. Likert organizes organizational styles into four systems ranging from a purely exploitative, authoritarian, hierarchical approach (System 1), to one which is less exploitative but still authoritarian (System 2), to a more consultative approach (System 3), to a participative approach (System 4). (Likert's use of the word "system" refers to a category, or type of approach, rather than to the overall structure of an organization, as the term is used in this book.)

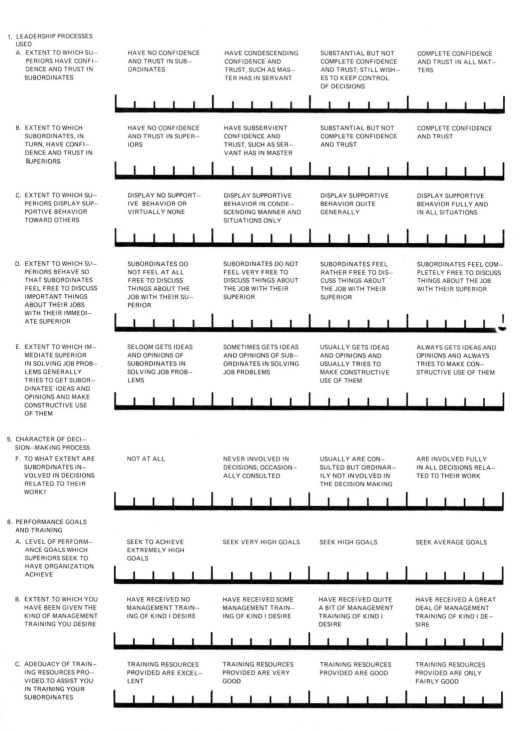

Figure 6.1. *Items added to the profile of organizational and performance characteristics.* (From **Human Organization** by R. Likert, pp. 120-121. Copyright © 1967 by McGraw-Hill. Used with permission of McGraw-Hill Book Company.)

Likert has developed a scale, or set of questions, to measure the position of an organization or organizational component on this continuum between the exploitative (authoritation) approach and the fully participative approach. Figure 6.1 shows some of the items Likert uses to determine an organization's position on the continuum. Although this table gives only a short excerpt from Likert's questionnaire, it serves to identify some of the differences among his four systems.

The System 1 manager has little confidence or trust in his subordinates. Most of the organizational decisions and goal-setting are determined at the top and then transmitted directly down the chain of command. Fear, threats, and other types of coercive power are used to force subordinates to work. Since the control process is rigid and authoritarian, subordinates can influence methods and goals only through the informal system, which frequently acts to oppose the goals and aims of the formal organization. There is no cooperative teamwork except on a very informal and *sub rosa* level.

At the other end of the continuum, management has almost complete trust and confidence in subordinates. Decision-making is widely dispersed throughout the organization, although mechanisms exist to ensure that decisions are well integrated. Information and communication flow occur freely both vertically and horizontally. Workers are motivated by their opportunity to become involved and participate in setting goals, improving methods, and evaluating their own progress toward established goals. There is a great deal of interaction between subordinates and supervisors, with a high degree of mutual confidence and trust. Responsibility for the control process is not centralized, but is widespread, with the lower units of the organization fully involved. This means that the formal and informal segments of the organization are often identical, and all of the social forces within the organization support the efforts to achieve the goals of the organization.

Likert has used this questionnaire to study a number of different organizations. His basic findings show that management systems leaning toward System 4 are more productive (higher output, less waste, and better labor relations), have lower costs, and have more favorable attitudes toward supervision and the organization than do organizations leaning toward System 1. Likert asserts that the overall consistency of his findings indicates that System 4 has widespread applicability and although its application in different organizations may vary, the basic principles of System 4 management can be applied to all types of situations.

One of the most useful aspects of Likert's analysis is his stress on management systems. He stresses the fact that if a company or other organization wants to apply the results of organizational research, it is necessary to shift from one coordinated system to another. Thus, if it

wishes to shift its operations from System 1 to System 2 to System 3 or 4, it should plan to modify all *of its operating procedures: leadership, decision-making, communications, coordination, evaluation, supervision, compensation, organizational structure, motivation, etc. . . . A well-integrated system of management should emerge.*[15]

However, as we shall see in the chapters on organizational improvement, Likert's statements that System 4 is the best approach in *all* parts of *all* organizations need to be modified.

3. Robert Blake and Jane Mouton.   These two authors have developed a concept of leadership best described as "the managerial grid," which states that there are several universal characteristics of organizations: (1) purpose—all organizations have some sense of purpose, or goal; (2) people—all social organizations have people who are involved with accomplishing the purpose of the organization; (3) hierarchy—all organizations have bosses and followers.[16] They also describe the ways in which these universals are interconnected: first, the amount of concern for production; second, the concern for people; third, a manager's set of assumptions in using the hierarchy to achieve production. In other words, different managers have different attitudes about using their hierarchical position.

As shown in Fig. 6.2, there are two basic dimensions of leadership: the extent and degree of the manager's concern about people; and his concern with production. The first dimension, roughly comparable to "consideration" as described earlier in this chapter, is shown on the vertical axis of the diagram. The manager's concern with production, i.e., of getting things done through his subordinates, is roughly comparable to "initiating structure."

Figure 6.2 also shows that concern for both people (vertical axis) and production (horizontal axis) can range from very low (1) to very high (9). It is therefore possible for a manager to have a high degree of concern for production while showing little or no concern for people. Or, a manager may exhibit very little concern for either people or production (1,1). As Blake and Mouton point out, it hardly seems possible that a manager could disregard both dimensions, but some actually do—although they are a part of the business, they do not really function within it.

For Blake and Mouton, the most desirable is the 9,9 manager, who exhibits a concurrent high concern for both people and production. As does Likert, however, they stress that this 9,9 approach to management cannot be attained without the systematic development and improvement of the entire organization.

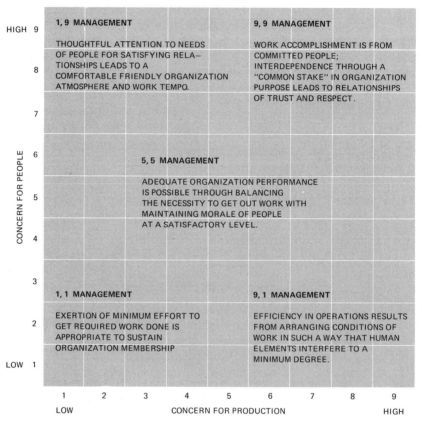

Figure 6.2. *The managerial grid. (Reprinted by permission from R. R. Blake and J. S. Mouton,* The Managerial Grid, *Houston: Gulf, 1964, p. 10.)*

Such systematic development generally occurs in six phases.

Phase 1 *of the six-phase approach involves studying the managerial grid as a theoretical framework for understanding behavior dynamics of the corporation's culture. In* Phase 2, *the behavior dynamics of actual organization teamwork is studied and tested in settings of actual work against the Grid model for the perfection of problem-solving methods. The same kind of application is made in* Phase 3, *but to the interworkings between organized units of the company where cooperation and coordination is vital to success. The top team in* Phase 4 *engages in a study of the properties of an Ideal Strategic Corporate Model necessary to bring corporate profitability logic to a maximum-thrust condition.* Phase 5 *involves implementation tactics for converting the corporation from what it has been to what it will become under the Ideal Strategic Corporate Model. Phase 6 measures changes in conditions from pre-Phase 1 to post-Phase 5 for the evaluation and stabilization of achievement and for the setting of new goals and objectives of accomplishment for the future.* [17]

In short, although the authors point to the 9,9 manager as the epitome of management style, they also stress that the manager is working within a total system and that the system itself must be changed before the 9,9 style of management can be fully utilized.

4. Fred E. Fiedler. The fourth major theorist in the field of leadership style is Fiedler, who has developed a "contingency" ("it depends") theory. In marked contrast to the "one best approach to management" stressed by McGregor, Likert, and Blake-Mouton, Fiedler asserts that appropriate management style depends on the subordinates, the set of conditions in which the manager finds himself, and the particular situation. Viewing management primarily in terms of leadership, Fiedler defines leadership as "a personal relationship in which one person directs, coordinates and supervises others in the performance of a common task."[18]

Management, therefore, comprises not only leadership, but also responsibility for the results. Although this is overly simplified, a manager can lead his group in either of two ways: (1) he can be highly directive and tell people exactly what to do and how to do it, or (2) he can involve his group in the planning and execution of the task, thereby sharing his leadership responsibilities. Since these are opposite ends of a continuum, several intermediate styles of leadership are also possible. However, the most appropriate style of leadership can be determined only by the circumstances.

Since the most appropriate leadership style varies with the circumstances, the manager must either adapt his leadership style to the situation or make the job compatible with his leadership style. Fiedler notes that it is easier to change the situation than leadership style and that part of the job of upper management might be to transfer a particular lower-level manager to a job which better fits his individual style.

Fielder has developed a questionnaire (consisting of a set of adjectives which an individual can use to describe the co-worker whom he least prefers) in order to determine an individual's leadership style. Fiedler's studies have shown that the individual who describes his least-preferred co-worker (LPC) in relatively favorable ways tends to be considerate, permissive, and oriented toward human relations; one who describes his least-preferred co-worker in more unfavorable ways (thereby getting a low LPC score) tends to be task-centered, manages closely, and is less concerned with human relations.

In his studies of surveying parties, military combat crews, steel companies, basketball teams, and members of boards of directors, Fiedler found that he could identify three variables which affect the favorability of a situation for the leader.

1. Leader-member relations. This is the degree and extent to which the leader and the members of his group like and trust one another. This conforms to our definition of a charismatic leader; it seems clear that if a leader is trusted and well liked, he does not have to have a superior rank in order to get the task accomplished.

2. Task structure. The task can be either spelled out very explicitly so that it can be done "by the numbers" or left rather vague and poorly defined. It is more difficult to exert leadership influence over a poorly defined task, however, because neither the leader nor his followers has a clear idea about the nature of the task or criteria for accomplishing it. If the task is clearly defined, on the other hand, the leader's authority is backed up by the organization, and he finds it much easier to lead.

3. Position power. This factor refers to the leader's legitimate, as distinct from his charismatic or personal power. Obviously, the leader's job is made easier if he has a great deal of position power.

Having defined these three dimensions of the situation, Fiedler proceeds to relate the two basic management styles to the following variables—good versus poor leader-member relationships, structured versus unstructured tasks, and strong versus weak leader position to permissive, considerate leadership versus controlling, active, structuring leadership—which determine the favorableness of the given situation.

Figure 6.3 shows Fiedler's summary of a number of group studies in which the groups were performing well but which used differing styles of leadership according to the situation. The range of leadership styles (as measured by the LPC) is given in the vertical axis; variables of the situations are shown in the horizontal axis. Fiedler found that either the nondirective and human-relations style of leadership or the managing, directive, task-oriented type of leadership can be effective. The degree of effectiveness of the leadership style depends on the favorableness of the situation. His general conclusion is that task-oriented leaders perform best in situations which are very favorable or unfavorable and that human-relations oriented, egalitarian leaders perform best in situations of intermediate favorableness.

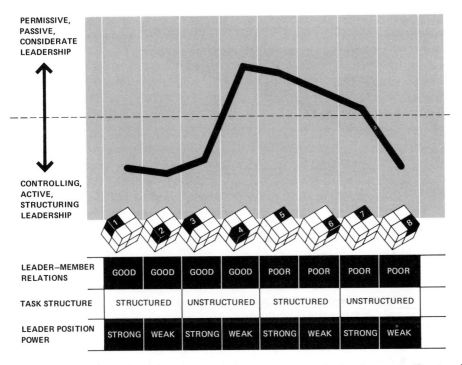

Figure 6.3. *How the style of effective leadership varies with the situation. (Reprinted by permission from F. E. Fiedler, "Engineer the Job to Fit the Manager," Harvard Business Review, 43, 5, Sept.-Oct. 1965, p. 118.)*

Fiedler identifies three approaches to getting the job done. First, the leader's position power can be changed by giving him more or less power, depending on the leader's style. Second, the task structure can be altered to fit the style of the leader. Finally, the leader-member relationships can be modified by either bringing in subordinates with similar attitudes and beliefs, thereby increasing the homogeneity of the group, or by decreasing the homogeneity of the group by bringing in subordinates whose culture, language, and background are different.

In their application of Fiedler's contingency theory, Shiftlett and Nealey used 132 male undergraduates at the University of Illinois divided into three-man laboratory groups to explore Fiedler's suggestion that the leadership situation should be engineered to provide a better match between leadership style and the task to be performed.[19] The leaders were assigned on the basis of their very high or very low LPC scores; group members were students with intermediate LPC scores. In addition, groups were divided into "high" and "low" ability

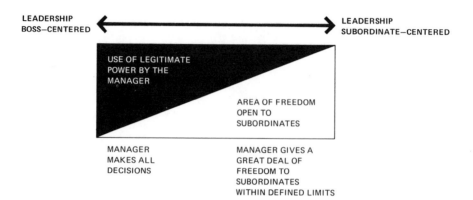

Figure 6.4. *Continuum of leadership behavior. (Adapted from R. Tannenbaum and W. Schmidt, "How to Choose a Leadership Pattern,"* Harvard Business Review, *36, 2, March-April 1958, pp. 95-110.)*

groups based upon a verbal ability test. The groups were checked for compatibility, whereupon 12 of the original 44 groups were dropped because of their relatively poor interpersonal relations.

The position power of the leader was established primarily through verbal instructions which gave him either strong or weak power. Group productivity predictions obtained from Fiedler's contingency model were supported only in the low-ability groups. The researchers conclude that "situational engineering still may be a viable idea," but that the specific application of the idea still requires further work.

The four theories—by McGregor, Likert, Blake and Mouton, and Fiedler—do have some points in common. Each postulates a continuum of leadership pattern from highly supervisor-centered to highly subordinate-centered. A composite of these four theories, developed by Tannenbaum and Schmidt, is shown in Fig. 6.4[20] At one extreme is the boss-centered manager who uses a great deal of authority and power (legitimate power) and gives relatively little freedom to his subordinates to make decisions. At the other extreme is the subordinate-centered leader who allows subordinates a fair amount of freedom to make decisions. Fiedler and Tannebaum and Schmidt all agree that the most appropriate leadership style depends on three key variables: the manager's attitudes and personality; the subordinates and their attitudes; and the situation. For example, some managers are extremely authoritarian, and expecting them to change their style would be virtually impossible. Some subordinates *want* to be told what to do and perform best with authoritian leadership. Recent research indicates that the nature, structure, and design of the organization have a profound influence on appropriate managerial styles. Careful studies usually indicate that leadership is highly specific to the circumstances and the tasks demanded of the leader. In some circumstances, the best leader may be the one who exercises "human relations" skills; in other circumstances, the best leader may be one who has expert power.

IV. SUMMARY AND CONCLUSION

In this chapter, we have looked at some of the determinants of leadership. Of the five different types of power, some depend on position, whereas others depend on access to others or on knowledge. We also made distinctions between successful and unsuccessful leadership attempts.

There are several distinct approaches to leadership styles, most of which come from studies describing authoritarian, democratic, or *laissez faire* (literally, "to leave alone") approaches. Three of the major theorists feel that the one-best-way approach is appropriate; one believes that a contingency approach is necessary, i.e., the "one best way" varies according to the manager, his followers, and the situation.

The most current thinking favors a contingency, or situational, approach toward leadership. If leadership style represents an open system, we can analyze the inputs (position power, task definition, leader-member relationships) and then decide on the most appropriate style of leadership for the given circumstances. Just as there is no clear answer to the question "What motivates this particular person at this particular time," there is no clear-cut answer to the question, "What is the most appropriate leadership style?" As Fiedler would say, "It all depends."

REVIEW

1. Compare and contrast Likert's systems theory, Blake's managerial grid, and Fiedler's contingency theory.

2. Look at leaders within your organization or university. Identify some formal and informal positions and specify what kinds of power the leaders are using.

3. Think of real-life situations which might serve to illustrate Fiedler's contingency theory.

4. If you were a consultant on leadership style, what would you advise a pharmaceutical company to do concerning an appropriate style?

5. Under what circumstances do you feel a Theory X approach to management might be appropriate?

6. Observe a group in interaction. Can you pick out a task leader and a social leader? How do their behaviors differ?

Critical Concepts

Legitimate power

Expert power

Referent power

Reward power

Coercive power

"Initiating structure"

"Interpersonal consideration"

Ohio State University studies

University of Michigan studies

Joan Woodward, English industries studies

Theory X

Theory Y

Likert's "systems"

Managerial grid

Fiedler's three-dimensional contingency theory

REFERENCES

1 R. Nader, *Unsafe at Any Speed* (New York: Grossman, 1965).

2 J. French and B. Raven, "The Basis of Social Power," in *Group Dynamics: Research and Theory,* 3rd ed., ed. D. Cartwright and A. Zander (New York: Harper & Row, 1967).

3 H. Leavitt, *Managerial Psychology* (Chicago: University of Chicago Press, 1964).

4 R. Kahn and D. Katz, "Leadership Practices in Relation to Productivity and Morale, in *Group Dynamics: Research and Theory,* 2nd ed., ed. D. Cartwright and A. Zander (Elmsford, N.Y.: Row, Peterson, 1960).

5 E. Fleishman, E. F. Harris, and R. D. Burtt, *Leadership and Supervision in Industry* (Columbus: Ohio State University Press, 1955).

6 E. Fleishman and E. F. Harris, "Patterns of Leadership Behavior Related to Employee Grievances and Turnover," *Personnel Psychology,* 51 (1962):45–53.

7 J. Woodward, *Management and Technology* (London: Her Majesty's Stationery Office, 1958).

8   E. Fleishman and R. Peters, "Interpersonal Values, Leadership Attitudes and Managerial Success," *Personnel Psychology,* 15 (1962):127–143.

9   P. Lawrence and J. Lorsch, *Organization and Environment: Managing Integration and Differentiation* (Boston: Harvard University School of Business Administration, Division of Research, 1967).

10 G. Graen, F. Dansereau, Jr., and T. Minami, "Dysfunctional Leadership Styles," *Organizational Behavior and Human Performance,* 7, 1 (April 1972):216–236.

11 J. Lorsch and P. Lawrence, eds., *Studies in Organization Design* (Homewood, Ill.: Richard D. Irwin and The Dorsey Press, 1970).

12 D. McGregor, *The Human Side of Enterprise* (New York: McGraw-Hill, 1960).

13 D. McGregor, *The Professional Manager,* ed. C. McGregor and W. Bennis (New York: McGraw-Hill, 1967).

14 R. Likert, *New Patterns of Management* (New York: McGraw-Hill, 1961).

15 R. Likert, *The Human Organization* (New York: McGraw-Hill, 1967).

16 R. Blake and J. Mouton, *The Managerial Grid* (Houston: Gulf, 1964).

17 R. Blake and J. Mouton, *Building a Dynamic Corporation Through Grid Organization Development* (Reading, Mass.: Addison-Wesley, 1969), p. 16. Reprinted by permission.

18 F. Fiedler, "Engineer the Job to Fit the Manager," *Harvard Business Review,* 43, 5 (Sept.–Oct. 1965), p. 118.

19 S. Shiftlett and S. Nealey, "The Effects of Changing Leadership Power: A Test of 'Situational' Engineering," *Organizational Behavior and Human Performance,* 7, 3 (June 1972):371–382.

20 R. Tannenbaum and W. Schmidt, "How to Choose a Leadership Pattern," *Harvard Business Review,* 36, 2 (March–April 1958):95–101.

7
THE
MANAGER
IN
THE
ORGANIZATION

I have nothing to offer but blood, toil, tears and sweat.

WINSTON CHURCHILL

I. INTRODUCTION

It is clear that the role of the manager in today's society is becoming more important and complex. As our society has become increasingly urban, there has been a corresponding growth of social organizations—hospitals, universities, governmental units, insurance companies, industrial establishments, and a myriad of other organizations—which all need to be managed. At the same time, there have been several major corresponding shifts in the structure and composition of these organizations. First, the number of "unskilled," blue-collar workers has decreased while the number of technical, professional, and clerical personnel has increased. These "white-collar" workers now outnumber the "blue-collar" employees. Second, organizations are becoming more complex, with the steadily increasing number of component subsystems that need to be managed. Finally, there has been a trend away from the owner/entrepreneurial manager to the manager as an administrator within an existing organization. The "owners" of the enterprise are farther and farther removed from the actual operation of the social organization, e.g., the stockholders of a large industrial organization have relatively little to say about the day-to-day management of the organization.

As a result of these and other forces, the job of the manager has become increasingly more important and complex. The practice of management is becoming less an art and more a science, a profession. Someone must establish the goals and directions for the social organization; someone must shape a productive enterprise out of human and material resources; someone must coordinate the various subsystems of the organization; someone must solve, or cause to get solved, the myriad problems facing any organization; someone must make certain that the total work of the organization and each of its subparts is accomplished.

This does not mean, of course, that the "top manager" does all this alone. Obviously, in a formal organization there are managers at all levels. Higher-level managers may have to be more conceptually and entrepreneurially oriented while those at the lower levels make the technical, "how to" decisions.

II. WHAT IS A MANAGER?

Having looked at some of the demands made on the manager, we can define a "manager" as the person within a formal organization who has at least one other person working for him. A subordinate may, in turn, also be a manager.

This topic—the job of a manager—has taken up a large portion of the literature over the past 30 years. Most definitions of the manager's job deal primarily with manager-subordinate relationships. In one of the best-known management texts, Koontz and O'Donnell say that the functions of a manager are essentially the same at all levels (from president to foreman) and consist of: planning, organizing, staffing, directing, and controlling.[1] These functions are primarily formally organized supervisor-subordinate relationships. Koontz and O'Donnell go on to point out that although there may be differing types of operations in an organization (manufacturing, engineering, selling, and purchasing), managerial functions are common to all types of operations.

Barrett notes that " 'planning' and 'organizing' involve a number of activities which the manager engages in by himself or with his peers or superiors." However, the use of such terms is an "old and inadequate description of the manager's roles which does not communicate adequately the complexity and variety of activities that managers actually engage in" when considered from a systems approach. In addition, "the more recent notion that a manager spends all of his time relating to subordinates is also too restricted, since many of his activities involve subordinates only indirectly or not at all."[2]

In his study of a manager's activities, Ponder found that 12 highly rated and 12 lower-rated supervisors in an electrical equipment manufacturing plant had an average of 457 interpersonal contacts during each eight-hour day, although most of these contacts lasted for only one or two minutes.[3] Thus, each supervisor spent about 13% of his time with his subordinates, including group leaders, 3% of his time with his immediate boss, and more than 30% of his time with peer-level individuals or groups. Moreover, Ponder found that the more effective supervisors spent a higher percentage of their time with representatives of such lateral groups, whereas the poorer supervisors tended to focus their efforts and time with their subordinates.

In a similar study, conducted in an automobile manufacturing company, Walker and his associates found that the manager had a high daily number of interpersonal contacts (387) and that the managers in the automobile assembly plants spent a large percentage of their time dealing with people in lateral, peer-level contacts.[4]

Strauss examined the behavior of purchasing agents, (functional managers in charge of purchasing departments) and found that their management function could be better analyzed in terms of *work flow* rather than by either the hierarchial boss-subordinate relationship or the typical concepts of staff-line relationships, even though the purchasing agent is technically a staff-line member.[5] Normally, one assumes that the work flow goes in only one direction. Sales receives an order; engineering designs the product and develops blueprints; production-scheduling establishes the manufacturing schedule, and the purchasing department places orders for the parts and other raw materials needed. Therefore, the purchasing agent has two basic functions in the hierarchy. First, he negotiates and places orders; and second, he expedites orders if they are late.

Most purchasing agents, however, are highly dissatisfied with this arrangement; they believe that if they could be involved with engineering at an earlier date, they could suggest specifications or types of parts which would reduce costs substantially. Furthermore, they feel that the production schedule does not allow sufficient time to buy the necessary parts, thus forcing them to choose from a limited number of suppliers or to pay premium prices. As a result, the purchasing agent strives to reverse the "normal" work flow and to exercise influence much earlier in the work-flow cycle.

Strauss points out that the more successful purchasing agents are able to do a better job of reversing the "normal" cycle and to exercise influence on others at a lateral level. The successful agents have developed a variety of techniques for dealing with other departments, some of which are tactics which considerably distort the established rules of the organization.

These studies show that the normal definition of a manager (planning, organizing, staffing, directing, and controlling the work of subordinates) is not adequate to explain a manager's true activities, as the study of purchasing agents clearly shows. Most of the purchasing agent's time, for example, is spent with lateral rather than vertical contacts. The results of such studies indicate that we need to change our concept and definition of a manager. For example, the authors of this text have found that managers spend more than 50% of their time with people either within or outside the boundaries of the organization other than their subordinates. Sayles would go even further; he believes that 25% or less of a manager's time is spent interacting with his subordinates, whereas close to 75% of his time is spent working with other levels of management or associated staff or service groups, primarily at the lateral level. He studied a group of engineering managers in a large corporation and found that they had to maintain contacts with as many as 30 different groups, each of which had its own manager.[6] In the course of speeches to various groups, one of the authors has asked his audiences: "In the course of a month, how many different people, excluding subordinates, have you had work-related contact with, either by phone, letter or memo, or personal visitation?" The answers range from a low of about 30 to a high of over 500, with a median of about 200. Obviously, then, the manager's role is highly complex and involves frequent interaction with a large variety and number of people, primarily at the lateral level.

In other words, the empirical studies demonstrate that what managers actually *do* in large, complex organizations is quite different from the activities they are supposed to be engaged in according to the classical definition, i.e., oversee the activities of subordinates.

What causes this difference? The more traditional definition resulted from failing to consider the organization as a network of interdependent and inter-

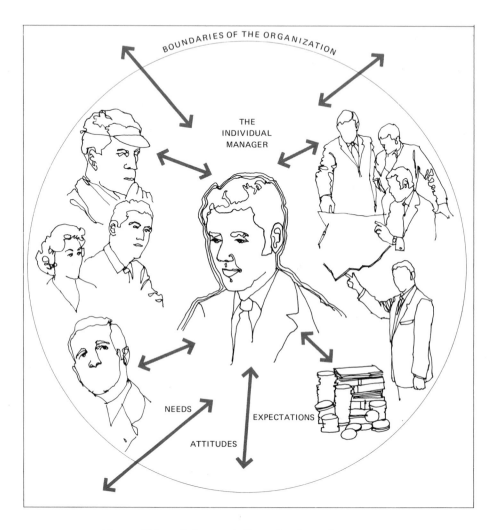

Figure 7.1. *Role expectations placed on the manager.*

related subsystems. However, if we take a systems approach and consider the three perspectives—structural-design, flow, and human—of a social organization simultaneously, we can begin to understand why the manager's activities cut across all of the perspectives. In other words, the manager's true function is to serve as the linking mechanism whereby balance among subsystems is maintained. For example, Kahn *et al.* propose that the formal job in an organization be considered as an office and that a manager's expected behavior be defined as a "role."[7] We can then ask, "What other people are linked to this manager within the operating organization?" and "Who does he associate with in performing his organizational role?" The manager's work relationships with supervisors, subordinates, peers, vendors, and customers constitute his "role set" (Fig. 7.1.). And by extending this concept, the organizational system becomes a set of overlapping and interlocking role sets both inside and outside the boundaries of the organization. A "role" is thus the sum total of expectations placed on the individual manager by supervisors, subordinates, peers, customers, vendors, and others, depending on the particular job. For as we mentioned earlier, the manager can have contact with 30 or more other groups in a month.

Since the average manager has contact with so many different groups and people, each with a different set of expectations, he must be able to integrate these expectations, as well as his own, into a coherent psychological contract if he is to perform successfully. If, however, he does not clearly understand what others expect of him, he has "role ambiguity." But if he understands these expectations and they conflict with one another and/or his own expectations, he has "role conflict" and will be unable to satisfy some of the expectations.

The importance of role conflict and ambiguity was thoroughly explored by House and Rizzo in their study of an organization manufacturing large, heavy equipment.[8] After having first developed a model of organizational behavior, the hypotheses associated with the model were tested on 80 supervisors and managers and 530 salaried employees. Perhaps their most important finding was that although role conflict and role ambiguity have a high degree of influence on perceptions, attitudes, and behavior, future studies on behavior in organizations should "place more emphasis on role ambiguity and less emphasis on role conflict."[9] The researchers found that role ambiguity links formal organizational practices and leadership behavior on the one hand with such factors as organizational effectiveness, job satisfaction, anxiety, and the tendency to leave the organization on the other. Therefore, organizational stability and personal satisfaction can be enhanced by working actively to reduce role ambiguity.

Role conflict and ambiguity can cause severe stress, a condition which accounted for a loss of 36 million work-days in Britain in 1971. In his study of the importance and impact of managerial stress, Pettigrew suggests that some managerial roles cause greater stress than others.[10] Since role ambiguity, conflict, and overload increase the stress under which a manager functions, Pettigrew recommends that organizations identify the jobs with high stress potential to analyze both the job and the incumbent. Then, either the job can be redesigned to suit the manager or a new manager can be selected; in either case, the goal is to ensure a better fit between the individual and his role in the organization.

A manager may react to role conflict and ambiguity and the resulting stress in several ways, all of which reduce his effectiveness. He may become aggressive and make "too many waves" in his impatience to get the job done. Or, he may try to resolve the conflict by withdrawing and trying to isolate himself from the conflict demands placed on him, e.g., taking longer lunch hours. Similarly, a college student who is doing poorly may respond by cutting classes and avoiding his professor. Unfortunately, however, the existing structure in most organizations provides little in the way of mechanisms for resolving either role conflict or role ambiguity.

Having discussed managerial role relationships and expectations, we are now ready to define the job of the manager. Sayles has suggested that the manager's job can be separated into three distinct functions, or categories of activity.[11] First, the manager is a participant in external work flow. Second, he is a leader, and third, he monitors the activities of others.

A. The Manager as a Participant in External Work Flow. As we pointed out earlier, a manager can have hundreds of contacts with different people inside and outside the organization, frequently at the lateral, or peer, level. It is at this lateral level of interaction that the manager spends most of his time. In these relationships with peers and with people outside the organization, the manager is providing the "connective tissue" that helps to coordinate the organization's activities. The first-line supervisor, for example, works with people in the scheduling, production control, quality assurance, and engineering departments. The purchasing agent works closely with vendors, customers, and the engineering and production control groups. The head of the industrial engineering department works with such internal groups as design, production, and marketing and such external groups as equipment manufacturers.

In these lateral relationships, the manager's efforts are directed largely toward negotiations with other work groups which in turn must make adjustments before the manager can shift his attention elsewhere. The result is a continuously shifting process whereby the demands by any one manager must be brought into line with those of other managers; in turn, each manager makes compensating moves and adjustments. This never-ending cycle of securing new agreements, commitments, and assurances in response to the demands made by others results in a decision-making process which can be characterized as a "continuous and *intricate process* of brokerage" within the open system.[12]

For example, a manufacturing manager is trying to get the research and development group to improve the design of a new model so that it is easier to manufacture; concurrently, he is pushing on the industrial engineering depart-

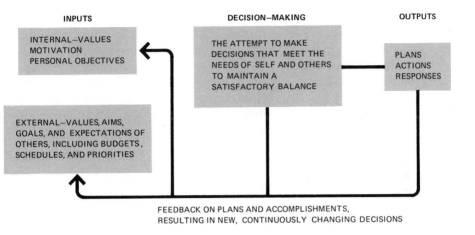

Figure 7.2. *The manager's activities.*

ment to give him better equipment; attempting to negotiate with the maintenance group to make quicker repairs; attempting to make certain that the
purchasing people expedite his order for parts that have been holding up the
production schedule; working with the quality assurance group who insist on
higher quality; fighting with the finance people to get a bigger budget for
training and employment; attempting to accomodate the requests of salesmen
for more samples to be used in the field; and working with the union steward
to settle labor grievances. Each decision or negotiation affects other decisions
and work groups—priorities change as a result of the on-going process of decision-making.

If we consider the manager as an open subsystem, engaged in a series of role
relationships and role expectations with other subsystems, all of which are also
open, changing, and dynamic, it is easy to see why more than half of a manager's
time is spent in negotiations in lateral-level relationships. Figure 7.2 shows the
managerial process in the work flow. Decisions are determined by both internal
and external inputs. The results, or outputs, of his decision-making process
affect other subsystems, and as a result, both the manager and other subsystems
may be forced to negotiate new plans and decisions. Since the manager must
always strive to maintain some sort of balance among these shifting, changing
inputs, his decision-making may be geared toward satisfying as many people as
possible rather than trying to find an optimal solution.

B. The Manager as a Leader. The typical manager spends about 25 to 35% of his time working with his subordinates. His designation as a "manager" automatically places him in the power structure of the formal system and gives him formal authority over people who may or may not themselves be managers. However, since the manager is an open system, his interaction with subordinates is varied and reflects not only his interactions and negotiations at the lateral level, but also the similar activities of his subordinates. Therefore, we can discern at least three different types of behavior that the manager engages in with his subordinates.

1. Leadership as direction. This portion of the manager's job is described in the classic definition of a manager, i.e., getting subordinates to respond to his initiative, actions, and directions. Through his position in the formal structure of the organization, the manager is truly directing, motivating, controlling, and coordinating subordinates' activities in attempting to meet organizational goals. However, if we consider the manager within a broader systems point of view, there are at least two other activities in which he must engage as a leader.

2. Leadership as response to subordinates. A manager's decisions are influenced by the inputs he receives as a result of interaction with subordinates. A manager not only tells people what to do, he must also respond to their needs and expectations; they are not merely passive individuals, and they have requests that they make of their own boss or supervisor. Students may request that their college professor explain a particular part of a text or postpone a scheduled paper. A department chairman may need to respond to a faculty member who asserts that one of his classes is too large for the style of teaching he is using. A first-line supervisor must respond to a subordinate's information that he needs additional parts. An engineering manager must respond to a subordinate who complains of difficulty in getting drafting help from another part of the engineering department.

3. The manager as a representative. When the manager/leader is unable to handle a matter brought up by a subordinate, he must act on behalf of that subordinate, and this may require him to negotiate with his peers or his own superiors. Thus, the manager as a representative is dealing at both the vertical and lateral levels in response to initiation and inputs from his subordinates. For example, a manager must recommend pay increases for his subordinates to his own boss. A sales manager may respond to complaints from his salesmen about slow delivery time by negotiating with manufacturing for faster delivery. A first-line supervisor may try to get the parts shortage reduced by having purchasing expedite orders.

A department chairman may convince the dean that more faculty members are needed to handle an influx of new students.

C. The Manager as a Monitor. In a sense, this function overlaps considerably with the other two functions: participating in external work flow and overseeing the activities of subordinates. Here, however, the manager must set up either formal or informal monitoring subsystems to determine "how things are going" —he must be sensitive to possible sources of trouble and decide whether he will intervene personally or ask others to do so. The manufacturing manager cannot wait until the day a new product arrives on the manufacturing floor to determine whether research and development has come up with a workable design. The retailing manager must monitor sales of certain items to determine how they are selling so he will know when to reorder and in what quantity. In short, the manager must develop both methods for detecting possible disturbances in the work system and criteria for signaling when these disturbances are significant. He must then develop patterns of corrective action and be able to assess the effect of these corrective actions. This recurring cycle of detection, assessment, and correction is what we called feedback in an earlier chapter—it is used to predict what new approaches or changes will occur to which the organization or the subsystem will have to adapt.

III. REVISED CONCEPTS OF MANAGEMENT

Use of the systems approach clarifies the concept that the manager is a subsystem within the total system and that a multiplicity of role expectations are placed on him by other subsystems within the organization and by outside influences. In describing the manager's role, we defined the manager's job as participating in external work flow, leading subordinates, and monitoring their work by developing both positive and negative feedback approaches. Since more than half of a manager's time is spent in work-flow relationships, there are some concepts in more traditional approaches to the manager's job which need to be revised.

A. "The parameters of a manager's job can be bounded and compartmentalized into a job description." The inaccuracy of this belief has been amply demonstrated; in actuality, the multitude of the manager's role relationships and the trading and negotiation that he must carry on make it impossible to compartmentalize his job. The manager is a subsystem interacting and relating with a large variety of other subsystems. In any given month he may have literally hundreds of contacts with a variety of different groups and individuals in an ever-changing set of relationships.

B. *"A manager takes orders from one boss."* In the traditional structural-design perspective, a manager has only one immediate supervisor. However, by describing the organization in systems terms, it becomes evident that the manager is an open subsystem interacting with other subsystems both within and outside the boundaries of the system and that each of these subsystems influences the behavior of the individual manager. Thus, in a sense any one manager is "bossed" by each of the other people or groups with whom he comes in contact —the manager's role is to adjust to and balance these multitudes of role expectations and demands.

C. *"The manager's authority is commensurate with his responsibility."* This is one of the most cherished concepts of the classical management theorists. However, the manager's job, or responsibility, is to get a particular job done within his own subsystem, and this requires continuous negotiations with other subsystems over which he has no formal authority. Therefore, it is obvious that the manager's ability to fulfill his responsibility comes not from his authority over other groups, but rather from his skill in negotiating, adjusting, and persuading others.

D. *"Staff people have no real responsibility or authority."* Traditionally, most of the writers on management have been concerned primarily with the concept of hierarchical, Perspective I organizations, which tend to be stable. As a result, they developed a series of concepts postulating that the "staff" serves only an advisory function. The systems approach to work flow, however, may make the entire concept of line and staff obsolete: the finance manager in today's organization may well have more power and authority than a manufacturing manager; marketing research, and research and development groups exert a tremendous power and authority over the manufacturing department which must, in essence, manufacture the products determined by these two groups. As Fisch points out, it no longer makes any sense to consider research and development departments as "staff departments."[13] By using a systems approach, however, we can see that each of the groups, or subsystems, within an organization has a tremendous impact on all the other subsystems.

E. *"The manager spends most of his time with his subordinates."* As we pointed out at the beginning of this chapter, the traditional definition of a manager emphasizes his planning, organizing, controlling, motivating, and directing relationships with his subordinates. But as we have stressed, the manager does not spend the majority of his time with his subordinates; rather, he spends most of his working time in both internal and external lateral, work-flow relationships.

F. *"Formal leadership is closely related to experience."* Another fallacious belief is that formal leadership is closely associated with experience and that the more experience a leader has, the better he will be as a formal leader. In his summary of both laboratory experiments and field studies of the Post Office, shop craftsmen, meat markets, grocery departments, heavy machinery production, and research chemists, Fiedler used data on 385 managers to test the relationship between length of supervisory experience and leadership effectiveness as measured by the group's "performance of its major assigned task."[14] Fiedler was unable to find any relationship between leadership experience (in years) and group effectiveness (productivity); the "median correlation" across the different samples was −.12.

In anticipation of criticism arising from both tacit and explicit assumptions that time and leadership experience should have a high positive correlation (some organizations even specify the number of years a manager must hold a particular job before being promoted), Fiedler reworked his data in a number of different ways. All the variations, however, cast profound doubts on the earlier assumptions and raised questions about the traditional criteria for managerial selection and development.

In a related study, Wheatley set up four different types of employer-employee problem-solving groups based on leadership style: (1) participatory, in which the leader encouraged group members to take an active role; (2) supervisory, in which the leader established procedures and an agenda but did not otherwise contribute to the group's efforts; (3) silent, in which the leader's only contribution was to provide instructions to the group; and (4) leaderless, in which the leader left the room after giving instructions for solving the problem.[15] These various leadership styles provided no measure of effectiveness of problem-solving; however, the level of interaction within the group rose significantly when the leader was either silent or absent. Wheatley concluded from this that group effectiveness "might be improved when no leader from management is present."

Although there is widespread belief in the six concepts we have listed, they are, at best, only half-truths, and their acceptance has led to a genuine misunderstanding of the manager's job. Managers have felt extremely uncomfortable with the traditional definition of their job, for it implied that they were not doing their job because they were spending too much time with lateral, work-flow relationships. As one very competent manager expressed it: "I got nothing done yesterday because I was all tied up in meetings. However, I feel great today. I had a staff meeting with my subordinates and got five letters written, in between meetings." In other words, although this manager was regarded as

highly effective by others in the organization, he felt uncomfortable because he
was operating under several obsolete concepts, particularly that which says that
"the manager spends most of his time with his subordinates." Although this is
always an unwritten dictum, it has had an overly strong influence on the way
managers have perceived their job.

IV. SUMMARY

Some management theorists feel that a manager should plan, organize, staff,
direct, and control his subordinates. However, research indicates otherwise:
managers have a large number of interpersonal contacts per day and spend much
of their time with lateral rather than vertical contacts; the better managers spend
more of their time in the lateral, work-flow process than do less successful
managers. These findings verify Sayles' description of a manager as: (1) a participant in external work flow, (2) a leader, and (3) a monitor. Accordingly, some
commonly held beliefs about a manager's role need to be revised. In actuality,
a manager takes orders (is influenced by) many persons, and usually he cannot
have authority equal to his responsibility. Similarly, the line-staff separation is
frequently blurred, and there seems to be little, if any, relationship between a
formal leader's experience and his success.

The most valid concept of management depicts the manager's role as a
complex, shifting set of relationships whereby decisions must continually be
renegotiated. In our culture the manager has multiple roles which require a great
deal of interaction with many people at a variety of levels inside and outside
the organization.

REVIEW

1. Give an example of both role conflict and role ambiguity. Show how each
   affects behavior.

2. Interview a manager and get his definition of a manager's job. Does this
   agree with the definition given in the text? If not, what do you think makes
   the difference?

3. We have distinguished between a "leader" and a "manager." Is this distinction valid? Explain.

4. If a manager spends much of his time interacting with peers and others in
   the work flow, what implication does this have for managerial development?

5. In the previous chapter we described various types of power and influence.
   Under what circumstances may a manager use one type of power rather
   than another?

Critical Concepts

Basic managerial functions
Manager versus leader
Role
Role conflict
Role ambiguity

REFERENCES

1 H. Koontz and C. O'Donnell, *Principles of Management* (New York: McGraw-Hill, 1968).

2 J. H. Barrett, personal communication.

3 O. Ponder, "Supervisory Practices of Effective and Ineffective Foremen," (Ph.D. diss., Columbia University, 1968).

4 C. Walker, R. Guest, and A. Turner, *The Foreman on the Assembly Line* (Cambridge, Mass.: Harvard University Press, 1956).

5 G. Strauss, "Tactics of Lateral Relationships: The Purchasing Agent," *Administrative Science Quarterly*, 7, 2 (Sept. 1962):161-186.

6 L. Sayles, *Managerial Behavior* (New York: McGraw-Hill, 1964).

7 R. Kahn, E. Wolfe, R. Quinn, and J. Snock, *Organizational Stress: Studies in Role Conflict and Ambiguity* (New York: John Wiley, 1964).

8 R. House and J. Rizzo, "Role Conflict and Ambiguity as Critical Variables in a Model of Organizational Behavior," *Organizational Behavior and Human Performance*, 7, 3 (June 1972):467-505.

9 *Ibid.*, p. 500.

10 A. Pettigrew, "Managing under Stress," *Management Today* (April 1972):99-102.

11 L. Sayles, *op. cit.*

12 *Ibid.*, p. 28.

13 G. Fisch, "Line-Staff is Obsolete," *Harvard Business Review*, 39, 5 (Sept.-Oct. 1961): 67-79.

14 F. Fiedler, "Leadership Experience and Leader Performance—Another Hypothesis Shot to Hell," *Organizational Behavior and Human Performance*, 55, 1 (Jan. 1970):1-14.

15 B. Wheatley, "Leadership and Anxiety: Implications for Small-Group Meetings," *Personnel Journal*, 51, 1 (Jan. 1972):17-21.

PART III

ORGANIZATIONAL GOALS, PERSONNEL SELECTION, AND TRAINING

An organization's objectives and control systems and its programs for personnel selection and training cannot be compartmentalized into the framework of the three perspectives; rather, they include elements from all three. However, since each of these functions is an open subsystem, we have grouped them in Part III of the text. Although the concepts presented in Chapters 8 and 9 are traditional in nature, they are necessary for understanding certain organizational and personnel functions more completely.

OBJECTIVES AND CONTROL SYSTEMS (CHAPTER 8)

An organization's objectives emerge from the various states in its development and are determined by several interacting factors: (1) the desires of management and workers; (2) the environmental needs provided by the organization; (3) the skills and abilities of the personnel team; (4) the technologies currently available; and (5) the funds available for conducting operations. "Official" objectives may differ from the "actual" objectives, and these two types of objectives may be reflected in the organization's approach to meeting its goals. Thus, a "forward-looking" (proactive) approach may be used with "official," or long-range, objectives; a "reactive" approach may be used for "actual," or short-term objectives. One other approach, which is gaining widespread acceptance, is "management by objectives," i.e., programs and methods for translating objectives into operational guidelines. Thus, techniques for appraising personnel performance are closely related to a management-by-objectives program and may be used for setting pay scales and personnel selection and training.

PERSONNEL SELECTION AND TRAINING (CHAPTER 9)

Most organizational behavior theorists have ignored personnel selection. However, since this is such a critical aspect of organizational life, procedures for personnel selection and training need to be considered in some detail. Perhaps the most important concept developed in Chapter 9 is that selection can be an open system with its own control devices for both testing the effectiveness of the selection procedures and modifying them as needed.

Once new personnel have been selected, they must be trained. There are several techniques available for assessing training needs, as well as for training, administering, and evaluating training programs. Using pilot studies and periodic performance evaluations after training has been completed, one can easily determine which training techniques are most appropriate for various job situations.

8
OBJECTIVES
AND
CONTROL
SYSTEMS

You may depend upon it, the more oath-taking, the more lying generally among the people.

S. T. COLERIDGE

I. INTRODUCTION

In this chapter we examine the problem of organizational objectives and their interrelationship with the internal and external environments of the organization. We look at the problem of multiple objectives, the distinction between "official" and "actual" objectives, and distinguish between proactive and reactive approaches to objectives, pointing out the importance and necessity of each type. Using Maslow's need hierarchy as a model, we describe how organizational objectives can and do change at different stages of organizational life. The concept of management by objectives is one method for making organizational objectives operational, and we point out some of the advantages and pitfalls of such an approach. Finally, we briefly discuss the concept of performance appraisal as an overall control measure and note some of the uses and abuses of performance appraisal as a control mechanism.

II. ORGANIZATIONAL OBJECTIVES

Every system needs objectives, or goals. Nearly 30 years ago, Gulick noted that "A clear statement of purpose universally understood is the outstanding guarantee of effective administration."[1] Some 16 years later, Etzioni modified this statement only slightly by pointing out that "An organizational goal is a desired state of affairs which the organization attempts to realize."[2]

The important part of Etzioni's definition is that it points to "a *desired* state" that the organization "*attempts* to realize." The organization may not reach the goals or desired state, but it does have direction and purpose. Of course, the objectives will vary with the nature and type of organization. An industrial organization may well have a different set of goals and objectives from a hospital or a social-welfare organization.

The objectives of any organization are complex, and no organization has a single set of objectives. Figure 8.1 shows that organizational goals result from a complex interaction of external and internal forces. Although most industrial managers assert that the objective of their organization is to make a profit, such a statement is an oversimplification which ignores the influence of both the external environment and the internal subsystems within the organization.

Laws and regulations have a tremendous influence on the objectives of an organization, as do the demands and expectations of the consumer, as witness the untimely death of the Edsel, a car on which Ford lavished a great deal of time and money. More recently, the refusal of the Congress to fund the SST (supersonic transport) caused a tremendous change in the objectives of a number

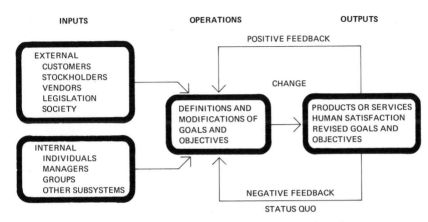

Figure 8.1. *Complexity of organizational goals.*

of different organizations. Similarly, the work of Nader and his "Raiders" has caused many organizations to change some of their stated objectives.

Furthermore, there is wide variation between what managers *say* and what they *do* within the organization, as is demonstrated in "Exercise Objectives" developed by Bass.[3] First, managers are asked to make decisions about several organizational problems; then, they are asked, as a group, to give percentage weights to six possible company objectives. Table 8.1 shows the results of a modified version of the exercise administered by one of the authors. These data

Table 8.1 Response of managers to "Exercise Objectives"

Objective	Percentage of weight given
Profits	35
Growth	11
Community welfare	21
Improve operations	22
Meet competition	11

Adapted from B. M. Bass, "Exercise Objectives," in *A Program of Exercises for Management and Organizational Psychology*, Pittsburgh: Management Development Associates, 1966.

were obtained from 60 managers in two industrial organizations. Although profits received the greatest weight, community welfare and improving operations also ranked high. Women executives of a telephone company gave much higher weight to employee welfare and service to the community than to profits; male executives of transit companies gave the highest weight to community welfare and improving operations.

In other words, although people may *say* that profits are the main objective of an organization, they do not *act* that way, either in exercises such as the one described here or as demonstrated by their actions in the organization. Furthermore, the objectives shift, depending on the type of organization in which the person is working.

A. Organizations Have Multiple Objectives

The results of the Bass exercise and the fact that the organization is an open system with interrelated and interdependent subsystems which receive inputs from the outside environment to produce a changing, uneasy balance demonstrate that an organization has multiple objectives. Drucker notes that industrial organizations must develop objectives in eight key areas: "market standing; innovation; productivity; physical and financial resources; profitability; manager performance and development; worker performance and attitude; and public responsibility."[4] Although the areas cited by Drucker are for a profit-making, or utilitarian, organization, *any* organization needs objectives in every area which affects its survival and effectiveness. It is also clear that since the social system is composed of interrelated subsystems, its objectives will also be interrelated. Thus, for example, market standing and innovation are highly related, as are profitability and worker performance, even though the short-term objectives in one area may contradict those in another area.

Perrow, taking a much broader, sociological approach than Drucker, identifies five categories of organizational goals:[5]

1. Societal goals—refer to society in general and large classes of organizations rather than to single organizations, i.e., the generating and maintaining of cultural values, maintaining order, as well as producing goods and services.

2. Output goals—such consumer functions as business services, consumer goods, education, and health care. For example, some industrial organizations have undertaken "contract education" for school systems. As Perrow points out, however, one societal norm is that an organization not take on too many diverse functions, e.g., a "company town" in which housing, recreation, and retail stores are controlled by the organization. Similarly, the Tennessee Valley Authority, which generates electric power and manufactures fertilizer, has been opposed by

some businessmen because it represents governmental intervention in the "private sector" of the economy.

Ford Motor Company found it difficult to shift its output goals from automobiles to small appliances when it purchased Philco; most of the top men at Philco left, and there was a massive transfusion of Ford executives into Philco. But since these executives had no experience in the appliance field, Ford had to bring in someone with the necessary experience. Similarly, organizations accustomed to working under government contracts have had difficulty in making consumer goods and have found it necessary to diversify through purchase of existing consumer-oriented companies rather than use their own people to start such organizations. The parent companies have discovered that the rigid rules and fixed procedures applicable to work on government defense contracts hinder successful operation in a consumer-oriented environment.

3. System goals—the organization's design and operation methods. Some organizations emphasize rapid growth; others emphasize stability and a high rate of profit. Some organizations are loosely controlled; others are tightly controlled. An organization that places a premium on being "the first" with rapid product changes has as its system goal the desire to be an industry leader. Another organization may place little emphasis on research and development, preferring to imitate designs developed by other organizations.

Perrow uses two utility companies to illustrate differing concepts of system goals and strategies for dealing with the environment. Consolidated Edison of New York, the largest gas and electric utility in the nation, relies on its political influence in New York City and Albany. Consequently, "Con Ed has the worst earnings record, service record and general public relations of the utility industry."[6] By contrast, American Electric Power Company, located in depressed Appalachia with only four cities of more than 100,000 people, relies on advanced technology and marketing techniques; because of aggressive promotion of all-electric homes and the introduction of innovations such as high-voltage transmission and heat pumps, it now generates more electric power than any other utility in the world and has steadily increased the quality of its service and lowered its rates, which "run from 25 to 38 percent below the nation's average."[7]

System goals need to change with the times, but this is sometimes quite difficult to do, as illustrated by Perrow's history of Eastern Airlines. The World War I flying ace Eddie Rickenbacker controlled and managed Eastern from 1935 to 1959. Unlike most other airlines, Eastern showed profits for 25 consecutive years as a result of Rickenbacker's system goal of economy. He managed to keep costs under control by stressing the importance of saving even mills (one-tenth of one cent). This was a desirable system goal in the early years, since Eastern had a near monopoly on its most profitable routes, especially the run from New

York to Miami. However, cutting costs could be achieved only by reducing services. Eastern delayed introducing new and better aircraft; scheduling and maintenance were tight and done at the convenience of the company rather than that of the customers; seating on its planes was more cramped than on other airlines; coffee and cookies rather than breakfast were served; and overbooking flights was more extensive than the usual industry practice. While Rickenbacker was concentrating on saving money, other airlines were spending money for pretty stewardesses, better food, more convenient schedules, nonstop service, and bigger, faster, and more comfortable planes.

When the Civil Aeronautics Board decided to strengthen smaller lines and increase competition by allowing them to operate on the busier and more profitable routes, Eastern was hard hit. From 1960 to 1963, Eastern lost increasing amounts of money. Although Rickenbacker had retired from active management in 1959, he stayed on as chairman of the board until 1963. When Floyd Hall took over in 1963, he made sweeping changes which stemmed the pattern of revenue losses. In 1964 Eastern lost $5.6 million; in 1965 the company's profit was $29.7 million. As Perrow points out, Rickenbacker's system goal of cost reduction and little innovation was an excellent one in the early years, but it became disasterous when changes in the environment required a system goal of growth and innovation.

4. Product goals—such "product-characteristic goals" as quantity, quality, styling, cost, type, and availability. Some clothing manufacturers specialize in "one-of-a-kind" dresses; others specialize in mass production. Some steel companies produce only high-quality steel; others manufacture steel in a wide range of quality.

Sometimes product and system goals conflict. For example, Perrow cites the case of a textile company that continued to turn out high-quality material on 500 looms when the market could support production of that material from only 50 looms. The company was taken over by another organization whose primary system goal was to make a profit. The conflict was quickly resolved by converting a product goal (manufacture of high-quality material) to a system goal (profit). However, it is not always easy to shift from one type of goal to another. Management may object ("We're in the woolen business"), or workers may object ("We're making high-quality products"). Gar Wood, for example, specialized in making custom-built, high-quality boats. When they decided to make cheaper, mass-produced boats in order to compete with Chris-Craft, the workers could not make the required transition; finally, Gar Wood had to build a new plant staffed with new people to turn out the lower-quality boat.

5. Derived goals—the ways in which the organization uses its power to pursue other goals. Organizations, especially large ones, have a great deal of power

which they can use to influence either their own members or the environment, as the controversy generated in the spring of 1972 over International Telephone and Telegraph's proposed takeover of Hartford Insurance illustrates so well.

Perrow points out that this categorization of goals is not as clear-cut as could be desired and that some goals could just as easily be placed in one category as another. His chief message is that organizations pursue a variety of goals and that some system of classification is helpful for categorizing goals.

The fact that organizations do pursue several types of goals is also stressed by Mohr who, after an exhaustive review of the literature, concluded that the goals of organizations need to be "viewed as multiple rather than unitary, empirical rather than imputed and to be dichotomized into outwardly- and inwardly-oriented categories."[8] Mohr calls the outwardly-oriented categories "transitive" and the inwardly-oriented categories "reflexive." Although most people as well as organizations have both transitive and reflexive goals, they may not give equal emphasis to both. For example, an organization with transitive goals may be highly oriented toward providing a product or service to its environment, whereas a reflexive organization such as a recreational club or fraternity exists primarily for the "mutual benefit of its members." This category also includes groups that have had extreme influence in developing both organizational and political theory. Such organizations include labor unions, marketing associations, professional societies, trade organizations, and political interest groups. One of Mohr's chief thrusts is that clear distinctions need to be made between the two, since studies made on reflexive organizations may not be relevant when the results or inferences of the studies are applied to transitive organizations or to the mix within organizations. For example, as we mention in the section on proactive versus reactive approaches to objectives, a company president may have ambivalent feelings about taking on a risky new product (transitive goal) and maintaining his own job security (reflexive goal).

B. "Official" versus "Actual" Objectives

An organization's multiple objectives may include both "official" objectives (drawn up for public consumption by a specially selected blue-ribbon committee, signed by the president or the chairman of the board of directors, and then framed and hung on the walls of executive offices and in the lobby) and "actual" objectives (those toward which the organization is actually directing its energies). Perrow describes "official goals" as the organization's "general purposes" as stated in annual reports, the official charter of the organization, and other authoritative pronouncements; "operating" goals, on the other hand, are those which guide the organization's activities, "regardless of what the official goals say are the aims."[9]

An interesting illustration of this distinction occurred when the president of an organization employing about 1500 people was asked to be a member of a panel on employment of the disadvantaged. When he stated that "our organization is not interested in your educational background, your race, color, or creed. We are interested in what you can do!" a member of the audience asked the president if he really meant that statement. The president said yes, whereupon, the questioner remarked, "I wish you would tell that to your employment manager. Last week, I filled out an application blank for your company and when the employment manager looked at it, he said, 'I see you haven't finished high school. We hire only high school graduates.' I didn't even get an interview." Frequently, once the "official" objectives have been established, they are seldom referred to again.

Whatever criteria are used to categorize an organization's goals, however, it must be kept in mind that in and of themselves, *organizations* do not have objectives; rather, *people* have objectives, stemming from their own views and motivations. Thus, so-called "organizational objectives" are really uneasy and shifting compromises among the individuals within the organization and the demands made by the outside environment. As Katz says,

Every *strategic action must strike a balance among so many conflicting values, objectives and criteria that it will* always *be suboptimal from any single viewpoint.* Every *decision or choice affecting the whole enterprise has negative consequences for some of the parts.* [10]

This contradicts the point made implicitly, if not explicitly, by advocates of the formal Perspective I approach who stress that objectives are developed at the top and then passed down and accepted unquestioningly through the chain of command to the lowest-level subordinate. However, it is obvious that such a viewpoint is erroneous, for even within the formal perspective there are many conflicting points of view. The research and development department may prefer excellent, elegant, "state of the art" designs; marketing may want a large variety of products in their catalog; manufacturing may wish to concentrate on a few, high-volume products in order to reduce costs; the president of the firm may want to mimimize risks while the research director wants to increase the rate of new product development and introduction. One possible result of such conflict was described earlier in the story that a large computer company's top management decreed that research work stop on the random-access memory that is now the basis of the third-generation, real-time computer. However, the research people continued their work under "bootleg" conditions until they had perfected the process.

The same types of conflicts occur in nonindustrial organizations. There may be strong differences of opinion between an administrator in a university who wants to reduce costs by having each faculty member carry a full teaching load and individual faculty members who wish to spend more time on their own research or writing projects. And in one large state mental institution, there continues to be serious conflict between those who favor admitting patients to facilitate the training of psychiatric residents and those who prefer admitting less curable patients requiring long-range custodial care.

Even within two organizations which ostensibly have identical purposes and objectives, vast differences can occur. Blau describes two different employment agencies which had the same official objectives.[11] But because of the differing nature of the director and the work force in the two organizations, one agency emphasized cooperation among employees and service to the "customer," whereas the other agency fostered competition and secrecy among employees and emphasized individual rather than total organizational performance, to the detriment of the "customer."

It is clear, therefore, that organizations have multiple objectives and that these objectives emerge from continuous renegotiations among the organization's personnel. Cyert and March point out that such mutual bargaining and perpetual conflict cause the members of the organization to be dissatisfied (a satisfied need is not a motivator); each member has a list (which may not be particularly well organized) of demands which pop up at different times. As a result, most organizations have goals that are highly contradictory but are not really recognized as such because they are rarely considered simultaneously. Such realization occurs only if there is a well-established ordering of priorities, which is rare because attention is given only to the goals relevant at the moment. Thus, for example, they raise the philosophical question about the entire concept of objectives: "To what extent is it arbitrary that we call wage payments costs and dividend payments profits rather than the other way around?"[12]

III. PROACTIVE VERSUS REACTIVE APPROACHES TO OBJECTIVES

Koontz and O'Donnell relate the story of a corporate president who decided not to embark on an expansion program, even though there was good potential for a great deal of profit to the company.[13] His rationale was that if he continued making only moderate profits, the stockholders would remain satisfied; if, on the other hand, taking this conservative route resulted in lower profits, he could then blame external political or business conditions, whereas if the expansion proved successful, the stockholders would merely assume that he was doing his normal job and therefore would not reward him properly for his effort and risk. However, if the expansion program failed, the stockholders might fire him. Since his primary goal was to remain as president of the company, he decided to maintain the status quo, thereby forfeiting the almost certain profits resulting from the expansion program.

Two points can be made from this story. First, profit is not always the manager's chief motive in making decisions about the goals and objectives of his organization. Second, and more important, this story illustrates the distinction between proactive and reactive approaches to objectives.

In Chapter 2 we pointed out that the behavior of individuals and social organizations has multiple causes and that the seeking for balance is a dynamic process. The internal balance of a particular subsystem is threatened by pressures from both other subsystems within the organization and external forces. Feedback, the flow of information back to the subsystem about its performance, is necessary for maintaining a dynamic balance within the individual subsystems and the total system. We also pointed out that a social organization strives for *balance,* but not *optimal balance.*

While organizations strive to maintain the balance of the organization and the subsystems within it, there appear to be two necessary but conflicting forces at work in establishing and maintaining objectives. One is the force that resists change and works toward preserving the status quo, or "reactive," force. The other is the force that works toward change in the system, or "proactive" force. These seemingly contradictory forces actually complement each other; an organization needs to grow and change, but it also needs a stabilizing force to keep it from "going off the deep end" by too sudden and rapid change. Thus, the organization is always struggling to maintain the proper balance between stability (reactive forces) and growth and improvement (proactive forces).

The reactive and proactive forces are analogous to positive and negative feedback loops. Figure 8.1 showed that objectives are affected by inputs from both external and internal sources. One series of feedback loops is directed toward maintaining the organization's direction, i.e., toward maintaining the status quo. Another series of feedback loops is directed toward fostering change, modifying organizational objectives, and thereby changing the organization's direction. For example, if one salesman reports that a customer is unhappy with a certain product, this input may have little or no influence on the organization; if, however, many salesmen make similar reports and sales of the product fall off drastically, this input may well represent positive feedback and result in change in organizational objectives.

In his discussion of reactive forces in social organizations, Leavitt describes the tendency of the railroad companies to consider themselves in the *railroad* rather than the *transportation* business.[14] When trucks and airplanes began to be used to transport goods, therefore, the railroads resisted change and lost customers because they refused to shift their objectives—they were oriented toward railroads rather than toward transportation and customer needs. Leavitt also cites the movie business, which initially regarded TV as a competitor for the movie business rather than as another component of the entertainment business. Leavitt criticizes the oil companies for considering themselves part of the oil rather than the "energy" business. As a result, most of the work on fuel cells is conducted not by either oil companies or utilities, but by other organizations.

In other words, some reactive forces cause organizations to cling to objectives or procedures that are actually harmful to the organization. Another type of reactive force is the variety of "control systems" within organizations. One such control system is the accounting approach used in most organizations. For its purposes, the accounting subsystem insists that the books be closed on a monthly or other regular basis so that profit and loss can be computed at short-term intervals. However, this is dysfunctional for the manufacturing susbsystem. For example, in a firm with a four-week accounting cycle, great stress is placed toward the end of the period on meeting the established production schedule. Thus, on a regularly predictable basis, department managers and first-line supervisors reschedule their work in order to meet the "quota." They "rob the line" that is, do work in the most rapid rather than the most effective sequence in order to meet production goals. They will, at times, knowingly pack defective products, just to meet the quota for the period. Similarly, it is not uncommon for the inspection subsystem to get 50% or more of its work in the last week of the accounting period.

As Fig. 8.2 shows, there is relatively little productivity in the first week of the next production period as first-line supervisors and workers repair the damage done in the last week of the previous accounting period, and this cycle is repeated with each new accounting period. This cycle is recognizable by almost every manufacturing manager and first-line foreman; almost all of them disagree with this pattern and believe that a better method should be used. However, the feedback for positive change is not sufficiently strong to overcome the status quo; most managers accept the use of the accounting period as a "given" condition of the control system, and feel that there is little they can do about it.

Unfortunately, in most social organizations, the control systems for negative feedback are more carefully developed than those for positive feedback. Most control systems are established to ensure that predetermined objectives are met in timely, appropriate fashion, albeit with dysfunctional results. Few "control systems" exist to ensure planned change, improvement, and optimal balance in the system. Leavitt points out that although the marketing department of an organization should perform part of this function, too frequently it suffers from the same myopia that affects the rest of the organization.

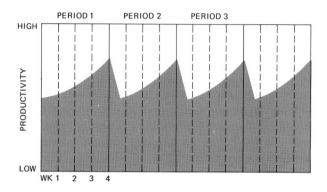

Figure 8.2. *Productivity during accounting periods.*

Most organizations are now beginning to recognize the need for establishing better methods of positive feedback. For example, it used to be almost unheard of for people on the manufacturing floor to get any feedback about what the customer thought of the product; now, more and more organizations are posting salesmen's reports on the bulletin boards for all to see, including those on the manufacturing floor. Much of the proactive change will come about through planned interaction among the three perspectives. The development of improved lateral information flow will have a positive influence, as will the deliberate design of organizations to better fit their environment. Much of the change will come about through greater attention to the human perspective. For example, when Tannenbaum surveyed organizational control in about 200 different organizational units, he found that employees at all levels wanted more opportunity to exercise self-control over their own work.[15] As to be expected, the largest gap between the amount and degree of external control and self-control is at the rank-and-file level.

IV. OBJECTIVES AT DIFFERENT STAGES OF ORGANIZATIONAL LIFE

According to Maslow's hierarchy of needs (Chapter 3), lower-level needs generally must be satisfied before higher-level needs can emerge. Since needs or motives are highly complex, a particular action may satisfy a number of different motives, e.g., a bachelor taking a beautiful woman out to dinner may be simultaneously satisfying physiological needs (hunger) and ego needs (being seen in public with a "real doll").

This duality was first discussed by Robert Michels, who noted that organizations tend to displace goals for other goals and that sometimes the means to a goal becomes a goal and the original goal becomes a means.[16] An organization originally set up to cope with a problem (goal) may become an end in itself (keeping its members employed). In *The Bridge over the River Kwai,* the British colonel believed that the strict discipline required for building a bridge would keep his men from becoming demoralized. The bridge, however, became an end in itself, and the officer bitterly resisted the attempt of other British officers to destroy the bridge.

A somewhat different type of goal displacement is occurring in the industrial world; companies originally concerned primarily with profits are becoming more concerned with keeping the government off their backs and becoming ecologically responsible. Even if such changes occur because of a continuing concern with profit, it nonetheless becomes a less immediate goal. As Anthony notes, many corporations are less concerned with profit because of their other transactional relationships with the society as a whole.[17]

A. Physiological and Safety Needs

Although organizations do not have physiological needs as such, their members do have needs for safety and survival. For example, the primary concern for members in an organization just getting started may be survival of the organization (and their jobs). Thus, they will be highly motivated to get enough captial to start the business and enough sales to ensure its survival.[18] At this stage in the organization's development, there may well be a charismatic, entrepreneurial manager with high achievement needs and as sole owner and manager, he will work long and hard to keep the business going, paying little attention to the other needs of the business.

The need for survival may also arise when the main purpose and objectives of a well-established organization have been attained. For example, the original purpose of the "March of Dimes" campaign was to eliminate polio. Logically, the organization could have been disbanded when this goal was accomplished. However, to ensure its survival, the organization modified its original objectives and is also working on birth defects.

B. Social Needs

Few social needs emerge until survival needs have been met. However, when the organization has grown and prospered to the point that its survival is assured, social concerns emerge. At this stage, the organization begins to join trade associations, puts on Christmas parties and picnics, begins to send its managers to outside training programs, etc. At this level of organizational development, the entrepreneurial manager may well be replaced by layers of managers who are concerned with administration rather than with entrepreneurship.

C. Ego and Esteem Needs

At some level of organizational development, objectives again shift; now the organization seeks to enhance its reputation and become esteemed by other organizations and the community. Indeed, some of the organization's activities at this level have no discernible relationship to profits. The organization may seek to become a member of the New York Stock Exchange, both a mark of prestige and a method of obtaining more capital. It may engage in prestige advertising which seeks to give the company a "good name." Philanthropic donations increase. The organization may prepare educational material without any advertising for free distribution to school systems. Paper companies may make their privately owned forest land available to campers at no cost.

D. Self-Actualization Needs

Economic motives have no role in an organization's self-actualization activities; many of the activities of the Ford Foundation, for example, could be perceived as contradicting the profit-making function of the Ford Motor Company.

In short, one can see a parallel, although not exact, between an individual's need hierarchy and that of an organization. The objectives, goals, aims, and values of the organization change over time, depending on its stage of development.

V. MANAGEMENT BY OBJECTIVES

Whatever the level of an organization's objectives, they must be made operational, that is, they must be translated into action. Coordination and control are necessary to ensure that the objectives are reached, a process Drucker called "management by objectives and self-control" whereby the goals of each manager and his unit can be tied in to the total objectives and success of the enterprise and the needs and objectives of individuals and groups can be more closely meshed.

First, however, we need to briefly define what March and Simon have called the means-end chain.[19] Any decision about what goals are to be achieved must be accompanied by a decision as to the means of reaching those goals. This set

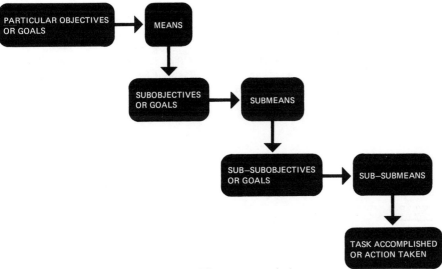

Figure 8.3.　*The means-end chain.*

of means, in turn, becomes a set of subgoals—and some means of attaining *them* must be established. These secondary means then become *sub*-subgoals, and the chain of means-end continues until the specific work is done or concrete action is taken, as shown in Fig. 8.3.

As we mentioned earlier in this chapter, one set of objectives may conflict with another set of objectives. In addition, there may be communication loss or misunderstanding or resistance to the means-end chain. For example, a supervisor conducting a staff meeting may outline a course of action and see all of his subordinates nodding their heads. However, the head-nodding may have different meanings: "Yes, boss, I agree"; or "Yes, boss, I hear you, but I don't agree." The boss may well prefer to conclude that there is unanimous agreement, although in fact there is conflict.

Working toward management by objectives does a great deal to reduce the "management by crisis" problem which occurs because the subordinate and his supervisor perceive the former's job differently. A classic study of the differing perceptions of the same job by high-level executives, conducted by Maier *et al.,* involved manager/subordinate pairs just below the vice-presidential level and showed a high degree of misunderstanding between them about some parts of the job.[20] Table 8.2 shows the areas of greatest disagreement.

Table 8.2 Perceptual agreements and differences between supervisor-subordinate pairs on basic areas of the subordinate's job

	Agreement on less than half the topics	Agreement on about half of the topics	Agreement on more than half of the topics
Job duties	15.0%	39.1%	45.9%
Job requirements - subordinate qualifications	36.3%	40.9%	22.8%
Obstacles in the way of subordinate's performance	68.2%	23.6%	8.1%

Adapted from N. R. F. Maier, L. R. Hoffman, J. J. Hoover, and W. H. Read, *Superior-Subordinate Communication in Management*, New York: American Management Association, 1961.

Management by objectives makes objectives operational. It motivates and develops managers and ensures that the job gets done better, that overall objectives are met, and that organizational objectives more closely fit individuals' objectives—thereby motivating the individual also. Odiorne defines this process as a way of having the supervisor and his subordinate managers jointly define the common goals of the organization and define the individual's major areas of responsibility in terms of the results expected of him, using these measures as guides for determining both the contribution of each member as well as the unit as a whole.[21]

In installing a management-by-objectives program at General Electric, Huse and Kay used a slightly different definition, describing the program as consisting of periodic meetings between manager and subordinate which are "oriented toward the daily work and result in mutual planning of the work, a review of progress and mutual solving of problems which arise in the course of getting the job done."[22] The basic steps in this process are as follows:

1. The manager sits down with the subordinate and the two of them determine the subordinate's specific areas of responsibility for the end results desired. This step is necessary to ensure that both agree on the specifics of the task to be accomplished.

2. The manager and his subordinate must agree on the standard of performance for each area of responsibility.

3. The manager and his subordinate must agree on a work plan for achieving the desired results in each area of responsibility, always in accordance with the overall objectives of the company.

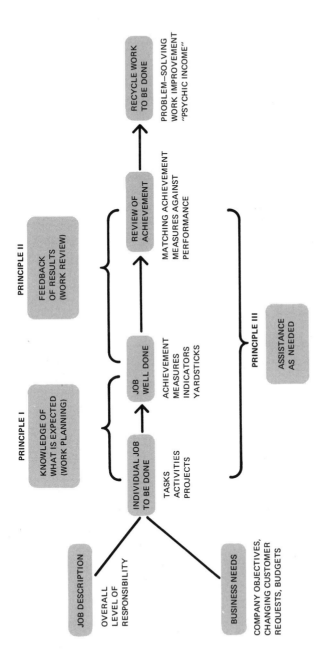

Figure 8.4. *Work planning and review ("psychic income"). (Reprinted by permission from E. Huse and E. Kay, "Improving Employee Productivity Through Work Planning," in The Personnel Job in a Changing World, ed. J. Blood, New York: American Management Association, 1964, p. 305.)*

The cyclical nature of this process is predicated on three basic psychological principles, as shown in Fig. 8.4.

1. A subordinate can improve his job performance only if he knows what is expected of him. The process provides him with better information about priorities, expected results, the methods by which results will be measured, and the resources available to him.

2. In order to improve his job performance, a subordinate needs feedback about how he is doing. This is the most basic of the three principles, since knowledge of results, or feedback, is essential for improving job performance.

3. A subordinate must be able to obtain coaching and assistance when and as needed in order to improve his job performance. This means that the climate must be changed from management by crisis so that the manager can act as a helper rather than as a judge.

The proper utilization of management by objectives can have considerable effect on management development. The research by Huse and Kay has shown that as a result of proper installation of a management-by-objectives approach, subordinates report (at a statistically significant level) greater goal involvement, and there is substantially greater agreement between the boss and subordinate about the job to be done and ways of improving their current job performance.

Other research has added weight to these findings. Reporting on the results of two studies which implemented a goal-setting and self-control program in a large firm, Raia found that the program had a number of positive results: shifting from a more personal to a more job-centered evaluation of performance; increased productivity; better identification of problem areas; better mutual understanding between supervisors and subordinates; and improved communications.[23]

Tosi and Carrol used a questionnaire to follow up on a management-by-objectives program in an organization manufacturing tools.[24] Their results were similar to those of Huse and Kay and Raia in that the managers reported such advantages as better planning, better identification of problem areas, more objective performance measures, and improved communications. In other words, the emphasis of management by objectives on clear understanding of results expected in terms of productivity objectives generally tends to result in higher motivation, improved performance, and greater identification of individual and organizational goals.

However, management by objectives is not a panacea. Thoughtful and realistic critics have pointed out that an incorrectly applied management-by-objectives program can have highly negative and unintended results. If, as

Levinson points out, a management-by-objectives program based on a reward-punishment psychology backed by power rather than reciprocity is used to both attain company objectives and appraise subordinates' performance, the results can be psychologically damaging.[25] If subordinate goals are designed to make the manager or unit look good rather than to contribute to the company's overall objectives, the effectiveness of management by objectives will be reduced. Similarly, techniques must not be allowed to overshadow the concept, as has happened in a number of organizations. Finally, individual objectives must not be made overly tangible and specific, thereby reducing effort on less tangible objectives. For example, although managers may be rewarded highly for meeting immediate, short-term results, few receive credit for an outstanding job of developing the potential of their subordinates.

Ridgway cites a number of cases in which overuse of tangible measurements led to serious dysfunctional consequences. He concludes that the stress on quantitative performance measurements can have highly undesirable consequences for overall organizational performance.[26] This stress on quantitative measure is what leads to the high productivity at the end of the accounting period, even though defective work is allowed to be packed and shipped. As one foreman remarked, "Just tell me what you want my boss to look good on, and I'll make it happen, even if something else goes by the board."

To summarize, control systems (now primarily a product of the Perspective I approach) must take greater account of their impact on the other two perspectives, especially the human perspective. Thus, Likert and Seashore stress that traditional accounting and control measures tell only half the story; such intervening variables as morale, attitudes, and motivating factors must be continuously and carefully measured as a part of the control system.[27] They point out that in the attempt to meet the cost squeeze, many organizations react by exerting stronger pressure throughout the organization on tighter budgets, shorter job-timing, and less stringent standards. Their major point is that in the short run, this can have an immediate impact on profits and profitability, but in the long-run, human resources are depleted as subordinates develop hostile reactions; over time, the organization may lose more than it gains by a "cost-reduction" program. They stress that control systems must do a better job of measuring the intangibles in the system, especially the human resources of the organization, in order to avoid dysfunctional consequences.

VI. PERFORMANCE APPRAISAL

Although related to management by objectives, the term "performance appraisal" is broader, implying judgment of others which may go beyond and be more inclusive than management by objectives. All organizations use some type of performance appraisal; people are always judging the performance of others —peers, subordinates, and managers. Subordinates are continually judging and evaluating the performance of their supervisors, e.g., students continually evaluate their professors. By the same token, a manager's recommendation of a raise for a subordinate is based on his evaluation of the subordinate's performance. In other words, whether the process is formal or informal, performance appraisal is an on-going process.

Theoretically, a systematized approach to performance appraisal should be better than a nonsystematized, informal approach. However, the literature is filled with a growing concern that classical performance appraisal techniques have not been particularly successful. McGregor, for instance, attributes the failure of performance appraisal to the reluctance of managers to "play God."[28] In the study reported earlier, Huse and Kay found that a very formalized performance appraisal in one company actually did more harm than good; subordinates' defensiveness to criticism of their performance increased in direct proportion to the number of criticisms. They also found that greater criticism in the appraisal discussions resulted in *less* performance improvement during the next three to four months. Similar findings were made by Thompson, who points out that many performance appraisals lead to cynicism, alienation, and discouragement on the part of the employee being appraised.[29] In one case, an organization had a "pay-for-performance" program whereby employees were given ratings (A, B, C, D, etc.) which determined their salary level. A new, young engineering graduate was hired and did an outstanding job. At his six-months review, he was given a substantial salary increase despite his "D," or below average, rating. His manager explained that the 15% increase accorded the "D" rating would have jumped to a 50% for an "A" rating. Although the engineer was pleased with the 15% increase, he soon quit because he did not want to have a "below average" performance rating on his record.

In his summary of the current status of performance appraisal, Kay notes that: (1) appraisal systems are multipurpose; (2) the rationale for appraisals is not clear, strong, or convincing; (3) the measurement or judgment of performance still remains a problem; and (4) there is little or no evidence that appraisal systems are meeting their objectives.[30]

Huse notes that the fundamental reason for the failure of performance appraisal is "the failure of management to clearly define objectives and to establish specific techniques of performance appraisal designed to accomplish these objectives."[31] He goes on to cite five different objectives of performance appraisal:

1. Meeting organizational objectives and improving performance—the subordinate needs to know what his objectives are and to obtain feedback about his performance and areas for improvement;

2. Proper salary administration—the manager needs to review the performance of his subordinates in order to recommend proper salary action;

3. Collecting and storing for future administrative actions on promotions, transfers, and demotions or discharges.

4. Identifying training needs—the organization needs to maintain accurate, current information about the strengths and weaknesses of its employees in order to develop timely and appropriate training programs;

5. Improving the selection of new employees—if an organization is to have a systematized, valid selection system, it needs proper criteria against which to validate its selection instruments.

A different technique or appraisal approach may be required for each of these objectives. Some of the standard techniques as well as their advantages and disadvantages are summarized in Table 8.3. However, most organizations have attempted to use an all-purpose form for performance appraisal which forces the manager to be a judge rather than a counselor. (The supervisor of the young engineer was forced to "judge" his performance for salary administration, which severely hampered his ability to act as a counselor or helper.) However, the very act of making salary recommendations forces the manager to be a judge. But if he has been successful in meeting the other goals of the management-by-objectives program, he will have a much better understanding of his subordinates' performance than he would otherwise. But as the research has clearly demonstrated, the techniques for the two may be vastly different. In one organization, a highly formalized procedure was used to determine and recommend salary action. The managers handled the problem very simply—they decided how much of an increase they wanted to recommend and then completed the performance appraisal form to defend the action they had already decided on. In other words, instead of using the form to help determine the reasons for salary action, they used it as a justification for their proposed action to the personnel department.

The problem of developing criteria for selection and promotion is highly technical and may be developed for a special purpose and usage, as discussed in the next chapter. However, the value of these criteria for selection research may be destroyed by attempting to use them as an administrative tool for other purposes.

Table 8.3 Types of performance appraisal techniques

Technique and examples	Advantages	Limitations
Objective measures		
Absences	Simple, reliable, objective	Doesn't reflect different types of absence (medical, unauthorized), doesn't reflect individual differences in quality or quantity of work
Productivity	Simple, reliable, objective	Difficult to measure at managerial level; at nonmanagerial level it does not take account of working conditions, incomparability of machines used, etc.
Subjective measures		
Graphic rating scales (Each dimension being measured has several precise descriptions of varying performance on that dimension.)	Clear, easy to counsel from, multidimensional	Subject to rater biases—leniency, central tendency (rating everyone in the middle), halo (having the rating on one dimension affect all others either positively or negatively), fakable
Checklists (The rater checks the various descriptions of behavior found in the particular job. Responses are given weights which are added up to obtain a final score.)	Same as graphic rating scales, may cover more ground	Same as for graphic rating scales, time-consuming
Forced-choice scales (The rater is usually asked to pick one of two or three grouped favorable statements,	More difficult to fake multidimensional	Difficult to construct, antagonizes the rater, forces him to choose between two undesirable alternatives, may force

Technique and examples	Advantages	Limitations
only one of which is considered critical to job performance. There are many varieties of this type of scale.)		differences where none exist or are insignificant
Critical-incident scales (These scales are constructed by obtaining unusual behaviors which are either very good or very bad and are central to the level of job performance.)	Greater agreement between raters, doesn't force differences, makes raters think about specific behaviors which can be rated	Somewhat difficult to record for the rater, somewhat time-consuming to construct
Ranking Methods (The rater rank-orders persons on one or more dimensions of effectiveness.)	Conceptually simple	Forces differences, cannot tell the differences between ranks, someone must be ranked last
Forced distribution methods (The rater is told that his ratings must conform to a predetermined distribution, e.g., normal distribution.)	Helps eliminate bunching, makes rater aware of response biases	Unless there is a very large group, this may not represent the real situation, forces differences
Simulations		
Situational exercises, trade tests (proficiency test), in-basket (consists of an in-basket full of memos, calls, letters, etc., which must be responded to by the test-taker.)	Allows for control during periods of evaluation	Situation is contrived and rarely corresponds to the real world, gets at best, rather than normal performance

Table 8.4 Guide to employee performance appraisal—performance degrees

Performance factors	Far exceeds job requirements	Exceeds job requirements	Meets job requirements	Needs some improvement	Does not meet minimum requirements
Quality	Leaps tall buildings with a single bound	Must take running start to leap over tall buildings	Can only leap over a short building or medium with no spires	Crashes into buildings when attempting to jump over them	Cannot recognize building at all, what's more jump it
Timeliness	Is faster than a speeding bullet	Is as fast as a speeding bullet	Not quite as fast as a speeding bullet	Would you believe a slow bullet?	Wounds self with bullets when attempting to shoot gun
Initiative	Is stronger than a locomotive	Is stronger than a bull elephant	Is stronger than a bull	Shoots the bull	Smells like a bull
Adaptability	Walks on water consistently	Walks on water in emergencies	Washes with water	Drinks water	Passes water in emergencies
Communication	Talks with God	Talks with the angels	Talks to himself	Argues with himself	Loses those arguments

To summarize, there are a number of different objectives of performance appraisal, each of which requires a different technique to meet the specific objective. For example, having the personnel department review the forms or data generated by the management tends to destroy the objectives of a work planning and review program. If such data are kept in the personnel files, they lose their usefulness for meaningful and constructive dialogue between the manager and his subordinates, because the *objective* has now been changed, i.e., now, the manager must please and impress the personnel department and writes his reports accordingly. The role of personnel in a management-by-objectives program is *not* to keep or review the data generated between the manager and his subordinate, but rather to *help* the manager do a better job of management by objectives.

It is beyond the purpose and scope of this book to provide a detailed manual for performance-appraisal techniques for each of the objectives we have listed. Rather, we merely stress that the technique used depends highly on the *purpose* of the performance appraisal. A more detailed, theoretical treatment of the liabilities and advantages of these techniques is provided Blum and Naylor.[32] The work by Whisler and Harper provides a "how to do it" approach to performance appraisal for those interested in constructing their own measures of performance.[33] Finally, in an attempt to keep this whole subject in proper perspective, an anonymous wit devised some spoofs on factors to be considered in performance appraisals (Table 8.4).

REVIEW

1. Listen to a speech by a prominent public figure or to a group discussion of a problem. List the reactive comments being expressed in proactive terms.

2. Does the concept of "management by objectives" fit in with the earlier concept of the "psychological contract"? Elaborate.

3. How would you design a control system to "ensure planned change, improvement, and optimal balance in the system"?

4. Give examples of Perrow's five types of goals.

5. From your own experience, elaborate and give examples of the differences between "official" and "operational," or "actual," objectives.

6. Using Fig. 8.1 as your guide, study a group or other small organization and analyze its goals.

7. Elaborate on the statement, "Organizations do not have goals, people do." What implications does this statement have for understanding organizations?

Critical Concepts

Organizational goal

Official vs. actual objectives

System goals

Product goals

Transitive vs. reflexive goals

Proactive forces

Reactive forces

Management by objectives

Performance appraisal techniques:
in-basket
critical incidents
forced-choice technique

REFERENCES

1. L. Gulick, *Administrative Reflections from World War II* (Tuscaloosa: University of Alabama Press, 1948), p. 77.

2. A. Etzioni, *Modern Organizations* (Englewood Cliffs, N.J.: Prentice-Hall, 1964), p. 6.

3. B. M. Bass, *A Program of Exercises for Management and Organizational Psychology* (Pittsburgh: Management Development Associates, 1966).

4. P. Drucker, *The Practice of Management* (New York: Harper and Brothers, 1954), p. 62.

5. C. Perrow, *Organizational Analysis: A Sociological View* (Belmont, Cal.: Wadsworth, 1970).

6. *Ibid.*, p. 155.

7. *Ibid.*, p. 156.

8. L. Mohr, "The Concept of Organizational Goal," *American Political Science Review*, in press.

9. C. Perrow, "The Analysis of Goals in Complex Organizations," *American Sociological Review*, 26, 6 (Dec. 1961), p. 855.

10. R. L. Katz, *Management of the Total Enterprise* (Englewood Cliffs, N.J.: Prentice-Hall, 1970), p. 13.

11. P. Blau, *The Dynamics of Bureaucracy* (Chicago: University of Chicago Press, 1955).

12. R. M. Cyert and J. G. March, "A Behavioral Theory of Organizational Objectives," in *Modern Organizational Theory*, ed. M. Haire (New York: John Wiley, 1959), p. 80.

13 H. Koontz and C. O'Donnell, *Principles of Management* (New York: McGraw-Hill, 1968).

14 T. Leavitt, *Innovation in Marketing* (New York: McGraw-Hill, 1962).

15 A. S. Tannenbaum, *Control in Organizations* (New York: McGraw-Hill, 1968).

16 R. Michels, *Political Parties* (New York: Dover, 1959).

17 R. N. Anthony, "The Trouble with Profit Maximization," *Harvard Business Review*, 38, 6 (Nov.-Dec. 1966):126-134.

18 M. Weber, *The Theory of Social and Economic Organization*, ed. T. Parsons, trans. A. M. Henderson and T. Parsons (New York: Oxford University Press, 1947).

19 J. C. March and H. A. Simon, *Organizations* (New York: John Wiley, 1958), pp. 194-195.

20 N. Maier, R. F. Hoffman, L. Hooven, and W. Read, *Superior-Subordinate Communication in Management* (New York: American Management Association, 1961).

21 G. Odiorne, *Management by Objectives* (New York: Pitman, 1965).

22 E. Huse and E. Kay, "Improving Employee Productivity Through Work Planning," in *The Personnel Job in a Changing World*, ed. J. Blood (New York: American Management Association, 1964), pp. 301-302.

23 A. Raia, "Goal Setting and Self-Control," *Journal of Management Studies*, 2, 1 (Feb. 1965):34-58.

24 H. Tosi and J. Carrol, "Management Reaction to Management by Objectives," *Academy of Management Journal*, 11, 4 (Dec. 1968):415-426.

25 H. Levinson, "Management by Whose Objectives?" *Harvard Business Review*, 48, 4 (July-Aug. 1970):125-134.

26 V. Ridgway, "Dysfunctional Consequences of Performance Measurements," *Administrative Science Quarterly*, 1 (1956):240-247.

27 R. Likert and S. Seashore, "Making Cost Control Work," *Harvard Business Review*, 41, 6 (Nov.-Dec. 1963):96-108.

28 D. McGregor, "An Uneasy Look at Performance Appraisal," *Harvard Business Review*, 35, 3 (May-June 1957):89-94.

29 P. Thompson and G. Dalton, "Performance Appraisal: Managers Beware," *Harvard Business Review*, 48, 1 (Jan.-Feb. 1970):149-157.

30 E. Kay, "A Review of *Performance Appraisal: Research and Practice*," *Personnel Psychology*, 16 (Spring 1963):81-83.

31 E. Huse, "Performance Appraisal—A New Look," *Personnel Administration*, 30, 2 (March-April 1967):13-18.

32 M. Blum and J. Naylor, *Industrial Psychology, Its Theoretical and Social Foundations* (New York: Harper & Row, 1968).

33 T. Whisler and S. Harper, eds., *Performance Appraisal: Research and Practice* (New York: Holt, Rinehart and Winston, 1962).

9

SELECTION
AND
TRAINING

When a great many people are unable to find work, unemployment results.

CALVIN COOLIDGE

Mating of man and company.

I. INTRODUCTION

Industrial psychologists have traditionally played a major part in the area of selection and training because it represents an application to the practical problems of industry the psychologist's interest in individual differences in ability and achievement and in theories of conditioning and learning. Personnel selection and training are important aspects of organizational life. Unless these two processes are closely related, filling job vacancies and training persons to perform effectively on the job lose meaning. Although personnel selection and individual training comprise an open system, they do not fit very conveniently within the framework of the three perspectives.

This chapter consists of two major parts—the problems associated with traditional approaches to personnel selection; and the nature of individual training, underlying psychological principles, and the types of techniques which are appropriate for individual training. We then discuss the means for evaluating the effectiveness of training programs. Finally, we present an integrated approach to selection and training, stressing the common elements needed to perform both functions.

II. THE SELECTION PROCESS

An organization's selection process consists of a number of interrelated steps: manpower planning, selection, and placement. First, however, it is necessary to define four basic terms—predictor, criterion, reliability, and validity.

A *predictor* is anything that forecasts an event or an outcome. A job applicant, for example, is frequently given a psychological test which forecasts his success or failure in a particular working situation. Another widely used predictor is the College Entrance Examination Board (CEEB) tests, which attempt to forecast how students will fare in college.

A *criterion*, the measure of success or failure, is related to the predictor. Most schools use the grade-point average as the criterion, sometimes referred to as the dependent measure, and this criterion measures the accuracy of the predictor. For example, although widely used, the CEEB tests are far from perfect predictors of success in college; many students with high CEEB scores do not have high grade-point averages, and some who do poorly on these tests go on to have highly successful college careers.

Sometimes, a measure of success or failure can be used as either a predictor or criterion. For example, colleges and universities use a student's grades as the *criterion* of his college performance, whereas businesses and other organizations use this criterion as a *predictor* of the student's later job success.

In order to be worthwhile, both the predictor and the criterion must have *reliability,* i.e., there must be "consistency in measurement." Any predictor which does not measure consistently over time is of no use, since it cannot be depended on to give accurate results. A criterion measurement which is not reliable will throw off the most highly accurate predictor.

In addition to reliability, a predictor must have *validity*; it must do what it purports to do. If an intelligence test actually does measure intelligence, it is valid. If it does not measure intelligence, it is invalid. Reliability is thus a prerequisite for validity. A measure is valid only if it is also consistent. However, the converse is not true; a measure can be reliable even though it is not valid.

A. Historical Orientation

Originally, the process of selection was considered important only for low-level workers in semiskilled or skilled jobs. Managers or supervisors obtained their positions through family or friendship connections. Following the Industrial Revolution, however, two distinct selection problems emerged. The first is the more familiar one, or selection of low-level workers; the second is the selection of managers.

Before the emergence of a separate department, personnel functions were handled by line supervisors; the foreman hired, fired, and paid his workers and developed his own procedures for getting the job done. As industrial organizations grew larger, however, this task became a burden, and a staff position was created to advise and carry on this personnel function. Since the Perspective I approach was the only one in operation at the time, there was a clear dichotomy between line and staff functions. Personnel policies were dictated by the line, and the embryonic personnel department was limited to bookkeeping and payment functions. However, with the growth of unionization, the distinction between line and staff blurred somewhat, and personnel procedures began to come from the personnel department. Human concerns, such as keeping the worker happy and productive, emanated from the personnel department and were expected to be upheld by the line function. It was at this point in the development of organizations that an attempt was made to select personnel for organizations in a scientific manner.

In the United States, systematic personnel selection for lower-level employees began with work done for the Army during World War I, when Army officials, faced with the problem of inducting thousands of people, needed a reasonably effective method of selecting men with the potential to be good officers. As a result, two tests were developed. Army Alpha tested literates, and the Army Beta tested illiterates' potential success in the armed services.

Since that time, selection procedures have multiplied and have become much more sophisticated; tests administered during World War II not only selected officers and noncommissioned officers, but also classified men according to the service branch and specialty for which they were best suited.

The selection of upper-level personnel and persons for unique or very flexible job routines has been less scientific because of the few numbers involved. However, over the years this procedure, too, has become more systematized.

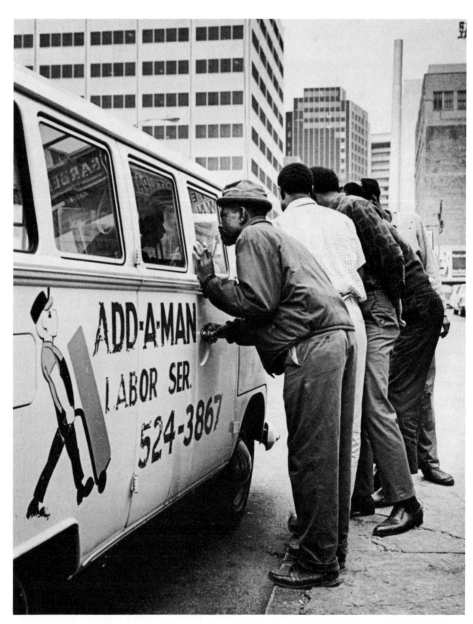

The process of selecting personnel is frequently haphazard. (Photograph courtesy Christian Science Monitor*)*

B. Manpower Planning

As we discussed in the preceding chapter, the establishment of organizational objectives determines organizational goals and the use of resources to accomplish these objectives. Once the objectives of the organization have stabilized, it is possible to plan the structure of the organization. To a great extent, the structural design of the organization influences the design of jobs within the organization. However, we have also noted the possibility of following Fiedler's recommendations to "engineer the job to fit the manager."

Manpower planning is necessary to determine the numbers and types of people in the organization and how they may be best utilized. Since organizational structure influences job design, organizations differ in the mix of personnel and styles of leadership which maximize their ability to meet organizational goals. Selecting people for positions in an organization is difficult and is frequently done haphazardly. There are various techniques, however, which can be used to create a more orderly, rational selection process.

C. Model for the Selection of Large Numbers of Personnel

1. Overview. Although most organizations do not have problems of the same magnitude as the Army's in selecting personnel, many industrial positions are filled by large numbers of people doing well-defined and repetitious work. In these cases, a traditional predictor-validation procedure is appropriate to find the most efficient way of filling these jobs with effective workers. Korman's recent text provides a good outline of suggestions for selecting large numbers of persons to fill well-defined jobs.[1] A slightly modified version of the outline follows.

a) Determine the job requirements. Job analyses can be used to identify and isolate those aspects of the job which are necessary for effective performance and to establish their relative value and importance to the job. These measures of success are known as job criteria.

b) Develop hypotheses of characteristics needed on the job. This allows rational choices about predictor variables to be made.

c) Create the "predictor variables." In the normal selection process, the measures used to predict job success include the application blank, the interview, and various types of psychological tests.

d) Obtain enough candidates to get a range of performance on the predictor variables. The best way to do this is to either hire an "unmeasured" group of candidates and administer the predictor variable to them or administer the "tests" before employment, but without using them in making the employment decision. A commonly used but less satisfactory way is to apply the predictors to people already on the job and to hire only those whose scores are similar to those of the proven workers, rejecting applicants whose scores match those of poorer workers. In either case, it is necessary to get a group of individuals who range from high to low on each of the predictor variables.

e) Develop adequate criteria. Criteria for good performance might include students' college grades, workers' merit ratings, or such clearly defined variables as absences, tardiness, rate of productivity, waste, accidents, and grievances. The criteria must, of course, reflect what is important for the given job or activity in question. To be adequate, criteria must be reliable, relevant to the particular job, and free from biasing influences. For example, "quantity sold" is a biased criterion if the sales territories are unequal and the prospectives consumers are nonequivalent. If in filling out a performance-evaluation form, a foreman and his assistant cannot agree on who is their best worker, the form and procedure are unreliable.

f) Establish the relationship between job performance (the criteria) and predictor variables. If the relationship or correlation between the two is too low, the "predictor" is of no value in forecasting the success of personnel on the job. Incidentally, in this step it is normal for more than half of the variables which were assumed to be predictors to show little or no relationship to the criteria of success. Variables such as these should be discarded from further consideration.

g) Cross-check or cross-validate the predictors. Using a different group of candidates, determine if the original relationship between predictor and criterion variables holds up. If it does not, the relationship originally found was probably due to chance factors and therefore cannot be trusted.

h) Select future candidates on the basis of the predictors identified. After the relationship between the predictor and criterion variables has been checked and double-checked (validated and cross-validated), the predictors can then be used to select future candidates.

Following these eight steps will materially increase the accuracy of selection of lower-level personnel with well-defined job descriptions. However, these steps are quite technical and should not be attempted by someone who has not had training and experience in research design and statistics. The proper identification and selection of the job criteria (personnel-performance measurements) is the most crucial and important step in the process, because this is the step on which all else hinges; the untrained person usually gives this step least weight and importance. If there is no properly trained person in the organization, an outside expert should be consulted.

2. Other Validation Procedures for Large Numbers of Personnel

a) *Concurrent validation.*   This is a much quicker method of validating a test. The battery of predictors and the criteria are administered simultaneously to people already on the job. The validation and cross-validation are done with current employees. The problem, however, is that the people already employed may not be similar to the applicants. In the course of doing their jobs, the employees may have learned something which differentiates them from those wanting to be hired, or their motivation in taking tests may be different. The problem is especially acute if the tests are achievement rather than aptitude tests. In addition, the motivation of present employees to do well on the test may be vastly different from those people who want to get the job. Therefore, the concurrent-validation method is a good deal less satisfactory than the traditional predictive method. The only advantage is that it takes less time.

b) *The use of utility theory in selection.*   As shown in Fig. 9.1, there are four possible results from using a single cutoff in the selection process. A person may score high on the test and do well on the job; he may score high on the test and not do well on the job; he may score poorly on the test and do poorly on the job; or, he may score poorly on the test and do well on the job. Although we have treated all errors in prediction as simply undifferentiated errors, it is obvious that prediction errors can be of two types. Overprediction occurs when the individual performs poorly on the job after scoring high on the test; underprediction occurs when a person does well on the job but had a low score on the test.

Some of the newer models do approach error differentially. Overprediction on an airline pilot would be a disaster, yet underprediction would not be very costly. If utility is measured in dollars, it is much more expensive to select a pilot trainee who then crashes the airplane than it is to not select someone who would have been good. Similarly, there may be jobs for which underprediction is more costly than overprediction.

c) *Moderator variables.*   Another of the newer considerations in prediction is the moderator-variable approach, which is used to "predict predictability." This separates two groups of people—the behavior of one group is more predictable than the other. For example, suppose you are trying to predict success for taxi

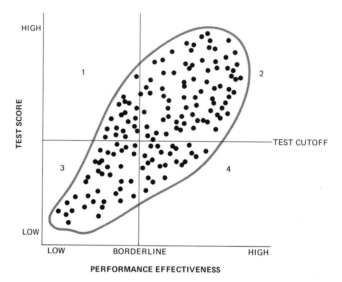

1. OVERPREDICTION — RESPONDENT TESTS WELL BUT PERFORMS POORLY
2. RESPONDENT TESTS AND PERFORMS WELL
3. RESPONDENT TESTS AND WOULD PERFORM POORLY
4. RESPONDENT TESTS POORLY BUT WOULD PERFORM WELL

Figure 9.1. Use of utility theory in selection.

drivers and your prediction validity is a low .15 to .25. But even though you have what you consider an adequate criterion, you continue to get these poor relationships. If you then look for some common characteristic of those who have been predicted well and who do well on the job, you are using the moderator-variable approach. Such a characteristic may be military service or a personality trait; the important thing is that it improves prediction. If a predictor variable is used first and the test or predictor is such that some of the people go unpredicted, new tests or new predictive devices may have to be developed in order to include the total group in the prediction.

d) Synthetic validity. Another approach which is becoming increasingly common is synthetic, or self-contained, validity. Here, the researcher identifies the behavioral dimensions of a job and tries to find already existing tests which predict those behavioral dimensions of the job. Although this approach is less time-consuming and is easier to administer, the criterion is less certain than in a more standard method. This technique may be useful in developing hypotheses of characteristics needed on the job (step 2 of the traditional selection method).

D. A Procedure for Selecting Small Numbers of Personnel

For employment situations requiring an individualized procedure—selecting a store manager or corporation president—the traditional validation scheme is inappropriate. Whenever the number of jobs to be filled is relatively small (under 50) *or* the job itself is defined by the incumbent, reliable evaluation is all but impossible, and it will be necessary to use the *clinical model* of selection. This simply means that the psychologist or other person trained in clinical-selection methods evaluates the characteristics needed for success on the job and decides whether the applicant has the needed characteristics. Although it is difficult to systematize this procedure mathematically, most psychologists working in this area follow certain set procedures. Although the clinical model makes use of testing, interviews, the in-basket, assessment centers, and references, their relative weights are determined more through personal judgment than are more strictly statistical approaches.

E. Commonly Used Selection Devices (Predictor Variables)

Each of these devices is used to improve the selection process, and as predictor variables, they all should be related to a performance measure. Although these selection tools—the resume, the interview, the application blank, psychological tests, personal or professional references, assessment centers, and in-basket techniques—are all "tests," the term is usually used in a much narrower sense.

1. The Resume. The resume, an instrument widely used in the selection process, particularly at the professional and managerial levels, can be defined as a life history, written by the candidate, of the details of his personal, educational, and experiential background that he believes important for employment. The resume is used as a screening instrument by the employment manager, who receives large numbers of them each year. He reviews the resumes in light of his employment needs and decides whether to invite the candidate in for an interview and further processing or write him, explaining that the organization has no need at the moment for someone of his particular skills and talents.

There has been little investigation of the reliability and validity of the resume in the selection process. One such study was conducted by Gaudet and Casey, who investigated the accuracy of judgments made about the resumes of industrial engineers for a large manufacturing company, all of whom had been hired by the organization.[2] Half of the engineers were successful; the others were failures whose employment had to be terminated. The three studies conducted by Gaudet and Casey indicate that the "evaluators" could have obtained the same results by tossing a coin to predict the success or failure of the new employees.

2. The Interview. The interview is the most widely used selection tool. Most frequently, the personnel department conducts the preliminary interviewing and thus screens the applicants; those who "pass" are referred to the appropriate line personnel, usually the immediate supervisor, who makes the final selection.

The interview is highly important, since it gives the organization an opportunity to obtain face-to-face information about the prospective employee. At the same time, it gives the prospective employee an opportunity to find out many of the things he needs to know about the organization in order to make a decision about the job and the organization.

There are a number of different types of interviews. Usually, the interview is a one-to-one situation. Sometimes, however, an applicant may be faced by a panel of interviewers. Some organizations place a group of candidates in a room and allow them to interact freely with one another as they discuss a particular case or exercise.

These types of interviews can also be classified according to the specific technique used: highly structured (directive) or less structured (nondirective). The "directive" interview usually follows a prescribed format in which the interviewer follows a specific, detailed check-list of items during the interview. In effect, he follows almost exactly the same procedure and routine with every interviewee. The nondirective interview is, by definition, much less structured, and the interviewer's primary technique is to follow the applicant's lead, probing further as necessary. Most interviews, however, fall between these two extremes. Thus, although the interviewer may have a list of specific questions, he may decide to probe more deeply into a particular area brought up by the applicant, thus changing the direction of the interview from that originally intended.

The research on the interview indicates that the more patterned the interview and the more highly trained the interviewer, the more valid the interview findings. Yet, two review articles by Ulrich and Trumbo, and Mayfield summarizing published studies of interviewing indicate that the interview is not very reliable and hence cannot be very valid.[3] Part of the problem arises from the human tendency of interviewers to pride themselves on being able to pick people successfully. Since most people do not apply for jobs they cannot handle and interviewers tend to "forget" their selection failures, the research findings may be somewhat biased. For example, in an effort to ensure the selection of

Application for Employment

POSITION(S) APPLIED FOR_____ DATE_____

NAME IN FULL_____ _____ TELEPHONE_____

ADDRESS_____

HAVE YOU HAD A MAJOR ILLNESS IN THE PAST 5 YEARS_____ IF SO, DESCRIBE_____

DO YOU HAVE ANY PHYSICAL DEFECTS?_____ IF SO, DESCRIBE_____

_____ SOCIAL SECURITY NUMBER_____

HIGH SCHOOL_____ YEAR GRADUATED_____

COURSE OF STUDY_____

COLLEGE_____ YEAR GRADUATED_____

MAJOR COURSE_____ DEGREE_____

SCHOLARSHIPS, HONORS, EXTRACURRICULAR ACTIVITIES _____

_____

OTHER EDUCATION_____

DO YOU SPEAK LANGUAGES OTHER THAN ENGLISH?_____

HAVE YOU COMPLETED YOUR REQUIRED MILITARY TRAINING?_____ EXPLAIN YOUR STATUS_____

ARE YOU A U.S. CITIZEN?_____ DO YOU HAVE ANY SPECIAL SKILLS OR QUALIFICATIONS THAT YOU FEEL WOULD ESPECIALLY

FIT YOU FOR WORK WITH US? _____

_____

SKILLS: DICTATING MACHINE ☐   FILING ☐   TYPING ☐ W.P.M._____

BOOKKEEPING MACHINE ☐   CALCULATOR ☐   SHORTHAND ☐ W.P.M._____

SWITCHBOARD ☐   BOOKKEEPING ☐   OTHER_____

PLEASE LIST BELOW YOUR FORMER EMPLOYERS, STARTING WITH THE MOST RECENT.

NAME AND ADDRESS OF EMPLOYER		NAME AND TITLE OF IMMEDIATE SUPERVISOR	
DATES OF EMPLOYMENT (FROM – TO)	TYPE OF BUSINESS OR ORGANIZATION	EXACT TITLE OF YOUR POSITION	
DESCRIPTION OF WORK (EXPLAIN SPECIFIC DUTIES PERFORMED)			
SALARY	EXPLAIN ANY BONUSES OR ADDITIONAL SALARY RECEIVED		
REASON(S) FOR LEAVING			

PERSONAL REFERENCES

PLEASE LIST BELOW THE NAMES, ADDRESSES, AND TELEPHONE NUMBERS OF THREE PEOPLE WHO HAVE KNOWN
YOU FOR AT LEAST FIVE YEARS.

NAME	ADDRESS	TEL. NO.

An application blank typically asks for a wide variety of information about a candidate for employment.

applicants with high success potential, interviewers may give too much weight to negative information about the applicant. In response to earlier research supporting this trend, Hollman found that whereas such negative information is processed accurately, interviewers do not give enough weight to favorable information about the applicant.[4]

3. The Application Blank and Biographical Data. The application blank is the second most widely used selection technique, or "test." It is a printed form which asks the applicant for a wide variety of educational, experiential, and personal background. Some organizations use different forms for different classes of applicants. The application blank is most commonly used to prepare the interviewer; it gives him the applicant's background history and information and in many cases saves him from asking questions that can be recorded more conveniently elsewhere.

Little is known about the reliability and validity of the application blank when used in this fashion. However, there has been continuing research (e.g., Buel, Scott and Johnson) on the reliability and validity of the application blank and biographical data as a "test" by itself.[5] A number of firms have conducted statistical studies to determine the extent to which various items on the application blank are related to success in a wide variety of jobs and professions. The weight of the research evidence indicates that the validation of the application blank has been of considerable value in improving the selection process for a wide variety of jobs. Indeed, some researchers believe that the use of personal history data obtained from an application blank or similar device will ultimately turn out to be the best single predictor of job success. Owens and his associates, for example, have found a way to considerably improve job success for large groups of people by using such information as a method of grouping people with similar backgrounds.[6]

The usefulness of biographical questionnaires for selection purposes is supported by Buel, who suggests that they be used as an alternative to psychological testing procedures, particularly in view of recent Supreme Court and other rulings about job-related validity.[7] He demonstrates that statistical analysis of biographical-information questionnaires shows high validity. He concludes that an applicant's "biography can add strength to existing methods of selection" or can act "as a replacement for them."

4. Psychological Tests. Not only have psychological tests been widely used in industry, they have also generated more pro and con discussion (and research) than has almost any other selection instrument. Although all selection techniques are "tests," most people reserve the word "test" for psychological tests. Such tests can generally be classified into five categories—aptitude (potential

Reprinted by permission of King Features Syndicate.

Personality tests may or may not give an accurate prediction of a candidate's success on the job.

ability), achievement (present knowledge), mental ability (intelligence), interest, and personality inventories—although there is considerable overlap in this classification scheme.

An organization's use of such tests can be either actuarial or clinical. A test is used actuarily when it has been carefully validated. Most of the research on personnel selection demonstrates that the proper actuarial use of a test materially improves the selection process. However, relatively few firms have spent the necessary time and money to go through a really good validation procedure. This effort is required because a test which predicts well for a given job in one organization may have no validity in predicting success for the same job in a different organization. Just as important is the fact that some tests discriminate against nonwhites and women; organizations using nonvalidated tests may be wide open for serious charges of discrimination and unethical hiring practices.

When used clinically, test scores are used in conjunction with other data about the person by the psychologist, who then draws on his professional experience and background to make predictions about the individual based on test scores, interview data, and other material. Research by Campbell, *et al.* has shown that the "clinical" use of test data by a psychologist has validity approaching, but not equaling, that of the "actuarial" approach.[8] However, when relatively untrained nonpsychologists use this clinical approach, the results may be highly misleading and dangerous. But when psychological tests are properly validated or are used by trained professionals, such instruments can greatly increase the validity of the selection process.

5. Assessment Centers. A variation of the clinical use of tests, the assessment-center technique, is gaining popularity in the selection of personnel for positions in which traditional validation is impossible. This procedure attempts to identify characteristics of able personnel which might predict their success in a different position.

Although the procedure varies from organization to organization, about a dozen persons are nominated by their supervisors to take part in the assessment-center proceedings. For several days the participants go through a series of cases, tests, and exercises designed to expose behaviors which are deemed important for managerial success. Several assessors watch the behavior and make notes. After completing the exercises, cases, and tests, the participants return to their original jobs, and the assessors spend additional time sifting through the material, which forms the basis of a report. Designed for use by the supervisor, the participant, and the organization, this report details recommendations for development of each participant's ultimate potential.

Assessment centers have generally been developed and used only within large companies. In their report of one design of an assessment center used in a bank, an electronics manufacturing firm, an auto manufacturer, a retail store, and a paper manufacturer, McConnell and Parker report high reliabilities among raters and concurrent validities.[9] The overall management score from the assessment procedure ranged from .28 to .64 in four organizations, with a total validity of .57 for the 70 participants. This relatively high validity is very useful in selection. The authors conclude that a standardized assessment program can be developed for use in a variety of organizations and that the "initial tests indicate that it is a significantly valid and reliable procedure for identifying and evaluating management abilities."[10]

In his review of the literature on management-assessment centers, Kraut describes a typical assessment-center process and examines the acceptance and validity of such programs.[11] He finds growing acceptance of the assessment center as a technique for "really getting at the abilities important to being a manager" in such diverse areas of the world as Japan, the United Kingdom, Germany, as well as the United States. He concludes that the validity of such programs has been amply demonstrated by a variety of validation procedures and that it contributes significantly to the promotional techniques currently being used, as was described in the study by McConnell and Parker.

6. The In-Basket. Because of the inherent problems of using ability tests for personnel selection in the middle-management range, within the last few years there have been many innovative attempts to find techniques which could be properly validated with this level of employee. One of these techniques is the in-basket. Here, a candidate for selection sits down at a desk with an in-basket full of letters, memos, and notes and responds as if he were already a manager in a particular position. Following this, the in-basket is objectively scored and is related to some performance criteria. In his discussions of the in-basket as a tool for selecting middle-level managers in a large corporation, Meyer found that there was a significant correlation between parts of the in-basket and performance criteria for supervisory functions.[12] However, although the correlations were significant, only about one-eighth of the total variance in the criteria was predicted. Since the in-basket technique cannot predict seven-eighths of the variance, this procedure must be used in conjunction with other predictors.

7. Reference Checking. Reference checking, another technique used by modern organizations to improve the selection process, consists of obtaining information about an applicant from someone who has known him in either a personal or work capacity. Of the two, the personal reference is the less useful, because most applicants, at any level, can find two or three persons who are willing to say that the applicant is a fine person. For "face validity," reference material obtained from a previous employer is more credible than a personal reference.

References can be checked by either telephone or letter. Although there is little research evidence about the reliability or validity of either technique, information obtained by a telephone call is probably more useful, since the respondent is much more likely to be candid if he does not have to commit himself in writing. However, there is little research evidence to back up this assumption.

F. Problems in Personnel Selection

1. Discrimination and Minority Group Hiring. One of the major problems encountered in personnel selection is how to accomplish the task equitably. In the past, many tests were culturally biased. As reported by Ash, this problem came to a head in 1963 when a black, Leon Myart, applied for a job in an Illinois plant of the Motorola Corporation. This case, heard by the Illinois Fair Employment Practices Commission, dealt with the use of a test which had been validated on an advantaged group some years earlier and hence was considered inappropriate by the Commission.[13] The company was ordered to cease using the particular test and if it wished to resume testing, its tests would have to be culturally fair.

This case was prominent in the debate over the amendment to Title VII of the Civil Rights Act of 1964, which stipulated that tests should be developed by professionals. To some psychologists and the Equal Employment Opportunity Commission, this implied that whenever possible, the test be related to a criterion; otherwise, construct or content validation would suffice. The net effect of this ruling was that tests would have to show *some* relevance to effective job performance.

In a second case, this one reaching the U.S. Supreme Court in 1971, the Duke Power Company, a southern utility, was brought to court because of allegedly discriminatory tests.[14] The Court held unanimously that even though the tests were fair in form, they were not fair in operation. The Court's main point was that in writing the Equal Employment Act, Congress had specified that such considerations as race, national orgin, sex, and religious persuasion are irrelevant to employment practices.

The Court did not forbid the use of testing, nor did it suggest that less qualified persons be hired simply because of their minority origin. Rather, it clarified some of the ambiguities of employment practices surrounding the issue of personnel selection. Even though racial discrimination is the focus of this issue at the present time, the practitioner must remember that all kinds of discrimination are forbidden by both the Civil Rights Act and the Equal Employment Opportunity Commission guidelines. Undoubtedly, other kinds of discrimination such as sex and age will come to the forefront in the years to come.

It is clear that the last word has not been spoken on this issue. If it is true that selecting students for matriculation in a university is a special case of personnel selection, is it then possible for a university to use tests which have not been specifically validated at the particular universities and at the various levels? We suspect that there will soon be a case involving a student versus a national testing service and a university. For example, suppose a student wishing to go to law school does poorly on a selection test and that the university rejects his application because he did not meet the minimum score (which may have been established by an accrediting agency). The law school, relying on general research of the testing service, has little or no data indicating that scores on the particular test are related to success in *that particular* law school. Therefore, the law school will be in clear violation of the intent of the Equal Employment Opportunity Guidelines that tests be validated prior to their use in a personnel-selection procedure. In addition, the American Psychological Association has decisively condemned the use of unvalidated tests as unethical.

2. Other Problems in Personnel Selection.   One of the major problems in personnel selection is that the correlations between predictors and criteria are frequently very low. Only rarely is the correlation above .50. Schein cites four possible reasons for this.[15] First, since jobs are complex and interdependent, finding adequate criteria to measure performance may be very difficult. A related factor is that since the criteria selected may be inadequate, it is difficult to relate the test scores to these criteria. Although many techniques have been used in order to improve the selection of managers, the data available are still inconclusive. Third, since many jobs are fluid in nature, it is difficult to test for adaptability, and it is even more difficult to develop criteria which reflect a changing job description over time. Finally, there is the problem of time. Because results are usually needed quickly, a predictive validation may be done over a short period of time; indeed, there have been few long-term validations. As Schein notes, "the correlation between the short-term and long-term performance tends to be low."[16]

There are other, more hidden pitfalls. Although work is dynamic, a testing procedure is a static look at a person. Testing appears to be a cold and impersonal method of selection which may discourage an applicant. Finally, there is the ethical question of the gathering and use of private information for organizational decision-making.

Despite the many problems, the testing process should not be stopped. However, new approaches to overcome the problems will have to be considered. At the very least, organizations using testing techniques need to be aware of the implications of their use.

G. A Classic Selection Study

In 1961 Standard Oil Company of New Jersey conducted a study on 443 of its managers on the early identification of management potential.[17] Some standard predictors used were: (1) the Miller Analogies Test, an intelligence test which emphasizes verbal aptitude; (2) a spatially oriented, nonverbal reasoning test; and (3) the Guilford-Zimmerman Temperment Survey, a personality inventory. Other predictors included biographical data, a management judgment test similar to the in-basket, a survey of management attitudes, a self-performance report, and a projective test (designed to examine types of motivation) in which respondents supplied meaning to a group of ambiguous pictures.

The primary subcriteria, or dependent measures, were position level, a ranking of managerial effectiveness, and salary history. Among the other subcriteria were whether the person was in a managerial position, the unit he was working with, his functional activities, a work-pattern profile, and his age. A statistical procedure called factor analysis, which finds the underlying dimensions of the criteria employed, was used to establish a single, scorable success criterion, i.e., various subcriteria correlated to a greater or lesser degree with the underlying dimension determined by the factor analysis and were, in effect, statistically weighted in order to be included in one, overall measure of success.

Whatever tests and specific test items did not distinguish between the good and poor managers were discarded in the validation procedure. A cross-validation, the procedure whereby the respondents are divided into two groups and scoring keys are developed for each group, was performed to weed out still more items which correlated with success by chance. Whenever there was a different keyed response for a given item or subtest in each of the groups in the cross-validation, the item or subtest was dropped. In this manner researchers were able to verify that the predictors really predicted success.

Of all the predictors used, only the projective test was excluded in the final, overall predictor battery. The rest were weighted in order to maximize the difference between the successful and unsuccessful workers. Persons were given weighted predictor scores and were then charted by quintiles (groups of 20%), and a probability of success was calculated for each quintile. Figure 9.2 shows a manager's chances of being in the top half of the criterion of success rating for any given quintile.

This study illustrates the process by which tests and other predictors are validated and shows how one can arrive at a probability statement of success as a manager. However, the one weakness of the study is that it is a concurrent study, that is, personnel who were already good managers were tested to see what differentiated them from persons who were not effective managers. These results were then applied to managerial applicants, even though in the future different sorts of predictors would probably be more valid than those used to predict the success of present managers. Also, it is likely that responses from those already on the job are different from those lacking training or experience.

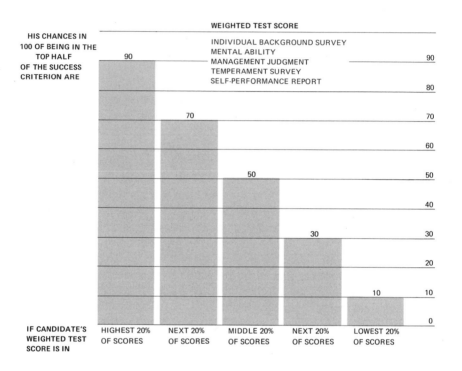

WEIGHTED TEST SCORE

HIS CHANCES IN
100 OF BEING IN THE
TOP HALF
OF THE SUCCESS
CRITERION ARE

INDIVIDUAL BACKGROUND SURVEY
MENTAL ABILITY
MANAGEMENT JUDGMENT
TEMPERAMENT SURVEY
SELF-PERFORMANCE REPORT

IF CANDIDATE'S
WEIGHTED TEST
SCORE IS IN

HIGHEST 20% OF SCORES	NEXT 20% OF SCORES	MIDDLE 20% OF SCORES	NEXT 20% OF SCORES	LOWEST 20% OF SCORES

Figure 9.2. Expectancy chart: predicting top half of success criterion by weighted test score. (H. Laurent, Early Identification of Management Potential, *New York: Standard Oil Company, New Jersey, August 1961, p. 24. Reprinted by permission.)*

In brief, despite the problems inherent in a concurrent study, the Standard Oil case demonstrates the usefulness of such an approach, and personnel departments would do well to begin with a study such as this and at the same time collect data for a longitudinal predictive study.

III. INDIVIDUAL TRAINING

A. Overview

The problem of criteria is inherent to the processes of both selection and training because the two processes are inseparable. Training, like selection, may be

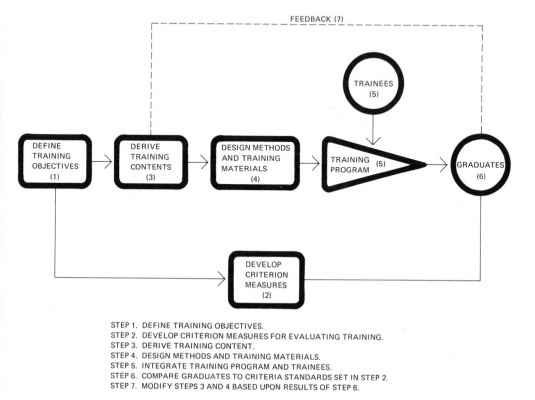

STEP 1. DEFINE TRAINING OBJECTIVES.
STEP 2. DEVELOP CRITERION MEASURES FOR EVALUATING TRAINING.
STEP 3. DERIVE TRAINING CONTENT.
STEP 4. DESIGN METHODS AND TRAINING MATERIALS.
STEP 5. INTEGRATE TRAINING PROGRAM AND TRAINEES.
STEP 6. COMPARE GRADUATES TO CRITERIA STANDARDS SET IN STEP 2.
STEP 7. MODIFY STEPS 3 AND 4 BASED UPON RESULTS OF STEP 6.

Figure 9.3. A systems approach to training. (G. A. Eckstrand, "Current Status of the Technology of Training," AMRL Document Technical Report 64-86, September 1964, p. 3. Reprinted by permission.)

considered as a series of subsystems. Procedures must be set up to check on the effectiveness of training and to modify the training programs as needed. Figure 9.3 shows Eckstrand's system model which pinpoints the phases of constructing a training program and incorporates techniques for modifying the program.[18] This model serves as a useful guide for thinking about training which allows for change when change is needed.

In this section, we focus on some of the traditional, hierarchical, formal perspective concerns of training, namely, the structure of the training program, its implementation, and some of the human perspective concerns, e.g., research findings in animal and human learning generalized to the training situation.

B. The Assessment of Training Needs

McGehee and Thayer note that in order to discover all of a company's training needs, one must study the problem from three angles: organization analysis, job analysis, and manpower analysis.[19]

1. Organization Analysis. This simply means the examination of the entire organization—its goals, resources, and the kind of environment in which it exists. Normally, this process requires determining what the short- and long-range goals are for the company as a whole, as well as for its departments and divisions. Beyond this, one needs to look at how these goals are being met in terms of a specific factor such as the amount of money spent to produce a particular unit of output. Finally, one must examine the environment from a systems point of view and discover the ways in which the organization interacts with the environment or influences it. The analysis must include those factors over which the organization has some control and those over which it has none, i.e., relevant social, political, economic, and geographical factors. This enables the analyst to be aware of everything on which training might have a bearing *and* vice versa.

2. Job Analysis. A job analysis is simply a breakdown of the tasks a worker performs in a given job. A job description for training purposes is a little different from a job description for selection purposes in that the former describes what a person needs to know in order to do a job effectively. Occasionally, a job description provided by a job analysis will be used for both training and selection and perhaps even for the establishment of pay scales.

3. Manpower Analysis. Manpower analysis is the assessment of individual training needs. What tasks does he already perform well? For what tasks is training needed for technical proficiency? In addition, as Bass and Vaughan suggest, one needs to know whether the persons to be involved are capable of benefitting from training or whether they should instead be transferred so that persons who are already trained can take over the job.[20] Finally, a decision needs to be made whether training or automation will best serve the needs of the organization.

C. Research Findings Applicable to Human Learning

Bass and Vaughan begin their discussion of learning with conditioning, which sheds light on "some of the basic principles of learning."[21] They then move on to discuss four approaches to complex human learning: trial and error, modeling behavior, mediation, and problem-finding. *Trial and error* refers to situations in which a person tries to find the correct solution in a random, haphazard fashion.

Driver training programs are generally based on the concepts of modeling and mediation. (Photograph by Edgar F. Huse)

Modeling behavior occurs when the individual watches others perform the task. When learning to drive, for example, the student may watch the instructor's demonstration of how to let up the clutch and thereby learn how to do it correctly. *Mediation,* unlike modeling, is any communication that helps the learner, e.g., verbal instructions, a road map, or anything else that helps the individual perform the task. *Problem-finding,* a more advanced method of learning, requires the learner to ask questions, create problems, and devise solutions. This type of behavior occurs when a person or group wonders why something is the way it is, proceeds to find out why, and perhaps do something about it, e.g., Ralph Nader's work in automotive safety.

D. Issues in Learning

There are a number of issues in learning that early research has helped clarify. These are: (1) generalization versus discrimination and transfer of training; (2) feedback, reinforcement, and motivation; (3) rate of learning over time; and (4) massed versus distributed practice.

1. Generalization, Discrimination, and Transfer of Training. If one is first taught to drive a standard-shift car and then an automatic, both generalization and discrimination occur. The processes of steering, braking, and accelerating are the same in both types of cars (generalization) and represent a transfer of training. However, since the automatic does not require the driver to shift gears or engage the clutch, he must learn not to perform these operations (discrimination) in an automatic car. Transfer of training also takes place when a novice salesman applies the techniques he has learned in training sessions to the work situation. Having learned how to approach a customer and finalize a sale, he transfers these techniques from the safe, friendly atmosphere of the "laboratory" to the hostile, "real" world.

2. Feedback, Reinforcement, and Motivation.   Extensive research with animals and children has shown that although punishment is sometimes necessary, it is not as effective as a positive reinforcement or reward in promoting learning. Punishment simply indicates to the learner that a particular behavior is not desired; it does not tell him anything about what *is* desired. Therefore, feedback is required. Immediate, positive feedback serves as a reward, whereas no feedback usually has negative consequences and indeed may serve to initiate other forms of less desirable behavior. Lack of praise for an employee's good work may foster sloppiness and a "What's the use?" attitude. In other words, feedback can be used as a reinforcement, or reward, which in turn is used by the recipient as a motivator to continue his good work.

3. Rate of Learning over Time.   Most learning situations follow a predictable pattern: a person learns quickly for a while, then his progress slows down (reaches a plateau), and finally it quickens again until he has mastered the particular technique to be learned. For instance, a new typist may start off with a fast rate of learning and then seem to take forever to reach a typing rate of 60 words per minute. Theorists differ as to what really goes on during the plateau period: some feel that learning is being consolidated prior to a new stage of learning, and others feel that learning is taking place, although it cannot be measured in terms of behavioral output.

4. Massed Practice versus Distributed Practice.   Any training program must incorporate a plan for organizing the time most effectively. According to Bass and Vaughan, learning is enhanced when provision is made for rest periods (distributed practice).[22] They suggest that: (1) rest periods be shorter early in training and longer later in training; (2) distributed rather than massed practice is especially desirable when the material to be learned is difficult; (3) distributed practice is especially effective with less capable trainees; and (4) retention of material is greater with distributed practice than with massed practice.

E. Types of Individual Training Programs

1. On-the-Job Training Techniques. *Apprenticeship training* is closely regulated by the craft unions. A trainee is accepted in a program which may last for one to four years. During this period, the trainee, or apprentice, works with an experienced worker, or master. When the apprentice has finished his training with the master and has completed any ancillary classroom work, he becomes a journeyman and may work on his own.

Two variations of the apprenticeship model are *job instruction training,* and *internship.* Job instruction training includes a step-by-step breaking in on a job and was used extensively in World War II. The internship, or assistantship, is generally reserved for the professions, but is very similar to craft apprenticeships.

All such training programs involve the participant in a way that few other techniques do. Usually, the trainee receives fairly direct feedback about his progress, and he may be allowed to proceed quickly to those aspects of the job which are more difficult. Normally, practice continues until the trainee has mastered the skill to be learned. However, such individualized training is usually costly and time-consuming, and this procedure does not permit large numbers of trainees to go through a particular training sequence together.

2. Off-the-Job Techniques. Although such techniques as lectures, films, and television may be appropriate with large groups of trainees, they do not actively involve the learner in the education process. His only feedback is from tests, if any are given. Techniques suitable for smaller groups include case study, conferences, and special study. Although these training procedures have the advantage of active learner participation, they are much more costly.

Off-the-job *vestibule training,* a technique which originated in industry—in the vestibule of the plant where the work was being done—is generally used to familiarize the trainee with the machines used in production. This technique enables a trainee to become proficient in a job before he is sent to the production floor. Although this technique has only limited applicability, its major advantages are the direct transfer of training which occurs and its usefulness in manufacturing plants where a large number of people are hired at one time. The major drawback of this technique is its cost.

A final off-the-job training technique is *programed instruction,* whereby the learner sets his own pace as he proceeds through the material. Frequent responses are called for, and the learner gets immediate feedback on the correctness of his response. Many self-instruction programs provide additional instruction (branches) when an incorrect response is made. Programed instruction is both inexpensive and effective, although the learner does not benefit from the learning and interaction inherent in group situations.

F. Administration and Evaluation of Training Programs

1. Administrative Considerations. Bass and Vaughan discuss three major issues which need to be confronted in the establishment of a training program.[23] First, it must be decided whether a training program is really needed. Job enrichment, which is discussed later in the text, may well be a viable alternative to training in some circumstances and may be conducted on an informal, on-the-job basis. Or, long-term costs may be reduced by substituting machines for personnel who need to be trained.

Second, training must be coordinated with selection and placement needs. If training success, e.g. examinations, job sample tests, etc., is used as a criterion for selection, it must be kept in mind that although certain predictors correlate well with *training,* they do not correlate well with measures of *success* on the job.[24] In other words, training and job performance involve different sorts of abilities. Certainly, in considering the long-term criteria for training success, one could develop measures of job success, which could in turn be used as criteria for selection.

Third, there is the issue of top management's commitment to training. They are in the best position to promote training and change the reinforcement structure. If they give only tacit approval or do not fully support training efforts, the learning may be "unlearned" when the individuals get back to the shop. This notion is supported by Mosel, who stresses that unless the organizational structure rewards training, it is not worth the effort.[25]

Fleishman obtained similar findings in his study of human relations training to improve a foreman's consideration for his workers and to decrease his initiation of structure at an International Harvester plant.[26] Immediately after the training, the foreman provided higher consideration and lower initiating structure, but these trends were reversed with the passage of time, surpassing those of the control group, which had received no training. Another finding was that the long-term behavior of a foreman correlated with that of his boss (modeling).

A third study which shows the importance of organizational climate in relation to training was conducted by Gomersall and Myers, who compared conventional on-the-job training with a revised method which stressed anxiety reduction.[27] New workers were given a special orientation which confronted and defused the typical anxiety they had as novices. The results were dramatic; workers who had been given the special orientation attained job competence more quickly and had fewer defects in output than those who had received conventional on-the-job training. In effect, the special orientation had told the new workers what to expect and thereby provided them with a very supportive introduction to the organization.

Finally, in a study of the identity stress experienced by college graduate recruits, Mansfield found that it is mitigated when the recruits form friendships with other recruits.[28] The stress is resolved, however, only when the recruit adopts a specific *occupational* identity which is accepted by others who are established in the organization. Mansfield does not regard this process as necessarily negative; indeed, it provides the recruit with first-hand evidence that he has changed, i.e., a process of unfreezing and then refreezing when the established members of the organization accept his new identity.

2. Designs for Evaluation. It is critical that appropriate criteria be developed not only to determine the effectiveness of the selection procedure, but also to determine the effectiveness of the training programs. Several research designs commonly used for examining the results of training have been outlined by Campbell and Stanley.[29] In modifying and simplifying their presentation of these designs, we have used the following notation: (1) zero refers to an observation or measurement of effectiveness; when no zero appears, there is no measurement of effectiveness; and (2) R indicates random assignment to separate treatment groups.

The first design looks like this:

	Time 1	Time 2
Group 1	Training	0

Since there is no control group, it is impossible to tell what life was like before the training program or at the time the training took place. There is no way of comparing observations to find out whether there was improvement or how any improvement could be related to the training program or to a different factor.

The second design is as follows:

	Time 1	Time 2	Time 3
Group 1	0_1	Training	0_2

Although at first glance this appears to be an improvement over the first design, this design does not really show whether the measure of effectiveness resulted from the training program or from such other factors as history, maturation, effects of measurement of 0_1 and 0_2, changes in the measuring instrument, or even a regression effect.

The third design is as follows:

	Time 1	Time 2
Group 1	Training	0_1
Group 2	No training	0_2

A serious problem with this design, however, is that perhaps the groups were not equally proficient prior to training.

One of the best designs is the following:

		Time 1	Time 2	Time 3
Group 1	R	0_1	Training	0_2
Group 2	R	0_3	No training	0_4

This design has none of the serious problems associated with the preceding ones. It also has a check such that if the two groups are not really random, comparison of 0_1 and 0_3 will expose that difference.

If there is a situation in which one needs to know whether there is an interaction between training and the measurement of proficiency, the following design, known as the Solomon four-group design, can be used.

		Time 1	Time 2	Time 3
Group 1	R	0_1	Training	0_2
Group 2	R	0_3	No training	0_4
Group 3	R		Training	0_5
Group 4	R		No training	0_6

The final design, the bottom two groups of the preceding design, can be used whenever randomization of the critical variables, in this case job proficiency, is certain.

		Time 1	Time 2
Group 1	R	Training	0_1
Group 2	R	No training	0_2

We have described these experimental designs because the use of such procedures is the only way of ascertaining the factor that caused changes in behavior. Such experiments, however, may be very expensive and may be disruptive to the on-going operations of the organization. Therefore, in considering an appropriate design to follow in evaluating a training procedure, one must look at the situation. Since not all training programs contribute to training or learning theory, it is permissable to use a design which is subject to some bias.

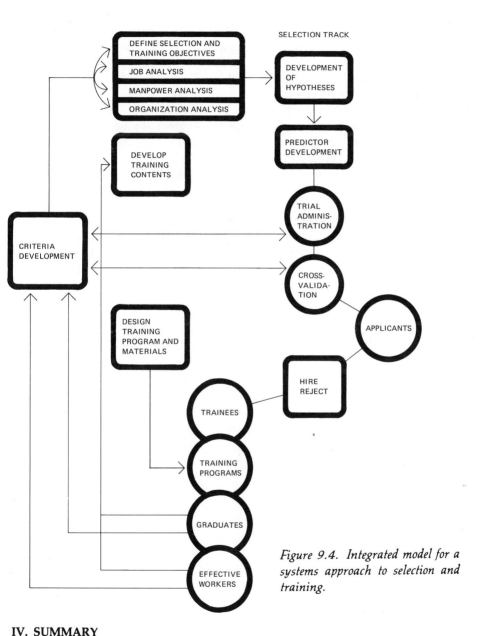

Figure 9.4. Integrated model for a systems approach to selection and training.

IV. SUMMARY

In this chapter we have presented models for selection and training. Both of these can be considered as part of a large, open-system model with some internal checks for effectiveness. Each model stresses the importance of development: in selection, criteria are needed to assess the value of the predictors; in training, criteria provide a method of assessing the effectiveness of the training program. These criteria serve as internal checks on the effectiveness of both selection and training procedures.

Each model uses an independent variable: in selection, this is the predictor scheme; in training, it is the actual training program. To be sure, the models differ slightly in that in selection, one is dealing with a prediction model, and in training one is working with an experimental group-control group to find the effects of training versus no training. The checks within each system enable one to modify the system in order to arrive at a better solution.

Figure 9.4 shows a systems approach to selection and training. Certain phases of selection interact with training, i.e., the effects of a selection procedure may influence the training outcome. Conversely, the effects of training success or failure help determine who will be selected in the future. The interesting feature to note is that criteria development is central to both procedures.

REVIEW

1. Suppose you are considering hiring a consultant for your canning company in order to install and validate a training program. How can you ascertain that he is professionally competent?

2. What explanation might there be for the negative findings of Gaudet and Casey about the resume? What implications does this have for selection?

3. List a number of on-the-job training techniques. Put them in order of priority in terms of their effectiveness, as you see them.

4. What do you think some of the most serious problems in selection will be in the next decade? In training?

5. What are some of your personal opinions about "personality testing?" Discuss.

6. Visit a local organization and examine how they select and train their personnel. How does their approach compare with that described in the text?

Critical Concepts

Predictor
Criterion
Reliability
Validity
Types of validation

Moderator variable
Utility theory
Clinical model of selection
Types of tests
Assessment center
In-basket
Organization, job, and manpower analyses
Types of complex learning
Generalization, discrimination, and transfer of training
Feedback
Reinforcement
Learning plateau
Massed versus distributed practice
Types of training procedures
Evaluation techniques

REFERENCES

1 A. Korman, *Industrial Organizational Psychology* (Englewood Cliffs, N.J.: Prentice-Hall, 1971).

2 F. Gaudet and T. Casey, "How Much Can You Tell From a Resume?" *Personnel,* 36 (July-August 1959): 62–65.

3 L. Ulrich and D. Trumbo, "The Selection Interview Since 1949," *Psychological Bulletin,* 63, 2 (1964): 110–116; E. C. Mayfield, "The Selection Interview—A Reevaluation of Published Research," *Personnel Psychology,* 17, 3 (1964): 239–264.

4 T. D. Hollman, "Employment Interviewer's Errors in Processing Positive and Negative Information," *Journal of Applied Psychology,* 56, 2 (1972): 130–137.

5 W. D. Buel, "Voluntary Female Clerical Turnover: The Concurrent and Predictive Validity of a Weighted Application Blank," *Journal of Applied Psychology,* 48, 3 (1964): 180–182; R. D. Scott and R. W. Johnson, "Use of the Weighted Application Blank in Selecting Unskilled Employees," *Journal of Applied Psychology,* 51, 5 (1967): 393–395.

6 W. A. Owens, "A Quasi-actuarial Approach for Individual Assessment," *American Psychologist,* 26, 11 (1971): 992–999.

7 W. D. Buel, "An Alternative to Testing," *Personnel Journal,* 51, 5 (May 1972): 336–341.

8 J. T. Campbell, J. L. Otis, R. E. Liske, and E. P. Prien, "Assessments of Higher-Level Personnel II: Validity of the Overall Assessment Process," *Personnel Psychology,* 15, 1 (1962): 63–74.

9 J. McConnell and T. Parker, "An Assessment Center Program for Multi-Organizational Use," *Training and Development Journal,* 26, 3 (March 1972): 6–14.

10   *Ibid.*, p. 14.

11   A. Kraut, "A Hard Look at Management Assessment Centers and their Future," *Personnel Journal,* 51, 5 (May 1972): 317–326.

12   H. H. Meyer, "The Validity of the In-basket Test as a Measure of Managerial Performance," *Personnel Psychology,* 23, 3 (1970): 297–307.

13   P. Ash, "The Implications of the Civil Rights Act of 1964 for Psychological Assessment in Industry," *American Psychologist,* 21, 8 (1966): 797–803.

14   F. Ruch, "What Impact did the Supreme Court Decision in the Duke Power Case Have on Employment Procedures?" (Address delivered to Edison Electric Institute, May 26, 1971.)

15   E. Schein, *Organizational Psychology,* 2d ed. (Englewood Cliffs, N.J.: Prentice-Hall, 1970).

16   *Ibid.*, p. 27.

17   *Early Identification of Management Potential Research Project* (Social Science Research Division, Employee Relations Department, Standard Oil Company, New Jersey, August 1961).

18   G. A. Eckstrand, "Current Status of the Technology of Training" (Army Medical Research Laboratory Technical Report AD608-212, September 1964), pp. 64–86.

19   W. McGehee and P. Thayer, *Training in Business and Industry* (New York: John Wiley, 1961).

20   B. M. Bass and J. A. Vaughan, *Training in Industry: The Management of Learning* (Belmont, Cal.: Wadsworth, 1966).

21   *Ibid.*, p. 14.

22   *Ibid.*

23   *Ibid.*, pp. 138–139.

24   E. E. Ghiselli and C. E. Brown *Personnel and Industrial Psychology* (New York: McGraw-Hill, 1955), p. 183.

25   J. N. Mosel, "Why Training Programs Fail to Carry Over," *Personnel,* 34, 3 (Nov.-Dec. 1957): 56–64.

26   E. A. Fleishman, "Leadership Climate, Human Relations Training, and Supervisory Behavior," *Personnel Psychology,* 6, 2 (1953): 205–222.

27   E. R. Gomersall and M. S. Myers, "Breakthrough in On-the-Job Training," *Harvard Business Review,* 44, 4 (July-August 1966): 62–72.

28   R. Mansfield, "The Initiation of Graduates in Industry," *Human Relations,* 25, 1 (1972): 77–86.

29   D. T. Campbell and J. C. Stanley, *Experimental and Quasi-experimental Designs for Research* (Chicago: Rand McNally, 1966). Reprinted from *Handbook of Research on Teaching,* ed., N. L. Gage (Chicago: Rand McNally, 1963).

PART IV

A

SYSTEMS

APPROACH

TO

ORGANIZATIONAL

IMPROVEMENT

INTRODUCTION

Managers are always trying to improve the operation of their organization, whether it be a local service station, a men's store, a motel, or General Motors. First, however, we need to distinguish, as Etzioni has done, between organizational *effectiveness* and organizational *efficiency*.[1] Organizational effectiveness is the degree to which a particular organization realizes its goals and objectives. Organizational efficiency, on the other hand, refers to the amount of resources an organization must use in order to produce a unit of output. In other words, although the two concepts are interrelated, they are not interdependent. An organization may be very effective in meeting its goals and highly inefficient because it uses up far too many resources in meeting its goals. Conversely, a plant may be highly efficient in its operation but not be very effective, as evidenced by its declining sales and decreasing profit margin. In part, of course, an organization's effectiveness depends on its objectives, their relevance to the environment, and conditions in the environment. In discussing organizational improvement and development, therefore, we must include both terms, since it is important that an organization be both effective in meeting its goals and efficient in using its resources wisely. The "competent" organization is both effective and efficient.

Elements of all three perspectives are needed for an organization to maximize its competency. Perspective I—the structural-design approach—looks *downward* in the organization and is concerned with organizational design and structure, including such subsystems as marketing, production, and finance. Perspective II—the work-flow approach—looks *across* the organization and emphasizes the flow of material and information. Perspective III—the human approach—focuses on the human process of managing, i.e., individual behavior and motivation, group dynamics, managerial and leadership style, and organizational design. This difference in emphasis has led practitioners and theorists to substitute "development" for "improvement" in describing organizational change.

Each of these three viewpoints of the organizational system is legitimate, and it is important to keep these three differing (and overlapping) sets of perspectives in mind, because an organization's work is performed by managers and subordinates through a series of interrelated and interdependent subsystems connected by work flows. Thus, the organization must be considered from a number of points of view in assessing its effectiveness and efficiency.

Analyzing an organization from only one perspective leads to the definition of only one set of problems and particular approaches to improvement of the organization. Analysis of the organization from a different point of view leads to a second set of problem definitions, a different set of solutions, and a different design based on a different set of assumptions. *Optimal* problem definition, *optimal* solutions, and *optimal* organizational designs are reached only when all three perspectives and all three sets of assumptions are considered simultaneously, with emphasis placed on differing points of view at appropriate points in time.

CURRENT CONFUSION IN MANAGEMENT THOUGHT

As one surveys the literature in the field, however, one is reminded of the old story about the six blind men of Indostan who went to "see" the elephant. One of the blind men felt the trunk and reported that the elephant was much like a snake. Another, feeling the tusk, said that the elephant was similar to a spear. A third, touching the ear, concluded that the elephant was very like a fan, and so forth. Similarly, it is apparent that many of those who write about organizations and organizational improvement and effectiveness have a strong tendency to take a specialized point of view, to the exclusion of others equally valid. Koontz points this out very clearly when he suggests that the welter and variety of differing approaches to management and organizational theory have led to a "kind of confused and destructuve jungle warfare" in which it seems to be the style of management theorists to "downgrade, and sometimes misrepresent, what anyone else has said, or thought, or done."[2]

Perhaps this is to some measure inevitable, since the scientific study of management is still very young. In addition, the plethora of books and articles in this field makes it impossible for any individual to really keep up with what is going on. Consequently, both the student and the business man are confused, and legitimately so.

ORGANIZATIONAL IMPROVEMENT—A DEFINITION

There are many definitions of organizational improvement—probably as many definitions as there are theorists in the field. However, an eminently practical one is that offered by Lawrence and Lorsch, who say that when we talk about improving organizational effectiveness and efficiency, "we are implying that we want to change the organization from its current state to a better-developed state."[3]

Before discussing the varying approaches to improving organizations, we want to again stress that the three perspectives for analyzing the organization are really artificial divisions made for the sake of greater clarity: any organization, large or small, exists as an entity and must be managed as such. Indeed, the three approaches overlap considerably and must therefore be considered simultaneously to arrive at *optimal* organizational competency. The vast majority of managers are concerned with improving information and work flow; all too few are concerned with improving the productivity and personal growth of their subordinates.

ORGANIZATIONAL IMPROVEMENT—PERSPECTIVE I (CHAPTER 10)

This chapter focuses on current research, theory, and application of organizational improvement from the point of view of the formal, structural-design approach. After a brief review of the history of organizational improvement in terms of organizational design, some of the newer, research-based approaches to organizational design are described. Chapter 10 concludes with a contingency theory of organizational design, i.e., there is no one best way to design an organization. Rather, organizational structure and design depend heavily on the interchange between the organization and its environment, and the design that works best for one type of organization may be dysfunctional for another type of organization.

ORGANIZATIONAL IMPROVEMENT—PERSPECTIVE II (CHAPTER 11)

This chapter describes current efforts to improve the flow processes through the organization by the use of such techniques as mathematical models, operations research, and computers. Some of the assets and liabilities of these approaches are examined in the context of the organization as a total system.

ORGANIZATIONAL DEVELOPMENT—PERSPECTIVE III (CHAPTER 12)

Focusing on the human side of the organization, this chapter describes organizational development, the term preferred over organizational improvement by practioners in this area. Chapter 12 stresses the necessity for proper diagnosis before action can be taken on organizational development. Following a description of some currently popular approaches to organizational development, we examine several criticisms of this area and point out some of the myths about this topic that have developed within the past few years.

TOWARD AN INTEGRATED THEORY OF ORGANIZATIONAL DEVELOPMENT (CHAPTER 13)

This chapter integrates the approaches to organization development described in the three preceding chapters. After illustrating some of the ways in which the three different perspectives can be combined to improve organizational competence, we conclude with two case studies which use these overall principles.

A CASE STUDY OF ORGANIZATIONAL DEVELOPMENT (CHAPTER 14)

The presentation of the case history provides further amplification of the principles of organizational development. In this case, a number of different approaches to organizational development were used at varying times. By describing both the successes and failures encountered in this study, we hope you will get a better understanding of the application of principles for organizational development.

REFERENCES

1 A. Etzioni, *Modern Organizations* (Englewood Cliffs, N.J.: Prentice-Hall, 1964), p.8.

2 H. Koontz, "The Management Theory Jungle," *Journal of the Academy of Management,* 4, 3 (1961): 174–178.

3 P. Lawrence and J. Lorsch, *Developing Organizations: Diagnosis and Action* (Reading, Mass.: Addison-Wesley, 1969), p.4.

10

ORGANIZATIONAL IMPROVEMENT— PERSPECTIVE I

All nature's structuring, associating, and patterning must be based on triangles, because there is no structural validity otherwise.

R. BUCKMINSTER FULLER

I. INTRODUCTION

The development of thought about organizational structure, design, and improvement has occurred gradually and inevitably, concurrently with the evolution of fairly simple and stable organizations into complex organizations operating in rapidly changing, quickly moving, and uncertain environments. Orginally, it was believed that there is "one best way" to organize a social system; this concept has been modified to a "contingency" theory of organizational structure and design, which recognizes the fact that not all types of organizations require the same type of structure and design.

This chapter traces the evolution of management thought, briefly discusses the historical roots of organizational design, and ends with a contingency theory. Throughout, our concept of organizational improvement is the enhancing of organizational effectiveness and efficiency. Although such aspects of organizational life as better budgeting or cost-accounting techniques and improved machine design are important considerations in organizational improvement, we restrict ourselves in this discussion to the structural design of the organization.

The main thrust and concern of early writers in this field reflected their knowledge of organizations as they existed in history and in the first part of the twentieth century. Thus, many of the classical "principles" of management were derived from the Roman and Prussian military models and from early industrial organizations. But of course, organizations and concepts of organizational design have changed considerably since then, as demonstrated in the current research and literature. However, the different theorists in the field have tended to ignore one another; indeed, in the 1950s and 1960s some of the Perspective III proponents seemed to "throw out the baby with the bath" by ignoring some of the writings of the early theorists. As Bennis indicates, early Perspective I management theorists described "organizations without people," whereas the later, Perspective III theorists were concerned about the interpersonal relationships between workers and tended to focus on "people without organizations."[1] This characterization, although overdrawn, illustrates the fact that many of the early organizational-design theorists were concerned with something akin to the machine-economic model of man to the almost total exclusion of the social or growth models of man. Similarly, modern behavioral theorists were, until relatively recently, concerned with self-actualizing man to the almost total exclusion of rational-economic man.

II. TRADITIONAL THEORY

A. The Classicists

The traditional, classical theorists were concerned with a variety of concepts—the structure of the organization, distinctions between line and staff, the division of labor, and managerial functions. Fayol lists 14 principles of management useful for all organizations, although he does note that these must be flexible rather than absolute.[2] These are listed in Table 1.1, p. 11.

1. Structure. This term refers to the way in which an organization is formally designed in order to ensure orderly specialization among its subsystems. Early theorists were fairly adamant about the fact that there was one best way to organize. Fayol, for example, says that "the same framework is appropriate for all individual concerns of whatever kind, employing the same number of people," although he also states that the same general appearance does not require exactly the same detailed structure and that implicit in this concept is the difficulty of "how to find essential personnel and put each where he can be of most service."[3]

Implicit to the notion of structure is the distinction made between line and staff, a distinction borrowed from military organizations. The line organization is the primary chain of command which comes directly from essential functions, or subsystems, of the organization, e.g., manufacturing, finance, and distribution. Staff activities are purely advisory to line functions. Definitions of line-staff relationships are, however, varied and have changed throughout the years. For example, early definitions made it clear that a line officer exercises *authority* over the entire organization and that "staff" activities are purely *advisory*. According to Mooney and Reiley, "It is the function of the staff merely to counsel; that of the line, and the line only, to command," although they do point out that this is oversimplified, since the line "represents the authority of man; the staff, the authority of ideas."[4] That this concept has undergone considerable change is demonstrated by Fisch's conclusion that the changing mix of organizations may well make the line-staff concept obsolete. "Research, development and engineering can surely no longer be considered as staff departments . . . they are of equal importance and hence require equal authority with manufacturing and sales."[5]

2. Division of Labor. Obviously, work must be divided into different segments, or components; otherwise, every job would be so broad and inclusive that effective performance would be impossible. Accordingly, Perspective I

One of the first applications of the moving assembly line was this magneto assembly operation at a Ford plant in 1913. Magnetos were pushed from one workman to the next, thereby reducing production time by half. (Photograph courtesy Ford Motor Company)

theorists have been concerned with whether an organization should be centralized or decentralized, set up by product or function, etc. Since the concept of division of labor extends from the top to the bottom of the organization, it may appear to be overly "formalistic" to spell out exact job description and positional interrelationships, but as Mooney and Reiley state, it is necessary for total efficiency.[6]

3. The Coordinative Principle. Since division of labor is essential to the proper functioning of a large, complex organization, unity of action for achieving organization goals can be achieved only through proper coordination. Initially, it was assumed that each superior was in charge of coordinating the work of his subordinates. As Fayol said, "For any action whatsoever, an employee should receive orders from one superior only . . . the rule of unity of command . . . is at least equal to any other principle whatsoever."[7]

Although he recognized the need for contact and communication across the formal hierarchy, Fayol stressed that informal communication was helpful so long as there was no conflict.

So long that F and P [two subordinates reporting to different managers] remain in agreement, and so long as their actions are approved by their immediate superiors, direct contact may be maintained but from the instant that agreement ceases or there is no approval from the supervisors, direct contact comes [immediately] to an end and the scalar chain [vertical chain of command] is straightaway resumed.[8]

In other words, conflict is resolved, in theory at least, only at the top.

4. The Scalar Principle. This concept prescribes a hierarchical chain of superior-subordinate relationships such that each subordinate has only one superior. According to Mooney and Reiley, "Wherever we find an organization even of two people, related as superior and subordinate, we have the scalar principle. This chain constitutes the universal process of coordination, through which the supreme coordinating authority becomes effective throughout the entire structure."[9] What follow from this, of course, are the principles of leadership, delegation (of authority), and functional definition, which refers to the superior's definition of his subordinate's function in the organization.

5. The Functional Principle. In contrast to the scalar principle, the functional principle refers to the differentiation of duties on a nonhierarchical basis. The vice-presidents for finance and marketing may be on the same level of the organization chart, but they have different functions within the organization.

B. The Structuralists

The structuralists' approach to the problem of management is very different from that of the classical theorists. The classicists used deductive reasoning to prescribe a conceptually clean organizational design and description of how each person within the organization *should* behave. The structuralists, on the other hand, examined existing organizations and used inductive reasoning to generalize about the true nature of organizations—their descriptive, or normative, approach focused on what organizations are *really* like rather than what they *should* be like.

One of the best-known early structuralists is Max Weber, who characterized organizational rules in terms of an "ideal" bureaucracy. (However, as Etzioni

Weeding out the bureaucracy

notes, the degree of an organization's bureaucratism may change in accordance with the times.)[10] Weber notes that the ideal type of bureaucratic organization has the following characteristics:[11]

1. "A continuous organization of official functions bound by rules."

2. "A specified sphere of competence." This means that bureaucrats have highly differentiated functions and the necessary authority to carry them out.

3. "The organization of offices follows the principle of hierarchy." This concept is similar to the scalar principle, i.e., no office is left to "drift" in an organization, and each office reports directly and solely to a higher-level office.

4. "The rules which regulate the conduct of any office may be technical rules or norms." In an editorial comment, Parsons suggests that the rules deal with constraints which promote efficiency in an organization, whereas norms in Weber's thinking probably are concerned with defining the conduct on grounds other than efficiency. However, it is important to note that Weber emphasized prescribed rules in bureaucracies.

5. Ownership of an organization and the administrative and production functions should be separated. In other words, the administrators in a bureaucracy

do not own the equipment needed for production or administration, e.g., a clergyman does not own the church he serves, and a governor does not own the state of which he is chief executive.

6. An incumbent must not be allowed to control either positions or trappings of office. Such a rule preserves the independence and freedom of an organization from the particular incumbent at a given time.

7. "Administrative acts, decisions and rules are formulated and recorded in writing, even in cases where oral discussion is the rule or is even mandatory." This, of course, is to stress the impersonal nature of a bureaucracy and ensures that the rules will be applied consistently in all situations.

To summarize, it is interesting to note that there are many features common to both the structuralist and classical approaches. The major difference appears to be the way in which the concepts were obtained.

III. EVOLVING CONCEPTS OF ORGANIZATIONAL IMPROVEMENT—PERSPECTIVE I

Early theorists, such as Gulick, Mooney, Reiley, and Weber examined organizations as they knew them from a limited background of research. Current concepts of organization improvement have been heavily influenced by expanding knowledge about human behavior, organizational design, including the concepts of formal and informal organization, and the human relations movement. Research and theory in this area have led current theorists away from a "one-best-way" approach and toward a contingency theory of organizational design.

Koontz and O'Donnell give an excellent review of organizational thought and history and show how research has heavily influenced current thinking about organizational improvement.[12] Another excellent presentation of organizational thought and history is given by Scott. He traces the underpinnings of the classical theorists, briefly describes the division of labor, the scalar and functional processes, structure, and the span of control under the rubrics of "The Classical Doctrine." He then describes what he calls the "Neoclassical Theory of Organization," which accepted the classical theory, but superimposed "modifications resulting from individual behavior, and the influence of the informal group" and introduced the concepts of social man and the informal organization, which had been largely ignored by the classicists.[13]

Worthy studied span of control (the number of people reporting to one boss) in two different types of Sears Roebuck stores.[14] Both types of stores had approximately 150 to 175 employees, but one type was organized along conventional lines—store managers, section managers, and approximately 30 department heads. The other type of store had a much flatter structure with a much wider span of control—approximately 30 department heads reported directly to the store manager. In terms of such criteria as profitability, promotability of department heads, and overall employee morale, stores with the "flat" structure were superior.

Unfortunately, Worthy's findings were reported anecdotally and were generalized well beyond the scope of the original study. In a compilation of studies about correlates of organizational structure, Porter and Lawler found no evidence to indicate that a flat organization improves both attitudes and performance on the job.[15] Rather, they found that a flat structure in smaller organizations appears to enhance satisfaction and productivity. From their review of the research, Porter and Lawler conclude that the advantages of having a flat organizational structure decrease, and even become a liability, as the organization becomes larger.

Porter and Lawler also found that upper-level managers were more satisfied than lower-level managers with the nature of their jobs. Additionally, insofar as it is possible to distinguish between line and staff jobs, line personnel felt better about their jobs, there was a much higher turnover of staff jobs, and line personnel were better informed about what was going on in the organization.

Porter and Lawler found that the size of subunits within the organization appears to be related to satisfaction; satisfaction and morale appear to be greater in small subunits, there is less absenteeism, and turnover is lower. Moreover, the larger the subunit, the greater the likelihood of labor disputes. Their findings about productivity, however, were equivocal; they were cautious about commenting on the relationship between an organization's total size and workers' attitudes and behavior. Similarly, there were no clearcut findings about the efficacy of a centralized or decentralized organization.

One of the interesting features about the work by Porter and Lawler is that even though their starting point was the Perspective I emphasis on structure, they took an inductive, research view of the correlates of structure, and many of the findings deal with the performance and feelings of individuals on the job. Their work exemplifies the blurring of the lines between Perspectives I and III. Perhaps the classical managerial theorists could argue that what was happening in the organizations studied should not have happened according to their principles, but the important thing to remember is that although prescriptions for behavior may be unrealistic, the data collected about the behavior do not lie.

In another evolutionary study, Hall found some confirmation of his hypothesis that organizational divisions or hierarchical levels with nonroutinized jobs are significantly less bureaucratic than those levels at which more routine activities take place.[16] Organizational flexibility and instability are thus negatively related to the rules of a bureaucracy as Weber envisioned them.

Among the important "follow-up studies" is Woodward's research on a large number of firms in a relatively small geographic area in England.[17] Using a sample of 100 firms which varied considerably in size and type, she and her associates found a wide range of organizational structures among successful firms in different industries with different technologies. For example, she found that the most successful firms and industries using unit- or batch-production technology had considerably wider spans of supervisory control with fewer levels of hierarchy than did successful firms with more stable, continuous-process technologies.

Burns and Stalker, who closely examined some 20 different organizations covering a wide variety of products and applications, found two basic types of organizational structures—"mechanistic" and "organic."[18] The mechanistic system, used in organizations operating under relatively stable external conditions, emphasizes well-defined rules, procedures, and functional roles. Since only those at the top of the organization have access to the overall knowledge and since the command hierarchy is well defined, interaction within the organization is vertical rather than horizontal. The "organic" system, on the other hand, operates in uncertain and changing environments, e.g., the electronics industry. Jobs are less clearly defined, and interaction tends to be lateral rather than vertical. Much more knowledge (and the power to make decisions) is contained at lower levels in the management hierarchy.

In the early 1960s Likert proposed his linking-pin theory, which is transitional because it takes both a structural and humanistic view of the organization.[19] However, even though it is based on substantive research, Likert's assumption is that there is *one best approach* to management of an organization. Likert notes that a superior in one work group is a subordinate in the next higher work group (Fig. 10.1). Thus, a foreman supervises his own work group, but he is a subordinate of the supervisor of foremen. In Likert's linking-pin approach, each work group has a head, or chief, who is tied in with the next higher group. The "linking-pin" is the chief who has contact with both groups.

One of Likert's key concepts is that of supportive relationships. He notes that a worker must feel wanted, needed, and important. The superior must understand the subordinate's expectations, and the superior must know how he is perceived by the subordinate. The feeling of support is the key to high motivation within a work group. A corollary of this is the key role of the work group. Likert states that since people want to achieve a feeling of value and personal worth, the supportive work group is *the* way to achieve this, noting that an organization will function best when workers function "not as individuals but as members of highly effective work groups with high performance goals."[20]

One of the interesting features of Likert's theory is that it integrates the structural and human perspectives. However, since it ignores the informal group

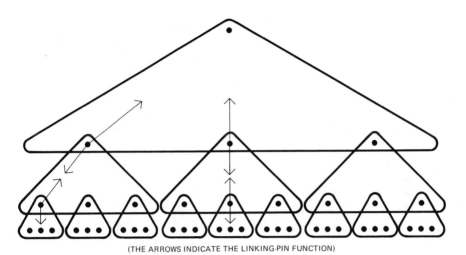

(THE ARROWS INDICATE THE LINKING-PIN FUNCTION)

Figure 10.1. Likert's linking-pin theory. (R. Likert, New Patterns of Management, *New York: McGraw-Hill, 1961, p. 113. Used with permission of McGraw-Hill Book Company.)*

and does not take account of extreme situations, its usefulness is somewhat limited.

The new contingency theory, developed from the work of Fred Fiedler and discussed in Chapters 1 and 7, is a model based on three variables: (1) leader-member relationships; (2) task structure or definition; and (3) position power of the leader.[21] Through extensive research, Fiedler found that when the work situation is either very favorable or very unfavorable for the leader, an author-itarian approach is warranted. When the situation is of intermediate favorable-ness, a democratic, or egalitarian, approach is justified. This early example of a contingency, or situational, approach to management was later expanded by Lawrence and Lorsch, who applied it to the organizational structure and to the roles to be maintained by individuals in the organization.

IV. A CONTINGENCY THEORY OF ORGANIZATIONAL IMPROVEMENT—PERSPECTIVE I

Perhaps the most exciting recent work to improve organizational effectiveness and efficiency according to Perspective I principles has been done by Lawrence and Lorsch, who used a *comparative, research-based* approach in their study of more and less successful companies.[22] Unlike many other theorists who examined only one organization, Lawrence and Lorsch studied organizations in the same and different industries.

Lawrence and Lorsch are concerned with the division of labor, or "differentiation," and with the coordinative principle, or "integration." However, their contingency theory differs considerably from most researchers' theories in its stress that there is *no one best way* to design an organization. Rather, the organization must be designed to fit its environment, and the most effective and efficient organizations are those which most closely fit environmental requirements. The more certain the environment, the more closely centralized the organization can be and can rely on a hierarchical decision-making process. Similarly, the more uncertain the environment, the less centralized the organization can be and the more decisions must be pushed downward to lower hierarchical levels.

In either case, an organization must achieve both *differentiation* and *integration.* To Lawrence and Lorsch, differentiation occurs in four dimensions:

1. Orientation toward particular goals or objectives, which may vary within the organization. For example, the manufacturing department may prefer a higher volume on fewer products; and marketing, a more diverse mix.

2. Time orientation, e.g., product development or research and development groups may be interested only in long-range thinking, whereas the manufacturing department is much more concerned about meeting daily schedules.

3. Interpersonal orientation, which Lawrence and Lorsch found to be much less important to manufacturing people than to sales and marketing personnel.

4. Formality of structure, which tends to be greater in the manufacturing and finance departments than in those involving long-range planning.

The authors point out that organizational integration (coordination) becomes more difficult as the various units become more highly differentiated. Successful organizations, however, are able to achieve both, although the ways in which this is accomplished vary from organization to organization because of its interaction with its environment. In short, organizational design must fit the environment.

An organization (and its products) exist at some point along an *environmental continuum* which ranges from relatively stable and certain to highly uncertain and complex. In addition, there are three general types of technologies extending *across* this continuum. At one end of the continuum is the container industry, which exists in a stable environment because the purchaser of containers (glass bottles, cans, etc.) has invested large sums of money in high-speed equipment to fill the container and does not want change. At the other end of the continuum is the plastics industry, which exists in an uncertain environment of complex, changing problems. Such an industry must develop a higher degree of differentiation and a correspondingly greater attempt at integration, which needs to be carried out at lower levels of the organization where the required knowledge and information are available.

At the stable end of the continuum, integration could be carried out through the managerial hierarchy, e.g., the more successful container company approached the prototype of the *classical* organizational model, in which all decisions are made through the formal hierarchy. Serious attempts in one of the less successful container organizations to push decision-making down into the organization had caused problems because this approach was inappropriate.

The states of differentiation and integration in effective organizations will differ, depending upon the demands of the particular environment. In a more diverse and dynamic field, such as the plastics industry, effective organizations have to be highly differentiated and highly integrated. In a more stable and less diverse environment, like the container industry, effective organizations have to be less differentiated, but they must still achieve a high degree of integration.[23]

In other words, the classical theorists may well have been correct in their approaches to unity of command, since they were dealing with relatively stable organizations. However, the contingency theory of Lawrence and Lorsch demonstrates very clearly that there is *no one best way* to organize and design an enterprise—rather, there may be a number of "best ways," depending on the environment of the organization.

Building on the work of Worthy, Woodward, Burns and Stalker, and Lawrence and Lorsch, as well as his own extensive work in the field, Perrow has expanded the concept of the contingency theory.* Perrow stresses that the *form*

---

*Although the contingency theories of Lawrence and Lorsch and Perrow heavily emphasize the importance of technology, other variables (size, vertical span of control, and specialization) are stressed in comparative work on organizational structure and design conducted by other researchers at the University of Aston in Birmingham, England. For a discussion of these variables, see D. Pugh, D. Hickson, C. Hinings, K. MacDonald, C. Turner, and T. Lupton, "A Conceptual Scheme for Organizational Analysis," *Administrative Science Quarterly*, 8, 3 (September 1963): 289–315. This work has been re-examined by H. Aldrich, "Technology and Organizational Structure: A Re-examination of the Findings of the Aston Group," *Administrative Science Quarterly*, 17, 1 (March 1972): 26–43; and J. Child, "Organization Structure and Strategies of Control: A Replication of the Aston Study," *Administrative Science Quarterly*, 17, 2 (June 1972): 163–179.

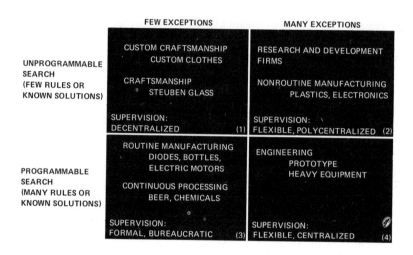

Figure 10.2. Technology, task, and organizational structure. (Adapted from C. Perrow, Organizational Analysis: A Sociological View, *Belmont, Cal.: Wadsworth, 1970, p. 83.)*

of the organization must follow its *function*, i.e., the form of the organization must reflect the "state of the art in each function and the changes required by the environments."[24] As Perrow points out, any organization is designed to produce something, whether it be slim buttocks for students in a charm school or the socialization and education of children in a public or private school. He therefore raises the question of how one can think about technology (in broad terms) as a method for transforming raw materials (which may be human, symbolic, or material) into some sort of desirable goods and services. The technology of the organization thus determines the form, or structure, of the organization. Successful complex organizations must adapt their structures to fit their current technology. Rather than using the simple environmental continuum of Lawrence and Lorsch, which ranges from stable to unstable, Perrow's typology uses two variables—"search" and the "number of exceptions," which can be examined independently or concurrently to construct a fourfold table, as shown in Fig. 10.2.

To Perrow, "search" can be either highly analyzable and routine or nonroutine and unanalyzable (few specific and well-established rules and guidelines). A craftsman blowing a unique piece of Steuben glass has a different search problem from one who makes ordinary glass bottles, for which the rules and procedures are well established.

Perrow's second category is the number of exceptions that an organization may have. An automobile factory with a myriad of different models, styles, and colors may have many exceptions, although after the model has been designed, the rules and procedures (search) may become highly routinized. Even though a research and development firm might have many exceptions, it could nevertheless fall in the category for which the rules and procedures are unknown (the unprogrammable search).

Perrow demonstrates that there is a high degree of relationship between the type of supervision required and the placement of an organization in a particular cell. For example, supervision in cell 1 needs to be decentralized; cell 2 requires flexible, polycentralized supervision; cell 3 calls for flexible and centralized supervision, and cell 4 requires formal centralized, highly bureaucratic supervision.

Perrow stresses that "before an organization's problems can be solved, it is essential to determine the nature of the organization." The way the organization is designed determines the appropriateness of its approaches to problem-solving. In practical terms, this means that techniques for solving organizational problems must be used selectively, since an approach or technique which is helpful for Organization A may be dysfunctional for Organization B.

V. CONCLUSIONS

In this chapter, we have discussed the problem of organizational improvement primarily from the point of view of organizational structure and design. The early "one-best-way" concepts of most of the classical theorists have been gradually modified through the years to the contingency theories described by Perrow and Lawrence and Lorsch, who point out that in fact there is no "one best way." Rather, the structure and design of a successful organization depend heavily on its technology and environment. An organization in a stable environment will generally be successful when its structure follows the classical bureaucratic pattern, but an organization in a highly unknown, unstable, and changing environment and technology needs to be designed and structured differently, since the problems of differentiation and integration are different. In other words, it is essential to take a comparative, situational approach to organizational improvement when the variables used are organization structure and design.

Creating a unique piece of Steuben glass is a nonroutine, unanalyzable task. (Photograph courtesy Corning Glass Works)

The process of removing impurities from petroleum cracking catalysts in the final filter area exemplifies a highly routinized procedure with many rules and known solutions. (Photograph courtesy W. R. Grace & Co.)

Assembling electronic components is a nonroutine task for which there are few rules or known solutions. (Photograph courtesy Corning Glass Works)

Prototype engineering represents a programmable search procedure with many rules and exceptions. (Photograph courtesy Boeing Company)

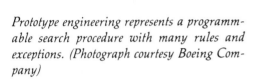

REVIEW

1. Give a brief description of Likert's linking-pin approach and two key concepts contained in it. What is its major drawback? Is Fieldler's approach better? Why or why not?

2. The Army has a very formal and rigid structure of supervision, but at the present time it is undergoing drastic changes in the environment in which it exists. If the Army applied Perrow's concepts, do you think a different type of supervision would emerge? If so, what type?

3. Describe the degree of differentiation and integration (high, medium, or low) that would probably characterize the following industries: chemical, computer manufacture, shoe manufacture, department store chain, corner grocery store, automobile manufacturer. What environment does each exist in?

4. Discuss the concepts of differentiation and integration as they are related to the older concepts such as the coordinative, scalar, and functional principles.

5. Read several of the articles cited in this chapter and critique their research approach, based on your current knowledge.

6. Can the Lawrence and Lorsch concepts be applied to a university? Elaborate.

7. List the information you would need to place an organization on the Lawrence and Lorsch continuum.

8. Pick several organizations that are local to your area. Where do each of these fall in the Perrow classification of organizations? Explain your reasons for classification.

Critical Concepts

Classicist principles

Structuralist principles

Classicists versus structuralists

Organic versus mechanistic structures

Linking-pin theory

Contingency theory

Differentiation and integration

Programmable versus unprogrammable search

REFERENCES

1 W. G. Bennis, "Leadership Theory and Administrative Behavior: The Problem of Authority," *Administrative Science Quarterly,* 4, 3 (September 1959): 259–301.

2 H. Fayol, *General and Industrial Management,* trans. C. Storrs (London: Pitman, 1949).

3 *Ibid.,* pp. 57, 58.

4 J. Mooney and A. Reiley, *The Principles of Organization* (New York: Harper and Brothers, 1939), p. 33.

5 G. G. Fisch, "Line/Staff is Obsolete," *Harvard Business Review,* 39, 5 (Sept.–Oct. 1961), p. 80.

6 J. Mooney and A. Reiley, *op. cit.*

7 H. Fayol, *op. cit.,* p. 24.

8 *Ibid.,* p. 35. Reprinted by permission.

9 J. Mooney and A. Reiley, *op. cit.,* pp. 14–15.

10 A. Etzioni, *Modern Organizations* (Englewood Cliffs, N.J.: Prentice-Hall, 1964).

11 M. Weber, *The Theory of Social and Economic Organization,* trans. A. M. Henderson and T. Parsons, ed. T. Parsons (New York: Oxford University Press, 1947), pp. 329–340.

12 H. Koontz and C. O'Donnell, *Principles of Management* (New York: McGraw-Hill, 1968), pp. 231–403.

13 W. G. Scott, "Organizational Theory: An Overview and an Appraisal," *Journal of the Academy of Management,* 4, 1 (April 1961): 7–26.

14 J. V. Worthy, "Organizational Structure and Employee Morale," *American Sociological Review,* 15, 2 (April 1950): 169–170.

15 L. W. Porter and E. E. Lawler, "Properties of Organization Structure in Relation to Job Attitudes and Job Behavior," *Psychological Bulletin,* 64, 1 (1965): 23–51.

16 R. H. Hall, "Intraorganizational Structural Variation: Application of the Bureaucratic Model," *Administrative Science Quarterly,* 7, 3 (September 1962): 295–308.

17 J. Woodward, *Management and Technology* (London: Her Majesty's Printing Office, 1958).

18 T. Burns and G. Stalker, *The Management of Innovation* (New York: Barnes & Noble, Social Science Paperbacks, 1961).

19 R. Likert, *New Patterns of Management* (New York: McGraw-Hill, 1961).

20 *Ibid.,* p. 105.

21 F. Fiedler, *A Theory of Leadership Effectiveness* (New York: McGraw-Hill, 1967).

22 P. Lawrence and J. Lorsch, *Organization and Environment: Managing Differentiation and Integration* (Boston: Harvard University Graduate School of Business Administration, Division of Research, 1967).

23 *Ibid.,* p. 108. Reprinted by permission.

24 C. Perrow, *Organizational Analysis: A Sociological View* (Belmont, Cal.: Wadsworth, 1970).

11

ORGANIZATIONAL IMPROVEMENT— PERSPECTIVE II

This new development (automation) has unbounded possibilities for good and for evil.

NORBERT WIENER

I. INTRODUCTION

This chapter discusses three major current thrusts in organizational improvement according to Perspective II, the flow perspective. The first is model-building, including the work of the operations researchers and the more recent work of Forrester; the second is the attempt at improving communications, material, and information flow through computerized management information systems; and the third is the recent work done on integration, including project management and the work by Lawrence and Lorsch on the importance and role of the "integrator."

II. MODELS AND MODEL-BUILDING

The term "model" has many meanings. To some, it connotes a beautiful girl; to others, it represents a small-scale version of an airplane, car, etc. And to yet others, the term "model" represents something less concrete and tangible. For example, as Forrester explains, each of us carries with us a mental image, or model, of the world.[1] This abstract model makes use of particular concepts or relationships to represent "the real thing." However, this type of model is fuzzy and incomplete and differs for each individual.

In this part of the text, we use the term "model" as an abstract representation of a system which attempts to give "reality" a mathematical rather than a verbal expression in English or some other language. For example, Einstein's formula $E=MC^2$ is an abstract mathematical model, not a verbal one. A model is a representation of a system and according to Emshoff, its primary purpose is to "integrate data about the system's behavior in a way that provides information about characteristics of that behavior."[2]

As many authors have pointed out, the attempt to build models at the level of the human and social system is very difficult. A clear example of this problem is given by Forrester, who notes that one can construct a computer model which ostensibly reproduces all the assumptions held by a particular person. When the model is used, however, it does *not* usually act in the way that the person himself acts; each individual has internal contradictions that lead to unanticipated behaviors. Indeed, Boulding, whose levels of systems were discussed in Chapter 2, seriously doubts that our present knowledge is sufficient to build more than the rudiments of theoretical systems, or models, much beyond Level 4 (a self-perpetuating open system such as a cell).[3] For Boulding, human and social systems are at Levels 7 and 8. Despite the inherent difficulties of model-building, however, several of the current approaches to organizational improvement do deliberately attempt to build models.

A. System Dynamics

Forrester made extensive use of models in order to describe the behavior of organizations resulting from the interaction of the organization with the outside environment.[4] He used a mathematical model comprising six interconnected networks, or subsystems—orders, materials, money, personnel, and capital equipment—all of which are interconnected by information flow. Using a systems approach to integrate the different functional departments within an organization (marketing, production, finance, and research and development), Forrester stresses that the interconnections and the interactions which occur among the components of the system will "often be more important than the separate components themselves."

Forrester believes that managing involves the primary tasks of designing and controlling an industrial system. Thus, industrial dynamics is an approach for management of systems analysis which involves the "time-varying interactions between the parts of the management system." There are four basic components of his model:

1. Information-Feedback Theory. This term is similar to "positive feedback," i.e., such a system exists whenever information from the environment causes a decision to be made that results in action. This action affects the environment and in turn influences future decisions. In later articles, he emphasizes the need for models in this area, because social organizations are involved in "multi-loop non-linear feedback systems" which the individual mind is not able to understand directly.[5] In other words, the policies and procedures which people follow are the very ones that get the organization into trouble, because the human mind is unable to adequately conceptualize "multi-loop non-linear feedback systems." (See Fig. 2.5, p. 44.)

2. Decision-Making Processes. This foundation, or basic premise, follows logically from information-feedback theory in that a model can be developed which provides formal rules for short-term tactical decisions. Forrester states that these formal rules are superior to those made by human judgment under the pressure of time, the absence of complete data, or in the rigidity of a large organization. (This may be true only in a self-contained system, however.)

3. An Experimental Approach to System Analysis. Since mathematical techniques are not as yet adequate for the development of general analytical solutions, the experimental approach is needed so that a simulation model can be used to try out different market assumptions and management policies which do not require the more sophisticated mathematical approaches.

Computers rapidly provide large amounts and types of information. (Photograph courtesy Bruce Anderson)

4. Use of Computers. Without the speed and capability of the modern computer, it would be impossible to use simulation models or to cope with a large number of variables.

Perhaps the most important concept in Forrester's industrial dynamics approach is the utility of his theories. He graphically illustrates that the use of intuitive judgment and "common sense" rather than the model may result in totally unnecessary cyclic swings in production. Small changes in retail sales, for example, may lead to totally unwarranted and wild swings in factory production so that a factory manager may at all times be able to produce more goods than are being sold to consumers; yet, he may be unable to fill the orders coming from the sales department. Using the model would reduce or eliminate the cyclic production swings resulting in hiring, overtime, and then layoffs.

Forrester has recently expanded and revised his concepts. He first substituted "system dynamics" for "industrial dynamics" and is now using the term "world dynamics," which reflects his belief that use of his model can have a marked effect on urban and world systems. Concurrently, the Club of Rome (an informal, international organization whose members have varying backgrounds) sponsored a book in which a global computer model is used to investigate five "major trends of global concern—accelerating industrialization, rapid population growth, widespread malnutrition, depletion of non-renewal resources, and a deteriorating environment."[6] Although this model is oversimplified and, of course, unfinished, data on the five strategic factors were computerized to determine the effectiveness of the model in assessing various alternatives for the future of mankind. The resulting predictions demonstrated that mankind is in serious trouble unless quick action is taken to achieve a state of nongrowth (global equilibrium) in which production and population are maintained in a careful balance.

This work, as well as that of Forrester, has been strongly challenged by Passell, Roberts, and Ross, who believe that the models rely on too many unproved assumptions, are overly simplified, and lead to unjustified conclusions.[7] For example, although the work done by the Club of Rome does stipulate that the model is incomplete, the review by Passell, *et al.* makes the criticism that " 'limits' pretends to a degree of certainty so exaggerated as to obscure the few modest [and unoriginal] insights that it genuinely contains." Nevertheless, we believe that this work has made an important contribution to the field.

B. Operations Research

Operations research, or management science, is an attempt to build mathematical models and use mathematical techniques to improve the welfare of the *entire* organization rather than merely certain of its components. As Hillier and Lieberman state, operations research attempts to "resolve the conflicts of interest *among the components** of the organization in a way that is best for the organization as a whole."[8]

Proponents of operations research stress that the method can be used in any type of an organization—hospitals, government, military, business, and industry. If one has a computer simulation of an oil refinery, for instance, it is far easier to use the mathematical model to try out different ways of operating the refinery to get different blends and mixes of gasolines and oils than it is to experiment with the refinery itself. The results obtained from using the computerized mathematical model can then be used in the real-life operation of the refinery.

Operations research began about 1940, when the British Army asked Nobel Prize winner Professor Blackett to assemble a team of scientists to work on operational problems. Their first problem was to determine what information should be collected from radar equipment in order to decide which gun sites would be most effective in preventing German attacks on the British mainland. The success of this effort prompted the United States military to undertake similar efforts. Since then, the usefulness of operations research has continued to increase; currently, most American universities have courses in OR, although they may be part of the engineering, management, statistics, or mathematics curriculum.

The larger the American business organization, the more likely it is to make active use of an operations research team. Such teams are heavily oriented toward the use of mathematics and models. Typically, the approach of an OR team is as follows:

1. Analyze, study, and observe the real-life system or structure that needs to be understood and explained. This includes identifying both the controllable and uncontrollable variables.

2. Structure the real-life situation so that a mathematical model (a generalized framework) can be developed which fits the observations and data obtained in the first step. This, of course, necessitates looking at the problem in the context of the entire system, including the objectives to be attained.

3. Check the model to find out how it will behave under conditions which have not yet been observed, but which could be observed if the changes were actually made.

---

*Italics added.

4. Modify and change the model to develop optimum approaches to reach the defined and desired objectives.

5. Test the model by developing experiments or changes in the actual system to determine whether or not the model actually *predicts*, i.e., determining whether or not the effects of the changes that are predicted by the model actually occur when the changes are made.

6. Refine and change the model as necessary.

7. Use the model as a guide to action in real life, i.e., use it to predict optimum solutions.

Ackoff and Rivett have noted nine organization-wide flow problems which they believe can be solved through operations research.[9]

1. Inventory. If we define inventory as idle resources, we can then define "resources" as anything which can be used to obtain something of value. Men, material, machines, and money are all inventory resources.

2. Allocation. The allocation subsystem is concerned with organizing the resources within the organization in such a way that the overall efficiency of the total system is maximized.

3. Queueing. The proper mix between the tasks to be performed and the facilities available to perform them must be obtained. For example, a bank needs to consider the optimum number of tellers' windows, which in turn depends on the number of customers expected. Costly waste results from having too many windows, but having too few windows increases the customers' waiting time.

4. Sequencing. The order, or sequence, in which operations occur depends on the queue discipline that has been selected. For example, if each of several products requires operations on two machines, the material flow can be sequenced so that maximum utilization of the machines is made. In other types of sequencing problems, priorities need to be considered.

5. Routing. In order to attain maximum efficiency of operations, the organization must determine how to best route its products through the manufacturing process, reach its customers, etc.

6. Replacement. Since parts break down or wear out over time, people leave, and equipment becomes obsolete, some organized plan of replacing these elements must be determined and ready if the need arises.

7. Competition. Within the organization, there may be competition for scarce resources; in the marketplace, there is competition for customers. Competition occurs from the effect on one decision-maker of decisions made by others. It may arise when the decision-maker's action is known in advance; it may involve choices when the competitor's decision can be predicted; or it can result when decisions have been unanticipated.

8. Search. This category involves the search for alternative actions or items to produce.

9. Mixed problems. An organization's problems can rarely be considered independently of one another; rather, since its subsystem are interdependent, its problems are interdependent.

Terms and techniques used by operations researchers are usually highly mathematical—linear programming, Markov chains, queueing theory, game theory, etc. This heavy reliance on mathematics and mathematical models is based on the precision, self-containment, logical structure, and convenience of the language of mathematics.

C. Criticisms and Limitations of Mathematical Modeling

One of the biggest problems facing those working on the "model" approach to the flow system is that the modern organization is constructed and organized along vertical rather than lateral lines. As a result, much of the effectiveness of operations research and similar "modeling" research methodology occurs within, rather than across, individual departments of the organization. For example, the use of linear programming as a tool in production and advertising cannot be readily applied to a consideration of the organization as a total system.

A much more serious criticism is that mathematical models, especially those used by operations researchers, depend primarily on mechanistic "output" models and not with more organic "input" models. An output model assumes known inputs and uses these known inputs to provide predictions of outputs. The extent to which the model makes accurate predictions is a measure of its usefulness. However, the validity of the "known" inputs cannot always be assumed; therefore, the predictions of the model may reflect unwarranted or incorrect assumptions.

A related criticism of the use of models is that it makes too many assumptions about human behavior. For example, Gruber and Niles criticize OR for inadequate attention to human factors, which are difficult to model mathematically.[10] Yet obviously, human factors are perhaps the most important factor in organizational life.

Simon criticizes what he calls "normative microeconomics" as being too mechanistic, pointing out that although it is carried forward under such labels

The high priest of the computer room.

as operations research or management science, the normative microeconomist acts as though he does not really *need* a theory of human behavior.[11] Rather, all he wants to know is how people *ought* to behave rather than how they actually *do* behave. In other words, the normative microeconomist makes the false assumption that one can ignore the human system while focusing on the model.

Emshoff extends this criticism by showing that the original work in operations research used mechanistic models, i.e., the input was known in advance (the rate of gunfire, the input from radar, etc.).[12] The problem was to combine these known inputs and to provide a better output from variables that were already known.

As operations research expanded into other fields, the model remained mechanistic—the inputs were generally known or could be easily identified. Therefore, the analysis was concerned primarily with how to handle the interaction among the input variables in the model so that the output of the model would be as realistic as possible.

However, as operations researchers began working on problems that were less mechanistic and more behavioral, their models became less successful as predictors, since solving mechanistic problems requires only a general knowledge of the behavioral factors, whereas solving behavioral problems requires an intimate understanding of human behavior. For example, the premium a person pays for a given amount of life insurance is generally governed by his age. This relationship is a statistical, actuarial, predictive model—it is known that the life expectancy of a person 75 years old is considerably less than one who is 25 years old. This output-based model does not require an understanding of the individual, only a knowledge of the behavioral factors involved, e.g., older people tend to die sooner than younger people.

However, as operations researchers and other model-builders have tried to apply their work to behavioral areas, they have tended to use the output rather than the input model. Emshoff explains that this is inappropriate, since "behavioral problems have fundamentally different characteristics from mechanistic problems and because of this, systems models for behavioral problems must be developed using an input-oriented research focus rather than the traditional output-oriented one."[13]

For example, it is well known in psychiatric circles that many girls become pregnant, not from lack of knowledge of birth control techniques, but because they want: revenge on parents, something (a baby) of their very own, or to get married. A model stressing control of pregnancies among unwed girls by means of better dissemination of birth control knowledge is an output model. An input-based model would focus more heavily on the reasons why unmarried girls become pregnant in the first place.

Emshoff insists that it is not sufficient to merely *describe* human behavior; one must also strive to understand human behavior and the reasons for it. Emshoff uses the goal of reducing traffic accidents to illustrate the operation of an input-based model. Insurance companies know that drivers under 25 have the highest accident rate. Psychologists know that the strongest influence on behavior for those under 25 is peer groups. Emshoff therefore postulates that increasing the penalties for traffic violations (output model) has little effect, since the influence of penalities is less than that of peer groups. Emshoff suggests that the accident rate for this age group might be reduced by using the force of peer influence. A probationary license would be issued to the applicant under 25, and it would have to be countersigned by two or more of the applicant's friends, each of whom also had a license and belonged to the same age group (input model). If one of the group lost his license due to a traffic violation, all of the cosigners would also lose their licenses. Emshoff theorizes that this might increase peer pressure to drive safely. Although the courts might find such a solution illegal, it does have the advantage of distinguishing between an output-based model—increasing the penalties for traffic violation, which treats everybody equally—and an input-based model—removing the drivers' licenses of peers, which takes into account peer pressure.

Another criticism that has been leveled at the model-builders, particularly the OR practitioners, is that OR models are usually structured to seek the optimum solution. Many organizations, however, seek only a satisfactory solution, since an "optimum" solution for a particular problem might conflict with other goals and objectives of the organization. Earlier, for example, we cited the case of the executive who refused to take a risk which would have benefitted the organization, but not necessarily the executive. An input-based model would take these factors into consideration.

Most models, and operations research in particular, have been successful *within* individual departments of a firm, but have generally been unsuccessful in resolving "the conflict of interest *among the components* of the organization in a way that is best for the organization as a whole." In fairness to the model builders, however, it needs to be pointed out that behavior models, too, have limitions of both theory and data, although Emshoff does give some suggestions for overcoming some of these "lacks."

III. MANAGEMENT INFORMATION SYSTEMS

Another main thrust of organizational improvement on the lateral, or flow, level is the integrated management information system, which uses the computer to provide information flow *through* the organization. With the advent of the computer in the late 1950s and its coming of age in the 1960s, the literature was filled with optimistic predictions that the computer would become the basic tool for developing management information systems which would in turn cut across the organization and provide managers at all levels with the knowledge and data necessary to make decisions about their jobs.

For example, Huse studied a major organization making a serious attempt to install a computerized, integrated, management system.[14] The integrated

Management information systems rely on computer facilities to provide information flow through the organization. (Photograph courtesy IBM)

system would take customer orders and, through a series of major computer programs, provide assembly and fabrication schedules, man-machine loadings, and other information through the factory. The system would then provide the purchasing department with requirements for orders from outside vendors. It was hoped that this system would replace or integrate a multitude of manual or partially mechanized systems already existing in the organization. Savings from the installation of the integrated management information system were expected to exceed $1,000,000 annually, since approximately nine man years

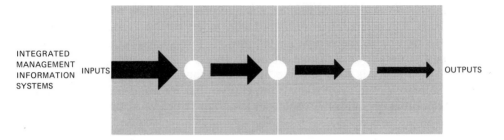

Figure 11.1. The traditional departmentalized structure and the use of an integrated management information system.

were required to make the 2,400,000 hand calculations needed to develop a single production planning schedule throughout the factory, and the frequent schedule changes required 40 working days to complete. The new system was expected to reduce the time necessary for a schedule change to about four or five days, including reviews for accuracy, and to require less than 100 hand calculations, with a corresponding increase in accuracy.

However, after several years and several million dollars, the program just "faded away," although it was never officially abandoned. The program failed, in part, because the company was organized on a classical, vertical basis, and the management information system was designed to cut across vertical lines and break down the departmental walls. However, as shown in Fig. 11.1, blockage occurred each time the program cut across departmental boundaries. Managers in one department refused to trust inputs from other departments and insisted on controlling their own data base. As a result, the resistance by middle managers blocked the installation of the program and caused it to fail. In other words, the attempt to impose a Perspective II concept on a Perspective I organization without corresponding changes in the total organization ensured the program's failure.

Many writers are becoming disenchanted with attempts to develop a total systems approach without first rethinking concepts about organizations. Kaufman has even suggested that the approach be given up as unsound and that attention be concentrated on more limited, but probably more manageable, approaches.[15]

Although the computer has been of great value within individual departments and sections of an organization, its ultimate value in providing information flow across departmental lines is still far from being realized. Thus, the computer is an excellent tool for handling the payroll or conducting scientific research, but such uses are restricted to intradepartmental needs. As a subsystem in its own right, the computer will not be truly successful in the lateral, flow system unless or until the present compartmentalized, vertical form of organizational structure is somehow modified and changed. For as Diebold has stated, "The new technology makes it imperative that we build information systems which break through the compartmentalized structure of the traditional business organization."[16]

IV. INTEGRATION THROUGH THE INFORMAL ORGANIZATION

In our previous discussions of the informal organization, we said that such groups and activities form a network of personal and social relationships which are not established or prescribed by the formal organization. Davis says that the informal organization "arises from the social interaction of people, which means that it develops spontaneously as people associate with each other."[17] And Bakke adds, "As factors influencing human behavior, the formal and informal systems are not separable."[18]

There are many reasons for the existence of informal organizations or groups: relatedness, affiliation, friendship, and security. Argyris contends that "the informal organization helps to decrease the basic causes of conflict, frustration and failure."[19] For example, Van Zelst found that carpenters and bricklayers who formed work groups voluntarily had higher productivity, lower costs, and considerably lower absenteeism; one worker said, "Seems as though everything flows a lot smoother . . . the work's a lot more interesting, too."[20] One of the possible reasons for this preference for informal work groups has been explored by Bowditch and King, who found that emotionally stable persons prefer to work with persons from similar backgrounds.[21]

As a method of improving work performance, the informal organization operates without an "official" set of rules or a formal manager. As a result, the members of the informal group work out among themselves approaches to accomplishing their tasks. Need an emergency repair on a machine? "Go see Jim and see if he can work it in between his scheduled jobs." Out of typing paper? "Rather than wait for a requisition to go through, borrow some from Mary." Stuck on a technical detail in R and D? "Drop over to see the mathematician in Section X—he may be able to give you some quick help." Want to get something done by a committee? "Drop in on Felix—he is the power behind the throne on the committee. If you get his O.K., he'll bring the rest of the committee around." Need an order expedited? "Call Bill, he will know how to get it done without having to wait for all the red tape."

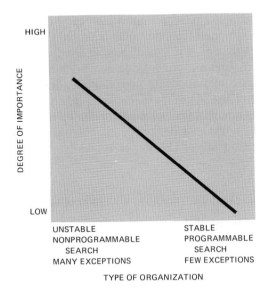

Figure 11.2. Importance of the informal organization in accomplishing work.

Of course, the informal organization does not *always* work for the good of the organization, as evidenced by the Hawthorne studies. There are many other well-documented cases of restriction in output and other dysfunctional approaches used by the informal organization. Perhaps one of the clearest examples of a dysfunctional approach by the informal organization occurred with a group of subordinates whose boss was highly disliked. One day at lunch, they decided to "get him" by *not* following their usual practice of getting the job done by some of the means just described. Instead, they decided to follow his orders to the letter. For two months, they did just that. From the official, formal organizational point of view, their behavior was impeccable. They did exactly what they were told to do, quickly and accurately. They followed the rules to the letter. Meanwhile, things in their section got worse and worse. Work backed up, and the manager found himself involved in crisis after crisis and in more and more trouble with upper management. He knew what was happening to him, but there was nothing he could do about it, since his subordinates were doing exactly what they were told to do, even though they knew that many of their "correct" actions would get their boss into even deeper trouble. At the end of two months, the boss decided to quit rather than to get fired.

Figure 11.2 shows that the importance of the informal organization in getting work done increases in direct proportion to the instability of the organization. In the nonroutine firm which has, to use Perrow's terms, unprogrammable search procedures and the need to deal with many exceptions, coordination among groups comes about through mutual adjustment as the need arises, and the interdependence of groups in the work-flow process is high. At the other end of the continuum, there is less need for the informal organization, because decisions can be programmed at the top, and there are few exceptions. Here, the informal organization serves social, safety, and affiliation needs rather than work-flow needs.

V. MORE FORMALIZED INTEGRATIVE APPROACHES

Since World War II, there have been numerous attempts to use formalized, nonmathematical approaches to integration. One such approach is the increasing use of project managers or program directors, especially in organizations having a variety of different products or uncertain environments, whose official task is to integrate the work-flow process across departmental or functional lines. Gaddis and Evans note that in some organizations, particularly those that are market-oriented, the program manager's job may be semipermanent, lasting as long as the product is on the market.[22] In other organizations, the program manager's job may be only temporary, having been established to make certain that a particular product is designed, manufactured, and delivered within a relatively short period of time.

The work of Perrow and Lawrence and Lorsch demonstrated that organizations can be improved through careful analysis of the interrelationship of technology, structure, and design. In addition, there are other, more formalized integrative devices which can be used. In some businesses in a stable environment with programmable search procedures, the organization is highly centralized, and most of the integration can be carried out from the top of the organization. Other organizations require greater differentiation (specialization) and tighter integration (coordination). Since these two needs are essentially antagonistic, the resulting complications demand new, more formalized and innovative approaches to bring about both differentiation and integration, which cannot be accomplished by the informal organization. The work of Lawrence and Lorsch shows the need for different integrative functions in different types of organizations.[23] Table 11.1 gives the results of their research.

This table shows three types of industries, ranging from least stable (plastics) to most stable (container), and that the need for differentiation increases with the need for adaptability to change, which results directly from the uncer-

Table 11.1 Comparison of integrative devices in three high-performing organizations

	Plastics	Food	Container
Degree of differentiation[*]	10.7	8.0	5.7
Major integrative devices	(1) Integrative department	(1) Individual integrators	(1) Direct managerial contact
	(2) Permanent cross-functional teams at three levels of management	(2) Temporary cross-functional teams	(2) Managerial hierarchy
	(3) Direct managerial contact	(3) Direct managerial contact	(3) Paper system
	(4) Managerial hierarchy	(4) Managerial hierarchy	
	(5) Paper system	(5) Paper system	

[*]High score means greater actual differentiation.
Reprinted by permission from P. Lawrence and J. Lorsch, *Organization and Environment: Managing Differentiation and Integration* (Boston: Harvard University Graduate School of Business Administration, Division of Research, 1967), p. 138.

tainty of the environment. As can be seen from the table, the number of integrative devices increases in direct proportion to the uncertainty of the environment; the container industry, which is the least differentiated, uses the managerial hierarchy and direct managerial contact as the basic integrative mechanisms. The plastics industry, on the other hand, requires many more integrative devices at all levels in the organization to accomplish the necessary integration, since it is the most differentiated of the three industries. These results illustrate the need for a new management function (the integrator or integrative department) in highly differentiated organizations so that high differentiation and high integration *across* the organization can be achieved simultaneously.

In their focus on the role of the integrator, Lawrence and Lorsch indicate that the integrator needs to have a balanced view of the differing time and goal orientations of various parts of the organization, e.g., the long-range time goals of the scientist versus the short-range time goals of the manufacturing department. In short, the integrator needs to have the following behavioral characteristics:

1. *Integrators need to be seen as contributing to important decisions on the basis of their competence and knowledge, rather than on their positional authority.*
2. *Integrators must have balanced orientations and behavior patterns.*
3. *Integrators need to feel that they are being rewarded for their total product responsibility, not solely on the basis of their performance as individuals.*
4. *Integrators must have a capacity for resolving interdepartmental conflicts and disputes.*[24]

In order to resolve conflict and bring about integration, integrators need to use both expert and referent power rather than to rely on their position, or "legitimate," power. Lawrence and Lorsch cite three basic ways of resolving interdepartmental conflict: smoothing—ignoring the problem in hopes that it will go away; edicting—using positional power to force a decision; and confronting—dealing with the conflict in open terms until a solution agreeable to all is reached. This is perhaps the most effective method for integration and conflict resolution, although forcing may be needed as a back-up method.

The approach recommended by Lawrence and Lorsch is one of the most important developments in the field of organizational improvement at the Perspective II level. Furthermore, the "integrator" concept is one way of integrating Perspectives I and II.

VI. CONCLUSION

In our discussion of some of the modern approaches to organizational improvement through the flow system, we have dealt with model-building, including system dynamics and operations research, and have described some of the difficulties with this approach. Attempts to improve lateral information flow with computerized management information systems may be hampered by the vertical structure of the organization and thereby reduce the effectiveness of such information flow which may, however, be facilitated by informal groups within the organization. In our exploration of formal integrative devices, we noted that such attempts to coordinate the organization must become increasingly complex and deliberate as the organization becomes more highly differentiated. We concluded by describing the role of the integrator, whose dual functions of conflict resolution and integration represent one of the most promising approaches to organizational improvement from Perspective II.

These are all ways of improving the flow of information, materials, and resources across an organization but, as we have stressed throughout the text, these approaches cannot be considered in isolation. Rather, they must be considered in the context of the other two perspectives—the formal and human perspectives. In the next chapter, we discuss organizational development from Perspective III, and in Chapter 13, we propose a unified theory of organizational development which integrates the approaches of the three perspectives.

REVIEW

1. Models of various "systems" are commonly observed in our complex modern world. Give examples of two such models and explain why they are beneficial to us. Do these models contradict Boulding's statement on the ultimate complexity of models or theoretical systems?

2. The computer is just a "black box" in which inputs lead to outputs that a human being would be able to determine if he had sufficient time. How can the results of a black box *not* be able to determine behavior and in fact cause interdepartmental conflict? Give an example.

3. Based on your knowledge of the results of applying coercive force, explain why the successful integrator uses confrontation before coercion. Can these two forces be applied in reverse order successfully? Why is "smoothing" used last?

4. According to Table 11.1, the container organization does not need the services of an integrative department. Why? Would an operations-research approach work in such a company?

5. Is the Lawrence and Lorsch discussion of conflict resolution related to the discussion in Chapter 5 of group task, maintenance, and self-serving activities?

6. Select an organization (club, fraternity, business) and observe how conflict is handled (smoothing, edicting, or confronting). What were the consequences?

7. From your own experience, give an example which shows how the informal organization has (a) helped and (b) hindered the organization. What caused the difference?

8. Give an example from your own experience that shows the difference between an "input" and an "output" based model.

9. We have given some reasons for the failure of total, computerized management information systems. Do you agree or disagree with these reasons? Elaborate.

10. How does the material in this chapter relate to the research by Sayles as described in earlier chapters?

Critical Concepts

Model

System dynamics

Information feedback theory

Operations research

Types of flow problems in organizations

Limitations of mathematical modeling

Output versus input models

Management information systems

Information flow

Informal organization

REFERENCES

1 J. W. Forrester, "Counterintuitive Behavior of Social Systems," *Technology Review,* Alumni Association, Massachusetts Institute of Technology, 73, 3 (Jan. 1971): 52–68.

2 J. R. Emshoff, *Analysis of Behavioral Systems* (New York: Macmillan, 1971).

3 K. Boulding, "General Systems Theory: The Skeleton of Science," *Management Science,* 2, 3 (April 1956): 197–208.

4 J. W. Forrester, *Industrial Dynamics* (Cambridge, Mass.: M.I.T. Press, 1961).

5 J. W. Forrester, "Counterintuitive Behavior of Social Systems," *op. cit.; idem.,* "Systems Analysis as a Tool for Urban Planning" (Paper delivered at the Symposium on the Engineer and the City, National Academy of Engineering, October 22–23, 1969, Washington, D.C.).

6 D. H. Meadows, D. L. Meadows, J. Ronders, and W. Behrens III, *The Limits to Growth* (New York: Universe Books, 1972), p. 21.

7 P. Passell, M. Roberts, and L. Ross, *"The Limits to Growth,* World Dynamics, and Urban Dynamics," *New York Times Book Review,* April 2, 1972.

8 F. Hillier and G. Lieberman, *Introduction to Operations Research* (San Francisco: Holden-Day, 1969), p. 5.

9 R. Ackoff and P. Rivett, *A Manager's Guide to Operations Research* (New York: John Wiley, 1963).

10 W. H. Gruber and J. S. Niles, "Problems in the Utilization of Management Science/Operations Research: A State of the Art Survey," *Bulletin of the Institute of Management Sciences,* 4, 2 (Jan. 1971): 12–19.

11 H. Simon, "Theories of Decision-Making in Economics and Behavioral Science," in *Managerial Economics,* ed. G. Clarkson (Baltimore: Penguin Books, 1968), pp. 13–49.

12 J. R. Emshoff, *op. cit.*

13 *Ibid.,* p. 25.

14 E. Huse, "The Impact of Computer Programs on Managers and Organizations: A Case Study," in *The Impact of Computers on Management,* ed. C. Myers (Cambridge, Mass.: M.I.T. Press, 1967).

15 F. Kaufman, "Date Systems that Cross Company Boundaries," *Harvard Business Review,* 44, 1 (Jan.-Feb. 1966): 141–155.

16 J. Diebold, "ADP—The Still-Sleeping Giant," *Harvard Business Review,* 42, 5 (Sept.-Oct. 1964): 60–65.

17 K. Davis, *Human Relations at Work* (New York: McGraw-Hill, 1962), p. 236.

18 E. Bakke, *Bonds of Organization* (New York: Harper and Brothers, 1950), p. 194.

19 C. Argyris, *Personality and Organization* (New York: Harper & Row, 1957), p. 230.

20 R. Van Zelst, "Sociometrically Selected Work Teams Increase Production," *Personnel Psychology,* 5 (Autumn 1952): 175–185.

21 J. Bowditch and D. King, "The Relationship Between Biographical Similarity and Interpersonal Choice," *Proceedings of the 78th Annual Convention,* American Psychological Association (1970): 381–382.

22 P. Gaddis, "The Project Manager," *Harvard Business Review,* 37, 3 (May-June 1959): 89–96; G. Evans, *The Product Manager's Job* (New York: American Management Association, 1964).

23 P. Lawrence and J. Lorsch, *Organization and Environment: Managing Differentiation and Integration* (Boston: Harvard University Graduate School of Business Administration, Division of Research, 1967).

24 P. Lawrence and J. Lorsch, "New Management Job: The Integrator," *Harvard Business Review,* 45, 6 (Nov.-Dec. 1967): 146. Reprinted by permission.

12
ORGANIZATIONAL DEVELOPMENT—PERSPECTIVE III

"The time has come," the Walrus said, "to talk of many things ..."

LEWIS CARROLL

I. INTRODUCTION

With our discussion of Perspective III, we introduce the term "organizational development" (OD), which more accurately reflects the orientation of the behavioral science practitioners in the field. However, both organizational improvement and organizational development have the same objective—to enhance the organization's effectiveness and efficiency.

Organizational development is a rapidly expanding field which is continually changing with new knowledge. Essentially, OD is a long-range attempt to improve an organization's ability to both cope with changes in its external environment and improve its internal problem-solving capabilities. However, unlike the other two perspectives, OD is directed toward integrating the needs, goals, and objectives of the organization with the needs of the individual for involvement, growth, and development on the job. This concern was evidenced in recent Congressional hearings. "One of the central themes of the hearings was the new concern for job satisfaction as an important factor in achieving greater productivity . . . The stakes are high . . . in the final analysis it is people and not machines which produce."[1]

An *explicit* part of the OD approach to improving organizational effectiveness is the deliberate and conscious effort to help human beings grow and develop in the organizational setting. This assumes that organizational effectiveness and efficiency can both be improved if certain conditions are met in the organizational setting.

1. Most people both need and desire growth and self-realization.

2. When basic needs have been satisfied, most individuals do not want or seek a soft, secure environment; rather, if given the opportunity, they become more concerned with work, challenge, and responsibility.

3. Organizational effectiveness and efficiency are increased when work is organized to meet the individual's needs for challenge, responsibility, and growth.

4. Increasing the openness of communication facilitates personal growth.

5. Shifting the emphasis of conflict resolution from "edicting" or "smoothing" to open confrontation facilitates both personal growth and the accomplishment of organizational goals.

6. As people working in groups become more open and honest with one another in a "caring" fashion, the group becomes increasingly able to handle problems in a constructive rather than disruptive fashion.

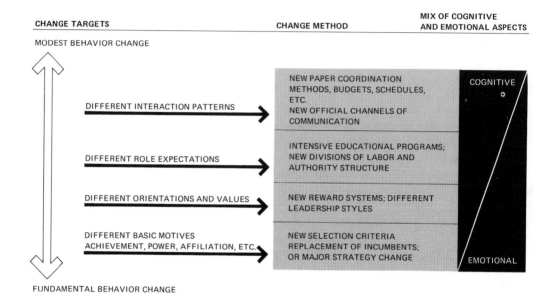

CHANGE TARGETS   CHANGE METHOD   MIX OF COGNITIVE AND EMOTIONAL ASPECTS

MODEST BEHAVIOR CHANGE

DIFFERENT INTERACTION PATTERNS → NEW PAPER COORDINATION METHODS, BUDGETS, SCHEDULES, ETC. NEW OFFICIAL CHANNELS OF COMMUNICATION   COGNITIVE

DIFFERENT ROLE EXPECTATIONS → INTENSIVE EDUCATIONAL PROGRAMS; NEW DIVISIONS OF LABOR AND AUTHORITY STRUCTURE

DIFFERENT ORIENTATIONS AND VALUES → NEW REWARD SYSTEMS; DIFFERENT LEADERSHIP STYLES

DIFFERENT BASIC MOTIVES ACHIEVEMENT, POWER, AFFILIATION, ETC. → NEW SELECTION CRITERIA REPLACEMENT OF INCUMBENTS; OR MAJOR STRATEGY CHANGE   EMOTIONAL

FUNDAMENTAL BEHAVIOR CHANGE

Figure 12.1. Elements of an organizational development program. (P. Lawrence and J. Lorsch, Developing Organizations: Diagnosis and Action, *Reading, Mass.: Addison-Wesley, 1969, p. 87. Reprinted by permission.)*

7. Organizational structure and the design of jobs can be modified to more effectively meet the needs of the individual, the group, and the organization.

8. Many "personality clashes" in organizations result from problems of organizational design.

II. THE NECESSITY FOR A DIAGNOSTIC APPROACH TO ORGANIZATIONAL DEVELOPMENT

Many organizations—Corning Glass, Esso, General Electric, TRW Systems, and Union Carbide, for example—have increased their effectiveness and efficiency by using OD programs. However, in almost all cases, behavioral scientists, or "change agents," were called on to initiate the OD program. Most of them agree that the approach to a particular organization depends on its present culture and value system. In other words, there are no "off the shelf" formulas for applying OD in a particular organization, since problems, technology, and culture differ among organizations. Therefore, the OD consultant, or change agent, adopts an action-research model which is designed to fit the needs, objectives, and present values of the organization.

The necessity for a diagnostic approach to organizational development

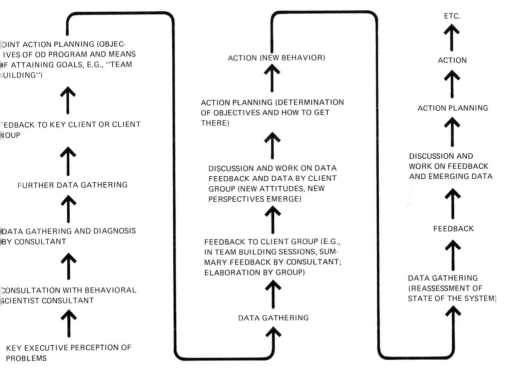

Figure 12.2. An action-research model for organizational development. (W. French, "Organization Development: Objectives, Assumptions and Strategies," California Management Review, *XII, 2, Winter 1969, p. 26. Reprinted by permission.)*

Figure 12.1 shows that the mix of cognitive and emotional aspects of an OD program stems directly from the amount and degree of behavioral change desired. The only general rule is that the method and approach must vary with the circumstances.

Figure 12.2 shows French's model for a diagnostic approach to OD, the key aspects of which are data gathering, preliminary diagnosis, feedback and discussion with the client group, preliminary action planning, action, and rediagnosis.[2] The diagnostic stage is tremendously important, for unless the consultant is highly sensitive to the prevailing culture of the organization, its state of readiness for change, its technology, and the expectations of the client system, he may seek to impose his own value system on the client system. Bennis documents three cases of OD programs that failed because the consultant did an incomplete and inadequate job of diagnosing the current client culture and readiness for change.[3] In one instance, which Bennis calls the case of "The Undercover Change Agent," an attempt was made to introduce laboratory training (sensitivity training) in an organization that was not ready for it. The president of the company summarily put a stop to the training, insisting that the training department revert to more traditional methods.

Diagnosis is highly important for another reason; since organizational subsystems are interrelated, changes in one subsystem will have an impact on the other subsystems within the organization. An illustration of the negative impact a change in one subsystem can have on other subsystems is in the "Hovey and Beard Company" case.[4]

The Hovey and Beard Company manufactured wooden toys—animals, pull toys, etc. The toys were cut, sanded, and partially assembled in the wood room. They were then dipped in shellac and painted. The partially assembled toys were spray painted in the paint room, an operation staffed entirely by female workers. Although the toys were predominantly two-colored, only one color was applied as the toy went through the paint room. Therefore, this process had to be repeated for each additional color, i.e., most toys required at least two trips through the paint room.

For a number of years, these toys had been produced entirely by hand. However, in order to meet the tremendously increased demand, the painting operation was re-engineered so that the eight girls who did the painting sat in a line by an endless chain of hooks which were in continuous motion past the line of girls and into a long horizontal oven. Each girl sat at her own painting booth, which was designed to carry away fumes and to backstop excess paint. The girl would take a toy from the tray beside her, position it in a jig inside the painting cubicle, spray on the color according to a pattern, then release the toy and hang it on the hook passing by. The rate at which the hooks moved had been calculated by the engineers so that each girl, when fully trained, would be able to hang a painted toy on each hook before it passed beyond her reach.

The girls working in the paint room were on a group-bonus plan. Since the operation was new to them, they also received a learning bonus which decreased by regular amounts each month. The learning bonus was scheduled to vanish in six months, by which time it was expected that the girls would be on their own, that is, able to meet the standard and to earn a group bonus when they exceeded the quota.

Over a period of time, the girls were given the authority to regulate the speed of the assembly line. Their participation was high, and productivity soared. However, the rest of the organization was not prepared for the change. Because the girls were on incentive pay, their pay was equal to or surpassed that of the more highly paid workers in the organization, e.g., tool and die makers. As a result, the manufacturing manager took summary action—he restored the slower assembly-line speed originally set by the industrial engineer. Within a short period of time, both the foreman and most of the girls quit for jobs elsewhere.

The importance of sensitivity to the client organization's culture, technology, and readiness to change has caused many OD practitioners to stress (although not all would agree) that the change process must start from the top down. Indeed, Beckhard defines OD as "an effort (1) *planned,* (2) *organization wide,* and (3) *managed* from the top, to (4) increase *organization effectiveness* and *health* through (5) *planned interventions* in the organization's 'processes,' using *behavioral-science* knowledge."[5]

A similar view is shared by Ferguson, who points out that "people problems" can seriously hurt, if not destroy, an organization if not properly handled; the task of OD is to identify, diagnose, and treat such problems.[6] To Ferguson, the crucial elements of OD are sensing, mutual coaching, and organizational display. He defines "sensing" as the attempt to use representative subgroups of the various units in the work force to ensure that managers "hear and understand the social dynamics of their employees" (which is similar to our use of the term "diagnosing"). "Mutual coaching" is the help individuals give one another to get the job done better, and "organizational display" is the attempt to bring organizational problems out into the open so that they can be clearly perceived and worked on, i.e., it is the "job of organizational development to search for and display organizational worms," since if they cannot be seen they cannot be treated.[7]

A slightly more conservative note is sounded by Kegan, who found the results of OD to be ambivalent; although a "proper" OD program increased trust toward peers inside and outside the work group while simultaneously keeping individuals task oriented, other data indicated that traditional bureaucratic norms conflicted with the program's development of norms of confrontation, choice, and collaboration.[8] Kegan notes that participants in an OD program must be aware of organizational hostility toward it and that this must be reflected in OD strategy.

The cyclical process of diagnosis, planning, action, and rediagnosis requires that the change agent, as a consultant, operate differently from most other consultants. In the more traditional mode, a consultant comes in, looks at a problem, makes his diagnosis, writes a report giving his recommendations, and then leaves, his task accomplished. In the OD process, the change agent generally does not write reports; rather, he usually prefers to work on on-going problems, acting as a resource person helping the organization to grow and develop and stand on its own rather than acting as either an internal or external consultant giving advice on specific problems. Thus, for example, the OD consultant and the management staff may work jointly in diagnosing the organization's problems and working out solutions.

III. APPROACHES TO ORGANIZATIONAL DEVELOPMENT

There are a variety of different approaches used in OD—laboratory training, team-building, job enrichment, organizational confrontation meetings, improved interdepartmental relationships, and inducing internal growth and change. In order for any of these approaches to be successful, efforts must be made to work with the organization as a total system and help it develop its ability to handle its own development in the future. It is also important that Perspective III changes mesh with organizational improvement approaches within Perspectives I and II.

A. Laboratory Training

Laboratory training, sometimes called sensitivity, or T-group training, is probably the most popular yet misunderstood technique used in OD. Indeed, to some people, laboratory training is synonomous with OD. As Bennis explains, "Most organization development cases that finally reach print focus almost exclusively on the T-Group as the basic strategy of intervention."[9] However, it is extremely difficult to define laboratory training, as is described by Schein and Bennis:

1. *Laboratories* vary tremendously *in goals, training design, delegate population, length and setting* . . .
2. *Laboratories attempt to provide a* total *and* integrated *learning experience for the participants, making it difficult to communicate . . . what actually occurs.*
3. *Laboratories are an attempt to provide a learning experience which is, in part,* emotional *and to provide the opportunity for the participants to explore the interdependence of emotional and intellectual learning.*[10]

Laboratory training first came into use in the late 1940s, largely because of the growing realization that the types of human relations training in vogue concentrated far more on the lecture method than on the more vital issues—the feelings and concerns of individuals—and that dealing with the latter was a more powerful form of education.

The objectives of laboratory training are of three types:

1. To increase the individual's interpersonal competence by helping him become more aware of his own feelings and emotions and those of others;

Getting at emotional responses.

2. To give the individual a greater awareness of his own and others' role within the organization, to increase his willingness to deal with and achieve collaborative relationships with others, and to help him increase his organizational interpersonal competence; and

3. To assist the organization in doing a better job of diagnosing, defining, and working on organizational problems and to help the organization improve itself through the process of working on the training of *groups rather than individuals.*

Although it is difficult to describe what happens in a laboratory training session, there is usually a trainer and group of people who form "stranger," "cousins," or "family" groups. In "stranger" laboratories, the participants do not know one another at the beginning. "Cousins" laboratories consist of people from the same organization who may be acquainted with one another, but who do not usually work together. "Family" laboratories consist of people who have direct working relationships with one another, e.g., a boss and a group of his subordinates. Obviously, the approach must differ considerably with the type of laboratory used.

A typical laboratory training session for "strangers" consists of four or five T-groups of 10–15 members gathered together under the auspices of an organization such as the National Training Laboratories. The T-group sessions may, at times, be interspersed with general-theory sessions, designed exercises, or management games.

At the beginning of the training session, the trainer announces that he is to serve as a resource to the group, and after a brief introduction he lapses into silence. With this dilemma of leadership and agenda, it is then up to the group to work out its own way of proceeding. What goes on in the group then becomes the basic data for the learning experience. The trainer will, as appropriate, intervene, but the nature and type of his interventions vary greatly, depending on the trainer and the nature and purpose of the laboratory. Most commonly, however, he encourages individuals to focus on and to understand their own feelings and to "level" with one another about what is going on in the group at the time. The emphasis is on the "here and now" experience rather than on anecdotes or "back home" experiences. It is through the emphasis on openness and leveling in a supportive and caring environment that the participants gain more insight into their own and others' feelings and the mechanics of group dynamics and can thereby begin to be more productive.

Most participants react positively to laboratory training sessions. Frequently, participants express a heightened awareness of self and others, increased ability to listen more intently, to accept feedback about themselves and provide it to other group members, and to feel less constrained by cultural norms about expressing and accepting a fuller range of emotions. Although laboratory sessions are brief, some participants are successful in achieving what Lewin calls unfreezing, experimentation, and refreezing of behavior patterns in rather significant ways.[11] Although participants are occasionally threatened or otherwise overwhelmed to such an extent that they do not benefit from the T-group experience, the causes frequently lie with their deep, unresolved psychological problems.

There are, of course, many variations in T-group training. Some laboratories extend for two weeks or longer. Others, "micro" or "marathon" labs, may last only a weekend or a day.[12]

The effectiveness of laboratory training appears to be mixed. House concludes that although such training has potentially powerful effects on both the individual and the organization, the effects vary widely with individuals and situations.[13] On the other hand, Campbell and Dunnette feel that such training may well have positive value for the individual, but that "the assumption that T-group training has positive utility for organizations must necessarily rest on shaky ground . . . the authors wish to emphasize . . . that utility for the organization is not necessarily the same as utility for the individual."[14]

More recently, Golembiewski *et al.* have described the success of such laboratory-style organizational development work initiated at a small plant and then expanded to a larger, more complex organization.[15] The program was started with divisional managers and during a 245-day period was extended to regional managers through to the top of the organization. The program design was a modified time series with six periods of observations following laboratory work. One of the important features of this work was that like the Blake and Mouton approach, organizational development was accomplished over time, starting with a subpart of the organization.

Although it appears that sensitivity training can be a powerful tool for influencing behavior, there is also abundant evidence that the transfer of laboratory learning to daily organizational life is sometimes difficult to achieve, if it can be achieved at all. It is clear that laboratories alone are an inadequate OD strategy and that other interventions are needed both prior to and following the laboratory training.

B. Team-Building

Much of a manager's time, as we have pointed out earlier, is spent working in groups or teams which can be either *vertical,* e.g., a boss and his subordinates, or *horizontal,* e.g., a task force working on a particular project. However, frequently groups are not as productive as they could be. Managers are often frustrated (and rightly so) because they waste so much time in meetings, which could be made more productive through the use of process observation and consultation, here defined as sitting in and observing a group and helping it to become more productive. To review briefly, there are two basic assumptions underlying team-building and process observation. First, in order for teams to be more effective and productive, the members of the group must coordinate and merge their efforts toward the accomplishment of mutually acceptable work goals (*group task*). Second, the personal welfare and emotional needs of group members must be met (*group maintenance*). If the emotional needs of the individuals are not met—if they are neglected or sacrificed—the group's effectiveness is considerably diminished and, indeed, the group itself may not survive.

In any team or group, events have two dimensions. One is *content*—the topic of conversation, the agenda, etc. The other is *process*—what is happening in the group, e.g., who is talking to whom, how the members feel about the group and one another, and the kinds of subgroups, coalitions, and alliances that have formed.

There are a number of different approaches to team-building, all of which require the help of a skilled process observer in increasing the effectiveness of the group's task and maintenance roles. One approach is for the consultant to interview each member of the team in advance about his feelings, attitudes, and perceptions of the team's effectiveness. A meeting is then scheduled, frequently away from the organization, where the consultant feeds back the information, and the group spends its time in working through the data, agreeing on basic problems, and setting priorities and action approaches toward resolving the problems.

Another approach is for the team to come together and for each member to discuss his role (or job) as he perceives it, with each other member of the team feeling free to make contributions, suggestions, or comments. This form of role identification and clarification can frequently be very helpful in clearing up misunderstandings and in making certain that each team member knows and accepts both his own role and that of the other team members. One of the authors, for example, recently attended a three-day meeting of the top boss with his subordinates. The first item on the agenda was the mutual establishment of organization goals; the second item was to review the role of each member of the staff, including the top manager. This portion of the meeting required about three hours of discussion for each job before mutual agreement was reached. Following this, the objectives of the organization were redefined. The last item on the agenda was to list problems facing the organization, assign priorities to them, and to agree on which subteams would work on each problem.

Another method of team-building often used in conjunction with that just described is for the consultant to attend regular staff meetings. Here, the consultant is a process observer who watches and observes how the team goes about accomplishing its group task and maintenance roles. Paying less attention to the *content* of the meeting, he focuses on the *process,* considering such variables as group atmosphere and the degree of trust and openness; task effectiveness, including the degree to which the group is working or "goofing off" and whether full use is being made of the talents and resources of the group; and the amount, degree, and nature of participation, e.g., whether only a few members participate, the extent and degree to which people interrupt one another, etc. In other words, the process observer looks at the ways in which the group goes about accomplishing both its *task* and *maintenance* roles, for both need to be accomplished if the group is to be effective.

Either during or following the meeting, the observer can give feedback on what he has observed or encourage the group to give its own feedback. For example, Schein describes a feedback technique whereby group members are asked to respond anonymously to a questionnaire about their feelings toward the group, its openness, and the degree to which group goals were accomplished.[16] After the questions have been scored and discussed within the group, it may become apparent that the questionnaire was inadequate, and new questions may be added. Such a process allows the group to change its direction and agenda somewhat and become more productive.

Feedback, whether given directly to the entire group or to individual members, must be supportive and nonthreatening. The purpose of the feedback is to help increase the effectiveness of both the group and its individual members. Therefore, it must be positive in tone and given in such a fashion that individuals and groups can use it, e.g., suggesting to an individual that he is continually interrupting and cutting off another person (behavior) is quite different from telling him that he "should get along better with people" (attitude).

C. Improving Interdepartmental or Intergroup Relationships

Although planned conflict is at times necessary for highly differentiated, integrated organizations, intergroup polarization and conflict can lead to the emergence of strong negative stereotypes. Thus, such attitudes as "it was their fault," "they are holding us up," or "*we* can't get any cooperation out of anyone in *that* group" are dysfunctional for solving mutual problems and accomplishing joint tasks.

The basic strategy of OD techniques for improving interdepartmental and intergroup relationships is to foster group discussion about the antagonisms and misperceptions that exist and to determine whether the group members want to work on these problems. If the process is to be handled on an informal basis, the two groups are asked to meet and openly discuss their attitudes and perceptions. A process observer then helps each group come to a better understanding of the other's perceptions and attitudes and explore ways in which relationships can be improved.

A more fully developed, formalized approach to the problem includes the following steps:

1. Agreement is obtained between the two groups to work directly on improving mutual relationships.

2. Each group writes down its perceptions of both their own and the other group.

Infighting.

3. The two groups are then formally brought together, and a representative from each group presents the written perceptions obtained in the previous step. Only the two representatives may speak, since the primary objective is to make certain that the perceptions and attitudes are presented as accurately as possible and to avoid the defensiveness and hostility that might arise if the two groups were permitted to speak directly to each other.

4. The two groups separate, each armed with four sets of documents—two representing their own group's perceptions of itself and the other group, and two representing the other group's perceptions of itself and the other. At this point, a great number of discrepancies, misperceptions, and misunderstandings between the two show up.

5. The task of the group (almost always with the help of a process observer) is to analyze and review the reasons for the discrepancies. In other words, the process observer works hard at getting the group to work at understanding *how* the other group could possibly have arrived at the perception they have, e.g., "What actions on your part may have contributed to that set of perceptions?

How did they get that way?" The emphasis is on problem-solving rather than on defensiveness.

6. The two groups are again brought together to share both the discrepancies they have identified and their problem-solving analysis of the reasons for the discrepancies. Again, the focus is primarily on the behavior underlying the perceptions. At this point, either the formal representatives may be used or the groups can talk directly to each other.

7. If formal representatives are used, the next step is to allow more open discussion between the two groups, with the goal of reducing misperceptions and increasing intergroup harmony.

A more complete version of this more formal approach is described by Blake *et al.,* who report, for example, excellent results in getting such mutually antagonistic groups as union and management to become more cooperative with each other, thus considerably reducing industrial strife.[17]

D. Job Enrichment

This particular approach to OD is directed primarily toward increasing the meaningfulness of the worker's job by allowing him to have a greater share in the "ownership" of his job. Sirota and Wolfson define job enrichment as the redesigning of jobs to provide the worker with more opportunity to assume responsibility, autonomy, and closure (a complete job), as well as more timely feedback about his performance.[18] They list 11 obstacles to the success of job-enrichment programs, many of which arise from managerial assumptions about the job and the nature of the work force. Other obstacles are the time and managerial interaction necessary for the successful completion of such programs. One of the major stumbling blocks is the fact that the concept of job enrichment has taken on a "quasi-religious flavor and fervor"; as a result, highly prescribed and ritualized procedures have been established despite the evidence that a variety of approaches may be suitable.

Most tasks have three elements: planning (deciding how something is to be done), doing (the actual work), and evaluating (feedback about the planning and doing steps and taking the necessary corrective action). Many jobs, particularly at the clerical and "blue-collar" levels, are designed so that the worker is involved in the *doing,* but has little or no share in the planning and evaluating stages. Indeed, the specialization of "doing" has progressed so far that as one industrial engineer said recently, "If an assembly-line job takes more than three minutes to complete, the job should be given to two different people, each of whom has a minute-and-a-half cycle."

Myers uses a bowling analogy to explain these three elements.[19] The bowler plans his own work—he decides whether to throw a straight or a curve ball, throws the ball, and observes (evaluates) the results. If he has a "split," he replans his work and tries to knock down the remaining pins with his second ball. Bowling is interesting, it is work, and people *pay* to compete with themselves (improving one's score) and with others.

However, if this model is applied in an industrial setting, the elements change radically. First, an industrial engineer might decide that right-handed bowling is the "one best way." Next, the foreman would decide exactly how and when the worker would throw the ball. A screen placed between the bowler and the pins at the end of the alley would ensure that only the inspectors in the quality assurance department could evaluate the worker's performance. Occasionally, the bowler would get some feedback, usually negative, e.g., "You've done a lousy job and have to improve."

In this industrial model, the planning and evaluating functions have been separated from the doing, thereby greatly simplifying the job. Therefore, people must be *paid* to bowl, and the *doing* becomes uninteresting and unchallenging; it's no wonder that people "aren't motivated." Actually, following practices developed by Frederick Taylor at the turn of the century in the scientific management movement, many jobs in industry, especially those on production lines, have been "simplified" to such a high degree that workers find them repetitive and unchallenging.[20] Although work specialization has contributed much to industrialization, it is clear that in many ways the process has been carried to an extreme. Job enrichment, as Herzberg notes, is an attempt to reverse this oversimplification by providing workers with greater opportunities for achievement, responsibility, and personal growth through the redesign of the job itself.[21]

A number of other authors have described the increased morale, motivation, commitment, and productivity resulting from various approaches to job enrichment. For example, Huse and Beer found that productivity increased 84% when a multistation assembly line was abandoned in favor of having each worker assemble the complete product.[22] At the same time, rejects dropped from 23% to 1%, and absenteeism decreased from 8% to 1%. Similarly positive results of job enrichment are documented by Paul, Robertson, and Herzberg, who report on five studies of British technicians, design engineers, and sales representatives.[23] In his study of 18 experiments involving clerical and other personnel in the telephone company, Ford reports that the results of 17 were positive and one was neutral.[24] Ford also outlines a complete training program for managers installing job-enrichment programs.

The increasing importance of job enrichment is documented in a recent magazine article which describes the growing alienation of assembly-line workers and the corresponding concern about this problem.[25] As the president of one UAW local commented, "Job monotony? Five years ago the union didn't even discuss it." Now, however, it is an important issue, especially since in some plants, absenteeism is as high as 13%, as compared to 3% a few years ago.

Not all workers respond positively to job enrichment, however. For example, Ford reports that although 90% of the workers in his experiments responded positively, some 10-15% did not.[26] As he points out, this small percentage of workers should be allowed to continue working at "nonenriched" jobs.

Job enrichment need not always result in expanded job content. For example, Roche and MacKinnon show that more extensive use of meetings, greater worker participation in overall departmental improvement, etc., can also have powerful effects similar to those of expanding job content.[27] Here, however, the focus is on involving the "doers" in the planning and evaluating aspects.

E. Organization Confrontation Meetings

This approach, which was developed by Beckhard, is designed to mobilize the resources of the entire organization to identify problems, set priorities and action targets, and to begin working toward them. Beckhard says that confrontation meetings are

particularly appropriate in situations where an organization is in stress; where, for example, there is a new top management, where there has been a loss of a major customer, or where the organization is going into a new product or new area of business. Organizationally, this [meeting] is most appropriate where the top group is relatively cohesive but there is a gap between the top and the rest of the organization.[28]

Although the model described by Beckhard involves only the managerial and professional people in the organization, technicians, clerical personnel, and assembly workers can also benefit from this approach, which includes the following steps:

1. A group meeting of all those involved is scheduled and held in some appropriate place. The reason for the meeting is discussed, and the task is assigned. Usually, the task is to identify problems about both the organization's effectiveness and the work environment it provides.

2. Groups consisting of members representing all different parts of the organization are appointed. Thus, each group might have one or more members from manufacturing, quality assurance, finance, purchasing, and sales. However, for obvious reasons, except for top management a subordinate should not be in

the same group as his boss, and top management should be together in its own group. Groups can vary from 5 to 15 members, depending on the circumstances, available meeting places, size of the organization, etc.

3. The groups are told, and the point is stressed, that they are to be honest and open and to work hard at identifying the problems they see in the organization. It is also emphasized that no one will be criticized for bringing up problems and that the groups will be judged on their ability to identify problems.

4. The groups are given an hour or two to identify the problems facing the organization. Generally, an OD practitioner goes from group to group, encouraging them, again stressing that they are to be open about problem identification and, in general, assisting the groups with their task.

5. When the groups reconvene in a central meeting place, each group reports the problems that it has identified and sometimes offers solutions. Each group hears the reports of all the others so that a maximum amount of information is shared.

6. Either then or later, the master list of problems is broken down into categories by all those present, by the individual leading the session, or by the manager and his staff. This process is necessary for eliminating overlap and duplication and separating the problems according to functional or other appropriate areas.

7. Once the problems have been categorized, they are divided up and given to problem-solving groups whose composition differs from that of the original problem-identification groups. For example, all manufacturing problems may be handled by people in manufacturing. Or, since the systems approach emphasizes the interrelatedness of organizational problems, task forces representing appropriate cross-sections of the organization may be used. Depending on circumstances in the organization, either team leaders are assigned or the task force selects its own leader.

8. Each group is asked to establish priorities among the problems given to them, to develop a tactical plan of action for solving the problems, and to determine an approximate timetable for completing this phase of the process.

9. Each group then periodically reports its list of priorities and tactical plan of action to the larger group, which may, in turn, make suggestions about priorities, timetables, etc.

10. Schedules for periodic (usually monthly) follow-up meetings are established. At these sessions, the leader of each team reports to either the other team leaders or the group as a whole his group's progress and plans for future action. The formal establishment of such follow-up meetings ensures both continuing action and the modification of priorities and timetables as needed.

Although the first nine steps can be accomplished within a very short period of time, e.g., one day, it may be preferable to spread the process out over a longer period of time, e.g., steps 1 through 5 in one afternoon; steps 5, 6, and 7 several days later; and steps 8 and 9 the next week. This allows the problem-solving groups more time for problem categorization, decisions about group composition, and development of action plans. Despite the many variations possible with this approach, the results appear, in almost every case, to be quite dramatic in mobilizing the total resources of the organization for problem identification and solution.

F. Introducing Internal Growth and Change Ability*

Because OD is a new field of applied behavioral science, much of the technology is being brought into organizations by external consultants, many of whom are university based. Although most consultants are involved with helping their client systems respond more effectively to current problems, they also see as one of their major goals the transmission of their knowledge and skills to key members of the organization, especially those who can be called "internal consultants," or "change agents."

One of the OD practitioner's underlying values is to help organizations become more self-sufficient. Although the organization may be momentarily relieved by the consultant's diagnostic and intervention skills in solving current problems, the organization will either need repeated help in the future or will soon return to its previous, less effective state unless the change agent encourages organizational personnel to acquire the tools and skills needed to sustain the change efforts he has begun. For unless the change agent makes a deliberate effort to make his services unnecessary, one of the long-term objectives of organizational development—self-renewal—will not be met.

Changing the culture, work flow, and dynamics in a large organization requires several years. Blake and Mouton, Likert, and others suggest that five years is a reasonable period of time for implementing a program of planned change in a large organization, and their approaches call for the development of large numbers of internal change-agent resources to sustain OD programs.[29] Since his visits to the client system are short and/or infrequent, the change agent cannot undertake a major, long-term development effort without the help of knowledgeable and skilled internal organizational resources.

In a field study of the career development of internal OD change agents who were teamed with external consultants, Lewis found that the most success-

*This section was written by John W. Lewis, III.

ful consultants had as a central part of their intervention strategy the tutorial development of their internal organizational partners.[30] Change-agent development occurred through processes of joint diagnosis and interventions in the client system, whereby the "trainee" was able to observe and emulate the model furnished by the consultant. The most significant growth occurred within the pair relationship itself, to which OD values, concepts, and behaviors were central to the interaction.

In the most effective internal-external OD pairs, the internal change agent gradually becomes the central figure in the effort toward planned change. As the role of the external consultant becomes less central, he can devote more time to teaching the internal change agent and other key members of the system how to use him as a resource. Increasingly, his time and efforts are spent more in reviewing OD objectives and strategies which have been developed and implemented within the system and less in making direct interventions.

The achievement of long-term change in organizations is made more difficult by the transiency of people within them and the fluid structures and role relationships within the system. This phenomenon of our time creates stress on the stability of the organization, which must nevertheless be maintained through a long-term change effort. An implication for OD is that conflicts continue to erupt even after they have been ostensibly resolved. A management team that has been developed gains new or replacement members and must be developed again. Problem diagnoses that are valid today may be stale or even obsolete tomorrow. Consequently, organizations must have competent internal change agents to continuously monitor the health of the system, diagnose symptoms and problems accurately and rapidly, and provide the skills and resources needed to sustain effective planned change.

IV. PROBLEMS WITH ORGANIZATIONAL DEVELOPMENT

A. The Tendency to Ignore Structure and Technology

Reading through the OD literature gives one the strong impression that sensitivity training and pushing decision-making downward through the organization are equally effective in all organizations and for all occasions. However, the work of Fiedler, Perrow, and Lawrence and Lorsch clearly demonstrates that this is not the case. Organizational development in a stable industry is, or should be, quite different from the OD approach used in an uncertain environment. Bureaucracy and the bureaucratic approach do have their place, despite the talk of many OD theorists and practitioners to the contrary. When Morse and Lorsch compared organizational effectiveness in two types of industries (stable, e.g., container, and unstable, e.g., research and development laboratories), they found that managers can achieve a sense of competency and growth in a stable, highly bureaucratic industry, e.g., "We've got the rules here for everything from how much powder to use in cleaning the toilet bowls to how to cart a dead body out of the plant."[31] They also found that successful research and development laboratories had many fewer such rules and regulations, whereas those less successful were attempting to use a more bureaucratic approach.

B. The Tendency to Use One Approach for All Situations

Although each practitioner *knows* that there are different techniques and methodologies available, he tends to use the methods that he is most comfortable with and knows best, regardless of the client's actual problems and needs. This tendency is apparent in one of the leading OD journals, the *Journal of Applied Behavioral Science*. Bennis, in discussing the overreliance on sensitivity training as a primary tool for OD, remarks, "When you read the pages of this Journal [JABS] you cannot but think that we're a one-product outfit with a 100% foolproof patent medicine."[32] Similarly, Sperling criticizes the tendency of practitioners who prescribe team-building for every organization.[33] Other practitioners may prefer management by objectives (MBO) and enthusiastically recommend that their clients adopt this approach.

Currently, "job enrichment" is seen by some as the panacea for all organizational problems. It is a powerful tool, but not in all circumstances for all organizations. Fitzgerald, for example, raises questions about whether or not job enrichment is in fact a subtle form of manipulation rather than an attempt to put meaning back into work.[34] He also raises questions about participation at work, saying that it might well be true that "the girls on the carton-folding operation really have nothing to contribute [of importance] about running a container company."[35] Carlson, voicing similar concerns, concludes that it seems quite possible that the concept of job enrichment will ultimately succeed only "when it's linked with something that job enrichers deride as 'lower-order needs': in other words, money."[36]

C. OD may be Overly Prescriptive and Culture-Based

Lee describes modern human resource management (MHRM) as consisting of the overlapping concepts and theories of McGregor, Herzberg, Argyris, Likert, Blake and Mouton, and Maslow.[37] He traces the development of management thought from Machiavelli through Adam Smith, Frederick Taylor, Mary Parker Follett, James Mooney, and others, pointing out that each theorist wrote in a cultural context and that the theories have changed as the culture has changed

—that the theorists follow rather than precede cultural change. He believes that the large majority of today's behavioral theorists advocating MHRM are professors whose "strong autonomy needs and antiauthoritarian bias govern much of their research approach and ideal model building."[38] Lee lists a number of sources of resistance to MHRM, using such fields as sociology and anthropology, industrial case analyses, research in industrial administration, experimental applications in industry, social psychology, and applied behavioral science to explain the reasons for this resistance. His general conclusion is that resistance to MHRM occurs because the culture changes slowly and unevenly and therefore the uses and applications of MHRM will also change slowly and unevenly. His eight-step approach for managers makes maximum usage of our current knowledge, however meager, of human motivation and behavior.

D. Some Myths about OD

Sperling has listed six myths that are relevant in concluding our discussion of organizational development:[39]

1. OD requires top management involvement and commitment. This is not necessary, since the OD consultant may become unnecessarily involved in the power struggles and politics of the organization.

2. The OD consultant is manipulative. Sperling feels that this myth arises because it is difficult for the consultant to be articulate and clear about his work. In order to dispel this myth, the OD specialist must be as open and candid about his work as possible. Specific ground rules should be established that the OD man is working for the organization rather than for a specific boss.

3. There is one best way to manage. The currently popular myth is that the "participative" manager is the only good one. As you now know, successful managers use a wide variety of methods, depending on the situation and their subordinates.

4. OD represents "seduction of artifacts." According to this myth, some sort of "formal program" must be developed and, preferably, be put into a manual. In fact, however, OD work is too "messy" to be this formalized. Merely listing the managers who have gone through training programs or the percentage utilization of company training facilities is, in essence, emphasizing the *form* rather than the *substance* of OD.

5. OD is a "doctor-patient model." This myth asserts that the OD consultant is like other consultants, that is, the client presents the problem, and the OD practitioner provides the answers. Rather, the OD practitioner works under the assumption that managers are competent and want to do a good job and that the practitioner is a resource person rather than a prescriber of solutions.

6. Organizational Development is a Panacea. OD is *not* the solution to all organizational problems. It is not a substitute for good market research or the development of good new products or sound financial management. Although OD can be of tremendous help to the organization, it is not a panacea. Organizational development will have a tremendous impact on the traditional personnel department because of the manager's three basic resources—physical, financial, and human. The proper use of human resources may be the edge he really needs to make him outstanding.

V. CONCLUSIONS

In this chapter, we have distinguished between "organizational improvement" and "organizational development," the term preferred by behavioral scientists working in this field. In discussing the basic assumptions underlying OD, we stressed that an explicit part of OD is the conscious effort to provide opportunities for growth and development of human beings in the organizational setting.

A diagnostic approach to OD is required, since the OD change agent must develop an action-research model designed to fit the needs, objectives, and present values of the organization. Some of the successful tools and techniques which have been used successfully in OD are laboratory training, team-building, job enrichment, organizational confrontation meetings, improving interdepartmental relationships, and inducing internal growth and change.

Although there are many advantages to using OD, there are also some problems associated with this approach. Some OD practitioners tend to ignore structure and technology; some use one approach for all situations; and OD may be overly prescriptive and culture-based. Finally, there are several myths that have emerged concerning the nature and concepts of organizational development.

REVIEW

1. Should the primary job of OD be to improve the individual or to improve the environment in which he must function? Are these two aims mutually exclusive?

2. Is an internal change agent or outside consultant of more long-term benefit to a company? For a short-term problem?

3. The text lists a number of approaches to organizational development. From your own experience, list some organizations in which each of these approaches may be functional or dysfunctional. Discuss.

4. How are the concepts described in this chapter related to those discussed in Chapters 10 and 11?

5. With your knowledge of perception, communication, and group dynamics, what factors do you feel would contribute to a T-group's success? To its failure?

6. Under what conditions would organizational confrontation meetings be an effective device? An ineffective device?

7. Read one or two articles in the *Journal of Applied Behavioral Science* and critique them on the basis of your knowledge and learning to date.

8. From your own experience, describe an instance when an attempt to improve an organization (Little League, Boy Scouts, or job you have held) failed because of improper diagnosis of the problems.

9. Select an organization with which you are familiar and map out a strategy of organizational development by an OD consultant. Contrast this with a strategy that might be used by a Perspective I organizational-improvement consultant.

Critical Concepts

Organizational development (OD)

Organizational effectiveness versus efficiency

Change agent

Sensitivity training (T-group laboratory)

Team-building

Task versus maintenance roles

Job enlargement versus enrichment

Organizational confrontation meeting

Myths about OD

REFERENCES

1 Subcommittee on Priorities and Economy in Government, Joint Economic Committee, *American Productivity: Key to Economic Strength and National Survival* (Washington, D.C.: U.S. Government Printing Office, 1972), pp. 7, 9.

2 W. French, "Organization Development: Objectives, Assumptions and Strategies," *California Management Review,* XII, 2 (Winter 1969): 23–34.

3 W. G. Bennis, *Organization Development: Its Nature, Origins and Prospects* (Reading, Mass.: Addison-Wesley, 1969).

4 W. F. Whyte, *Money and Motivation* (New York: Harper & Row, 1955).

5 R. Beckhard, *Organization Development: Strategies and Models* (Reading, Mass.: Addison-Wesley, 1969).

6 C. Ferguson, "Coping with Organizational Conflict," *Innovation,* 29 (March 1972): 36–43.

7 *Ibid.,* p. 42.

8 D. L. Kegan, "Organizational Development: Description, Issues and some Research Results," *Academy of Management Journal.* 14 (1971): 453–464.

9 W. G. Bennis, *op. cit.*

10 E. Schein and W. Bennis, *Personal and Organizational Change Through Group Methods: The Laboratory Approach* (New York: John Wiley, 1965), p. 10. Reprinted by permission.

11 K. Lewin, "Field Theory in Social Science," in *Group Dynamics,* ed. D. Cartwright (New York: Harper & Row, 1951).

12 E. Schein and W. Bennis, *op. cit.;* L. P. Bradford, J. R. Gibb, and K. D. Benne, *T-Group Theory and Laboratory Methods* (New York: John Wiley, 1964).

13 R. J. House, "T-Group Education and Leadership Effectiveness: A Review of the Empiric Literature and a Critical Evaluation," *Personnel Psychology,* XX, 1 (Spring 1967): 1–33.

14 J. P. Campbell and M. D. Dunnette, "Effectiveness of T-Group Experiences in Managerial Training and Development," *Psychological Bulletin,* LXX (August 1968): 73–104.

15 R. T. Golembiewski, R. Munzenrider, A. Blumberg, S. B. Carrigan, and W. R. Mead, "Changing Climate in a Complex Organization: Interactions between a Learning Design and an Environment," *Academy of Management Journal,* 14, 4 (1971): 465–495.

16 E. Schein, *Process Consultation: Its Role in Organization Development* (Reading, Mass.: Addison-Wesley, 1969).

17 R. R. Blake, H. A. Shepard, and J. S. Mouton, *Managing Intergroup Conflict in Industry: Foundation for Human Behavior* (Houston: Gulf, 1964).

18 D. Sirota and A. Wolfson, "Job Enrichment: What are the Obstacles?" *Personnel,* 49, 3 (May-June 1972): 8–17.

19 M. S. Myers, *Every Employee a Manager* (New York: McGraw-Hill, 1970), p. 48.

20 F. W. Taylor, *The Principles of Scientific Management* (New York: Harper & Row, 1911).

21 F. Herzberg, "One More Time: How Do You Motivate Employees?" *Harvard Business Review,* 46, 1 (Jan.-Feb. 1968): 53–62.

22 E. Huse and M. Beer, "Eclectic Approach to Organizational Development," *Harvard Business Review,* 49, 5 (Sept.-Oct. 1971): 103–112.

23 W. J. Paul, K. B. Robertson, and F. Herzberg, "Job Enrichment Pays Off," *Harvard Business Review,* 41, 2 (March-April 1969): 61–78.

24 R. N. Ford, *Motivation Through the Work Itself* (New York: American Management Association, 1969).

25 "Boredom Spells Trouble on the Line," *Life,* September 1, 1972, pp. 31–38.

26 R. N. Ford, *op. cit.*

27 W. J. Roche and N. L. MacKinnon, "Motivating People with Meaningful Work," *Harvard Business Review,* 48, 3 (May-June 1970): 97–110.

28 R. Beckhard, *op. cit.,* p. 38. Reprinted by permission.

29 R. R. Blake and J. S. Mouton, *The Managerial Grid* (Houston, Gulf, 1964); R. Likert, *The Human Organization* (New York: McGraw-Hill, 1967).

30 J. W. Lewis, III, "Growth of Internal Change Agents in Organizations" (Ph.D. diss., Case-Western Reserve University, 1970).

31 J. Morse and J. Lorsch, "Beyond Theory Y," *Harvard Business Review,* 48, 3 (May-June 1970): 61–68.

32 W. G. Bennis, "The Case Study—I, Introduction," *Journal of Applied Behavioral Science,* 4, 2 (1968): 229.

33 K. Sperling, "Getting OD to Really Work," *Innovation,* 26 (Nov. 1971): 39–45.

34 T. Fitzgerald, "Why Motivation Theory Doesn't Work," *Harvard Business Review,* 49, 4 (July-August 1971): 37–44.

35 *Ibid.,* p. 43.

36 E. Carlson, "Job Enrichment: Sometimes It Works," *Wall Street Journal,* December 13, 1971.

37 J. Lee, "Behavioral Theory vs. Reality," *Harvard Business Review,* 49, 2 (March-April 1971): 20–28.

38 *Ibid.,* p. 28.

39 K. Sperling, *op. cit.*

13

TOWARD
AN
INTEGRATED
SYSTEMS
THEORY
OF
ORGANIZATIONAL
DEVELOPMENT

I. INTRODUCTION

In Chapters 10, 11, and 12, we discussed current approaches to organizational development from the formal, flow, and human perspectives. Throughout the text, however, we have stressed that the organization is a total system of interrelated and interdependent subsystems and that the three different perspectives represent somewhat artificial and arbitrary ways of looking at organizations. We have already pointed out the vital importance of the linkage among organizational subsystems; a change in one subsystem causes changes, stresses, and strains in all of the other subsystems.

In this chapter, we show how the three perspectives fit together and can be used as an integrated theory of organizational development. First, we reexamine the concepts of organizational competence and describe some of the characteristics of a competent organization, together with some problems of attaining an optimal balance among the subsections of the system. We then list a number of recommendations for organizational development from a systems point of view. Finally, we present two case studies which illustrate how these recommendations have been used in real-life situations.

II. THE COMPETENT ORGANIZATION

Earlier, we said that the competent organization is both effective and efficient. Organizational efficiency can be defined as the amount of resources an organization must use in order to produce a unit of output, and organizational effectiveness is the degree to which a particular organization actually realizes its goals and objectives. In this section, we consider the characteristics of the competent organization as well as some of the forces that reduce organizational competence.

A. Characteristics

Schein, one of the authors who have addressed themselves to this topic, uses the term "organizational health" to describe organizational competence.[1] We, however, prefer the term "organizational competence," which includes the following elements:

1. Adaptability. This refers to the organization's ability to react quickly and to solve problems in the face of both external and internal changes.

2. A Sense of Identity. Organizational members have a clear understanding of the direction of the organization, its goals and purposes, and the extent to which the perceptions of the individual members coincide.

3. Capacity to Test Reality. A number of studies have shown that organizations need to considerably increase their ability to test reality and to sense the changing demands of the organization and the environment. This topic was discussed in some detail in Chapter 8.

4. The Need for Integration. Although the organization needs to be divided into subsystems, some mechanism must exist for ensuring that the subsystems work together in an integrative fashion.

5. Simultaneous Consideration of the Three Different Perspectives.
Throughout the text, we have repeatedly stressed that the competent organization must always bear in mind the interaction of the formal, flow, and human perspectives. Optimal organizational effectiveness and efficiency can be attained only when all three perspectives are considered concurrently. Similarly, organizational goals and objectives must be integrated with the needs and goals of employees at all levels within the organization.

B. Problems in Attaining and Maintaining Organizational Competence

Perhaps the biggest single obstacle to organizational competence is finding and maintaining an optimal balance for the organization at any particular point in time, as was discussed in Chapter 8. To Clark, the adaptive organization is one which is able to adequately handle the need for balance with the corresponding need for growth and change.[2] For example, the manufacturing department must strive for a stable, relatively unchanging production schedule so that costs can be reduced, and the sales department must be aware of changes in this schedule so that they can make an early delivery to an important customer. In this case, the manufacturing department serves as a reactive force to protect the status quo —the manufacturing schedule—whereas the sales department is a proactive force trying to bring about change in order to please an important customer. Both functions are necessary in a competent organization.

Clark notes that we sometimes confuse these two forces by failing to make the proper distinction between them. He cites the example of a group of women production workers who contributed about 120% profit to the firm through their effectiveness and efficiency. Their productivity had increased about 300% in two years, even though they were not on an incentive system. The openness, freedom, and trust within the group enabled them to solve problems that outside "experts" had been unable to solve.

However, top management and engineers became dissatisfied with the girls' freedom to switch around on jobs, design and operate their own test equipment, etc. As a result, their foreman was promoted to another job, and a new foreman was brought in to "really set the place straight."

Clark extensively quotes a new engineering executive who also had just been brought in. The executive couches his language in proactive terms, although it is clear from the interviews that his attitude is highly reactive. In essence, this manager says that since the girls have far too much responsibility, he will have to really "take the place over," remove the girls' testing and inspecting responsibilities, and make certain that every operation will be under close surveillance by engineering (despite a 120% increase in profitability and a 300% increase in productivity).

This example illustrates three things. First, Theory X assumptions about people, particularly production workers, are deeply embedded in many managers, who refuse to modify these perceptions and assumptions even in the face of such evidence as a 300% increase in productivity in two years. Second, this example reinforces the idea that a change in one subsystem causes stresses and strains through the entire system. Third, this case illustrates an overreliance on obsolete concepts about the role of the manager. As we discuss in the next chapter, structural and interpersonal changes must go hand in hand; the very climate of an organization must be changed if some of the developmental changes are to work.

Another barrier to organizational competence is the common fallacy that people resist change as such. This is not true; when people clearly recognize that the change is beneficial to them, they welcome it. Few students resist a professor's changing their grade from "B" to "A." Few managers resist a 25% increase in salary. Rather, what people resist is the real or imagined *threat* implicit in change. Thus, middle management may resist computerized integrated management information systems because they fear that they will lose control of their own data base and that the information will be used against them in a punitive fashion.

Yet the competent organization must be able to quickly accommodate itself to the rapidly increasing pace of change while still maintaining the status quo where this is necessary. Many authors feel that organizations that are not adaptive and flexible will quickly become obsolete and, indeed, may go out of business. The validity of this belief is evidenced by the fact that in less than a year, three major corporations (Penn-Central, Rolls-Royce, and Lockheed) either went bankrupt or were on the brink of bankruptcy.

III. USING SYSTEMS THEORY TO PROVIDE AN INTEGRATED APPROACH TO ORGANIZATIONAL DEVELOPMENT

In this section, we build on the material in the three preceding chapters to provide you with some guidelines for integrating the three perspectives for a more unified, comprehensive approach to organizational development. However, since no firmly established theory of organizational change exists, our recommendations must be regarded as tentative, especially since the field of organizational development is expanding so rapidly.

A. Broad, Organizational Approaches

Such factors as organizational design, informational flow analysis, task forces and temporary groups, and levels of organizational intervention and chance can be used in the five integrated approaches presented here.

1. Use of "Systems Theory" in Organizational Design. Any organizational system (industrial, service, nonprofit, or other) must be carefully designed to fit its environment and technology. The work of Lawrence and Lorsch and Perrow has demonstrated that there is no "one best way" to design an organization as a total system. Although formal research on organizational design is in its infancy, the evidence is clear that a contingency theory of systems must be applied. An organizational structure and design that "fit" a business making glass bottles (stable environment), for example, must be different from the design for a firm manufacturing plastics or electronic instruments (unstable environment). Recent work on applying these concepts to such other types of organizations as municipal governments and educational systems is described by Lorsch and Lawrence.[3] Clearly, the real research on organizational structure and design is just beginning, and within the new few years, we will know much more than we do now about systems theories of organizational structure and design. We do know now, however, that the pattern of differentiation and integration *within* specific organizations must be modified to fit the internal and external environment of the firm.

We also know, as we discussed earlier, that the concept of line and staff may well be obsolete for a systems approach. Indeed, in discussing different types of organizations, Etzioni concludes that in a professional organization, e.g., a university, the traditional line-staff organization is reversed inasmuch as the real decisions are most frequently made by the faculty and that the traditional "line" organization, e.g., the president, deans, and department chairmen, serve primarily to provide resources to the faculty, or staff.[4]

2. Use of Systems Theory in Information and Related Flows. The use of a systems approach to improve information flow may result in a redesigning of the organization. But although major advances in organizational improvement have resulted from the use of models and the computer *within* particular departments, the results have generally been disappointing when such approaches

Plant operations such as gas preparation, synthesis, and other processes can be monitored from this central control panel. (Photograph courtesy W. R. Grace & Co.)

have been applied across departments and organizations. Deardon points out, for example, that although every organization has a number of formal and informal information systems, it is impossible to design, develop, and implement an integrated, computerized management information system (MIS).[5] The creation of such a "supersystem" requires the input of too many principles and details, even though such concepts are being advocated in many business schools. The University of Minnesota, for example, has both a Ph.D. program and a research center in MIS.

One of the major difficulties is that organizations rarely make a careful analysis of their information and related flows. Mockler describes a case in which a large mail-order house carefully analyzed its information and paper flow prior to purchase of a computer.[6] As a result of its thorough self-analysis, the firm reorganized itself to *fit* the needed information and materials flow. Mockler points out that superficially, at least, the organization looked much the same as it had before but that in reality, there was a strong shift from an "authority-centered" to a "systems," job-centered organization. Reorganization also caused major adjustments to be made in the grouping of functions *within* departments and in the daily working arrangements *among* departments.

The benefits of work-flow analysis are illustrated by a consultant's work for the Bureau of Vital Statistics in a large municipality. The organization was designed to accomplish three basic tasks—receive and issue birth certificates, receive and issue death certificates, and report vital statistics to the state government. However, the Bureau was six months late in getting these data to the state and two months tardy in issuing birth certificates.

The director of the Bureau requested three new employees to supplement his twelve-man staff, but his request was denied. In order to help justify his plea for additional people, he then sought the help of a consultant retained by the organization. Subsequently, they decided to use documents published by the U.S. Government Printing Office for studying paper-work flow. The employees (all of whom were under Civil Service) carried out the actual work, with a small amount of pretraining. Within a few weeks, the work load had been considerably reduced so that the average time lag for sending out a birth certificate was only two days. Two employees eventually transferred out of the Bureau (only because better jobs opened up), and it was found that only nine of the ten remaining people were really needed to carry out the Bureau's work. In other words, through proper analysis, the Bureau was able to reduce its work load, which resulted in a 25 percent reduction in its work force.

3. Use of Systems Theory to Combine the Formal and Informal Organization. Throughout the text, we have discussed the concepts of formal and informal organizations and groups. This approach is less effective in the more stable, bureaucratic organization than in the less stable, nonprogrammable organizations, as was indicated in Fig. 11.2 (p. 277). The use of informal structures in organizational development can be called the "decision center" approach, and it emphasizes redesigning the organization to improve the interrelatedness of the formal, flow, and human perspectives.

The use of decision centers includes the following steps:

a) Determine "natural" work units. First, the work flow must be analyzed to identify the interrelatedness and interdependence of work tasks and units, irrespective of the existing "formal" organizational structure. Such "natural" work units can be grouped together within the existing formal structure to capitalize on the fact that certain segments of the work are more closely related than others.

b) Develop work team "decision centers." Once natural work units have been identified, the members of those groups should be brought together geographically to form the new, natural work teams. The teams should consist of six to fifteen members, depending on the work unit, the technology, and other situational constraints. In manufacturing, for example, such a decision center might consist of highly interrelated task groups in the manufacture, assembly, and inspection of a particular product. In purchasing, such a work team, or decision center, might consist of those involved with purchasing, scheduling, inventory control, and expediting for a particular product line.

Individual interaction and decision-making responsibility within the decision center should be maximized within the constraints of the situation. For example, although the decision center may not have the option of deciding to make "X" number of widgets and "Y" number of gadgets during the month, it can have the opportunity to determine its own daily schedule. Similarly, individuals within the decision center should be given the opportunity to "grow into" as much responsibility, challenge, and discretion as they are capable of handling; at the same time, it is wise to leave room to "back off" if the process moves too rapidly.

c) Provide for rapid communications flow. The flow of communications and information is both internal and external to the decision center. Rapid internal communication facilitates work accomplishment: work gets done better when people know what they are doing and why; when there is frequent and open interchange of ideas; when feedback is nonpunitive; and when group members trust one another and the accuracy of their information. For instance, in a manufacturing decision center, the frequent interaction of team members can be maximized by making sure that members working on one stage of fabrication or assembly are close enough, geographically, to others working on other stages of production so that mistakes or errors can be quickly detected and corrected through rapid feedback. Whenever possible, data and solutions to problems should be generated in common so that group conflict can be avoided.

Proper external communication is needed to ensure that the group members get the information they need in the time span, form, and shape in which they need it. Too often, information goes to the wrong person for the wrong reason. Frequently, a higher-level manager receives information which should have been sent to individuals within the decision center. For example, it might be more appropriate for customers' comments about product quality to go directly to the appropriate decision center rather than to management.

4. Greater Use of Task Forces and Temporary Groups. Formal and informal organizations can be combined through the use of decision centers, which remain relatively stable as a part of the formal organizational design. Industry and business are also making greater use of less stable groups—"task forces" or "temporary groups"—that are formed to handle a specific problem or problems and are then disbanded. The growing use of terms such as "product" or "project manager" illustrates the increasing use of such temporary groups. The use of such groups occurs most frequently in organizations with relatively unstable environments, although their use in stable organizations is increasing.

The accelerating pace of change will require much more extensive use of such temporary groups, frequently under the leadership of a product or program manager. Bennis predicts the growing use of such temporary groups and task forces, especially in enterprises that are in a state of rapid technological change or which exist in an uncertain or unclear environment.[7] Although his work was done independently, his recommendations appear to closely parallel the work of Lawrence and Lorsch in their description of the work and role of the integrator.

The use of temporary groups or task forces has several important advantages.

a) Greater use of the human resources of the organization. If the members of the task force are chosen carefully, they will represent the resources necessary to get the job done. For example, one of the authors is currently working with an organization using such an approach for special projects. There is a chairman, or "integrator," for each such project or program, and members of the task force represent key areas of the organization involved with the project. A particular group might consist of engineers, production workers, representatives from purchasing, etc. When the task force meets, the "integrator" reports on the present status of the project and as problems come up and are identified, specific individuals are assigned to begin work on the problem. For example, at one point vendor problems delayed delivery of a vital part to the organization until four days before the product had to be shipped. A key production worker learned of the problem two weeks in advance and began to make plans for ensuring that he could get his job done in time. He therefore requested that a worker from another area of the plant be a consultant for at least half a day after the part arrived, and the production worker was thus able to get his job done on time.

In another organization, $250,000 had been spent in three months in an effort to solve a problem on a product that would be sold for $250,000. It was imperative to ship the product, even at a considerable loss, since the customer also purchased many other products. Yet in all that time, the key people involved had never met as a group to even discuss the problem. As a result, each member of the production effort was able to "cast the blame" on the others, since a mutual problem-solving, task force approach had not been used.

b) Greater involvement of the personnel involved. The involvement of the individual members of a temporary team is usually extremely high. Their motivation comes from the "authority of the task" rather than from the "authority of the boss." Generally, temporary teams work harder and put in longer hours than they do on their regular jobs.

c) Greater ability to innovate and consider new approaches. In the more stable work group, there is a greater need for maintaining the "status quo." However, task forces more readily accept new, innovative approaches than do more stable, permanent groups.

d) Greater effect on the major, more permanent organization. By bringing together representatives from various parts of the organization, there is a greater likelihood that the solutions and recommendations arrived at by the temporary group will be accepted by the larger organization, since the proponents of the change or new approach act as "ambassadors" for the change and are more effective in combating the status quo. For example, a committee was assigned to consider a specific problem in a particular university. Representatives were brought together from all parts of the organization, including some who had been the strongest proponents of the status quo. During their deliberations, the committee consulted with a number of people within the university. After they had written their recommendations, the committee held a public hearing for open discussion of the problems involved and the reasons for their recommendations. As a result, changes which had been bitterly resisted by the larger organization for at least ten years now took place within three months.

e) Increased communication and information flow. When task forces are properly constituted and used, the lateral flow of information is highly increased. The early identification of problems that must be solved to ensure successful completion of the project is made possible by use of a task force whose members come from every key area of the organization. Although some authors have questioned whether such temporary groups can be successful, Fine has shown that given the proper conditions, they can be effective and do not require more enduring, long-term work relationships.[8]

5. Use of Systems Theory in Organizational Intervention and Change.
Harrison lists five intervention strategies along the dimension of "depth," which he defines as the extent of *overt emotional involvement* of the individual in the change process.[9] These five levels can be used for a systems approach to organizational development.

a) Operations analysis. This level is concerned with the roles and functions that are to be performed in the organization rather than with individual values and motivation. This strategy for change focuses on specifying tasks, resources, and power and also defining jobs for individuals and groups in the organization.

This first level of organizational development depends on the structural design of the organization and can be applied by any organization to ensure that its structure fits its environment. If the organization is properly designed to fit its environment, individuals are more likely to get a great deal of job satisfaction and sense of competence from performing the job. As Morse and Lorsch indicate, individuals can be highly motivated and have a feeling of competence and achievement when there is a good organization task "fit," even though the organization may be highly bureaucratic in nature.[10]

b) Evaluating and controlling individual performance and behavior. This second level deals with the selection, placement, training, counseling, and appraisal of individual employees. Here, the focus is on observable performance rather than on the individual's personal characteristics. Attempts to bring about change can include use of such external rewards and punishments as salary increases, promotions, or organizational transfers. Management by objectives is another illustration of this type of strategy for change.

This strategy of intervention and organizational development is probably applicable to all types of organizations, although it is generally most useful in stable organizations in which external rewards are of major importance. This strategy may be "wasted" on research and development organizations, for example, in which the scientists already have a high degree of freedom and autonomy, as was discussed in Chapter 10.

c) Concern with work style. At this "depth" the concern is with work performance and the method, style, and processes by which it is achieved. This level includes such "human" factors as how the individual does or does not delegate authority, the extent of his competition or collaboration with others on work-related issues, and how and if he communicates information to others.

Intervention at this level involves attempts to change work behavior and working relationships among individuals and/or groups, and this includes the satisfaction or dissatisfaction which organizational members derive from others' work behavior. Such intervention frequently requires intergroup or interpersonal bargaining and negotiating and is likely to result in changes in either the formal or informal group norms about communication, collaboration, and methods for resolving present and future conflicts. Such intervention is probably less effective in the more rigid, bureaucratic structures than in less stable environments in which rules, procedures, and policies are not rigidly defined and in which the informal organization plays a greater part in the processes of integration and work flow, as was discussed in Chapter 11.

d) Interpersonal relationships. Harrison's fourth level of overt emotional involvement focuses on the attitudes, feelings, and perceptions which members of the organization have about one another, i.e., their warmth or coldness toward one another and their awareness and expression of such feelings as trust, suspicion, rejection, and acceptance. This is the first intervention level at which the personal feelings of organization members are a direct focus of the intervention strategy. It is at this level that laboratory training and similar approaches can be used to bring these feelings out into the open and work on them.

This strategy is most appropriate for highly differentiated organizations in which authority is decentralized and the subsystems have a fair amount of latitude to deal rapidly and flexibly with frequent changes in the environment. This strategy is also effective with individuals who do not receive immediate feedback, work on unique tasks which cannot easily be evaluated by comparison to others, and who have job security, unique skills, or the opportunity to move easily from one organization to another.

e) Intrapersonal analysis. At Harrison's deepest level of intervention, the consultant works with the individual on his deeper values and concerns about his own identity, experience, and competence, helping him to increase the range of experience he can bring into awareness and begin to cope with. Thus, the intervention strategy may be on either a one-to-one or group basis, e.g., marathon laboratory sessions or task-group therapy. This strategy of intervention occurs when the individual is not dependent on economic and bureaucratic pressures, but instead seeks more internal and self-determined rewards to increase his sense of autonomy, competence, and worth.

In concluding his analysis of depth strategies, Harrison suggests two criteria for choosing the most appropriate interventional depth:
1. to intervene only at the level necessary to produce lasting solutions to the problems facing the individual and/or the organization; and
2. to use a level of intervention strategy at which the resources and the energy of the organization can be directed most appropriately to change and problem-solving.

Figure 13.1 shows Harrison's intervention strategies superimposed on our typology of system design according to environment, structure, and task. An organization or its subsystems at the right-hand side of the continuum is highly stable and bureaucratic, and therefore the depth of intervention strategy may remain relatively superficial. Thus, laboratory training and similar approaches might not be appropriate at this stage. As one moves across the continuum, deeper levels of intervention may become more appropriate, including such approaches as job enrichment, team-building, and other strategies discussed in

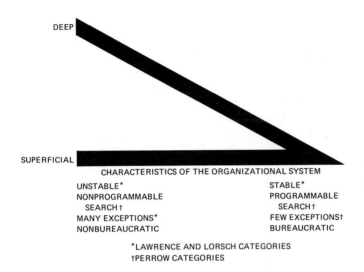

DEEP

SUPERFICIAL

CHARACTERISTICS OF THE ORGANIZATIONAL SYSTEM

UNSTABLE*	STABLE*
NONPROGRAMMABLE	PROGRAMMABLE
SEARCH †	SEARCH †
MANY EXCEPTIONS*	FEW EXCEPTIONS†
NONBUREAUCRATIC	BUREAUCRATIC

*LAWRENCE AND LORSCH CATEGORIES
†PERROW CATEGORIES

Figure 13.1. *Depth of intervention and change strategy.*

Chapter 12. For organizations at the far left-hand side of the continuum, such approaches as tighter rules and more bureaucratization may well be dysfunctional, just as "pushing decision-making down" and laboratory training may be dysfunctional at the far right side of the continuum.

B. Individualized Approaches

The two approaches described in this section focus more on the individual as an integrative factor in organizational development.

1. Use of Systems Theory in Formal Leadership Style. In Chapter 6, we concluded our discussion of leadership with Fiedler's contingency theory, according to which different types of leadership style are effective, i.e., result in high group performance, under different conditions—the quality of leader-member relationships, the amount and degree of task structure, and the amount of the leader's position power.[11] In general, task-oriented leadership is associated with high performance under extreme conditions, whereas relationship-oriented leadership is more effective under middle-range conditions.

In their study of more and less successful organizations at either end of the continuum, Morse and Lawrence found that task-centered leadership is more effective, but that the leadership style must vary.[12] In the high-producing container industry, for example, top managerial behavior must be directed toward the task and enforcing specific rules and procedures; in the high-producing research laboratory, on the other hand, leadership style must be directed more toward the individual than toward enforcing depersonalized rules and procedures. This leadership style emphasizes coordinating and focusing the group's attention on the overall task to be performed.

Vroom found that people who have weak independence needs really do not want to be, nor are they, influenced by the opportunity to participate in making decisions.[13] By contrast, persons who either have strong needs for independence or are more egalitarian are more highly motivated in their performance by the opportunity to participate. Similarly, a person's personality may influence his choice of a job. For example, Vroom found that truck drivers want to be told by the dispatcher where to go on their next trip, whereas package handlers become more involved and more highly motivated when they can participate in the decision-making process.

Perrow's belief that the type of leadership required depends on the technology and structure of the organization is depicted in Fig. 10.1, p. 253.[14] By combining the variables of technology, task, and organizational structure, he concludes that supervision in firms with few rules or known solutions and many exceptions, such as research and development firms, must be flexible and polycentralized, whereas supervision in organizations with few exceptions and many rules or known solutions needs to be formal and bureaucratic.

These studies clearly indicate the need for both a systems approach to leadership and a leadership style that varies according to the situation. Fiedler points out that even within particular subsystems of the organization, the situation may vary and therefore require different types of leadership style.[15] He notes, for example, that the manager of a fairly routine operation can prescribe well-defined rules for his subordinates to follow. However, when a crisis occurs, the leader is likely to call together his staff for a conference, at which time his behavior becomes more nondirective and permissive until the crisis has passed. The reverse of this procedure occurs in a research planning group, whose leader under normal conditions is permissive and encourages his subordinates to participate, speak up, give suggestions, and offer criticisms. However, when a specific research plan has been developed with the full participation of the subordinates, the manager becomes more directive in accordance with the more highly structured situation. As Fiedler remarks, "Woe be to the assistant who decides to be creative by changing the research instructions."[16]

Fiedler thus stresses that the appropriateness of leadership style depends on the situation, although at the same time it may be that a person's preferred style may make him a better manager in certain types of operations. Etzioni echoes this point of view by advocating that the situation, rather than people, should be changed.[17] He notes that $88,000 is spent per "life saved" in driver training (an attempt to change people), whereas $87 per car is now spent on safety devices such as seat belts and other devices, which do a far more effective job of saving lives. In short, "Solving social problems by changing people is apparently less productive than accepting people and changing their circumstances instead."[18] Since, as Hersey and Blanchard note, there is a great deal of mobility if the manager is a "producer," it may be necessary for the organization to make a careful assessment of his *styles* as well as his *capabilities* before assigning him a "permanent" position in an organization.[19]

In conclusion, then, leadership style, when considered from a systems point of view, must be varied to fit the situation, the attitudes and feelings of subordinates, and the amount of power that the leader has. As Schein has said:

The most successful manager must be a good diagnostician and value a sense of enquiry . . . He may be highly directive at one time and with one employee but very nondirective at another time. He may use pure engineering criteria in the design of some jobs, but let a worker group completely design another set of jobs. In other words, he will be flexible, and will be prepared to accept a variety of interpersonal relationships, patterns of authority and psychological contracts.[20]

In other words, it is the formal leader who has direct control over the psychological contract, and his style of leadership must reflect the circumstances, the task, the motivation of subordinates, and the relationships among these variables. Since the manager's role is so critical, it may be appropriate to consider either putting the leader in a job that fits his style or reconstructing his job to better fit his style rather than trying to fit the leader to a specific job.

2. Use of Systems Theory in Management Development. In Chapter 7 we stated that in many organizations, whether stable or unstable, the manager spends most of his time as a participant in the lateral work-flow process rather than as a supervisor. We also cited research which confirms that the better managers do become more involved in the work-flow process.

However, since most management texts stress the manager's supervisory functions, little has been done to help him either understand his vital linking function or become fully effective in peer-level relationships. Therefore, the OD practitioner's use of such techniques as sensitivity training and team-building is a direct attempt to help managers become more effective with others in the network of lateral relationships. But this is not sufficient. Universities, personnel departments, and outside training agencies need to place much more emphasis on helping the current manager to understand and deal with his linking role; and college students in management programs should be given much more understanding about group behavior and how to work and deal more effectively with their peers.

IV. APPLICATION OF THE SYSTEMS APPROACH TO ORGANIZATIONAL DEVELOPMENT

In the preceding sections of this chapter, we presented some characteristics of the effective and efficient organization and listed a number of recommendations for using systems theory to provide an integrated approach to organizational development. The validity of these recommendations is demonstrated in the two case studies which follow.

A. Non-Linear Systems

For about eight years, Non-Linear Systems had been a successful manufacturer of digital converters, electronic test equipment, and other complex electronic devices. The company was organized along conventional Perspective I lines with such "line-staff" functions as engineering, manufacturing, and purchasing. However, in the early 1960s, Andrew Kay, president of the company, became dissatisfied with this arrangement because he wanted to "put more meaning into work for the individual employees."[21]

Combining the three perspectives

Taking a "systems approach" to organizational design, he brought in several consultants representing diverse backgrounds and approaches; using their advantages as well as his own intuition, Kay decided to redesign the company's structure to better fit the firm's unstable, rapidly changing environment.

Choosing an appropriate level of organizational intervention

Figure 13.2 gives a simplified version of the organization's "before and after" designs. Although there have been some changes and modifications of the new design in the past ten years, it has remained essentially unchanged.

Use of systems theory in organizational design

Before the change, the engineering department was subdivided in the traditional manner into specialties in mechanical design, electrical design, etc. Under the new

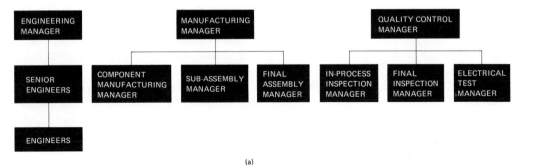

(a)

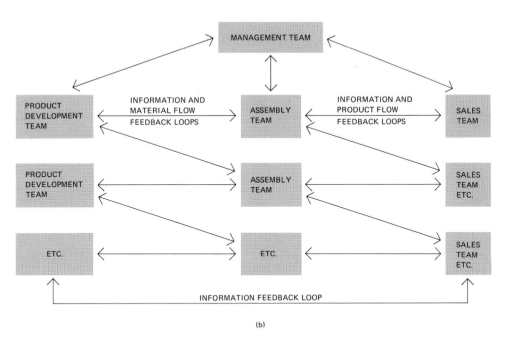

(b)

Figure 13.2. *Non-Linear Systems' organizational design: (a) before, and (b) after the change process.*

design, engineering project teams were established, each of which contained all the resources—designers, engineers, machinists, draftsmen and, when necessary, production workers—needed to design and develop a complete product. In effect, after the management group requested the development of a particular product, the project team was given responsibility for designing it, and the design engineer in charge of the project was allowed to purchase some experimental parts directly, without having to go through the normal purchasing-agent channels.

At the time of the reorganization, there were about 12 such teams, each consisting of 10 to 12 members. Each team worked independently, but was able to draw on the resources of the total organization as necessary. Mr. Kay reports that this was difficult for some members of the organization to accept, since this approach highlighted individual capability and acceptance of responsibility.

The assembly-line operation was broken down into eight or nine teams of six or seven workers. Each team had its own work area—a 12-by-20 foot cubicle.

Use of systems theory in information and related flows

When prototypes were developed by the design team, some were given to the marketing teams for display and sale to customers. The assembly teams were also given a prototype model and in essence told to "make it like this one." Rather than working according to the highly detailed instructions and rigid job descriptions typical of most assembly-line operations, each team was free to decide how the work load would be shared. Individual job enrichment as well as the team concept were encouraged, and the assembly team was allowed to assemble, inspect, sign, and pack its own instruments for distribution to customers. Inspection of the product by "outside" inspectors was limited to areas mandated by government requirements.

Sales teams assigned to different regions of the country were freed from having to write detailed reports. Instead, they were encouraged to use the telephone for direct, personal communication with the plant, including the assembly teams.

To lessen status differences among employees, all were put on salary, thus making labor costs fixed and known. Indeed, by reducing the complexity of the pay system, the organization was able to correspondingly reduce its costs of preparing the payroll by having it done at the bank.

1. Integration of the Three Perspectives

a) Structural-design perspective. The reorganization was undertaken so that the company would better fit its changing, unstable, and complex environment (electronics). The new organizational structure was extremely flat, consisting of 12 product development teams. Decision-making was pushed downward in the organization, whereas formerly it had been more centralized at the top.

b) Flow perspective. The new organizational structure resulted in great improvement in information, material, and related flows. For example, rather than having specialized groups in engineering, all the people directly involved in the design and development of a new product were on the same team and in the same geographical location. This immediately reduced communications blockages between such specialized groups as the electrical and mechanical sections. Since all aspects of the manufacturing process were represented on one team, there were few communication difficulties between the development and assembly teams or within each team. Since the sales teams (assigned by geographic area) were encouraged to call the plant directly and could call the appropriate people, the information flow between sales and the project and assembly teams was materially improved. Direct communication by telephone increased the speed, accuracy, and amount of feedback.

c) Human perspective. The new design merged the formal and informal structure of the organization. Furthermore individual workers received much more satisfaction from involvement in their jobs through the use of such approaches as increased individual responsibility, team-building, job enrichment, etc. The psychological contract clearly changed from a rational/legal contract to a more normative one. After all personnel had been put on salary, increases were relatively large, but usually occurred only for exceptional performance, promotions, or similar reasons.

The president of the company points out that although this is participative management, it is also "tough" management in that high, difficult goals are established and maintained. Incompetent performers are discharged.

2. Evaluation of Results

a) Managerial time. Because of the increased emphasis on group and individual decision-making and responsibility, managerial time was freed for more long-range planning. As the individuals and groups gained proficiency, they were consistently able to expand their ability to assemble a wider variety of products of higher quality in a shorter period of time.

b) Productivity. The design change was made quickly. As a result, although productivity initially dropped, it was back to normal within a few months and continued to climb until it leveled off to about 40% above what it had been prior to the change. Since the production workers were more highly involved in their jobs and got prompt feedback from the field, customer complaints dropped off sharply.

c) Employee morale and commitment. When manufacturing workers were put on salary, they were given the same sick-leave benefits as management people, and their absenteeism rate dropped from about eight percent to about one percent. Avoidable turnover became nearly nonexistent. Marked improvement was seen in employee morale and commitment, as evidenced by not only the turnover and absentee reduction, but also more requests for training and greater involvement in the task. One difficulty has been noted in this area, however. Some of the attempts at individual job enrichment went too far—some workers became discouraged when it took three weeks or longer to assemble an instrument. Therefore, for the more complex instruments, team effort has been substituted for individual job enrichment. The workers themselves decide on the size of the segment they wish to handle.

B. Plant X

This study involved extensive changes in the flow and human perspectives. Plant X had been in existence for three years and had consistently lost money (as is to be expected for a time in most new subsidiaries or plants). However, top management was becoming concerned because the earnings rate was not improving, and a consultant was brought in to diagnose the situation and make recommendations.

Use of systems theory to determine depth of intervention

Within a month, the consultant had recommended that the top management team spend several days away from the plant to build a management team that could work more effectively together. Their first task at the off-site session was to identify plant objectives. Their second task was to discuss the role expectations that each member of the management group had of each other member. As might be expected, this exercise

Use of systems theory in management development

revealed a large number of differing role expectations. Each job required three to four hours of discussion to iron out the differing and conflicting role expectations to the satisfaction of everyone in the group. Next, the group redefined organizational goals, since the role discussions had indicated that this was now necessary. The redefinition of organizational goals resulted in a much sharper and clearer set of goals than had resulted previously. Finally, the group listed problems facing the organization and developed ways of solving these problems.

Use of systems theory in formal leadership style

During the next several months following his arrival in April, the consultant worked with the management staff on establishing leadership styles more appropriate to their particular jobs. It became apparent that although top management had improved their working relationships, conflicts and misunderstandings still existed at lower levels in the organization, thereby reducing the effectiveness of not only information and other flows, but also the morale of the individuals and work groups. As a result, it was decided to try to improve both the flow and human perspectives simultaneously by building a more cohesive work force.

Choosing the level of organizational intervention

It was decided to use a modification of the organizational confrontation meeting (described in Chapter 12) to accomplish both of these objectives simultaneously. In August the plant was shut down for an afternoon, and teams were established to identify plant problems. Every member of the organization excluding top management was involved. In order to achieve the greatest mix, each team had at least one representative from each department and included all levels of personnel: guards, manufacturing employees, engineers, janitors, clerks, and management personnel. The design ensured that a subordinate was not in the same group with his immediate boss. Since this was a union plant, union members were present in each group.

Greater use of task forces and temporary groups

The task of each group was to identify problems facing the organization, in terms of either its overall effectiveness or the work environment it provided to employees. At the end of the afternoon, the groups reported their findings and conclusions to the entire organization. There were, of course, overlapping problems, since more than one group identified some of the same problem(s). The problems were then sorted into functional categories. Two weeks later, the plant was shut down for another afternoon, at which time new, cross-functional employee groups were formed to work on specific lists of problems. During the next two months (September and October), the plant shut down every Friday afternoon to allow the groups to work on their lists of problems, which caused a 10% reduction in "productive" time.

The time span in each of the following diagrams is calendar year 1970 and the first period of 1971. The reason for this is that three corporate decisions were made in 60–70 days. Although the decision to close down the plant was made in November 1970, dramatic changes in the plant were already beginning to show up. Therefore, a decision to keep the plant open was made in December (period 13). In period 1 (January 1971), a third corporate decision was made to not only keep the plant open, but also to *add* a research and development facility and a sales and marketing group.

Figure 13.3 shows the reduction in manufacturing cost for each four-week accounting period.* (Sales remained relatively constant during this time span.) After the original problem-identification and problem-solving meetings were held during period 8, there was a marked drop in manufacturing costs, amounting to about 45% over the next few periods.

Figure 13.4 shows the increase in productivity dollars per man hour during the time we are discussing. It is obvious that productivity increased considerably.

Figure 13.5 depicts the dollar reduction in the scrap rate. The horizontal line represents the budget figure for scrap, an item budgeted by every manufacturing plant. As a result of organizational changes, the amount of scrap decreased considerably.

---

*To protect confidential company information, the figures in these diagrams have been modified by a constant.

Application of the systems approach to organizational development

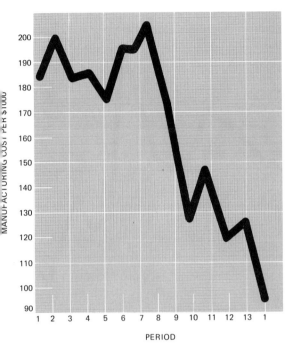

Figure 13.3. *Reduction in manufacturing costs per accounting period.*

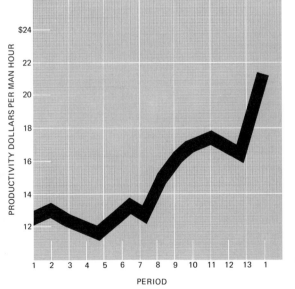

Figure 13.4. *Productivity dollars per man hour.*

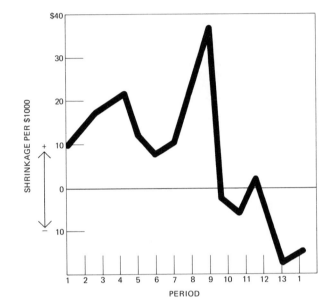

Figure 13.5. *Dollar reduction in the scrap rate.*

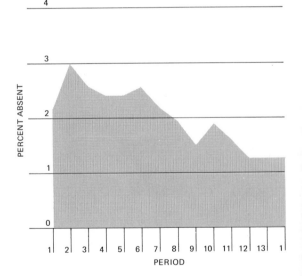

Figure 13.6. *Rate of absenteeism per accounting period.*

The percentage of absenteeism during the time shown is given in Fig. 13.6. Absenteeism decreased markedly, although the decrease preceded period 8, when the original organizational confrontation meetings were held.

In this case study, no attempt was made to change the organizational structure of the plant. Rather, time and effort were expended to simultaneously improve the flow and human perspectives. The results, we think, speak for themselves. The team-building at the upper-management level allowed the organization to be receptive to the concept of problem-identification and problem-solving meetings at all levels. These materially improved both the flow and human perspectives by bringing problems out into the open where they could be acted on.

V. CONCLUSION

In this chapter, we defined the effective and efficient organization as one which has: the ability to adapt, a sense of identity, the capacity to test reality, and the ability to be well integrated and to simultaneously consider the three different perspectives stressed throughout the book. In re-examining the concept of proactive and reactive forces affecting organizational balance, we pointed out that both are necessary. A major problem, however, is the inability, at times, to make a proper distinction between the two. Many managers have deeply embedded Theory X assumptions about people, and it is frequently difficult for them to alter their assumptions and perceptions, even in the face of directly contradictory evidence.

We then provided general guideline factors to be considered in a systems approach to organizational development. Systems theory can be used to restructure organizational design and information and related flows. It can also be used to combine the formal and informal organizations and to determine the most appropriate levels of organizational intervention and change. A final broad, systems approach to organizational development is the increased use of task forces and temporary groups.

In addition to these broad approaches which focus on the organization as a system, other, more individualized systems approaches can be used. Thus, systems theory can be used in both formal leadership style and management development to enhance organizational competency.

The two case studies presented in this chapter illustrate how the three perspectives can be integrated to improve organizational efficiency and effectiveness. In each case, the results provide dramatic evidence of the usefulness of an integrated approach to organizational development.

The extensive presentation of the case study in the next chapter describes in greater detail how an integrated systems approach to organizational development can result in a more adaptable and flexible organization with greater effectiveness and efficiency. Because this was an actual case study conducted under field conditions, it will not exactly parallel the recommendations presented in this chapter. Rather, Chapter 14 stresses the impact of the three different perspectives.

REVIEW

1. Using the same organization for which you devised an organizational-development strategy in the last chapter, redesign the strategy by taking into account structure and the various flow processes.

2. Compare Perspectives I, II, and III, and determine how each views the organization, the effect of one of the others, and give examples of each.

3. Describe how you would enrich the following jobs: a salesman in a hardware store, a cashier in a supermarket, a service station attendant, and a carpenter on a construction project.

4. This chapter lists several "principles" for organizational development. Based on your reading and experience to date, make up your own list of principles, which may differ from those given in the text. Explain the reasons for your list.

5. Select an organization and show how the principles listed in the text (or your own) can be applied.

6. Select an organization to assess for competence. What criteria would you use on each dimension?

7. Choose five organizations you wish to improve. Describe the depth of intervention and the intervention strategy you would use. Where on the Lawrence and Lorsch continuum does each organization appear?

8. Give a critique of one of the two cases presented in this chapter and indicate how you might have approached the problem differently.

Critical Concepts

Characteristics of a competent organization

Use of systems approach in organizational development

REFERENCES

1 E. Schein, *Organizational Psychology,* 2d ed. (Englewood Cliffs, N.J.: Prentice-Hall, 1970).

2 J. V. Clark, "A Healthy Organization," *California Management Review,* IV, 4 (Summer 1962): 16–30.

3 J. Lorsch and P. Lawrence, *Studies in Organizational Design* (Homewood, Ill.: Richard D. Irwin, 1970).

4 A. Etzioni, *Modern Organizations* (Englewood Cliffs, N.J.: Prentice-Hall, 1964).

5 J. Deardon, "MIS is a Mirage," *Harvard Business Review,* 50, 1 (Jan.-Feb. 1972): 90–99.

6 R. J. Mockler, "The Systems Approach to Business Organizations and Decision Making," *California Management Review,* XI, 2 (Winter 1968): 53–58.

7 W. G. Bennis, "Beyond Bureaucracy," in *The Temporary Society,* ed. W. G. Bennis and P. E. Slater (New York: Harper & Row, 1968).

8 B. D. Fine, *Comparison of Work Groups with Stable and Unstable Membership,* American Psychological Association, Experimental Publication System, December 1970, issue 9, Ms. No. 333–1.

9 R. Harrison, "Choosing the Depth of Organizational Intervention," *Journal of Applied Organizational Science,* 6, 2 (1970): 181–202.

10 J. Morse and J. Lorsch, "Beyond Theory Y," *Harvard Business Review,* 48, 3 (May-June 1970): 61–68.

11 F. Fiedler, "Engineer the Job to Fit the Manager," *Harvard Business Review,* 43, 5 (Sept.-Oct. 1965): 115–122.

12 J. Morse and J. Lorsch, *op. cit.*

13 V. Vroom, *Some Personality Determinants of the Effects of Participation* (Englewood Cliffs, N.J.: Prentice-Hall, 1960).

14 C. Perrow, *Organizational Analysis: A Sociological View* (Belmont, Cal.: Wadsworth, 1970).

15 F. Fiedler, *op. cit.*

16 *Ibid.,* p. 119.

17 A. Etzioni, "Human Beings Are Not Very Easy to Change After All," *Saturday Review,* June 3, 1972, pp. 45–47.

18 *Ibid.,* p. 46.

19 P. Hersey and K. H. Blanchard, "The Management of Change," *Training and Development Journal,* 26, 3 (March 1971): 28–33.

20 E. Schein, *op. cit.,* pp. 70, 71. Reprinted by permission.

21 A. Kay, personal communication.

14

AN
INTEGRATED
STUDY
OF
ORGANIZATIONAL
DEVELOPMENT

When there is no wind, row.

OLD POLISH PROVERB

I. INTRODUCTION

Before describing an organizational development program that took place in one company, we should first briefly review some of the concepts discussed previously. A social organization is a complex of interrelated and interdependent subsystems and can be analyzed from three different perspectives—the formal, flow, and human perspectives. These three sets of differing, but overlapping, subsystems are shaped in large measure by the way in which the organization is designed and how it approaches the problems of differentiation and integration. Analysis and design of the organization from one perspective lead to the definition and solution of problems in terms of that perspective. *Optimal* problem definitions, solutions, and designs are most likely to be reached only when all three points of view and the assumption underlying these perspectives are considered concurrently, with shifts in emphasis as appropriate. Such an integrated, or systems, model of organizations is shown in Fig. 14.1.

When this type of systems model is used as the basis for organizational change, we can consider the three perspectives as forming a pattern of inputs, organizational processes, and outputs, as is shown in Fig. 14.2. For example, the management hierarchy (Perspective I) converts the attitudes and potential brought to the organization in the form of individuals' needs and abilities so that they are compatible with the needs and goals of the organization. Similarly, the flow of information and resources (Perspective II) through the organization cannot exist independently of interpersonal variables (Perspective III), which are subject to managerial control.

Within this formal system, both interpersonal and flow-process variables are important for effective and permanent organizational change. For example, many studies have shown that managerial control systems over employees may lead to their restricting output, playing the "numbers game," and other dysfunctional practices. Too often, the effect of control systems on human behavior has not been adequately understood.

Since organizational outputs reflect the quantity and quality of both input and processes, it is obvious that organizational outputs can be increased by

This chapter has been modified from E. F. Huse and M. Beer, "Eclectic Approach to Organizational Development," *Harvard Business Review,* 49, 5, September-October, 1971, pp. 103–112.
Note: We would like to express our appreciation to the innovative and far-sighted managers and supervisors of the organization described in this chapter: J. Sabin, C. Wheatley, C. Barebo, L. Macarelli, R. Banach, D. Sweyer, and C. Carlozzi.

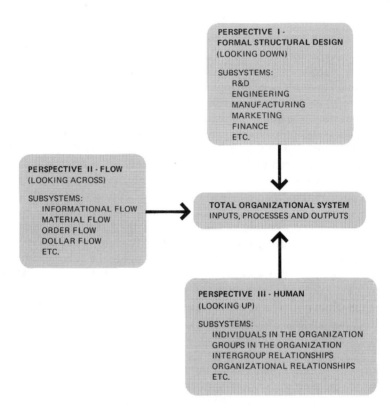

Figure 14.1. *Integrated systems model of the organization.*

improving the quality of the input, e.g., selecting people with higher levels of abilities and needs. However, the costs associated with selecting better personnel do not necessarily lead to greater organizational efficiency. Although the organization may improve its performance, this gain has been obtained only because the quality of people has been improved through better selection, not because there has been a change in the organization's use of its human resources.

Because organizations are open systems, outputs of organizational performance can usually be improved by modifying organizational flow processes so that more of the potential inherent in the human resources can be unleashed. Outputs normally increase because the conversion process has been made more

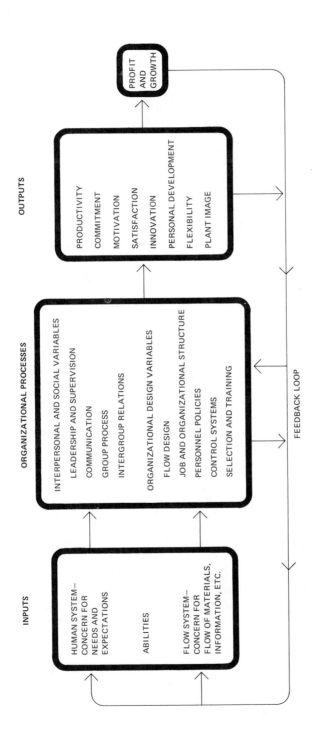

Figure 14.2. *Human- and flow-systems model of an organization.*

INPUTS

ORGANIZATIONAL PROCESSES

OUTPUTS

HUMAN SYSTEM—
CONCERN FOR
NEEDS AND
EXPECTATIONS

ABILITIES

FLOW SYSTEM—
CONCERN FOR
FLOW OF MATERIALS,
INFORMATION, ETC.

INTERPERSONAL AND SOCIAL VARIABLES

LEADERSHIP AND SUPERVISION

COMMUNICATION

GROUP PROCESS

INTERGROUP RELATIONS

ORGANIZATIONAL DESIGN VARIABLES

FLOW DESIGN

JOB AND ORGANIZATIONAL STRUCTURE

PERSONNEL POLICIES

CONTROL SYSTEMS

SELECTION AND TRAINING

PRODUCTIVITY

COMMITMENT

MOTIVATION

SATISFACTION

INNOVATION

PERSONAL DEVELOPMENT

FLEXIBILITY

PLANT IMAGE

PROFIT
AND
GROWTH

FEEDBACK LOOP

efficient. This can be done, for example, by changing the job structure to allow for greater challenge, better communications, and prompt feedback or by restructuring the formal system to improve materials or information flow. The adjustment of flow processes to more accurately reflect organizational and individual needs is one of the key objectives of organizational development.

II. THE APPROACH TO CHANGE

A. Background

The organizational development program described in this chapter successfully integrated the three perspectives of the organization as a social system. The results were increased plant productivity and profitability, improved product quality, reduced absenteeism and voluntary resignations, greater maturity of attitude and acceptance of responsibility by hourly workers, and fewer layers of supervision. In addition, such other outcomes as the increased satisfaction and motivation of the company's employees verify current research findings that these factors optimize an organization's long-term profitability and growth.

The organization studied is one of a 50-plant corporation with facilities both in the United States and overseas. This plant, which interacts with the parent corporation as well as with the outside environment, manufactures a variety of electronic and electrical instruments and related equipment that are used in medical and laboratory products. The products range from relatively simple hot plates to a highly complex instrument (containing more than 500 parts and 12 printed circuit boards) which is used to perform blood analyses and give a visual, electronic readout.

Prior to its program for development, the plant followed the traditional structural model, i.e., there was a plant manager and such structural departments as plant engineering, manufacturing, personnel, quality assurance, and materials control (including purchasing, plant planning, and scheduling). Since its products were primarily electronic, the plant purchased most of the needed components, e.g., transistors and capacitors, and was therefore oriented toward assembling rather than manufacturing parts. One section—the glass shop—of the plant, however, did manufacture parts out of glass tubing for use in electrodes. A machine shop built and repaired equipment.

Because of the fast-moving nature of the electronic instrument business, the plant was continually faced with the problems of introducing and changing new products and modifying and improving existing products. Some products, of course, did remain stable for a considerable period of time.

Most of the hourly assembly workers were women, most of whom had less than a high school education. The research and development, marketing, and sales groups reported to supervisors whose chain of command differed from that of the plant manager.

B. Assumptions Underlying the Change Program

1. This organization falls on the left of the Lawrence and Lorsch continuum, i.e., it operates in an unstable, rapidly changing environment.

Use of systems theory in organizational design

2. Organizations should improve if they work actively to meet the needs of people (change the psychological contract) and the organization. Under such conditions, individuals at all levels will grow and mature.

3. Simultaneous attention should be paid to the three basic perspectives; one cannot be stressed to the exclusion of the others. Each approach to change has an appropriate place in a total organizational development program, and no single tool or technique should be the paramount vehicle for change. For example, although sensitivity training has been widely used as an instrument for organizational development, it was not used at this plant and, indeed, may never be used unless it appears appropriate at a particular point in time.

Use of systems theory in organizational intervention and change

4. Most managers want to do a good job and improve their own performance and that of their subordinates. As a result, they will try out, and continue to use, techniques which help them to get their job done better. The individual manager will cease taking what he perceives to be nonbeneficial actions. The manager should therefore be more concerned about results than about "theory" as such.

5. The role of the change agent should be directed toward helping the operating manager do his job better. The change agent can do this by acting as a resource person rather than by telling a manager how to do his job.

Use of systems theory in management development

6. The most effective and permanent learning comes after the individual has experimented with new approaches. This is consistent with research indicating that behavioral change precedes attitudinal change. By working with a change agent, a manager may experi-

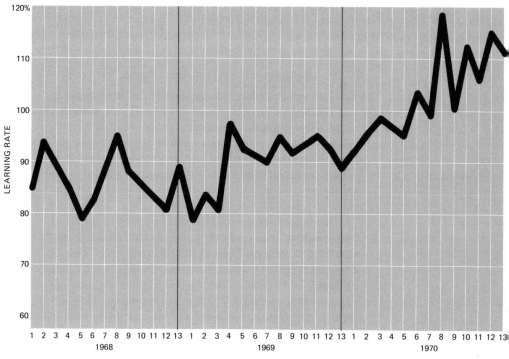

LEARNING RATE

PRODUCTION REPORTING PERIODS

A. Plant efficiency

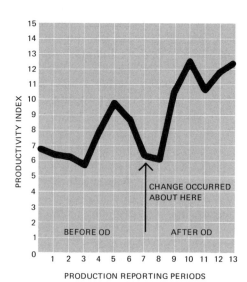

PRODUCTIVITY INDEX

CHANGE OCCURRED
ABOUT HERE

BEFORE OD

AFTER OD

B. Productivity in the hot-plate department

PRODUCTION REPORTING PERIODS

C. Other results during 1968-1970 period

Hot-plate department
Productivity increase 84%
Controllable rejects drop . . . . 23% to 1%
Absenteeism . . . . 8% to 1%
Elimination of "weekly" inspector

Glass shop
Productivity increase 20%

Materials control department
Parts shortage list reduced from 14 IBM pages
to 1 page

Instrument department

Four new products introduced in eight months
with only a slight drop in overall
productivity. New product efficiency[*]
now never less than 80%
Productivity increase 17%
Quality increase 50%
Absenteeism reduced 50%

Supervision
Elimination of job of manufacturing manager
Elimination of 1/3 of first-line supervisory jobs[†]

Incremental profit
One of the best among 50 plants
in corporation

[*]Measured in terms of speed in learning new production tasks.
[†]Vacant jobs not filled after promotion of individuals.
E. Huse and M. Beer, "Eclectic Approach to Organizational
Development," *Harvard Business Review*, 49, 5 (Sept.-Oct.
1971). Reprinted by permission.

Exhibit 14.1. *Economic impact of organization development.*

ment with new means of communication, job enrichment, or organizational structural change. Successful
experiences begin in a subtle way to change the culture
and norms of the plant, thus initiating a continuously
evolving cycle of change.

C. The Change Team

The organizational development team consisted primarily of three people. There
were two "external" change agents—the manager of organizational research and
development for the parent corporation and an organizational development
consultant. In addition, there was an "internal" change agent—the personnel
manager of the plant. A fourth person, who visited the plant periodically, was
a researcher who conducted interviews and gathered data for use in diagnosis,
feedback, and research.

The basic approach of this team was for the two "outside" change agents
to establish working relationships with individuals at all management levels
within the plant and to present themselves as resource persons available to help
solve specific, on-going problems or to initiate small-scale experiments in management practices. The change team wanted to get someone or some organizational component to begin implementing the managerial concepts shown in Fig.
14.2. With the help of the change team, a few individuals in various parts of the
organization began to apply these new concepts. These initial experiments were
successful, thereby reinforcing both the individual and the organization's commitment to the change program, which in turn enhanced their interest and
motivation to continue with the change process.

The change team conducted surveys and used survey-feedback techniques
throughout the change period, but the initial, continuing, and most important
changes were achieved through the consulting-counseling approach, which focused on helping operating managers solve their problems in ways that would
have both immediate and long-term effects. In other words, the change team had
two objectives—to help the manager with his immediate problems and to fit this
type of help to an integrated, systems model for organizational development.

III. RESULTS OF THE PROGRAM

The overall results of the organizational development program are given in
Exhibit 14.1. The exhibit is largely self-explanatory and will be referred to
throughout the remainder of the chapter.

One of the most significant results of this organizational development program was that hourly workers developed more mature attitudes and became

more willing to accept responsibility on the job. The change in these workers is even more marked when they are compared to hourly workers in conventional organizations which are managed according to Theory X assumptions.[1] The following are typical reactions of workers at all levels to the development program.

Since I've been working here, my husband is a much better supervisor in his plant. I tell him what he should do to make his people more interested in what they are doing, based on what our supervisors do here. (Assembly worker)

I wondered about this organizational development approach when I got here and kinda thought it was for the birds. But the thing that convinced me was how those new products go into production. In any other plant I've worked in, it would have been a complete fiasco. (Engineer)

The more I get into this thing, the more I see that it is going to be a way of life for me from here on. Everybody wins. (Plant manager)

A. Changes in the Human Perspective

Although we discuss the organizational changes that occurred within the framework of three distinct perspectives, it is important to stress that we do so only for the sake of clarity. In fact, the three perspectives are interdependent, and work on all three proceeded simultaneously.

In order to bring about changes in the human perspective, the change team had to work on organizational processes having to do with interpersonal and social variables—the needs and motivations of individuals within the organization. Therefore, the change agents focused on improving the leadership and supervision potential in the plant, enhancing the vertical and horizontal flow of information, expanding workers' jobs, establishing and developing more effective work groups, and improving intergroup relationships.

Use of systems theory in formal leadership style

1. Communications. One of the first tasks of the change agents was to open up better communication channels so that the organization members could develop mutual trust and understanding before new and more profound changes were made. Although the organization already made use of staff meetings and other types of traditional communication channels, the change agents wanted to do more.

a) Departmental meetings. With relatively little training, individual supervisors at all organizational levels began to hold monthly meetings with their subordinates. At first, these meetings consisted only of the supervisor's telling his subordinates what was going on in the plant and in his department. The supervisor stated the organization's monthly objectives and the status of progress toward these goals; he also described the relationship between departmental and organizational goals. The supervisor tried to get feedback in the form of ideas, comments, and suggestions about the things he had discussed and tried to get subordinates' views about what was going on in the plant.

Over a period of several years, these meetings evolved into truly two-way communication sessions; discussion shifted from "mini-gripes" to "mega-gripes." The subordinates began to be concerned about such questions as: "What is our product being used for?" "Who is using it?" "What do they think of it?" "Are the quality standards high enough?" "How do the customers feel about it?"

b) *"Coffee with the Boss."* Every week a sample group of hourly and weekly employees (on a rotating basis) met with the plant manager in an effort to close the communication gap at the top. Over time, the same shift in concerns emerged as it had in the departmental meetings.

Use of systems theory in information and related flows

c) *Plant tours.* As the content and openness of meetings changed, it became apparent that employees at all levels wanted more information about their jobs, their place in the organization, and how the business was doing. Therefore, plant tours were initiated so that employees could see what was happening in other departments. Significantly, hourly employees began to conduct the tours for both employees and visiting dignitaries.

d) *Use of charts.* At the major traffic point in the plant, charts were put up every month to show actual versus budgeted programs in sales, inventory, plant effectiveness, etc. Although no dollar figures were given, all employees could see where the organization was in relation to its objectives, and this openness contributed to employee morale. As one assembly worker commented, "We're proud of where we are."

e) Mutual goal-setting. Goals for each department were derived from plant objectives, and weekly or monthly goals for individuals or work groups were set after discussion by the boss with his subordinates. This process of mutual goal-setting enabled workers to understand how their own production goals were related to the goals of the plant. As a result, there was less need for close supervision for long periods of time.

2. Group and Intergroup Relationships. These factors were an important aspect of increasing effectiveness, communications, and trust. In order to help managers become more effective, change agents sat in on manager-staff meetings. After the meeting, the change agent could give the manager suggestions for making future meetings with his staff more effective.

The plant routinely used a "Rate the Boss" form on which subordinates rated their immediate superior on a number of variables. Change agents then discussed these forms with the managers, clarifying the meaning of the ratings and making suggestions for increasing the manager's effectiveness.

Use of systems theory in organizational intervention and change

When the organizational development program was initiated, professional and supervisory personnel felt that interdepartmental relationships needed to be improved. Therefore, a meeting (attended by the change agents) of department managers was held so that each manager could discuss his perception of his own and others' departments.

This first frank discussion was followed by other meetings at which the format and style were expanded. For example, periodic cross-department meetings were held at which the "monthly" personnel of one department discussed their expectations, perceptions, and their strong and weak points with the "monthly" personnel of another department. Most employees agreed that such meetings were helpful. As one employee explained, "Before we had these meetings, I really wasn't concerned about the people in 'X' department. Now, I'm beginning to understand some of their problems. I'm beginning to listen to them and work with them."

Depth of intervention

Although T-groups were discussed as a "family group," the plant personnel felt that they really did not need such an approach. The other approaches were accomplishing a level of openness that was sufficient for their purposes.

3. Job Enrichment. The change agents wanted to create opportunities for employees to satisfy their individual needs on the job. A process of job enrichment was developed to enlarge jobs, to give individuals more opportunity to handle the whole job, and to give them responsibility for the planning, doing, and evaluating of their own work. The change agents felt that people at all levels in the organization should be given interesting and challenging work for which they could assume full responsibility. Since such an approach obviously depends not only on the situation and the individual but also his job, the change agents felt that job enrichment should be determined by circumstances and could be accomplished by using either a team or individual approach.

a) The hot-plate department. An engineer who became excited about this idea wanted to try it out. Both he and his first-line supervisor wanted to do something about the layout of the hot-plate department, which assembled several models of hot plates for laboratory and hospital use.

Use of systems theory in organizational design

At the time, this operation was already pretty well streamlined into the normal assembly-line approach, with each girl having a small part in the total assembly process. The line was balanced, and management was generally satisfied with the department's rate of productivity. After considering and discussing several alternatives with others in the organization, the first-line supervisor and the engineer developed a radically different design—they decided to have each girl assemble the entire hot plate. The only change in the department was that each girl was expected to do the entire job, to which the girls responded positively, e.g., "Now, it is *my* hot plate."

The results of this job redefinition were dramatic (see Exhibit 14.1). First, there was a drop in controllable rejects from 23% to less than 1%. Second, absenteeism dropped from about 8% to about 1%, where it has remained for several years. Third, productivity rose sharply, as Exhibit 14.1 shows. When the average productivity for the first and second halves of the year are compared, it becomes evident that there was an 84% gain in productivity. (The temporary increase in productivity in periods 5 and 6 was caused by emergency pressure to get the product out to meet a sudden, unexpected increase in sales.)

By all criteria, the development program in the hot-plate department was successful. Having each assembly worker be responsible for the total product had marked effects on productivity, efficiency, quality performance, and morale. In fact, the quality of the workers' performance increased so much that inspectors were no longer needed. Now, each girl does her own inspecting and signs her own name to "brag tags" which go directly to the customer.

b) The glass shop. In this department girls work on lathes to form glass for electrodes. Because of the nature of this operation, the supervisor decided to try the team approach to productivity. At the beginning of the change program, team formation and the effectiveness of cohesive work units had been discussed, and the supervisor simply went ahead and divided his people into teams, with minimal discussion with outsiders, although the supervisor's boss and the plant manager had given their approval to the change beforehand.

The supervisor's approach was very simple. After he had formed the teams, he told the girls,

Use of systems theory to combine the formal and informal organization

Look, I think we ought to organize around teams, and you four girls are responsible for the "X" electrode. You three girls are

Each person is responsible for assembling the total product. (Photographs courtesy Corning Glass Works)

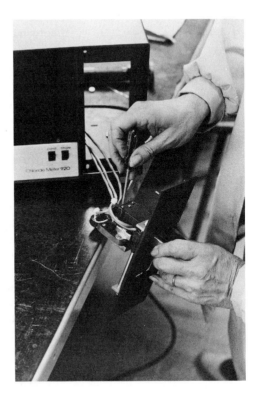

responsible for the "Y" electrode. You are going to be responsible for the total task; I want you girls who are working on the "X" electrode to know that we're going to need 500 of these by the next accounting period, and you girls decide who's going to do what, how you're going to do it, and you schedule it.

The girls did not all react positively to this sudden change. Some saw it as a tribute to their capability and were enthusiastic. Others, who were not used to working in this kind of climate and with this type of supervisor, were suspicious and thought that the supervisor was abdicating his responsibility. (This kind of suspicion, which emerged from the researcher's interviews, existed in many of the stages of change.)

Despite some workers' apprehension, however, productivity soon showed a 20% increase. In addition, there were immediate and lasting changes in the involvement, commitment, and interest by the girls in their work. For example, they sometimes stayed late to discuss manufacturing problems and schedules over a cup of coffee.

Isn't it silly for a bunch of us housewives to stay here after work worrying about how we are going to make the schedule. We really should be home cooking dinner for our husbands.

Furthermore, one girl took the schedules home at night to type so that they would be neat, even though she knew that she should not work overtime without pay.

As time went on, the composition of the groups changed, and at one point the concept was almost abandoned when a new supervisor who had come in from another plant was dubious about the value of the team approach. However, within a year he had become an enthusiastic supporter of the work-team concept. His conviction was strengthened by the obvious contrast between the department he had managed previously and the glass shop. In the glass shop the teams knew their schedule, pooled their efforts, and swapped jobs as necessary to get the work done. In the other department, however, it was necessary for the supervisor to assign work at the beginning of the work day to each employee.

Inappropriate use of systems theory in organizational intervention and change

c) *The instrument department.* This department, which makes highly complex and complete systems ranging from relatively standard models to sophisticated electronic equipment, experienced both successes and failures in organizational development. To help him assign girls to various production areas, the department supervisor decided to use a sociometric questionnaire (which asks respondents to specify in rank order others with whom they would like to work). However, because the supervisor had neither prepared his people very well for this task nor established sufficient trust to carry out such a plan, the girls rebelled, saying that it was his responsibility to make work assignments. Underlying this negative reaction was the girls' feeling that they were not ready for this type of change and that they were unprepared to accept such a role.

Appropriate use of systems theory in organizational intervention and change

Some months later, this supervisor left the plant for a better job, and a new manager took over the instrument department. Unlike his predecessor, the new manager was extremely frank and open with his people in explaining why schedule changes were necessary. Using a team-building approach, he began discussions with his subordinates about how schedules could be met and began involving them in the planning process. In addition, he began working toward what he called the "total job concept," his term for job enrichment. Within a year, individuals were undertaking the complete assembly of complex instrument systems. With yet more complex instruments, he used groups of workers to do the assembly work.

After the job-enrichment program was initiated, four new instruments were introduced into the department. In contrast to the initial low productivity when new products go into the traditional assembly-line process, the introduction of the new instruments caused only a slight reduction in productivity.

Using data for several instruments that had been in production for at least two years prior to the job-enrichment program, the plant accountant was able to show just how effective the change in approach had been. The average productivity for the eight months preceding the change was used as a base. After the job-enrichment program had been implemented, productivity rose by 17%, or approximately $1500 per year per worker. Quality also improved; the number of rejects decreased from an average of 25% to an average of 13%, an increase in quality of about 50%. Absenteeism was reduced from 8.5% per month to 3.4%, a reduction of about 50%.

An engineer associated with the introduction of the new products asked the change agents how they could be certain that job enrichment would be better than the more traditional use of assembly lines, time standards, etc. When asked in return how the introduction of a specific new product would have been handled in a conventional type of plant, the engineer supplied the answer to his own question.

It would have been utter chaos. Under the circumstances, we just couldn't have gotten a normal assembly-line process going for months. At least with the girls making the entire product, they learned about the problem quickly; you had fewer people to talk to and train, and they were so involved that if they had questions, in most cases, they solved the problem by discussing it among themselves. I guess that's the kind of proof I needed.

These are examples of some of the improvements that occurred by initiating changes in the human perspective. Later, we will document the gain in workers' maturity and their increasing acceptance and willingness to take on additional responsibility. Certainly one evidence that workers' needs were being met was the considerably reduced absenteeism and voluntary resignation rate throughout the plant. As one worker said, "It's important to come to work in the morning. I'm interested in the team and what we can do to meet our production goals. Sometimes, when I'm sitting at home, I think about how we can improve our performance and better the goal."

In the next section, we discuss how changes in the flow perspective helped improve plant effectiveness. However, it is important to stress that these perspectives are interrelated and that many of the changes in the human perspective had a direct impact on the flow of information and materials throughout the plant.

B. Changes in the Flow Perspective

Here, the change team wanted to improve the lateral flow of information, materials, etc., through the plant in addition to the vertical flow of information discussed in the previous section. Obviously, some of these latter approaches improved the lateral flow as well. For example, the interdepartmental meetings greatly increased the amount of "informal communications flow" across departments, and departmental relationships improved accordingly.

In this section we discuss more direct approaches to improving communications, information, and other flows across the organization. These changes also affected the formal, hierarchical structure of the organization, as will be discussed in the next section.

Use of systems theory in information and related flows

1. The Matrix Organization. This approach, based on the research findings of Lawrence and Lorsch, includes the use of the integrator and the matrix organization. However, before going into detail, a little background is needed. In most industrial organizations, problem-solving, or production, meetings are usually attended by the heads of different functional groups and key production people in the organization. This plant was no different. The daily production meeting was attended by the plant manager and the heads of such departments as engineering, quality assurance, materials control, and the individual first-line supervisors as needed. Prior to the meeting each functional head and first-line supervisor held a briefing with his subordinates to become up to date in his own area. After the meeting, each manager communicated specific courses of action or problems to his subordinates. Such meetings served to help unify the plant, disseminate information to the departments, and ensure that production schedules were met.

However, the plant manager felt that this design could be improved and that he and his managers should spend more time in long-range planning. In addition, communication failures, delays, and misunderstandings occurred because the managers served as "communications carriers" to and from their own departments.

Several basic objectives evolved from discussions between the plant manager and the department managers.

1. Increase the effectiveness and rapidity of the information flow through the plant to make certain that the right people have the right information at the right time.

2. Move the decision-making and problem-solving processes down to the level of the person responsible for doing the work.

3. Increase the responsibility for the total job and push that responsibility as far down as possible.

Use of systems theory in organizational design

The design that evolved from these discussions was the matrix organization. Each production supervisor would be an "integrator" for a team consisting of representatives from each of the staff departments that serviced his production department. Those from engineering, materials control, and quality assurance, for example, were to be "doers" rather than supervisors or managers. A typical team might thus consist of a technician from quality assurance, a technical engineer from engineering, and one or more representatives from materials control.

The readiness of the plant's management for a major change of this magnitude was evidenced by the relatively short period of time in which the new structure was discussed and a decision reached. It seemed clear to everyone that the matrix structure more accurately combined and represented the informal, most effective communication links. Nevertheless, the change has not been totally successful to date, although there continues to be improvement.

In part, this lack of success was caused by management's failure to effectively train and prepare individuals for the change and their new roles. The matrix structure has worked best when the staff department representatives are competent, motivated, and skilled in working in groups. In addition, the head of one functional department was not fully committed to the change program, and therefore he did not delegate full responsibility to his subordinates on the team. Some integrators lacked clear understanding of their role and the means of influence and control open to them. Finally, neither the plant manager nor the change agents gave proper attention and follow-up to the changes that had been made.

The reasons for these difficulties were discussed with the change agents and the key people involved with designing the matrix. Following a diagnosis of the problems and subsequent discussion of the difficulties, it was agreed that most of the problems could be overcome. A decision was made to continue with the matrix because it fit operational needs, reflected management philosophy, and complemented the culture of the plant.

Use of systems theory in organizational change

Even though the introduction of this level of matrix organization did not totally meet expectations, it is important in several respects. First, that the organization was willing to undertake such a major change reflects management's adaptability as fairly sophisticated consumers of new managerial methods. Second, the ability to examine and diagnose failure reflects the openness of the plant and management's willingness to invest time in examining the organizational process, even in the face of continuing task pressures. Third, the failure itself supports the thesis that change must be preceded or accompanied by changes in individuals' abilities, motivation, role understanding, interpersonal skills, or other social and behavioral changes. In other words, change depends on the interaction of the formal, flow, and human perspectives.

2. New Product Introduction. Almost all manufacturing companies have difficulty in introducing new products—there are delays, misunderstandings, parts shortages, etc. The resulting conflict may cause the research and development group to complain, "We have given you (manufacturing) an excellent product—you loused it up." Manufacturing, in turn, may grumble, "If you gave us a well-designed product, we could build it." Elsewhere, we referred to the tactics of the purchasing agent who tried to ensure that he got as close to the design of the product as possible, even though in the more formal, traditional sense, his job was simply to order parts as cheaply as possible and to expedite their delivery.

When a new product goes into production in any manufacturing organization, cost standards are developed for the product, that is, labor and parts costs are estimated in order to give the organization some idea of the number of people needed to manufacture the product, selling prices, etc. In addition, most companies expect a learning curve, the time needed for the organization to learn how to build the product. Thus, the actual costs versus predicted costs in the first month or so of actual production generally result in a 20% efficiency rate. As Exhibit 14.1 shows, however, the efficiency rate of new product introduction in this plant never fell below 80%, a very high figure for highly complex products.

How was this efficiency rate achieved? A higher-level, modified matrix approach is now being used to integrate such diverse sectors of the organization as the marketing, research and development, materials control, manufacturing, and sales departments.

Greater use of task forces and temporary groups

This matrix consists of a product team for each new product. The task of the product team, led by an integrator, is to ensure that all the "bugs" are out of the product before it is manufactured. In addition, this team ascertains that the product is well designed and marketable, generates and stabilizes a parts list in order to give purchasing sufficient lead time, and ensures that the product fits the demands and needs of the marketing people. Interviews conducted in the plant in December 1970, as well as information obtained later in 1971, indicate that this approach is succeeding—many of the previous problems have been reduced, if not eliminated.

Although not all changes led to immediate improvement, the organization remained committed to the idea of change and has been willing to experiment. As one engineer put it:

I've never seen new products move so easily, quickly, and smoothly into the plant as they do now. We are taking care of the problems early that used to really plague us in the past. Sure, we have our conflicts, but they are brought out into the open early, and this lets us iron them out and get them solved before it's too late. I think that for the first time, we are really integrated.

C. Changes in the Structural-design Perspective

As we have seen, changes in the design perspective are highly dependent on changes in the other two perspectives. For example, the interdepartmental discussions initiated by the change agents improved interdepartmental relations and therefore brought the formal and informal organizations closer together. Although most of the formal, structural changes have already been described in the sections on changes in the human and flow perspectives, there are several areas which are most appropriately described in this section—the redesign of part of the formal organization, changes in leadership and managerial style, reduction in levels of supervision, and changes in the parent organization.

1. Changes in the Materials Control Department. This department had responsibility for purchasing, inventory control, scheduling, and expediting, and people were assigned to one of these four speciality areas. However, the plant was being plagued by parts shortages, which caused delays in production. (This was well before the development of the matrix organization or the new-product task forces.)

After experimenting with individual job enrichment, particularly for his secretary, the department supervisor decided that the entire departmental structure should be reorganized through job enrichment. As he said:

I don't think these people who are expediting really like expediting; it's not a very challenging kind of a job. In addition to that, I think my people are having tremendous problems communicating across functional lines.

Use of systems theory to combine the formal and informal organizations

The materials control manager then developed a plan of action. Rather than having each work group specialize in a particular functional area, he decided to formally organize his department around product-line teams. Each group would have total responsibility—expediting, scheduling, purchasing, and inventory control—for a particular product line. The manager felt that his change would reduce his parts shortage problem, solve his communications problems, and make the work more interesting for his people. Since this was a radical change, he moved slowly and discussed with the plant management, the change agents, and his people some alternative ways of implementing the structural change, the impact it would have on his people, and the need to go slowly and to keep the "back door" open in case he needed to retreat from the project-team approach.

When he made the change, people were ready. Within three months, the parts-shortage list was reduced from 14 large, computer-printout pages to less than one page (as Exhibit 14.1 shows), while the department maintained the same volume of business. Even though the total volume of business increased as more complex instruments were introduced and the absolute number of parts shortages increased correspondingly, the relative number of parts shortages still showed a considerable net decrease. The introduction of the new product teams at a later time also helped to significantly reduce the number of parts shortages.

Departmental personnel reacted positively to the changes brought about by job enrichment:

You no longer operate in a vacuum. I used to schedule with only one point of view— that of getting everything produced for delivery to a customer. I never thought about or was concerned about inventory problems or lead time involved in buying. I wasn't really concerned with other people's point of view. We just didn't communicate, and therefore there was very little cooperation.

Now, we can relate our successes to theirs (the manufacturing area). It gives you a great sense of satisfaction to know that you have coordinated the back-up work for an entire department.

My job is a lot more interesting since the reorganization. I no longer have to do the same things day after day, and things have real meaning for me.

Use of systems
theory in formal
leadership style

2. Changes in Management and Leadership Style.

There is no doubt that managerial leadership and supervision have an important impact on the motivation, commitment, adaptability, and satisfaction of employees. One of the aims of the change agents was to help the plant move toward a style of management which emphasized participation, consideration, and support of employees, with proper delegation of responsibility. As changes occurred in group processes, intergroup relationships, job structure, communications and information flow, and organizational structure, supervision in the plant became less centralized and increasingly participative and supportive. It is clear that leadership style is not merely reflected in the nature of communication flow, job structure, and organizational structure; it is in turn affected by them. In short, leadership cannot be isolated from the other variables.

a) Search for an appropriate managerial style. Since the plant's environment was uncertain, it appeared appropriate to push decision-making downward, a change that reflects the research by Lawrence and Lorsch that we discussed earlier. Perhaps the most interesting aspect in the development of participative management was the early difficulties encountered by the managers in understanding and applying the concept. After participative and supportive management had been discussed in seminars and with individual managers, the change agents found that some managers interpreted this to mean a hands-off, be-warm-and-friendly-to-everyone-regardless-of-the-situation approach, i.e., a *laissez-faire* style of management. This extreme shift in direction was most often reflected in increasing managerial uncertainty about how to handle problems and problem employees. For example, should a supervisor discuss lagging performance with an employee? Should he mention something about absenteeism and tardiness? In short, concern for people was being emphasized to the exclusion of concern for production. Occasionally, a manager's confusion could be seen in his abrupt "swing" in style from *laissez-faire* to highly structured directiveness. When, not surprisingly, *laissez-faire* and warm friendliness did not work, the manager's frustration would cause him to erupt in a new, tough, and (from the subordinate's point of view) quite unexpected approach to a problem. To the change agents, these swings were not surprising and reflected a trial-and-error learning process on the part of the managers.

The search for an appropriate managerial style reflects common managerial confusion about participative, or Theory Y, management. Participative management dóes not lie on a "hard-soft" continuum; rather, it is an integrated, simultaneous concern for both people and production. Participative management requires the mutual involvement, at all levels, of boss and subordinate in setting goals and making decisions that affect the employee. Concern for people is expressed by their involvement in making decisions, defining tasks, and setting objectives. Participative management is a third alternative which is more difficult to apply than directive leadership, under which the manager can simply "go by the book."

b) Installation of work-planning. Counseling and work by the change agents led to the use of a management-by-objectives, or work-planning, approach at all levels of the organization. For example, production and other goals were mutually planned and set by the plant manager and the production supervisors. Mutual goal-setting was also adopted with production workers, as we discussed earlier. Rather than having an industrial engineer determine standard piece rates, etc., departmental goals are now derived from the plant goals, and weekly or monthly individual and team goals are derived from departmental goals after the boss and his subordinates have discussed them. This process enables workers to clearly understand how their goals fit into the goal structure of the plant, and they can therefore work on their own for long periods of time without close supervision. Performance reviews, held periodically with all employees, including hourly workers, are two-way discussions. In addition, "Rate Your Boss" forms are also used.

c) Promotions and dismissals. The concept of participative management has been extended to include the handling of promotions and dismissals. The plant has a relatively high turnover rate for ineffective employees. When termination is deemed necessary, the employee is told frankly the reasons for his dismissal. This practice reflects not only the organization's concern for people and their needs for security and understanding what is happening, but also the company's assumption that most people are interested in doing a good job and are mature enough to understand the reasons for their termination.

Performance is the primary criterion for promoting an employee. Again, participative practices are used by management to make sure the employee knows why he has been promoted and has a clear understanding of his new responsibilities.

The concept of participative management has pervaded the "culture" of the organization. It has encouraged managers and subordinates to take a more realistic look at themselves and to assume individual responsibility for difficult decisions that in more traditional organizational cultures are often postponed or bucked upward.

d) Reduction in the work force. Perhaps one of the best illustrations of this change in the plant's culture is the approach that was used to reduce the size of the work force. During late 1970 and early 1971, sales were declining, and the plant was accumulating an inventory of unsold products. Top management therefore decided that a layoff was necessary. The management staff discussed a number of alternatives and then decided that since this was an "open" plant, these alternatives should be discussed with the production workers. The assembly workers had a major share in the final decision, which was to reduce the number of work weeks for individual employees. (To the best of our knowledge, this is the *only* time that a decision to reduce the work force in *any* organization has been greeted by spontaneous applause by those affected.)

3. Reduction in Managerial Personnel. When the program for change began, the plant hierarchy consisted of a plant manager and staff departments, including a production superintendent and first-line supervisors. As the study progressed and as workers and managers grew in maturity and willingness to accept responsibility, less and less close supervision was needed. As a result, when the original plant manager was promoted, the production superintendent was promoted to take his place. The latter's position was not filled, however, since by this time the first-line supervisors had grown more and more skilled and were able to take on greater responsibilities.

As the plant increased in size, consideration was given to employing an additional first-line supervisor, but it was decided that this was unnecessary. Finally, when one of the first-line supervisors was promoted, the two remaining supervisors felt that they would be able to supervise the entire plant floor, i.e., 80 production workers in several departments.

In other words, as people developed more mature attitudes and were increasingly able to assume responsibility at all levels, one layer of supervision (the production superintendent) and one-third of the first-line supervisory force were eliminated. This major change in the formal system resulted from the improvements that had been made at all levels in the human and flow perspectives.

4. Relationships with the Parent Corporation. In Fig. 14.2 we included both control systems and personnel policies in the category of organizational processes. So far, however, we have discussed this plant only as a system in its own right. Since this plant is part of an international corporation with about 50 plants in the United States, we can also consider this particular plant as one subsystem within the larger system, the parent corporation. Accordingly, some of the established policies, procedures, and controls of the parent company affected, and were affected by, this plant as a subsystem.

For example, most large corporations have well-established pay programs for hourly employees which are based on the assumptions that the manager leads and directs and that the hourly workers merely follow his directives. What kind of pay system should be devised for hourly workers whose jobs have been enlarged by their taking over the job of inspecting their own work? How can traditional methods of job evaluation take into consideration the fact that hourly assembly workers have grown and matured on the job so that they have taken over many of the calibration and related tasks that previously required the work of technicians who were paid on a weekly basis? Such problems illustrate the fact that a change in one subsystem creates stresses and strains throughout the entire system. In this case, the parent corporation is still considering what action to take with regard to the revision of pay systems.

IV. SUMMARY AND CONCLUSION

We have used this case study to show how concepts of organizational development were used and applied in a concrete, real-life situation. We have tried to show that organizations can improve and that individuals at all levels can grow and develop. In other words, the needs of the individual and the needs of the organization can be met through changing the nature of the explicit and the implicit psychological contract.

Perhaps more importantly, we have tried to demonstrate through concrete examples the entire concept of systems that we first discussed in Chapter 2. First, the organization is an open system composed of a number of interdependent and interrelated subsystems. Second, optimal problem definitions, solutions, and designs occur only when all three perspectives of systems are considered simultaneously, with emphasis being placed on differing points of view only as appropriate.

REVIEW

1. Compare the company in this case before and after change according to McGregor's Theories X and Y. Should the results which occurred in this case have happened according to theory? Were there other things that should have happened but didn't?

2. "Behavioral change precedes attitudinal change." How can action precede thought? What is the role of reinforcement in such a process? What is the role of feedback?

3. What was the purpose of the "brag tags" the girls signed and sent to the customer? What function did the concept of competition have here? Is this a return to the craft concept of manufacture? Under what circumstances will this solution prove feasible in the hot-plate department?

4. How is the managerial style of leadership related to the total system concept of organizational operations? What is the benefit of participative management in this context? Was it used in this case?

5. What were the primary functions of the change agent in this case? Should the agent solve the particular problem that is facing his client? What is the relationship between the outside change agent(s) and the internal agent?

6. From Fig. 14.2, determine the resultant change in outputs: (a) if the control systems were eliminated from the organizational processes; (b) if communication were eliminated; and (c) if the human system inputs were missing.

7. Select an organization and analyze it according to the human and flow systems model (Fig. 14.2). Indicate what is missing and the impact you think it has on the total system.

REFERENCES

1 E. Huse and P. Price, "The Relationship Between Maturity and Motivation in Varied Work Groups" (*Proceedings of the 70th Annual Convention of the American Psychological Association,* September 1970), pp. 587–588.

PART V
PROSPECTS
FOR
THE
FUTURE

15
TOMORROW

The true rebel in a society where the only certainty is change itself is the individual who resists change.

EUGENE JENNINGS

Reprinted through the courtesy of the Chicago Tribune-New York News Syndicate, Inc.

I. INTRODUCTION

All of us are continually predicting the future. When we turn on the radio, we are predicting that it will work; when we turn on the ignition of our car, we are predicting that the car will start. In the past, soothsayers examined the entrails of chickens or other creatures to predict whether the future would be favorable or unfavorable. Literally thousands of people visited the Oracle at Delphi in ancient Greece to obtain an understanding of their own personal future. Crystal balls, palmistry, astrology, and even highly sophisticated mathematical models have been used to foretell the future.

One of the difficulties with any prediction is that it may be based on improper or inaccurate assumptions. Another problem is that the data are often ignored. Many feel that the Pentagon Papers clearly show that many governmental assumptions about Vietnam were incorrect and that the data, although available, were incorrectly used. One editorial praising the reorganization of the government's intelligence agencies pointed out that the CIA and the State Department's Bureau of Intelligence and Research have been consistently more skeptical and more accurate than White House or military evaluations; however, only these latter sources were used.[1]

If the assumptions on which predictions are based are inaccurate and the available data are used improperly, the prediction will be inaccurate. In a parody of Tolkien's *The Lord of the Rings,* a birdbath is used as a type of crystal ball to predict the future. After Frito, the hero, has had a successful future predicted for him, he falls asleep.

The surface of the basin remained black for a while, then flickered and showed the triumphal reception of the S.S. Titanic *in New York Harbor, the repayment of the French war debt [World War I] and the [presidential] inaugural ball of Harold Stassen.*[2]

Some science fiction writers have been highly successful in predicting the future. For example, when the Manhattan Project to develop the atomic bomb was in progress during World War II, a science fiction writer accurately described the specific techniques for developing the atomic bomb, including the methods by which uranium 235 would be developed.[3] Shortly after this short story appeared in a magazine, FBI agents descended upon the hapless and surprised author, demanding to know how he had got hold of governmental top secret documents. By all accounts, it took quite a bit of explaining for him to convince the agents that his predictions had been derived from material available in the public domain and his own intuition.

This experience may have led to the hiring of six famous science fiction writers to assist a consulting company with "Project Delphi," an attempt to predict what the world will be like in A.D. 2000.[4] Thirteen client companies funded this project to project feasible alternatives that might be considered for the future, and the project's "consultants" were not only the six science fiction writers, but also the company's employees—from janitors to highly paid technical analysts and executives.

The impossibility of finding the single best answer is aptly demonstrated by Handler, who points out that especially in the living sciences, attempts to provide answers to questions invariably reveal another set of more sophisticated questions.[5] In other words, the greater our knowledge, the greater our ignorance.

II. TWO DIVERGENT WORLD VIEWS

A. The Pessimistic View

Such a view was expounded by George Orwell, who foresaw increasing depersonalization of the individual, thought control, and the accompanying loss of individual identity, both on and off the job.[6] The increasingly tight controls over the individual and society would result in man's being locked into a rigid, tight mold, with severe punishments for deviants. A recent confirmation of this view was given by Russell Baker, who described the FBI's investigation of a reporter who published articles disliked by the Administration and who warned against the "development of certain monarchical, absolutist tendencies" of the past three Administrations.[7]

Many people feel a sense of helplessness, alienation, and futility as they look at today's organizations. For example, many college freshmen regard their high schools as boring, meaningless, and depersonalized institutions. But their colleges are no improvement; they see only a rigid, outmoded, and "irrelevant" curriculum and a university structure that does not respond to their needs.

Many managers have similar feelings about industrial or other social organizations. They believe that today's organizations are becoming increasingly depersonalized, i.e., an individual going into a large organization will suffer a loss of identity and be forced to become an "organization man" who knuckles under and conforms to the "system," thus becoming less of an individual. In his description of the resulting dilemma and role conflict faced by many managers, Ericson notes that although such values as honor, trust, loyalty, individuality, and human dignity are highly important to the manager, these concepts do not fit in with his organizational experience.[8]

Bass reviewed field work conducted in the United States, Japan, and Australia and reports that managers generally see the need for (1) increased education, (2) performance having a more direct impact on reward, (3) better use of the computer, (4) more emphasis on interpersonal skills, (5) opportunity for both managers and the work force to have greater autonomy, and (6) increased attention to such external environmental factors as overseas markets, customer demands, and governmental regulations.[9] In addition, Bass sees the need for concern with the increasing importance of the role of women, change, and immediacy. The changing nature of the work force means that employees will be demanding more meaningful work which allows for personal growth and responsibility.

The magnitude of these problems has caused many people to feel that there is little or no possibility of changing "the system," whether it be politics or the modern organization. This leads to their feelings of apathy and powerlessness. As a result, many individuals have turned to communes and T-groups to fill the need for closeness with others.

The ever-increasing size and complexity of modern organizations provide further evidence of the Orwellian concept. The annual revenue of General Motors, for example, exceeds the gross national product of all but two foreign governments (England and Russia). With the increasing use of computers, the individual loses his "identity" to a multidigit figure which can become an input to computers throughout the country without his knowledge. The danger inherent in this national collection and dissemination of information on citizens is cited by Hey, who warns against "social security snooping."[10] Currently, there is little state or federal legislation controlling the widespread use of such information, although remedial action is being considered. The Soviet Union, however, intends to develop a computer network that would allow the Kremlin to take over and centralize larger sections of the nation's economy than has been possible in the past.[11] This would reassert the Kremlin's totalitarian control, which has been eroding since the death of Stalin in 1953.

Perhaps the most chilling recent book in the Orwellian tradition is *One Flew Over the Cuckoo's Nest*, in which the hero, McMurphy, is confined to a mental hospital even though he is perfectly sane.[12] McMurphy is determined not to passively accept the hospital "system" and to get other patients to reassert their sense of humanness and life. The "Big Nurse," who reigns over the hospital ward, is equally determined to maintain her dominance, the "system," and to "cure" McMurphy of his independence, freedom, and immense capacity to enjoy life. With the tacit help of the psychiatrist, McMurphy almost wins; but slowly, the system, personified by the nurse, prevails. McMurphy's struggle is seen as further evidence of his insanity, and he is given shock treatments "for his own good." When he still resists conformity, the Big Nurse has him lobotomized, leaving him a "vegetable" with his individuality, vitality, and sense of humor irretrievably lost. Such "fiction" is all too real to those Soviet citizens who have been confined to mental hospitals to "reform" their criticism of the regime.

Although he probably would disagree with his placement in this section, one advocate of the "more pessimistic" approach is Skinner, who believes that the environment determines behavior through operant conditioning.[13] He proposes a technology for the *design* of a culture which could bring about the complete control of human behavior, pointing out that this is "essential if the human species is to continue to develop." He feels strongly that this continuing evolution requires more rather than less control and that this is "an engineering problem of the first importance." Skinner insists that such control is essentially neutral and that its use is hindered by the inappropriate use of such terms as "freedom" and "dignity." He concludes by pointing out that we are still not fully aware of "what man can make of man."

According to these negative, or pessimistic, views, the world of the future will be depersonalized—except for the elite few, men will become automatons and slaves to a computer-dominated system. The application of this viewpoint to social organizations has been well articulated by Leavitt and Whisler, who predicted that a tight oligarchy of managers and innovators will form an organizational elite and that the gap between this small group and those lower in the organization will widen and become more sharply drawn.[14] Almost ten years later, Carroll pointed out that the intervening years had provided "little basis for disagreement with their prophecies. If anything, the mechanisms for fulfillment are clearer."[15]

B. The Optimistic View

The pessimistic view is not universally accepted. Some people believe that the future holds far more freedom for individuals. Similarly, the optimists predict that organizations of the future will change rapidly from the traditional, authoritarian structure in order to survive in a rapidly changing world. Therefore, bureaucracy as we know it will become dysfunctional in organizations, albeit with a few exceptions. This view is based on the premise that the rate, or pace, of change is rapidly accelerating and that new organizational structures must replace more traditional ones.

One of the most articulate writers in this area is Warren Bennis, who predicts the decline of bureaucracy and the emergence of new, adaptive systems that better fit the accelerated process of change.[16] According to Bennis, bureaucracy is based on a high degree of division of labor, a specified hierarchical authority with specific rules and procedures emphasizing impersonal relationships, and the use of technical competence as the primary criterion for selection and promotion. Therefore, bureaucracy leads to the development of "group thinking," which neither allows for individual growth and development nor provides for the proper handling of conflict, unanticipated problems, and rapid change.

Bennis feels that organizational structures of the future will be considerably different from what they are today in that the use of temporary groups will increase. An excellent example of such a temporary group is the operating-room "team." According to classic bureaucratic principles, the operating-room team cannot be effective, since there is no centralization of authority. Frequently, neither the surgeon nor the anesthesiologist is a hospital employee, but rather "contracts" his services to the patient. The nurses and orderlies assisting the surgeon are employees of the hospital and therefore do not "bureaucratically" report to either the surgeon or the anesthesiologist. Yet the team functions well, not because of bureaucratic rules and structure, but because of the "norms" of the team and the urgency of the situation. All members of the team concentrate on the patient, not the bureaucratic structure. Indeed, as one operation is completed, an entirely different "temporary group" may conduct the next operation.

Another writer with an optimistic view of the future is Reich, who uses the terms Consciousness I, II, and III to trace the evolution of American thought and beliefs.[17] For Reich, Consciousness I epitomizes the Puritan ethic of individual-

This rural town in Nebraska typifies the era of Consciousness I, when individualism and hard work were the tenets of the Puritan ethic. (Photograph by Edgar F. Huse)

ism and the release from the European customs of class and social status. The individual was his own sovereign and was almost completely responsible for his own fulfillment, achievement, and growth. Success, in the Horatio Alger tradition, was achieved by hard work, self-denial, and the development of character. Indeed, character was all-important, since it was from the individual's own character that the other virtues were derived.

Reich believes that Consciousness I failed because it was unable to keep up with the changing American realities—America outgrew its rural traditions, and individuality and the simple virtues became submerged in organizations. The resulting spirit of reform and the need for change led to Consciousness II—a striving for order and rationality through bureaucratic, rational organizational

Habitat, a shopping and housing complex built for Expo '67, represents the rationality and technology of Consciousness II. (Photograph by Felicity S. Bowditch)

processes. However, Reich believes that this has resulted in the "American Corporate State," a single, vast corporation of which everyone is a forced member. To Reich, the corporate state has only one value—"the value of technology-organization-efficiency-growth-progress," which results in the individual's nearly total subordination to the system.[18] He feels that this leads to a type of schizophrenia—the individual splits his working and private life, accepting the values of the corporate state while at work, but seeking to escape from them in his private life.

Reich believes that the corporate state is starting to destroy itself; manifestations of this are the individual's loss of interest and pride in his work, the growing concern with ecology, and the growing dissatisfaction (particularly among younger people) with things as they are. This corporate self-destruction will give way to a peaceful, bloodless revolution (Consciousness III) whereby the individual will refuse to passively accept the system and will strive for more personal liberty and accept more personal responsibility for society and himself. The aims of Consciousness III are a new sense of self, less acceptance of society as a "given," and a greater assertion of values that are considerably less material-oriented than are the values of Consciousness II, which are highly oriented toward material attainments and goals.

The emergence of Consciousness III is illustrated by the conversation one of the authors had with a young man who had completed all of his work for his doctorate but his Ph.D. dissertation. Rather than completing his degree immediately, the student decided to drop out for a year or two to travel across America and Europe in order to "get to know the land and the people and find out more about himself." Lacking money, he planned to take on odd jobs to support himself and had already held a variety of such jobs—janitor, short-order cook, and service-station attendant. He felt that by doing this, he would be able to "put my Ph.D. degree to more meaningful use."

Reich's highly controversial book led to a companion volume entitled *The Con III Controversy: The Critics Look at "The Greening of America,"* in which more than 30 authors, ranging "from the editors of Fortune Magazine to Herbert Marcuse," discuss the pros and cons of Reich's book.[19] Some of the commentators believe that Reich's points are valid, but others do not believe that Reich's "bloodless revolution" will come to pass.

Glasser, who goes beyond Reich, traces the 3.5 million years of man's history and identifies four clear, distinct phases: (1) primitive survival society, (2) primitive identity society, (3) civilized survival society, and (4) civilized identity society.[20] In Phase 1, the primitive survival society, man was preoccupied primarily with survival in a hostile, rigorous environment. Survival was possible only because man was able to cooperate with others for defense, hunting, and protecting the young. Man's need to cooperate intelligently with others slowly became instinctual, a condition which was necessary in order for man to survive the harshness of his environment.

After three million years, man began to gain more control over his environment; he was therefore less concerned with survival as such than with rest, leisure, and pleasure. During this primitive identity society (Phase 2), which evolved about 500,000 years ago, man began to develop religious beliefs, rituals, art, magic ceremonies, and dances. He was now using both his body and his brain in the pursuit of enjoyment and pleasure.

Phase 3, the civilized survival society which emerged as the population increased, is based on a power hierarchy which maintains a rigid, pyramidal

The Stonehenge, a circular formation of huge rocks, was built by prehistoric man for use in religious ceremonies.

social structure—a small elite, a somewhat larger middle class, and a vast laboring class. The development of agriculture and the decrease of available game to hunt meant that in much of the world, land and similar possessions became valuable. Men who were more aggressive were able to acquire more resources, and therefore aggression became a dominant theme in man's existence. (As Glasser points out, the American Indians were living in a Phase 2 society when they were overrun by the American frontiersmen, aggressive members of the civilized survival society.) Only a few members of Phase 3 society were rich enough to be concerned about identity, however; the masses were still scrambling for existence at a survival level.

Phase 4 is the civilized identity society, or what Reich calls Consciousness III. Here, particularly during the last 20 years in western culture, the more affluent societies have begun to move toward a society in which man can be more concerned with his own self-identity and his own self-expression, or what Glasser calls the development of a successful respect for individual integrity as opposed to the needs for security and survival.

In his predictions of the future, Toffler goes beyond Reich or Glasser by suggesting that the rate of change in all areas of society will increase rapidly in the next few decades.[21] Modifying the term "culture shock," which has been used to describe the impact on an individual's ability to adapt while moving from one culture to another, Toffler has coined the phrase "future shock" to describe the difficulty of adapting to changes caused by the passage of time. Future shock is the physical and psychological distress resulting from over-stimulation and the "overload of the human organism's physical adaptive system and its decision-making processes."[22] In other words, future shock causes a great deal of disorientation because the individual is subjected to far too much change in far too short a time.

Although he hedges some of his predictions by quoting an old Chinese proverb, "To prophesy is extremely difficult, especially with regard to the future," Toffler makes a good case for the fact that the next few decades will bring about an avalanche of change and that most people are almost totally unprepared for the vastly accelerated pace of change. To build his case, he reports on both physiological and psychological studies. Physiological studies, for example, have shown that the amount and rate of change an individual has been subjected to in a particular time span is closely correlated with his state of physical health. In other words, the greater the amount of change, the higher the probability that the individual will have a subsequent illness. Similarly, psychological studies have shown that the rate of change affects the mental well-being of the individual. In the same way that the body may react to the rate of change by subsequent illness, so also can the psyche crack under the strain, reducing the individual's ability to make rational decisions. In short, there is an optimum amount of stimulation which the human body and mind can take, and beyond this point the individual's ability to handle overload is considerably reduced. Toffler believes that the rising rate of confusion and emotional breakdowns, including the increasing use of drugs at all levels of society, the increasing rate of outbreaks of violence and vandalism, and the increasing popularity of mysticism, are all signs of future shock.

Toffler's conclusions are confirmed by recent research on the strong relationship between moving and depression in women.[23] Although many people believe that Americans are able to adapt to frequent moves with relative ease and little anxiety, moves generate a great deal of stress, particularly among women. The women studied rarely connected their mental illness to the moves; rather, they were likely to attribute their depression to such other causes as increased marital friction, problems with finances and children, and identity confusion. However, the research indicated that it was the move itself that caused the depression, with resulting effects on marital, child, and financial concerns.

Toffler sees a present and continuing superindustrial revolution which will result in an almost paralyzing surfeit of choice (overchoice). For example, he cites Marshall McLuhan's finding that for any specific make of automobile, there is such a proliferation of choice of different engines, accessories, color, upholstery, and other items that the sum total of available options is approximately 25 million! To verify this, we reviewed *Edmund's New Car Prices* for the 1971 Tempest series (all of which have the same basic body and chassis).[24] There are three different models in this series (Tempest, LeMans, and GTO); six types of engine; twenty-seven options on body style; eight different styles of mounted tire style and two types of spares; seven different transmissions; six radio options; and seven mirror styles. And this listing of accessories does not include the tremendous variety in color and upholstery. If the customer then tries to compare makes of cars, it is obvious that the varieties of choice go up astronomically. McLuhan may well be right.

Toffler also cites the overchoice apparent in the proliferating number of detergents and brands of cigarettes on the supermarket shelf. This increasing amount of choice and rate of change, coupled with the increasing rate of technological change, lead not to a 1984 concept of sameness, but rather to the problems of future shock.

III. ACCELERATED PACE OF CHANGE

In this section we discuss five areas of rapidly accelerating change: the knowledge explosion, product obsolescence, the changing composition of the labor force, the increasing concern about social issues, and the growing internationalization of business. Although these areas are interrelated, they are dealt with separately for the sake of clarity.

A. The Knowledge Explosion

More than 90 percent of all the scientists who have ever lived are still living. This has resulted in a tremendous acceleration in the development of knowledge —the "knowledge explosion." For example, for literally thousands of years, the wheel remained one of the most advanced inventions in transportation and,

The first transatlantic flight left Port Washington, New York, on June 28, 1939 for Marseilles, France. (Photograph courtesy Pan American World Airways)

indeed, was reinvented at various times by different peoples. The American Indian had not yet even invented the wheel when Columbus landed in this country less than 500 years ago. The Tasaday tribe in the Philippines, discovered in 1971, is still in the Bronze Age and has not yet invented the wheel. In the thousands of years that the wheel has been known to man, only minor improvements have been made, e.g., rubber tires. Yet in about 80 years, transportation has progressed to the invention of motor cars, jet airplanes, and rockets to outer space. Indeed, the *first* commercial passenger flight across the North Atlantic occurred on June 28, 1939, a little more than 30 years ago.

The development of the modern vacuum tube is relatively recent and was superseded by the development of transistors and microminiature circuitry, which in turn led to the development of solid-state circuits. The recent discovery of DNA may well make it possible in the near future for geneticists to "design" human beings *in advance*, by altering the sperm or the egg prior to conception.[25]

This highly sophisticated microminiature circuit is so small that an ant appears to be quite large by comparison. (Photograph courtesy Jet Propulsion Laboratory)

The result of the knowledge explosion is that an individual's knowledge can quickly become obsolete. In other words, it is almost impossible to keep up with new knowledge. Information learned in college courses may well be obsolete before the student has an opportunity to put what he has learned into practice. In the field of psychology alone, it is estimated that some 21,000 books, articles, and monographs are written each year, and it has been estimated that the rate of new information is doubling every ten years.

B. Rapid Product Obsolescence

Products quickly become obsolete as new knowledge is acquired. New products are invented, developed, and quickly become obsolete, just as the transistor became relatively obsolete with the development of microminiature circuitry.

Each year, on the average, a higher percentage of the gross national product goes into research and development than ever before. An industrial company develops, for example, a new, complex medical instrument only to find that within a few short months, a competing company has brought out a better instrument at a lower cost. And as more money is poured into research, the rate at which new products are developed increases. This is far different from the manufacturing of the horseshoe, the design of which remained essentially unchanged for hundreds of years.

Product obsolescence is growing at a rapidly accelerating pace. Meanwhile, products are becoming more and more complex and costly to produce. One of the reasons for the soaring cost of hospitalization, for example, is the vastly expanded use of instruments that were not even in existence 20 years ago.

C. The Changing Composition of the Labor Force

The United States has undergone a dramatic shift in population as the country has become increasingly urbanized. In 1825 only 10 percent of the American population lived in towns and cities. By 1960, however, 70 percent of the population lived on 1 percent of the land area. It is estimated that in the year 2000, 90 percent of the population will live on 2 percent of the land area. A recent response to such demographic trends has been the planned development of new cities. One such new city is Columbia, Maryland, where General Electric built a new distribution facility to serve the Northeast, in which 30 percent of the nation's current population is concentrated on 7 percent of the land.[26]

Paralleling the increasing urbanization is the rising educational level of the population. When Frederick Taylor did his pioneering work in 1900, most industrial workers were immigrants who did not know English. This work force, then, had little education and was accustomed to obeying orders without question. Today, however, it is estimated that 60 percent or more of the urban population is obtaining some form of higher education beyond high school. In fact, today's college diploma is roughly equivalent in value to a high school education of only a few years ago. The same shift is occurring at the graduate level. The United States Office of Education expects the nation to have 1.6 million resident graduate students in 1979, or nearly double the 889,000 in 1969, and almost five times the 331,000 in 1959.

Therefore, the employee of tomorrow will be considerably better educated than the employee of today, regardless of the type of organization in which he or she is employed. In practical terms, this shift in educational background means that the employee of tomorrow will not accept outmoded styles of management. For example, 33 military officers, among the brightest and most capable of those teaching at West Point, recently left the service.[27] A spokesman for the academy indicated that the resignations were disastrous, since these men "are the brightest—they are outstanding officers." All of the officers who re-

Many people fear that increasing urbanization will be accompanied by greater uniformity and population density. (Photograph courtesy Christian Science Monitor*)*

signed had been promoted faster than normal, but all felt that life outside the army would give them greater personal satisfaction. As one officer explained, "You have to play it safe for so long before you can become a general—and by that time you're a different person."

Another major change in the composition of the labor force is the decrease in the median age of the population, a direct result of the baby boom following World War II. In a few short years, the number of births in this country rose by about 50 percent. As a result, the median age of the work force is decreasing, and managers will have to become increasingly aware of the needs and concerns of their younger workers.

The fourth major change is the shift from "blue-collar" workers (laborers and semiskilled workers) to "white-collar" workers (managerial, professional, technical, sales, and clerical personnel). The year 1956 marked a watershed; for the first time, "white-collar" workers outnumbered "blue-collar" workers. The best guess is that the ratio will be about 3-2 in 1976 and will continue to increase.

D. Increasing Concern over Social Issues

People are becoming increasingly concerned about all types of social issues, e.g., school integration, air and water pollution, and ecological damage. Recently, for example, 23 major industries in Birmingham, Alabama, were found in violation of the Clean Air Act and were given direct court orders to cease fouling the air.[28] Similarly, on 14 June 1972, William Ruckelshaus, administrator of the Environmental Protection Agency, announced a nearly complete ban on the use of DDT in the United States because the agency believed that the pesticide's potential harm to the environment outweighed its benefits. The ban becomes effective on 31 December 1972, thus giving farmers time to make the transition to other pesticides which are not as toxic as DDT. Both industry and environmentalists are appealing the ban—the former because they believe "the ban is adverse to the interests of agriculture"; the latter because they believe a total ban should go into effect sooner.

This growing public concern with social issues has led to a decreasing acceptance of bureaucratic authority. The strong drive for civil rights, student strikes in universities, stress on strong legal action to safeguard the environment —including preservation of wild life, parks, undeveloped land—are all indications of the growing public concern about social issues and the traditional bureaucratic methods of handling these problems. Other indications are the growth of such organizations as Common Cause and the increasing public support of the work of Ralph Nader.

Large stockholders, especially universities and religious bodies, are coming under increasing pressure to use their investment leverage to force large corporations to take positive action on far-reaching social issues. For example, both Harvard and MIT own about 250,000 shares of General Motors stock. In 1971 the academic community exerted strong pressure on Harvard to endorse four proposals forcing GM to be more responsive on current social issues.[29] The five-man governing board of Harvard, however, decided not to endorse the four proposals.

One year later, in April 1972, the Administration Building of Harvard College was taken over by campus blacks who were trying to force Harvard to get rid of about $18.5 million of Gulf Oil Corporation stock. Their protest was based on the belief that Gulf allegedly supports Portuguese colonial rule in

Angola. Subsequently, the President and Fellows of Harvard College issued a statement asserting that Harvard would request Gulf to provide more information about its operations in Angola and would send a personal representative to Angola to obtain first-hand information about Gulf's performance and operations in the country. However, the college did not feel that selling its Gulf stock would be a useful move.

Such pressures have led to the formation of a new type of mutual fund that provides investment assistance for investors who do not want to put their money into organizations or industries that pollute, engage in racist hiring practices, or are involved in the "military-industrial complex.[30] Undoubtedly, such funds will continue to grow in the future. Just as student "sit-ins" in the office of a university president were almost unheard of a few years ago, it is possible that employees will "revolt" against their corporate employers. Athos predicts that this is likely to occur unless organizations take into account the concerns of today's students and what is likely to happen as they move into middle-management ranks.[31]

Athos' prediction has already come true. In the spring of 1972, a group of primarily black employees at Polaroid made serious attempts to dissuade the company from carrying out business with the South African government, calling such dealings imperialist and racist (Polaroid equipment and techniques are used in the identification cards the South African government requires all nonwhites to carry with them at all times). These employees called for a boycott of Polaroid products to support their demands. The company, which has a strong record of progressive social action, countered that their plants in South Africa actually helped improve the lot of nonwhites by providing them with jobs, which in turn helped improve their standard of living.

The growing concern with social issues occurs not only with students and middle managers, but also among members of the Young President's Club (a club for men who have become company presidents before age 40). In a series of interviews conducted with these men, Purcell found that they were concerned not only with business, but also with society, the community in which the corporation is located, justice, and idealism.[32]

Cuthbert and Elden stress that today's social unrest among students will have a strong impact on tomorrow's organizations.[33] They predict that employees of the 1970s, in particular, will be demanding more freedom, power, and social influence. Therefore, organizations must begin to build new organizational structures to solve the problems of tomorrow before they occur. The employees and managers of the not-so-distant future will be demanding a reward system that emphasizes excitement and relevance rather than security and money.

At this new, highly automated Vega plant at Lordstown, Ohio, the young workers have translated their dissatisfaction with their jobs into overt acts of sabotage, absenteeism, and hostility to management. (Photograph courtesy The Warren Tribune Chronicle*)*

The General Motors Vega plant in Lordstown, Ohio, has already experienced overt employee unrest. At this new, highly automated plant, the average age of the 6400 workers is about 23. But, as *Newsweek* points out, "Lordstown has turned out to be something of a nightmare" for G.M.; the work force disdains the traditional work ethic and has "no tolerance at all for the nit-picking discipline of the assembly line."[34] Absenteeism is climbing steadily, and one person, asked why he was working only four days a week, replied that he could not "make enough money in three." In addition, there are strong indications of increased polarization and hostility between management and workers, who commit overt acts of "sabotage" by snapping off trunk or ignition keys in the locks.

It is obvious that there is confusion about the nature of personal versus corporate and governmental responsibility in all kinds of activities. Boulding suggests we take care in examining what appear to be deviances from norms,

As business firms become international, they must also become multilingual. (Photograph by Edgar F. Huse)

because it is possible that the *norms* are shifting.[35] He also notes that the most important thing to prepare for is the unexpected, thereby guarding against the illusion of feeling certain in an uncertain situation.

E. Increasing Internationalization of Business

Business is becoming more and more internationalized, as the growth of the European Common Market indicates. For example, Bass suggests that "60 percent of all the world's business will eventually be done by international firms."[36] He predicts that the concept of the common market will vastly expand and that the typical manager of the future will be involved in a world of mixed economies, e.g., capitalist and socialist ideologies will be closer together, and the organization of the future will be doing business in many different countries, as is already happening in the expanding trade between the United States and Russia.

Table 15.1 Imports and exports in world trade (value in million U.S. dollars)

International investments	Imports	Exports
1938	25,400	23,500
1961	141,000	134,000
1968	251,000	239,000
United States		
1938	2,180	3,064
1961	14,703	8,700
1968	33,066	12,190

Source: Adapted from *Yearbook of International Trade Statistics*, New York, United Nations, 1970, pp. 12-13.

Table 15.1 shows the income receipts and payments resulting from international investments. The table clearly shows the vast increase in receipts and payments from 1938 to the present time, with the amount doubling in the seven-year period from 1961 to 1968. Not only is the United States investing more heavily abroad (to the concern of the Canadian government), but also other countries are investing more heavily in the United States. For example, although Mitsubishi Heavy Industries (a Japanese firm) encountered cultural difficulties when their aircraft assembly plant began operating in San Angelo, a small Texas town, the company in 1970 had 25% of the American market for executive turboprop aircraft and intends to increase production in the plant by 50% in 1972 to increase its share of the market.[37]

In his discussion of cultural barriers, Stone stresses the need to adapt interpersonal and intercultural communications in order to bridge the cultural barriers in international management.[38] Stone provides ground rules to such an approach and points out the need to consciously build a world-wide culture in which international well-being and cooperation can be achieved. Goodman and Moore, however, urge caution in undertaking such an approach.[39] They feel that the quality of cross-cultural managerial studies has been generally low because the theoretical delineation and operational specification of the culture (and subcultures) were neglected as moderating variables and that the data were not adequately analyzed.

F. Summary

In this section, we used five examples of the signs of accelerated change. In addition, there are such others as mass education and communication and mobility. These forces behind societal changes and changing values mean that organizations will have a younger, more highly educated labor force that is oriented toward white-collar and service organizations. Today's painfully gained knowledge may well be obsolete tomorrow. With the increasing amount and rate of product obsolescence, organizations will have to become geared to rapid change. Increasing concern about social issues will force organizations of all types to consider their environment much more carefully, either through conscience or social legislation. Finally, the increasing internationalization of business will force organizations to become more adept at dealing with a wider variety of cultures.

IV. DEALING WITH ORGANIZATIONAL CHANGE

The rapidly increasing pace of societal change will affect the organization of the future even more than it affects the organization of today. Tomorrow's hospitals, governmental units, and businesses will have to improve and increase their ability to cope with change in modern society in order to survive.

In Chapter 2 we discussed the tendency of organizations to seek an equilibrium, or balance. This process is made more difficult by the existence of two forces—proactive and reactive. The reactive forces resist change and work toward preserving the status quo; the proactive forces work toward change and the attainment of an optimal balance in the system. Using a "force-field analysis" approach, Lewin has established a method of analyzing the effect of these opposing forces.[40]

Figure 15.1 shows this process. The arrows represent forces, or vectors, applied to the body at rest. The length of the vector is equivalent to the strength of the vector. If the algebraic sum of the vectors is equal, the body will remain at rest, but if the strength of the vectors on either side changes, the balance point changes until the sum of the vectors is again equal. In other words, one can either increase the force on one side or decrease the force on the other side.

The same concept is true if this model is applied to social organizations. The organization can reach a new balance point if one set of vectors is either increased or decreased. However, the forces exerted on social organizations—feelings, attitudes, and emotions—cannot be quantified. For example, a foreman's demand for greater productivity (increased vector) is likely to be met by increased resistance, distrust, and hostility on the part of the workers, for if one "pushes" a man, he is likely to "push" back. For example, a group of high school

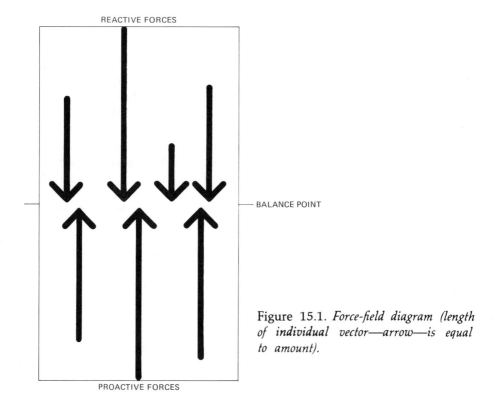

REACTIVE FORCES

BALANCE POINT

PROACTIVE FORCES

Figure 15.1. *Force-field diagram (length of individual vector—arrow—is equal to amount).*

boys were working as dishwashers and general kitchen help in a nursing home. When a new man was put in charge of the kitchen, he reduced lunch breaks, eliminated coffee breaks, and pushed hard for increased work in an effort to increase the workers' productivity. As a result, the boys slowed down their work and took even longer to accomplish their tasks than they had in the past. In this case, the equilibrium of productivity actually moved downward as a direct result of the pressure to move productivity upward. In other words, a simple, mechanistic model cannot be applied to the social organization, because increased pressure from one direction may result in increased counterpressure from the other direction.

Organizational equilibrium can be altered by either *increasing* the set of forces in the desired direction or *reducing* the set of opposing vectors. Table 15.2 shows some of the forces which affect the present balance of the social organization, e.g., the accelerated rate of knowledge expansion and product obsolescence, the changing values of the work force, and increased public pressure for cleaner air and water and greater social responsibility by business. Reactive

Table 15.2 Forces affecting organizational balance

Proactive forces	Reactive forces
Increasing rate of change, including product obsolescence, etc.	Rigidity of bureaucratic approaches
Increased pressure from public sector	Failure to use systems approach
Changing values of the work force, including managers	Overemphasis on single perspective
More laws and regulations	Obsolete managerial concepts
Increasing knowledge in behavioral and quantitative sciences	Need for stable manufacturing schedule
	Managerial myopia—clinging to outmoded concepts
	Fear and distrust of change
	Organizational inertia
	Theory "X" assumptions
	Conflicting objectives

forces may take the form of top management's refusing to seize an opportunity because of the inherent personal risks involved. Or, a manager may exert a reactive pressure by ignoring improvements that threaten his deeply held Theory X assumptions.

Argyris believes that the strongest reactive forces lie not only within the managers, but also in the other individuals within the social organization.[41] He believes that most individuals are "systematically blind" to their behavior and are therefore "culturally programmed" to behave in ways that reduce the probability of change. The strength of these reactive forces cannot be lessened simply by increasing the amount and degree of the proactive forces. Rather, a much more effective approach is to reduce the amount and degree of the resistance to change by reducing the strength of the reactive forces.

One alternative is provided by Gellerman, who uses what he calls cost-control and value-adding strategies.[42] For Gellerman, cost-control strategies include restricting behavior through the use of budgets, rules, reports, and standards. Value-adding strategies encourage actions which lead to change through the use of such proactive forces as job enrichment and increased participation. Although these two approaches are not necessarily mutually exclusive, the time may have come to emphasize the value-adding approach to increase human productivity.

Similarly, Buckley differentiates between "structure-maintaining" and "structure-elaborating and changing" features of the system.[43] He believes that the modern organization must shift its emphasis from structure-maintaining behavior to structure-elaborating behavior, asserting that this will help the organization to survive, grow, and prosper.

Sokolik's approach is more specific; he contends that the traditional personnel-department concept has failed and suggests that two separate and distinct types of personnel departments replace it.[44] One type of personnel department would deal primarily with such maintainence factors as pay and working conditions; the other would be responsible for growth needs. He also describes a second model for personnel departments, i.e., personnel activities would be grouped according to selected classes of workers, e.g., scientific and technical, culturally disadvantaged, and women. This second model is favored by Hall and Lawlor, who stress that scientific and research and development personnel must be managed differently from other types of workers, as Lawrence and Lorsch also note.[45]

All of these authors are stressing the need for change and improvement in organizations, not by increasing the forces for change, but rather by reducing the forces against change. Lane discusses the need to improve organizations by designing jobs that provide "pursuit of pleasure" on the job, believing that since current job designs are not coping with the rising frustration index of people on jobs, they are thereby destroying the "good life."[46] As he says, "It is this very asset that is continuously, assiduously plowed under . . . and kicked into sullen submission by 99% of employees today."[47]

A number of authors have discussed a broader, more general approach to change. For example, Greiner reviewed 18 studies of organizational change and found that the more successful attempts at change involved six major steps:[48]

1. Pressure and Arousal. At this level, there is a felt need for change, particularly at the top-management level. Such pressure comes from either external forces—competitor breakthroughs or stockholder discontent—or internal events—interdepartmental conflict, decreased productivity, or a union strike.

2. Intervention and Reorientation. This usually involves bringing in a newcomer, usually an outside consultant, who has a more objective viewpoint, can appraise organizational needs, and can reorient the thinking of top managers by getting them to re-examine their practices and procedures, thereby helping them define the real problems.

3. Diagnosis and Recognition. At this level of change, the newcomer, or consultant, helps the organization at all levels to do a better job of "seeking the location and causes of problems." In the more successful attempts at change, this is a shared rather than a unilateral or delegated approach; in the unilateral approach, the top brass make the decisions, whereas in the delegated approach, top management delegates, but remains uninvolved.

4. Invention and Commitment. Here, effort is directed toward developing more effective solutions to problems and using the shared approach to obtain full commitment for the implementation of the new solutions. Greiner stresses that successful change approaches involve intensive searches for new, innovative solutions which depend on the collaboration of a large number of people who provide their own solutions. In his study, Greiner found that none of the less successful attempts at change reached this stage and that rather than commitment, there was serious resistance to the proposed changes. (In other words, the *reactive* forces became stronger than the *proactive* forces.)

5. Experimentation and Search. Greiner reports that the successful change approaches used "reality testing" to determine the usefulness of the solution prior to the introduction of large-scale changes. He stresses that the concept of *shared power* ensures that a number of minor decisions are implemented at all levels of the organization. In short, the decision-making process is tentative rather than final.

6. Reinforcement and Acceptance. With successful change, there are clear improvements in organizational performance, with corresponding support for change from all levels of the organization. This has the effect of reinforcing the impact of the change, particularly as it involves a sense of experimentation and reward for those who continue with change efforts.

From these studies of successful and less successful change attempts, Greiner concludes that successful organizational change requires four positive actions:

1. The myth that organizational change must consist of a master blueprint designed and executed at the top by a "omniscient consultant or top manager" must be dispelled.
2. Managers too often assume that change is for those lower in the organization, who are seen to be less productive and less intelligent than those who are higher in the hierarchy.

3. Successful change efforts cannot rely on either unilateral or delegated approaches to change.

4. Those involved in the change must develop broader outlooks and become less parochial in their viewpoints towards change.

Greiner's findings, based on study of successful and less successful change efforts, closely parallel what Schein has called the adaptive-coping cycle, which consists of six steps: (1) sensing a need for change in either the external or internal environment; (2) ensuring that appropriate parts of the environment receive the information as soon as possible; (3) bringing about the appropriate change in the appropriate subsystems; (4) stabilizing the change while managing or reducing the undesired changes which have occurred in related subsystems; (5) exporting the new products or services resulting from the change; and (6) obtaining appropriate feedback on the success of the change.[49] Beer and Huse list 11 findings which generally agree with the reports of Greiner and Schein.[50] They, however, do not place as much emphasis as Greiner does on the need for high involvement by top management.

In summary, change can be brought about by either increasing the forces for change or decreasing the forces against change. The work of Greiner and Beer and Huse, in particular, demonstrates that the most effective change process occurs when the amount and degree of the reactive forces against change are reduced. It is more difficult and less effective to try to increase the forces for change.

V. THE ORGANIZATION OF THE FUTURE

It seems clear that the organization of the future will have generally the same form that it does today, although it will have to be carefully designed to fit its environment and will have to establish and maintain mechanisms for quickly adapting to change. This is particularly true for organizations at the more unstable and uncertain end of the Lawrence and Lorsch continuum. Organizations at the stable end of the continuum, such as the container industry, may well be able to maintain the more classical mode of operation. Even here, however, change and modification will be necessary to meet the demands of the changing composition of the labor force, including the changing expectations and values of younger managers and the increased pressures from the social and governmental sectors of the economy. Some of the major thrusts that will both affect the design of organizations and enable organizations to adapt more quickly to change are discussed in the following sections.

A. Increased Emphasis on the Overall Systems Approach

Organizations will become increasingly concerned about the differentiation and integration of the organization as a total system. At the same time there must be increased emphasis on a balanced viewpoint which incorporates the formal, flow, and human perspectives so that the organization can reach optimal efficiency and effectiveness. For example, many computerized information flow systems fail to work because they are superimposed on a classical, departmentalized structure. These organizations must be redesigned to take better account of the three perspectives.

B. Increased Use of Models and Model-Building

In pointing out the increasing usefulness of the operations-research approach, Vandell estimates that in 1970 there were only about 19,000 fully trained practitioners in the field but that universities will soon be graduating about 10,000 per year.[51] He concludes that the organizations "that will survive and prosper are the ones whose managers have mastered the techniques of generating and using perceptively the information that can be provided by the data banks."[52]

Similarly, we have already quoted Forrester in terms of what he calls the "counterintuitive behavior of social systems," which means that on many occasions, individuals are not able to cope with the data available because they lack the models with which to work. Roberts points out that the "boundaries of a management control system design study must not be drawn to conform with organizational structure merely because of the structure."[53] He feels that the designers of control systems frequently ignore models of man. Earlier, we discussed the necessity for models to be input-based rather than output-based if they are to be successful.

C. The Evolution of the Organic-Adaptive Structure

Earlier in this chapter we described Greiner's study, which demonstrated that the more successful change attempts in organizations involved joint participation at all levels rather than unilateral decisions made at the top. In almost all of his recent writing, Bennis has predicted the decline of bureaucracy as we know it. Both Bennis and Toffler forecast the decline of bureaucracy and predict that new, rapidly moving, rapidly shifting, and evolving organizational forms will emerge. Increased use of project groups, task forces, and similar approaches will become the norm. Bennis uses the term "temporary systems" to describe these new forms, whereas Toffler has coined the term "ad-hocracy" to describe such groups. Both warn that the accelerated pace of change and the rise of

As part of its reorganization program, the Army now allows the men to decorate their barracks as they wish. (Photograph courtesy Carl Iwasaki)

professionalism caused by the shift to a service economy will reduce employees' loyalties to the organization and increase their loyalties to the profession and to the specific task to be performed and/or the problems to be solved. Even the Army will be affected, and it is already attempting to reorganize to fit the changing times.[54] Officers and their men are now beginning to talk things out together, and in Army posts where these newer concepts are being used, reinlistment rates are double those on Army posts which still cling to the old traditions.

D. The Matrix Organization

One of the forms that the organic-adaptive structure may take is that of the matrix organization. Argyris describes the matrix organization as consisting of project teams which are created to solve a particular problem.[55] Each team consists of representatives from the functional departments which are relevant to the problem. The members of the team are expected to work together as a cohesive unit and share responsibility and power for solving the problem.

As Argyris points out, however, one of the difficulties with this approach is that individual members of the team may not work too strongly at representing their own groups. Or, team representatives may not be given sufficient opportuntiy for recognition within their own functional departments. Argyris lists other problems with the matrix approach, but stresses that the problem lies "in the everyday *behavior style that the managers have developed, in the past, to survive and to succeed within the traditional pyramidal organization.*"[56] Argyris believes that the real answer lies in the careful training of the matrix-team members.

It would seem apparent that the organization of the future will increasingly use matrix approaches to help solve the problems of change. Accordingly, traditional organizational concepts will have to be changed and modified to fit this new approach.

E. Reward Managers on the Accomplishment of Total Systems Goals

One of the difficulties with the matrix organization is that most managers have learned behavioral styles within the traditional pyramidal organization. Current accounting and budgeting practices force many managers to "play the numbers game" in order to make their own unit or group "look good," because this is the surest way to promotions and pay increases. However, there is mounting evidence that many such procedures are highly dysfunctional when the organization is considered as a total system. For example, Hawkins stresses that control systems need to emphasize management by self-control; inflexible rules and accounting systems are inappropriate in times of change, particularly when the organization is in a complex, changing environment.[57]

In order to reward managers for accomplishing total systems goals, it will be necessary to rethink the ways in which accounting and other control systems are established and to ensure that the "measurements" of accomplishment involve consideration of the total system from all three perspectives. This is especially true for an organization in a highly certain environment, which may look vastly different from one designed for a matrix organization in a highly complex, uncertain, and changing environment. Thus, Lawrence and Lorsch point out that the better integrators are those who *are* rewarded and recognized on the basis of the accomplishment of total systems goals.[58]

VI. THE MANAGER OF THE FUTURE

The manager is the most important link among the subsystems of the organization. The role of the manager in today's complex organization is threefold: to act as a participant in the work-flow process; to act as a leader to his subordinates, including directing, responding, and representing; and to act as a monitor, both within and outside his own subsystem. Managers actually spend more time interfacing with others in the lateral work-flow process than they do with their own subordinates. The manager, as leader, can exert several types of power and influence: legitimate, expert, referent, reward, and coercive power, and according to the contingency theory, each of these types of power is appropriate at different times.

Earlier in this chapter, we described the accelerating process of change and the corresponding modifications that this will bring about in the design of the organization of the future. At the same time, using a force-field analysis, we demonstrated that there are strong forces against change. Now, however, we will briefly describe some of the roles, tasks, and characteristics of the successful manager of the future.

A. Greater Ability to Deal with Conflict and Change

The increasing use of temporary groups, project management, and task forces will require that the manager of the future spend even more time than he does now in the work-flow process. He will probably belong to a variety of different groups and will have to interact with a wider variety of people. At the same time, organizational change and redesign will increase through the adaptive-coping cycle. As these changes lead to more and more employee participation at all levels, the manager of the future will have to rely increasingly on his social skills. Because of the increased interaction and use of temporary groups, the successful manager of the future will need to be able to move quickly and easily into new groups, develop working arrangements, and be prepared to become effective more quickly. In other words, he must be adept at dealing with conflict and change.

With this new role, the manager of the future will not be able to rely solely on position power, as Lawrence and Lorsch have pointed out.[59] In a task force, for example, all of the members will probably have relatively equal status. Therefore, the manager of the future will need to become more adept at solving conflict through confrontation (bringing all the facts out on the table and dealing with them openly and honestly) rather than through either edicting (use of position power) or smoothing (sweeping the problems under the rug). In turn, management-development programs must recognize the need for improvement in managerial skills and help managers to work openly and honestly with one another.

B. Broader Education and Viewpoint

There is an increasing tendency for managers to become more "professional" and to receive more and broader management training. Such training is especially important for those who have "come up through the ranks" and are suddenly expected to adopt a broader outlook. The rapid expansion of technical knowledge will require *all* managers, however, to continue their managerial education throughout their careers. With the advent of the four-day week, the manager may be able to combine the shortened work week with a one-day educational week.[60] For unless managerial personnel make a determined effort to discard old facts and ideas and replace them with more modern concepts, they will become managerial illiterates—unable to relearn and to assimilate new ideas.

Managers of the future will need to be knowledgeable about the concepts, ideas, and methodologies of each of the three perspectives we have discussed throughout the text. This is not to imply that each manager must become an expert on computers or on model-building or on behavioral science, but he will certainly need to be more conversant and knowledgeable about these fields than the average manager is today. Just as "war is too important to leave to the generals," so, too, "computers are too important to leave to computer people."

C. Greater Tolerance for Ambiguity

Under the bureaucratic model, organizations could operate successfully under set rules, and managers could, essentially, survive by following the rules. Although the bureaucratic model can still be followed in stable organizations, organizations with highly uncertain, quickly changing environments must be able to respond quickly to change. The manager who is a member of continually shifting, short-lived temporary groups cannot operate with a known set of rules. Rather, he must be able to withstand and tolerate ambiguity and to make decisions on the basis of his own knowledge and authority. He will have to make decisions even when much of the data are unknown or inaccessible. Since computers will make most of the routine, repetitive, programmable decisions, the manager will have to contend with the vague, the general, and the unprogrammable data.

D. Sharply Improved Diagnostic Skills

Forrester makes a good point when he says that his "basic theme is that the human mind is not adapted to interpreting how social systems behave."[61] This may well be the case, but given our present knowledge, the use of models is still severely limited and will continue to be so in the foreseeable future. As a result, the manager will need to greatly improve his ability to identify and diagnose problems. In discussing the problem of change and resistance to change, Lawrence points to management's need to do a better job of problem exploration and definition.[62] As he points out, when resistance to change does appear, it should be considered not as something to be overcome, but rather as a signal, a red flag, that something is going wrong. He stresses the necessity for better diagnosis and says that when this occurs, there will be "better performance in putting new ideas for technological change into effect."[63] For example, the engineering manager who was able to "overlook" a 300% increase in productivity showed no diagnostic or problem-solving skills at all; rather, he was being highly reactive and resistant to change. In other words, one of the biggest jobs of the manager of the future will be to improve his diagnostic and problem-solving skills so as to reduce the forces opposing change (Fig. 15.1).

E. Managing Within a Larger Environment

Not only is the modern organization becoming larger, more complex, and multinational, but it is also becoming increasingly involved in social and ecological issues. The manager of the future must become more aware of the fact that the social institution in which he works is part of a much larger system. The boundaries between social systems become blurred when this occurs, and the manager of the future will have to develop working relationships with other organizations, the public sector, and the governmental sector of the economy. As Bass says, "Managers . . . will have to negotiate even more than they do now with other large organizations and agencies."[64]

Staats puts it even more clearly when he states that the manager of the future will more and more become involved in carrying out public policy through a variety of means; he believes that the line "between public administration and private participation will be less clear than ever."[65] This means that the manager will have to walk the fine line between maintaining responsibility for his own organization while at the same time carrying out public policy.

F. Changing and Emerging Value Systems

Earlier in this chapter, we discussed the changing composition of the labor force, i.e., workers' increasing educational level and the increase of technical and professional people. Ericson gives the results of a number of studies which show the difference between the value systems which managers hold and those which they are allowed to display on the job.[66] In a more highly educated, professionalized society, the manager of the future will need to be more aware that the higher levels of Maslow's need hierarchy are becoming actualized and that more opportunities for satisfying ego, esteem, and self-actualization needs must be provided, for individuals at all levels in the organization will be seeking greater need satisfaction. The research has clearly demonstrated that although scientists and other professionals require special management techniques, even the ordinary employee has rising expectations which can be satisfied only through greater participation and autonomy.

The six major points of Bergey and Slower form a convenient summary to this section:[67]

1. The manager of the future must have greater knowledge about psychology and the social sciences, world affairs, and the humanities.

2. He must be a catalyst who can merge and integrate information technology and human resources.

3. Government and governmental intervention will be increasingly more influential, and business organizations and the government will become interdependent.

4. More managers will come from the universities rather than from the ranks.

5. With the increasing use of the computer to handle the routine details, the manager of the future will be freer to consider the long-range social implications of his (and the computer's) decisions.

6. Organizations will become more flexible in their capacity and ability to respond to a fluid, rapidly changing environment.

VII. CONCLUSION

In this chapter, we tried to peer into the future, chancy and risky though that might be. We examined the pessimists' view that the world will become more tightly regulated and the optimists' belief that the future will bring about more personal freedom, autonomy, and independence, and concluded that the latter trend is more valid. We then examined the accelerated pace of change, including such variables as the knowledge explosion, rapidly increasing product obsolescence, increasing concern over social issues, and the changing nature of the work force. Using a force-field analysis approach, we discussed handling the problem of organizational change, pointing out that it is more effective for social organizations to reduce the forces opposing change rather than to increase the forces for change. In examining the organization of the future, we cited the increasing emphasis on the overall systems approach, the greater use of models and model-building, the growth of the organic-adaptive structure, the matrix organization, and the need to reward managers on the basis of accomplishment of total systems goals. Finally, we noted that the manager of the future must be able to deal with conflict and change; he must develop a broader viewpoint and continue his education, and he must develop a greater tolerance for ambiguity and change. We feel that the job of the manager will become more difficult, and one of his major difficulties will be to avoid becoming obsolete.

REVIEW

1. The feedback of information is an important part of the efficient operation of a system. Why, then, do many people believe that the rapid exchange of information by computer is bad? What other aspects of an organization are ignored by individuals professing this viewpoint?

2. Do you think the future will bring "1984" or "Consciousness III"? On the basis of your choice, what do you think the major attributes of a manager of the near future will be? Will organizations as they exist today be able to cope successfully with the problems of the future? Why or why not?

3. What impact does the fact that white-collar workers outnumber blue-collar workers have on an organization? Do white-collar workers have specialized problems that cannot be solved by the general techniques used for blue-collar workers? What alternative methods could be used?

4. Describe the educational background a manager in the future will need. Draw up an educational plan to update the skills of a manager already on the job, including schedule, areas of improvement, costs, problems, etc.

5. Construct a force-field diagram for the proactive and reactive forces which are acting on your university or organization. Show how the balance point will move when you vary the length of specific vectors (or eliminate them).

6. We have distinguished between the "optimistic" and the "pessimistic" view of the future. Is such a distinction appropriate? Discuss.

REFERENCES

1 "Good Wishes, Mr. Helms," *Christian Science Monitor,* November 12, 1971.

2 H. N. Beard and D. C. Kenney, *Bored of the Rings, or Tolkien Revisited* (New York: Signet, 1969), p. 92.

3 S. Cartmill, "Deadline," *Astounding Science Fiction,* 33, 1 (March 1944): 154–178.

4 R. Wright, "Science Fiction Put to Work as Forecaster," *Christian Science Monitor,* July 26, 1971.

5 P. Handler, ed., *Biology and the Future of Man* (New York: Oxford University Press, 1970).

6 G. Orwell, *1984* (New York: Harcourt, Brace, 1949).

7 R. Baker, "Big Brother is Growing," *New York Times,* November 14, 1971.

8 R. F. Ericson, "The Impact of Cybernetic Information Technology on Management Value Systems," *Management Science,* 16, 2 (October 1969): 13–47.

9 B. Bass, "Organizational Life in the 70's and Beyond," *Personnel Psychology,* 25, 1 (Spring 1972): 19–30.

10 R. P. Hey, "Social Security Snooping," *Christian Science Monitor,* July 15, 1971.

11 "Soviet Computer Technology Bringing '1984' a Little Closer," *Boston Globe,* July 15, 1971.

12 K. Kesey, *One Flew Over the Cuckoo's Nest* (New York: Viking, 1962).

13 B. Skinner, *Beyond Freedom and Dignity* (New York: Alfred A. Knopf, 1971).

14 H. J. Leavitt and T. L. Whisler, "Management in the 1980's," *Harvard Business Review,* 36, 6 (Nov.-Dec. 1958): 41–48.

15 D. C. Carroll, "Implications of On-Line, Real-Time Systems for Managerial Decision-Making," in *The Impact of Computers on Management,* ed. C. Myers (Cambridge, Mass.: M.I.T. Press, 1967, pp. 140–167).

16 W. Bennis, *Changing Organizations* (New York: McGraw-Hill, 1966).

17 C. Reich, *The Greening of America* (New York: Random House: 1970).

18 *Ibid.,* pp. 89–90.

19 P. Nobile, ed., *The Con III Controversy: The Critics Look at "The Greening of America"* (New York: Pocket Books, 1971).

20 W. Glasser, *The Identity Society* (New York: Harper & Row, 1972).

21 A. Toffler, *Future Shock* (New York: Random House, 1970).

22 *Ibid.,* p. 1.

23 M. Weissman and E. Paykel, "Moving and Depression in Women," *Transaction Social Science and Modern Society,* 9, 9 (July-August 1972): 24–28.

24 *Edmund's 1971 New Car Prices* (Detroit: Edmund Publications, 1971), p. 60.

25 "Altering the Cell—The Vistas are Breathtaking," *New York Times,* October 31, 1971.

26 J. Rosenthal, "Columbia, Maryland—A Tale of One City," *New York Times Magazine,* December 26, 1971.

27 "Thirty-three Teachers at West Point Leave Army in 18 Months," *New York Times,* June 25, 1972.

28 "U.S. Orders First Emergency Pollution Curbs," *Boston Globe,* November 18, 1971.

29 "GM Stock Proposals Test Harvard's Stand on Business Social Roles," *Boston Globe,* May 17, 1971.

30 "Mutual Funds," *Time,* November 22, 1971, p. 100.

31 A. Athos, "Is the Corporation Next to Fall?" *Harvard Business Review,* 48, 1 (Jan.-Feb. 1970): 49–61.

32 R. V. Purcell, "Who Knows the Company President?" *California Management Review,* XI, 2 (Winter 1968): 6–8.

33 S. Cuthbert and J. Elden, "An Anatomy of Activism for Executives," *Harvard Business Review,* 48, 6 (Nov.-Dec. 1970): 95–100.

34 "Autos: The Bullet Biter," *Newsweek,* February 7, 1972, p. 65.

35 K. E. Boulding, "The Future of Personal Responsibility," *American Behavioral Scientist,* 15, 3 (Jan.-Feb. 1972): 329–359.

36 B. Bass, "Panel: Implications of the Behavioral Sciences on Management Practices in the Year 2000," in *Management 2000* (New York, American Foundation for Management Research, American Management Association, 1969), p. 160.

37 "Internationalization of Business," *Time,* November 22, 1971, p. 103.

38 D. Stone, "Bridging Cultural Barriers in International Management," *Advanced Management Journal,* 34 (Jan. 1969): 56–62.

39 P. S. Goodman and B. E. Moore, "Cross-Cultural Management Research," *Human Organization,* 31 , 1 (1972): 39–45.

40 K. Lewin, *Field Theory in Social Science* (New York: Harper & Row, 1951).

41 C. Argyris, *Management and Organizational Development* (New York: McGraw-Hill, 1971).

42 S. Gellerman, "Behavioral Strategies," *California Management Review,* XII, 2 (1969): 45–51.

43 W. Buckley, "Society as a Complex Adaptive System," in *Modern Systems Research for the Behavioral Scientist,* ed. W. Buckley (Chicago: Aldine, 1968).

44 S. L. Sokolik, "Reorganize the Personnel Department," *California Management Review,* XI, 3 (Spring 1969): 43–52.

45 D. Hall and E. Lawlor, "Job Characteristics and Professionals and the Organizational Integration of Professionals," *Administrative Science Quarterly,* 15 (1970): 271–281; P. Lawrence and J. Lorsch, *Organization and Environment: Managing Integration and Differentiation* (Boston: Harvard University Graduate School of Business Administration, Division of Research, 1967).

46 J. Lane, "Hedonistic Management," *Advanced Management Journal,* 34, 1 (Jan. 1969): 74–77.

47 *Ibid.,* p. 75.

48 L. Greiner, "Patterns of Organizational Change," *Harvard Business Review,* 45, 3 (May-June 1967): 119–130.

49 E. Schein, *Organizational Psychology,* 2d ed. (Englewood Cliffs, N.J.: Prentice-Hall, 1970).

50 M. Beer and E. Huse, "A Systems Approach to Organizational Improvement," *Journal of Applied Behavioral Science,* 8, 1 (Jan.-Feb. 1972): 79–101.

51 R. Vandell, "Management Evolution in the Quantitative World," *Harvard Business Review,* 48, 1 (Jan.-Feb. 1970): 83–92.

52 *Ibid.,* p. 92.

53 E. Roberts, "Industrial Dynamics and the Design of Management Control Systems," in *Readings in Management Strategy and Tactics,* ed. J. Hutchinson (New York: Holt, Rinehart and Winston, 1971), p. 322.

54 B. Ayres, Jr., "Army is Shaken by Crises in Morale and Discipline," *New York Times,* September 5, 1971.

55 C. Argyris, "Today's Problems with Tomorrow's Organizations," *Journal of Management Studies,* 4, 1 (Feb. 1967): 31–55.

56 *Ibid.,* p. 34.

57 D. F. Hawkins, "Behavioral Implications of Generally Accepted Accounting Principles," *California Management Review,* XII, 2 (Winter 1969): 13–21.

58 P. Lawrence and J. Lorsch, *op. cit.*

59 *Ibid.*

60 K. E. Wheeler, R. Gurman, and D. Tarnowieski, *The Four-Day Work Week* (New York: American Management Association, 1972); N. Ream, *Management 2000, op. cit.,* p. 59.

61 J. Forrester, "Counterintuitive Behavior of Social Systems," *Technology Review,* 73, 3 (Jan. 1971) Alumni Association of the Massachusetts Institute of Technology, pp. 52–68.

62 P. Lawrence, "How to Deal with Resistance to Change," in *Organizational Psychology —A Book of Readings,* ed. D. Kolb, I. Rubin, and J. McIntyre (Englewood Cliffs, N.J.: Prentice-Hall, 1971).

63 *Ibid.,* p. 387.

64 B. Bass, in *Management 2000, op. cit.* p. 123.

65 E. Staats, in *Management 2000, op. cit.,* p. 161.

66 R. F. Ericson, *op. cit.*

67 J. Bergey and R. Slower, "Administration in the 1980's," *Advanced Management Journal,* 34, 2 (April 1969): 25–33.

16
CONCLUSION

Man ultimately decides for himself, and in the end, education must be education toward the ability to decide.

VICTOR FRANKL

Perhaps the most important concept presented in this book is that all of us are born, live, work, and die within organizational frameworks, be they formal or informal. The individual can become more effective merely by recognizing this fact and understanding some of the ways in which organizations operate.

A. THE SOCIAL ORGANIZATION AS A TOTAL SYSTEM

Throughout the text, we have stressed that social organizations can be considered as systems with a number of subsystems, each of which acts on and affects the other subsystems. Explicitly recognizing that any organization is a complex of subsystems makes it more difficult to apply what has been called the "one best way," or "single-cause solution," to organizational problems. Therefore, we have stressed the need to view organizations and their problems from three perspectives. Although such a separation of organizations into the three different perspectives is artificial, it provides a useful theoretical framework for understanding the operation of organizations. Only by simultaneously considering the structural-design, flow, and human factors can one deal realistically and successfully with the complexities of organizational life. Thus, the most successful attempts to improve organizations take into account all three perspectives.

Just as unidimensional approaches are likely to fail, so, too, are model-building and operations-research approaches which neglect the inputs of human behavior. The failures occur because the output-based models, which work well in *mechanistic* systems, are not valid for use with *social* systems. Similarly, many attempts at computerized, management-information systems, which cut across departmental lines, fail because they concentrate on the flow perspective, with insufficient attention to either the structural-design or human perspectives.

B. THE VITAL IMPORTANCE OF THE MANAGER

All too frequently, the manager is thought of as a mere supervisor, and such a definition downplays his true, vital role in the organization. The manager has critical functions both in the work-flow process and as a leader. The manager's many roles will continue to expand and become more important in the face of the continually shifting, dynamic environment in which he functions.

Recognition of the tremendous role demands on the manager, with the accompanying role conflict and ambiguity, will force managers to become better trained in the most effective methods of lateral interface with their peers and others both inside and outside the organization. Managers will have to become better diagnosticians of systems problems, and new, better ways will have to be developed to reward them for accomplishing supraordinate goals.

Managers need to have a clearer understanding of the difference between proactive and reactive forces, and they must develop keener insight into their performance of either role. But since personality factors may influence their style and effectiveness of performance, it may be necessary to adopt a "contingency theory" of leadership so that the job can be molded to fit the manager rather than the other way around.

C. THE IMPORTANCE OF THE INDIVIDUAL AND THE PSYCHOLOGICAL CONTRACT

In Chapter 3, we discussed several models of motivation and described the importance of the individual as a subsystem within the organization. One concept is clear: every individual is *always* motivated by his own particular set of needs. Therefore, no one individual can "motivate" another. Since motivation is a process internal to the individual, it can be "tapped" by someone else only if he changes the situation. In other words, the clock-watcher who leaves promptly at 5 P.M. is highly motivated—to leave on time. From the organizational point of view, such motivation may be dysfunctional. Yet rather than trying to get the individual to give up his clock-watching habit, his "motivation" may be transferred to more functional outlets if his work situation is changed, i.e., if his job is enriched. This does not mean that the individual will now become "happy"; since man is a perenially wanting being, as soon as one set of needs is satisfied, another set emerges. However, there is a vast difference between the "minigripe" (the quality of food in the cafeteria) and the "maxigripe" (parts shortages). The "minigripe," or hygiene factor, is much easier to handle than the maxigripe, but the latter signifies a much healthier organization.

One of the most powerful factors influencing the individual's emotional response to his work is the psychological contract. Individuals learn very quickly about the psychological contract and react accordingly. If it is a rational-legal contract, the individual will put in "a fair day's work for a fair day's pay," although his concept of a fair day's work may differ from that of the organization. If an organization wants loyalty and commitment from an employee, it needs to set up a normative contract.

D. THE IMPORTANCE OF THE GROUP IN THE SOCIAL ORGANIZATION

In Chapter 5, we discussed the ways in which the group affects individual and organizational behavior. In later chapters, we discussed the use of such temporary groups as task forces or project teams in solving specific organizational problems, introducing new products, and integrating different departments on the lateral level. For example, we showed how the development of matrix task forces materially increases employees' work quality and productivity when complex new products are introduced. It seems clear that knowledge and understanding of group behavior and the facts of group norms and structure are vitally important to today's manager as well as to the manager of the future, whether the group is a part of the formal or informal structure of the organization.

If, as we believe to be the case, the use of temporary, ad-hoc groups will be necessary in the adaptive-coping cycle that many organizations must go through, this has profound implications for management and professional selection, development, and training. The problems associated with temporary groups are much different from those of stable, relatively unchanging environments and work groups.

E. THE NECESSITY FOR IMPROVED CONTINGENCY THEORY IN ORGANIZATIONAL DESIGN

We believe that a major breakthrough is just emerging in our shift from regarding the structure and design of an organization as a "given" to something highly contingent on the climate and environment in which the organization finds itself. We are really only beginning to see the implications of this concept, and the next few years should see a great expansion of research and thought in this area. The continuation of an adaptive, competent organization may require a continual review and re-examination of the structure and design of the organization in terms of the nature, type, and state of its relevant environment and the nature of the continuous interchange between the organization and its environment.

The entire problem of how best to differentiate and integrate an organization is one that has concerned management theorists for decades. This problem, and the research necessary to more clearly define the type of structure that is optimum for an organization at a given period of time, will receive an increasing amount of attention, and deservedly so. Although attention to organizational structure and design may be a major consideration in the survival of specific organizations, only now are we beginning to develop systematic and applied methods for examining this problem in greater depth.

F. THE NEED FOR BETTER UNDERSTANDING OF PROACTIVE AND REACTIVE FORCES

Organizations or their component subsystems seek to find a relatively stable balance, or equilibrium. However, this process is made more difficult by the action and reaction between proactive forces (those seeking to bring about change) and reactive forces (those seeking to maintain the relative, current status of the social organization). Explicit in this approach to force-field analysis is the entire problem of change and adaptation. Change in itself is neither good nor bad. The manager, however, must know and be able to clearly identify the difference between the proactive and reactive forces. In addition, it is important for him to realize that the organization *requires* the two opposing sets of forces: proactive forces allow the organization to change and adapt; reactive forces offer a restraint to wild organizational shifts in direction and purpose.

In order to bring about change, however, either the strength of the proactive vectors must be increased or the strength of the reactive vectors must be decreased. The successful manager must be an expert diagnostician to know whether to increase the strength of the proactive forces, decrease the strength of the reactive forces, and/or to work on both.

Nonetheless, conflict is inevitable. There are three basic ways of handling conflict—forcing, or edicting; smoothing, or sweeping the problem under the rug; and confrontation, or bringing the facts out on the table and discussing them openly. This last technique is perhaps the most useful, because it generally recognizes the validity of feelings and emotions and asserts that their denial is a type of smoothing. Thus, under normal circumstances, the best way of handling conflict and change is through confrontation, which "faces the facts" of feelings and emotions.

G. THE MANAGER'S NEED FOR CONTINUING EDUCATION

Change is ever-present and is increasing at an accelerated rate. This is particularly true of the "knowledge explosion," which creates the obsolescence of current knowledge. There is always a lag between the development and application of new knowledge. In the hard sciences, the lag is steadily decreasing, but in the behavioral sciences, the lag between the development and application of knowledge is much slower. For example, even though the Hawthorne studies showed that workers respond positively to being treated as individuals, today —40 years later—many organizations still treat their employees harshly, believing that any other mode somehow weakens the manager's proper authority and will lead to negative repercussions.

Relevant knowledge *is* being generated at an accelerated rate. The successful manager will be the one who can do a better job of continuing to educate himself and do a better and faster job of importing new knowledge into the organization at all levels, thus further reducing the lag between the generation and the application of knowledge.

REVIEW

1. This chapter lists some of what we feel to be the book's most important concepts. Develop your own list of the points that have been most important to you.

2. Apply the systems concept of an organization to a university and describe why a particular individual or group within the university has experienced certain successes and failures.

3. List (and be prepared to defend) what you consider to be the five most important questions a manager can ask about any given situation. These questions should also be applicable to a situation which might occur in the year 2000.

4. What is the contingency theory of leadership? Will it work for all types of managerial positions? Could the job of president of the United States be accomplished according to such a theory?

5. In your present organizational situation, what could be done in the area of "job enrichment"? What kinds of needs are being unfulfilled? Would a normative rather than a psychological contract help to improve your situation?

6. Using the organizational structure of your college or university, outline a management information system that would be adaptable to a change in the organizational environment of your school. Be sure to include feedback loops to allow for modifications necessitated by reactions to output from the external environment.

APPENDIXES: CASE STUDIES

THE CASE OF THE DUCK EGGS

A family with several children lived on a piece of highly wooded property near a large pond with a small island in it and a rustic footbridge to the island. Each winter the family fed corn to the pheasants, and each spring and summer the family threw corn into the shallow part of the pond for the wild ducks to eat.

One spring, a wild duck decided to build her nest on the island. She chose a spot under a pine tree whose lower branches were extremely close to the ground. The entire family began counting the days until the eggs hatched and the ducklings arrived.

Early one morning, about 4 A.M., the adults in the family heard the duck quacking continuously. Later, about 7:30, one of the boys, returning from his paper route, reported that he had counted 14 duck eggs on the nest. Remembering the commotion earlier in the morning and knowing that ducks do not lay that many eggs, the father suggested to his son that they go down to the island to investigate. The ground was covered with broken egg shells. Apparently, early in the morning, a fox or dog had eaten all of the eggs. However, the son had reported counting 14 duck eggs. When it was pointed out to him that there was nothing left of the nest, big tears rolled down his cheeks. It was only then that he perceived broken shells rather than unbroken eggs.

DISCUSSION QUESTIONS

1. Why did this occur?
2. What implications does this true story have for other situations?

CHANGING WORK PROCEDURES

This is a four-part case. It is strongly recommended that you not read beyond any single part until your instructor gives you the signal to begin.

PART I

The Harwood Manufacturing Company, located in West Virginia, produces pajamas, a process requiring frequent changes in production routine. All operators (mostly female) are on a piece-rate basis, with a standard, or minimum, of 60 units per hour, a rate which had been determined by a time study. (In other words, all work was converted to standard units for each task.) A girl exceeding the standard receives commensurate pay, e.g., a girl doing 25% over the standard rate is paid 25% above her base pay. In addition, the girls receive a special transfer bonus when they are transferred from one set of duties to another to ensure that they do not lose any money.

When task changes occur, however, a number of related events take place simultaneously. First, the workers whose tasks have been changed show evidence of hostility toward both their immediate supervisor and the organization. Second, their work rate decreases and is slow to reach the standard rate again. The recovery rate is so slow, in fact, that a new operator has a faster learning time than an experienced operator. Only about 38% of the operators whose jobs have been altered eventually reach the standard; the other 62% either quit during the relearning period or fail to reach the standard work rate.

PART 2

After analyzing these findings, the company decided to set up a series of experiments. They picked four groups that seemed to be about equal in productivity and capacity. Group 1, the "no participation" control group, followed the usual routine when a factory job was changed, i.e., the job was modified by the production department, and a new piece rate was established. Normal procedures were followed by bringing the group together to explain that competitive conditions necessitated the change, and the new piece rate was thoroughly

---

Adapted from L. Coch and J. R. P. French, Jr., "Overcoming Resistance to Change," *Human Relations*, I, (1948): 512–532.

explained by the time-study expert, who also answered any questions that workers might have.

The members of Group 2 were brought together, the reasons for the change in production methods were explained in a rather dramatic fashion, and the necessity for cost reduction was shared with the group. Then, management outlined a plan to eliminate unnecessary frills and fancy work from the garment by studying the present job, eliminating work that was unnecessary, training several operators in the new methods, and establishing piece-work rates by time studies on operators who had been specially trained. The group informally approved the plan and chose the operators who were to receive the special training. Everyone was cooperative and made a number of suggestions. After training, these specially trained operators instructed the other workers in the procedures for doing the new job.

All the operators in Groups 3 and 4 participated in the change process. Again, the need for a change in methods to reduce costs was made dramatically clear. Since these two groups were smaller than Group 2, all the operators were involved in planning and designing the new jobs, and they all were studied by the time-study observer. The "total participation" was so effective that the stenographer had difficulty in keeping up with the many suggestions and recommendations. The two groups approved the revised plan informally, although no official or formal decision was made.

PART 3

What were the results on productivity of the three different methods? The nonparticipation, or control, group began with an initial productivity of about 45 units and continued at about this level during the trial period. The usual resistance to the change occurred immediately after the change and continued during the 32 days of the recording period. In addition, there was a great deal of hostility and aggression against management. When grievances about the piece rate were filed, the standard was rechecked and found to be too "loose" rather than too tight. In the first 40 days, 17% of the workers quit, and those remaining never reached the standard production rate of 60 units per hour.

Group 2, with its specially trained "representatives," averaged 61 units per hour at the end of 14 days. Their productivity climbed steadily to a high of about 68 or 69 units at the end of the 40 days. The researchers felt that the figures for the group's learning period and productivity would have been even higher had work been less scarce during the first week of the study. The workers' attitude toward management, the methods engineer, and the supervisor was generally cooperative.

Groups 3 and 4, the total-participation groups, recovered more rapidly, and their productivity was considerably higher than that of either the control group or the representative group. One of the groups reached a temporary high of about 80 units, although the average for the total period was about 70-73 units per hour, an increase in productivity of about 14%. No workers in Groups 3 and 4 quit during the 40 days that records were kept on this variable.

PART 4

After the experiment, the control group was broken up, and individual members of the group were reassigned to jobs scattered throughout the plant. About ten weeks later, the 13 members of the group that still remained were brought together again for a second experiment, which consisted of giving the group members a new job based on the total-participation technique. The approach was much like that already explained for the two participation groups of the first experiment, and the new job was roughly comparable in complexity to the one they had had in the first experiment.

The result of the second experiment with the 13 remaining members of the original control, nonexperimental, group was in startling contrast to the first. Under the total participation method, the group started at a productivity level of about 55 units per hour, as opposed to the productivity of about 45 units in the first experiment. The productivity of the second group climbed and at the end of 18 days had reached a level of about 75 units, whereas in the first experiment, productivity had leveled off after 32 days at about 45 units per hour. During the second experiment there was no evidence of the hostility and aggression that these same operators had shown previously, and there was no turnover such as had occurred earlier.

Some time later, a similar experiment was conducted in Norway.* In this study, which was fashioned after the original Harwood study, the researchers found *no* significant differences between the productivity of the participative management condition and the nonparticipative management condition. In other words, an approach which was effective in the United States did not have the same positive effect in Norway.

DISCUSSION QUESTIONS

1. Why was this experiment a success in the United States?
2. Why did it fail in Norway?
3. What implications does this have for other parts of the text?

---

*J. R. P. French, Jr., J. Israel, and D. Ās, "An Experiment on Participation in a Norwegian Factory," *Human Relations*, 13, 1 (1960): 3–19.

CLEANING THE TANK

BACKGROUND

The Acme Company employs about 20 people, including 12 production workers. Because the company works with precious metals, all residue is pumped into a specially designed settling tank before the liquids go into the normal sewage system. Once or twice a year, depending on production, the tank must be drained and the sludge shoveled out into barrels to be taken to another plant for recovery of the precious metals. Unfortunately, because of the chemical process involved, removing the sludge is much like cleaning a septic tank—it is a thoroughly unpleasant, dirty, smelly, distasteful, and filthy process. Because the tank cannot be cleaned during normal working hours, whoever cleans the tank works on an overtime basis.

Because this is a role-playing case, you should not read ahead until your instructor has selected the two people who are to play the two roles.

ROLE FOR PETE

According to Acme custom, the person with the lowest seniority has the task of cleaning out the sludge tank. This worked equitably, as far as you can tell, when the company had normal turnover. But since jobs have been hard to find recently, turnover has been low. You have been on the job for three years and have had to clean out the tank five times. Bill, your predecessor, had to clean the tank only once, as did Sam, the man before that. After cleaning the tank, you feel dirty and unclean for several days, no matter how often or for how long you take a shower. Besides, it makes you almost physically ill while you are doing it, and afterwards you fight with your wife and are unpleasant to the children.

You feel strongly that you have done more than your share and that it is now time to let someone else "do the dirty work." You don't care whether it is a matter of drawing straws or flipping a coin or what, but you've cleaned the tank for the last time, and you're tired of the unnecessary ribbing you take for always getting stuck with the job.

You notice that the tank will need to be cleaned within the next several days, and this time, you are really going to "have it out" with the boss. You are under a union contract, and nothing in the contract says that the man with the least seniority has to clean the tank. Just because it has been done that way in the past doesn't mean it has to stay that way.

ROLE FOR ED, PRODUCTION FOREMAN

You notice that the sludge tank needs cleaning out, and you are about to call Pete in to get him to do it in the next day or so. You have been with the plant ever since it opened 15 years ago, and the man with the lowest seniority has always been given the job; now it is a "normal shop practice." Therefore, you have no hesitation about telling Pete to do it because he has the lowest seniority, and besides, you really don't like his attitude. Although he is a good worker and his productivity is high, he has an attitude you just don't like. However, you just can't quite put your finger on it. In the past few weeks, this attitude has somehow grown worse, and you don't really know why. Other than Pete, you have a good, loyal, cohesive work force, and most of the men have been with you for a long time.

THE COMPANY PRESIDENT
AND THE APPLICATION BLANK

A panel discussion was held as part of a program to help disadvantaged people and others find jobs. One of the panel members was the president of a medium-sized local company. During the course of his presentation, he repeatedly stressed that in *his* company, the only thing that mattered for selection and promotion was the ability of the individual. He made a special point of emphasizing that one's amount of education, race, and color were totally unimportant; only ability mattered.

When he finished his presentation, a member of the audience asked, "Mr. President, do you really mean that the amount of education a person has is unimportant in either selection or promotion?" The president assured him that he was truly sincere in what he had said.

The questionner then responded, "The day before yesterday, Mr. President, I responded to an advertisement in the paper from your company for unskilled labor. When I completed the application blank, the personnel man did not interview me. He merely looked at the application blank, noted that I had not finished high school, and told me that it was company policy to hire only high school graduates, so there was no sense in wasting time on an interview."

DISCUSSION QUESTIONS

1. Was the president sincere in what he said?
2. Can there be a difference between the beliefs of the man at the top and those on the "firing line," i.e., the personnel man?
3. What might the president say to the personnel man when he returns to his company? How might the personnel man respond?

EXERCISE CAREER VALUES

A. PURPOSE

In order to "motivate" someone else, it is necessary to know something about his own individual and unique needs. The purpose of this exercise is to see how well you can estimate some of the attitudes and feelings the members of your study group have toward their career values and also to provide you with feedback about others' perceptions of you.

B. PROCEDURE

First, read the definitions of various types of career values. Then, you will be asked to rank your own career values as you perceive them and then to rank the career values of the other members of your study group. Finally, you and the others in your group will announce and discuss the rankings. The discussion is the most important part of the exercise, since it will enable you to give and obtain valuable feedback about how you perceive others in the group and how they perceive you.

DEFINITIONS OF CAREER VALUES

Step 1: Read Definitions

Career values can be divided into a number of different areas. Listed below are nine such areas that involve a number of varying aims that an individual may have in life:

A. **Top Management**—Wants to rise to the top in an organization and be a high-level manager, even though subordinates may not like him.

B. **Competence**—Wants to be a competent specialist rather than a manager, so that he can make maximum use of his intellectual problem-solving abilities and see the applied results of his work.

Adapted and modified from B. Bass, "A Program of Exercises," (Pittsburgh: Management Development Associates, 1966).

C. **Affiliation**—Wants to contribute to the satisfaction of others and to be helpful to them.

D. **Leisure**—Wants the time and opportunity to really enjoy life, even if this means giving up some income potential with a lower overall rate of earning.

E. **Security**—Wants a job that is congenial and enables him to look forward to a stable and secure future.

F. **Risk**—Wants a career that has a potential of really making it big, although there is a correspondingly high possibility of a financial loss.

G. **Creativity**—Wants a career that permits him to be original, innovative, and creative.

H. **Independence**—Wants the opportunity to be his own boss, i.e., to be free from supervision by others.

I. **Analysis**—Wants to probe deeply and thoroughly into problems; is more concerned with the "why" than with the application of results.

Step 2. Complete Career-Values Ranking

First, rank your own career values. Give a "1" to the value or goal which is most important to your own career satisfaction and write it in the first column of Table 1. For example, if you decide that "risk" is most important, place the number "1" across from the letter "F" in the first column. If, on the other hand, you feel that "leisure" is most important to you, place the "1" opposite the letter "D." Then decide which career value is next most important to you and give it a rank of "2." Continue this process until you have ranked all nine career values.

An alternative way of ranking is to begin with the most important, giving it a rank of "1" and then ranking the least important, giving it a value of "9," thus working toward the middle. Do not tie any ranks. If you have to, guess; usually your first impression is most accurate.

Now, at the top of the second column write the name of the person sitting on your immediate right. Without consultation with him, rank his career values *as you perceive them.* Again, your first impression is generally the most accurate, so work quickly. When you have completed this ranking, use the third column for the next person on your right, etc., until you have completed all the rankings and recorded them in Table 1. Only when your group has ranked every person should you proceed to Step 3.

Step 3: Announce, Record, and Discuss Career-Value Rankings

As soon as everyone in your study group has finished all the rankings, you should begin announcing the rankings each of you has assigned to yourself and to the others. First, enter in the parentheses of Table 1 each person's self-ratings. As each member of the study group reports about you, enter his rankings of you in Table 2. You should repeat your own self-ranking (Table 1, Column 1) in Table 2, Column 1, to make subsequent comparison easier. To get an idea of how the others see you, you should complete Table 2 by totaling the values assigned to each row (excluding your own self-ranking) and finding the mean value. To do this, divide each total by the number of the members in your study group (excluding yourself). When you have completed this step, you should proceed to "discussion of rankings."

C. DISCUSSION OF RANKINGS

A. *Raters:*

Basically, there are four interrelated reasons why you made the rankings you did:

1. You are accurate in your perception of others, even on short acquaintance;
2. You "project" your own feelings onto others, that is, if you feel a certain way, others should also;
3. You use a few cues or mannerisms to influence all of your impressions about others;
4. You are influenced by "social" factors and rank yourself and others in what you think is a socially acceptable way.

B. *Ratees:*

Look at the ranks that others have given you. In many cases, you will find a great deal of "inaccuracy," i.e., their rankings do not agree with yours. Yet this may be the way you "come across" to others. You should then ask yourself, "Why?" Ask the other members of your group to give you feedback about their reasons for their ratings; you will find this extremely helpful and illuminating.

C. *Actual Life:*

One of the frequent comments following this exercise is that there has been insufficient time to get to know one another. In one sense, this is true. You have been together for only a limited period of time. Yet in real life, we are

Table 1 Career Value Rankings *By You* of Yourself and *By You* of Everyone Else in Your Study Group

(Do not write anything in the parentheses until directed to do so in Step 3)

	(1) Yourself	(2)	(3)	(4)	(5)	(6)
	Ratee name	Ratee name	Ratee name	Ratee name	Ratee name	Ratee name
A. Top Management	____	__( )_*_(	)__(	)__(	)__(	)__( )
B. Competence	____	__( )__(	)__(	)__(	)__(	)__( )
C. Affiliation	____	__( )__(	)__(	)__(	)__(	)__( )
D. Leisure	____	__( )__(	)__(	)__(	)__(	)__( )
E. Security	____	__( )__(	)__(	)__(	)__(	)__( )
F. Risk	____	__( )__(	)__(	)__(	)__(	)__( )
G. Creativity	____	__( )__(	)__(	)__(	)__(	)__( )
H. Independence	____	__( )__(	)__(	)__(	)__(	)__( )
I. Analysis	____	__( )__(	)__(	)__(	)__(	)__( )

*Parentheses are for inserting values assigned to you by each other ratee.

Table 1 (cont.)

	(7)	(8)	(9)	(10)	(11)	(12)	
	Ratee name	Ratee name	Ratee name	Ratee name	Ratee name	Ratee name	
A.	__(	)__(	)__(	)__(	)__(	)__(	)
B.	__(	)__(	)__(	)__(	)__(	)__(	)
C.	__(	)__(	)__(	)__(	)__(	)__(	)
D.	__(	)__(	)__(	)__(	)__(	)__(	)
E.	__(	)__(	)__(	)__(	)__(	)__(	)
F.	__(	)__(	)__(	)__(	)__(	)__(	)
G.	__(	)__(	)__(	)__(	)__(	)__(	)
H.	__(	)__(	)__(	)__(	)__(	)__(	)
I	__(	)__(	)__(	)__(	)__(	)__(	)

Table 2 How Other Study Group Members Rank You

	(1) Yourself	(2)	(3)	(4)	(5)	(6)
	Rater name	Rater name	Rater name	Rater name	Rater name	Rater name
A. Top Management	____	____	____	____	____	____
B. Competence	____	____	____	____	____	____
C. Affiliation	____	____	____	____	____	____
D. Leisure	____	____	____	____	____	____
E. Security	____	____	____	____	____	____
F. Risk	____	____	____	____	____	____
G. Creativity	____	____	____	____	____	____
H. Independence	____	____	____	____	____	____
I. Analysis	____	____	____	____	____	____

Table 2 (cont.)

	(7)	(8)	(9)	(10)	(11)	(12)	Total (row) (Exclude Col. 1)	Mean (row)
	Rater name	Rater name	Rater name	Rater name	Rater name	Rater name		
A.	——	——	——	——	——	——	——	——
B.	——	——	——	——	——	——	——	——
C.	——	——	——	——	——	——	——	——
D.	——	——	——	——	——	——	——	——
E.	——	——	——	——	——	——	——	——
F.	——	——	——	——	——	——	——	——
G.	——	——	——	——	——	——	——	——
H.	——	——	——	——	——	——	——	——
I.	——	——	——	——	——	——	——	——

frequently asked to make decisions about others with less data than you currently have. For example, the average campus interview lasts for about 20 minutes. You should ask yourself how this exercise can be applied to real life. For example, if you "projected," that is, if you showed a strong tendency to describe others as you see yourself, this may have a number of implications. You may, as a manager, try to "motivate" others with those factors which motivate you, although these may not apply to others. At meetings and conferences, you may "dance to your own music," that is, you may be insensitive to the needs, motivations, and reactions of others.

AN EXERCISE IN RATING SUPERVISORY BEHAVIOR

Today, we are going to discuss and rate first-line supervisory behavior. You are asked to *work as a group,* to *discuss,* and to *rate* the eight statements given below which might describe a supervisor's behavior.

The group should take about 10-15 minutes for the discussion and rating. You may take longer if you feel it necessary.

Place a "1" in front of the statement the *group* decides is the most important characteristic of the good supervisor, a "2" in front of the statement the group decides is the next most important, etc., until all eight behaviors have been rated.

You must work as a group—talk together and rate together.

Do not choose a formal discussion leader.

Record the rating as the group decides it.

Now: Read through the statements carefully and then begin discussing and rating *as soon as you are ready.*

____ He praises work when it is a job well done.

____ He communicates the reasons for important decisions to his men.

____ He encourages his people to make suggestions about his policies and practices.

____ He consults with his people before making changes affecting their work.

____ He shows no favoritism.

____ He reprimands subordinates in private, not in front of others.

____ He delegates authority to his people on matters directly affecting their work.

____ He backs up his people when they are in trouble.

THE EXPERIMENTAL PROGRAM

BACKGROUND

Over a period of several years, one plant of a large corporation had purchased a number of numerically controlled lathes, each costing about $250,000. Each "numerically controlled" lathe had its own minicomputer which controlled the operation of the machine and reproduced the actions of a skilled lathe operator. Despite management's expectations and a great deal of time, trouble, and attention, productivity leveled off at about 28% effectiveness, and the scrap rate was extremely high.

After discussion with the personnel department, an innovative manager made the crucial decision to turn the problem over to the workers, and this decision led to "the experimental program." Scheduled to last one year, the program focused on seven automatic lathes in the middle of the production floor. Twenty-one machinists and three "lead hands" were selected to participate in the program. There was to be no foreman in the work area, intershift communication would be facilitated by a 15-minute paid overtime, and participants would receive a 10% bonus over their normal, straight-time earnings for participating in the study.

The initial months of the program were chaotic. Utilization, productivity, and worker attitudes plummeted to record lows. Many of the men were confused about their new role expectations, whereas others seemed to be testing management's sincerity. Workers in "support" groups who were not otherwise participating in the program showed hostility to those in the special group. In addition, problems were caused by the extensive training required. Finally, there were problems with the quality of both incoming components and the computer tapes. All of these difficulties resulted in the uneven performance of the experimental group during the first two years of the study.

However, things began to stabilize when the union became a participant in the management of the program. The union's participation resulted from its dispute with management over the selection of a new work leader, which in turn led to the activation of a union-management steering committee for the program. A union counsellor's boastful remark that "too much management" was inhibiting progress resulted in the program manager's reassignment and the

Adapted from a true case prepared by a manager (Austin deGroat), a union representative (Peter Teel), and personnel representatives (Robert Curry and David Burton).

subsequent transferral of the foreman out of the group; thus, all immediate supervision was removed from the experimental group. Finally, management recognized the validity of the workers' assertion that *group* rather than the traditional individual measurements were most appropriate for managing this particular group.

Within three months, the group's performance had surpassed management's highest expectations. Machine utilization jumped from 40% to 70%, and scrap rates fell to new lows. Quality soared, and "operators" finally got involved. With no foreman or upper-level manager to "guide" them, the operators in the group soon were stepping forward to take the "role" of production supervisors, methods planners, production control foremen, and process-control engineers to deal successfully with the complex "support" systems around them. To demonstrate what they could do, program members eliminated a "backlog," brought in complex new work with unprecedented ease, and modeled worker-management relationships that quickly brought top-management attention, although not all of the latter was positive.

In 1971, the third year of the study, machine utilization dropped to a fairly consistent rate of about 60%, not because the operators were incapable of achieving higher productivity, but because this was the rate at which new pieces were coming in. Management "support" jobs around the unit had been eliminated, i.e., production planning and control people, methods planners, process engineers, the foreman, and the next higher levels of management.

Because of the program's success, management began to seriously consider extending the process to the rest of the automatic-lathe operators in the building. Enough data had been presented to management so that they could make a firm decision to institutionalize the experimental program, at least for the original members, by establishing a formal job classification and rate of pay.

ROLE-PLAYING SITUATIONS

With the background information that has been provided, you should be able to assume one of the roles described in the following pages. Now that the experiment has survived the initial chaos and uncertainty, jobs must be defined, fair rates of pay must be determined, and a decision must be reached about expanding the program into other areas of the company.

Management Team

The management team is charged with negotiating a job classification and pay rate for members of the experimental program. As a member of this team, it is clear to you, as it is to the others, that significant advances in worker-management relations have resulted from the program. It is also apparent that management's relationships with the union have improved significantly, and this is especially important in light of the plant-wide and company-wide strikes that have occurred in recent years. There are, however, several serious problems that must be ironed out with the union. Among these problems are the following:

1. fear that the last seven months of the program have been only a lengthy "up" period for the program and that a "down" period will occur again;

2. genuine concern about the dimensions of change, i.e., it may be possible to extend this type of "management" beyond the lathe operators;

3. uncertainty about whether you can measure a group's progress and provide pay rewards without adopting incentive pay plans, which you do not want to do because of your past experience in the organization;

4. genuine inability to peg the new job into the existing pay structure for hourly workers in the corporation—you cannot use the accepted "skill-care-effort" approach, and you are uncertain how to determine the job's value;

5. a sense of foreboding that "we" may be stepping out too far ahead of the rest of the company, especially since corporate headquarters has been sending "signals" about this;

6. concern that over the long term, the productivity gains may be eroded;

7. concern about how to manage the program, which seems to call for a "new" kind of foreman-manager, but you don't know where to find him or what his function should be;

8. a lingering gut feeling that "everybody needs a boss," despite the program's success without one.

As you enter negotiations with the union, you feel distressed. Looked to for leadership and an "answer," you are instead unsure and you do not have "the" answer that will put the issue to rest. You can't "cave in." You can't give away the shop. You want to reap the program's gains.

Roles Within the Management Team

Employee relations manager. This man, in charge of compensation programs for hourly and salaried employees, is a traditionalist who believes in the company-wide job-evaluation program that emphasizes skill, care, and effort as guidelines for measuring the value of production workers' jobs. This manager feels utterly frustrated about how to "measure," or evaluate, the worth of work done by the members of the experimental program—some of their activity is "exempt," some is "salaried," and some is "hourly."

Employee relations manager for union relations. A creative innovator, this manager believes that people want to work in a changed environment. He feels that the union is ready to work in a progressive approach with management to solve the many problems of managing the changed work force of the 1970s and to alleviate the union/management distrust typical of the immediate past. However, he fears that he may incur corporate hostility for being overly daring and innovative.

Program manager. Creative, willing to take risks, and aggressive, the program manager has lived with the program and watched it mature as "controls" were eased. He is committed emotionally to the Theory Y style of management and will press very hard to have the program implemented on a broader basis throughout the plant.

Plant manager. He is not exactly sure what the experimental program is or why it is working, but he is convinced that it is making very impressive productivity gains. He is being asked about the program by shop-operations managers in other buildings. Although he wants to implement the program on a broader basis, he is concerned about what will happen to displaced management personnel should the program be extended to other areas.

Union Negotiating Brief

The responsibility of the union local's negotiating committee is to work with local company management toward a just settlement of the experimental program. According to the agreement when the program was initiated, the 21 machinists are at job level 19 and receive a bonus of 10%. One operator is the designated tool setter, although he receives nothing extra. The three lead hands, one per shift, are paid at job level 22 plus 10%. In addition, an overtime factor of 2.5 hours a week allows a 15-minute overlap between shifts, which facilitates communications.

Under the terms of the initial agreement, the experiment would be evaluated after one year, and both the company and the union maintained the right to terminate the experiment at any time by mutual agreement. After the program had been evaluated, the company asked for an extension of the program because there were no meaningful data. The union agreed to an indefinite extension because in its view, the experiment had made some significant gains and was, indeed, a success.

The program's accomplishments have given the union some strong negotiating points:

1. The scrap and rework costs have been reduced from $8000 per month to $3500 per month while productivity has more than doubled.

2. Machine utilization in the first year rose from 28% to 45%. Now, in the second year, utilization is regularly 50-60%, depending on input from other parts of the plant, and you know that machine utilization can go even higher.

3. Operator attitudes have considerably improved, and absenteeism has been reduced. It is obvious that the operator's responsibilities have been considerably increased.

4. Various management levels have openly expressed their belief that the pilot program is an unqualified success.

After job classification and pay rates have been determined, the union must decide how seniority and bumping, upgrading, and other transfers will be handled for the experimental group and for other areas if the program is expanded.

Consulting Team

Your firm, Creative Human Resources, Inc., has been hired by the company-union negotiating team to help bring about a settlement of the "rate issue" for the program. You have been asked to offer a "creative, unfettered approach" to the establishment of a special pay rate for members of work groups operating numerically-controlled equipment. These operators are relatively independent and unsupervised, are responsible for managing their work area, receive a 10% bonus for participating in the experiment, are breaking all past records for productivity (especially as compared to other operators of the same equipment who are still at a low rate of productivity) and are exhibiting a worker-management relationship wholly uncharacteristic of the relationships you have encountered in the past.

It is obvious that these workers' jobs have been enriched. You will offer recommendations for establishing a job description and payment plan in keeping with these "new" jobs to your client, the company-union negotiating team. You will join the negotiations after they have been in progress for some time and will continue to work with the negotiators after you have offered your recommendation(s). It is likely that during this second phase you will serve principally as an "integrator" to help both sides arrive at an acceptable agreement.

Process Observer's Guide

During the exercise, you are to make notes on the processes operating at various times within the management team, the union committee, and the combined negotiating committee. You should also observe the response of both groups to the consultants and the way in which the consultants present their recommendations. Be prepared to discuss with all parties the nature and significance of your observations in the negotiations. You may find it helpful to refer to Fig. 5.2 on p. 134 as you make your observations.

FOLLOWING ORDERS

In a large metropolitan hospital, the chief surgeon was known not only for his technical competence, but also for his violent temper. During one operation, for example, he found something wrong with the instrument tray that had been prepared for that particular operation. Looking directly at one of the operating room nurses, he said, "Take that g.d. tray and throw it out the g.d. window." She opened the window and threw the tray out the window into the alley behind the hospital.

DISCUSSION QUESTIONS

1. Why did the nurse perform the action she did?
2. Was she justified in following such a direct order?
3. What implications do you see here for the nurse? For the surgeon?

GROUP CONFLICT

Three different groups—marketing, research and development, and manufacturing—were located in the same building, but reported to different bosses in the corporate organizational structure. Animosity and suspicion existed among the three groups, and their managers seldom spoke to one another. Indeed, on one occasion, the manufacturing manager locked his office door while the marketing manager stood outside pounding on the door and demanding to be let in. The research and development group felt that marketing was doing a poor job of predicting the market and that manufacturing was systematically lousing up "good designs," e.g., "There isn't a single man over there in manufacturing who knows what he is doing." In return, the manufacturing group felt that the research and development people were arrogant, did not know or realize manu-facturing problems, and were providing designs that were almost impossible to manufacture. They also felt that marketing was establishing a selling price for the equipment manufactured that did not include any profit for the plant.

A reorganization took place, and a new manager was put in charge of the three groups. He told them, in no uncertain terms, that from now on, they were to "get along with one another." The three managers merely nodded their heads and left the room.

DISCUSSION QUESTIONS

1. What do you think the results of the new manager's ultimatum will be? In the short term? In the long term?
2. Was this the best approach that could have been used?

THE GUNNERY PROBLEM

PART 1

At the turn of the century, the accuracy of naval gunnery was poor. For example, in 1899 five ships each fired for five minutes at the hulk of a lightship, at the conventional range of 1600 yards. After the 25 minutes of firing, two hits had been made on the sails of the hulk.

There were several problems. First, the gun pointer had to fire on the roll of the ship, since there was no easy way to raise and lower the cannon rapidly. Second, because the gun pointer had to anticipate the speed of the ship's roll, he had to make the decision to fire before the sights were actually on target. This caused a "firing interval," the time between the impulse to fire and the actual act of pressing the firing button. Third, since the telescopic sights were mounted on the guns themselves, they were seldom used because of the probability of the gun pointer's losing an eye during the recoil. Therefore, open sights were used.

In 1898 Admiral Sir Percy Scott was in command of a British ship, the *Scylla.* While watching gunnery practice, he noticed that one gun pointer was more accurate than the others and that this was caused in part by the fact that the pointer was using his elevating gear to compensate for the roll of the vessel. Recognizing the validity of such an action, Scott made a number of changes. First, he changed the gear ratio for the elevating mechanism so that the gunner could easily depress or elevate the gun to follow the target throughout the roll. Second, he ordered that the telescopic sights be mounted on sleeves that would not be affected by the recoil. Third, he instituted practice sessions, using small targets that could be moved up and down to simulate a moving target and mounted a small-caliber rifle in the gun so that the pointer could practice every day. Shortly, the *Scylla* established remarkable records for gunnery accuracy.

In 1900 Admiral Sir Percy Scott became acquainted with an American junior naval officer, William Simms. Simms modified and improved Scott's work and installed the gear on his own ship. Within a few months, his ship began showing similarly remarkable improvements in accuracy. ·

Adapted from W. E. Morison, "A Case Study of Innovation," in *The Planning of Change,* ed. W. G. Bennis, K. D. Benne, and R. Chin (New York: Holt, Rinehart and Winston, 1962), pp. 592–695. (Originally published in *Engineering and Science Magazine,* California Institute of Technology, April 1950.)

Discussion Question

1. If you were Simms, what action would you take to influence the U.S. Navy to improve its ordinance and gunnery doctrine?

PART 2

During the next two years, Simms wrote 13 lengthy official reports. In each report, he reiterated three major themes. The first was the increased accuracy of the British and American ships using the new method, and this was supported by reams of accumulated data. The second theme was the description of the mechanisms used and the training procedures followed to achieve greater accuracy. The third recurring theme was that the mechanisms currently used by the American navy were not designed for continuous-aim firing and needed to be changed and modified. Washington's response fell into three easily identifiable stages, and at each stage, Simms' behavior also changed.

Discussion Questions

1. What do you think will happen?
2. What are the three stages?

PART 3

The first response from Washington was "no response." The reports to the Bureau of Ordnance and the Bureau of Navigation were filed away because the claims and records of continuous-aim firing were simply not credible. Indeed, to his delight, Simms later found some of his first reports half eaten by cockroaches.

Simms despised being ignored and commented to a friend, "I want scalps or nothing and if I can't have 'em I won't play." The tone of his reports became much more strident. He also circulated copies of his reports to other officers in the navy, which meant that high officialdom had to respond. The Chief of the Bureau of Ordnance responded to Simms by rebuttal, Washington's second stage of response. The Chief rebutted by the use of "reason," i.e., the American equipment was as good as that of other Navies, the trouble had to be in the training of the gun pointers (which was the responsibility of ship's officers, *not* the Bureau of Ordnance), and the Bureau's own experiments at the Washington Navy Yard had demonstrated that it would take more than five men to produce the energy necessary to compensate for a five-degree roll in ten seconds. Therefore, Simms' reports were mathematically impossible.

The third stage was name-calling. As Simms' language became more forcible, so also did the response from Washington. Simms was labeled a crack-pot egotist and a deliberate falsifier of evidence.

Simms finally took the last resort—he wrote directly to the President, Theodore Roosevelt. Roosevelt responded positively and brought Simms back from China and gave him the job of Inspector of Target Practice in 1902, a job that Simms held as long as Roosevelt remained in office—six years. This, of course, raised a great deal of hostility and animosity against Simms within the navy.

However, one naval gunner, using the new methods in 1905, was able to score 15 hits on a target 75 X 25 feet in one minute at the 1600-yard range. Just as importantly, half of the hits were in a bull's eye 50 inches square. This was a far cry from two hits in the sails of the hulk after 25 minutes of firing.

Discussion Questions

1. What principles are involved here?
2. How can this be applied to other situations?

MR. HOLLY AND MR. MORGAN

PART 1

Frank Holly, the personnel director of Top Products, Inc., sat pondering a confidential note from Ed Patton, the general manager of a division of the company. An impending layoff would include Peppy Morgan, a 35-year employee with the company, and Holly would have to either find a place for Morgan in another division or lay him off. It was never a pleasant task to lay off a long-service employee, but this was going to be especially difficult. Anticipating that this might happen, Frank had already tried to locate a position for Peppy elsewhere in the plant, but without success. Both his high salary and "do nothing" reputation had closed many doors to Morgan.

Peppy Morgan had joined Top Products as a draftsman, and his skill and hard work had moved him rapidly upward in the drafting department. A minor disability kept him out of the military service, and during the war years he rose to the position of manager of a fifty-man design and drafting department in the company's aircraft parts plant. Although his superiors would have preferred to see someone else as manager, Morgan was the best of the choices available at the time. Following the war, Top Products rapidly converted to peacetime endeavors and had several successful years. Peppy continued in his position, received a substantial salary increase, and rose to a senior management level in the organization.

After 25 years with the organization, Morgan was moved into a special staff position and was replaced by a younger man in the drafting department. Peppy was quietly disappointed in the change, although for all appearances it looked like a promotion for him and in fact, he got a substantial raise. The next several years were difficult ones for Peppy. With each change in the organization, he usually wound up with a new title, more money, but less and less to do. Fewer people spent time with him, and he sometimes felt that if he stayed home for a week, no one would miss him. Only two things kept him from taking an early retirement. First, he wanted to get his 40-year service pin, a milestone few others had reached; and second, he wanted to pay off the mortgage before retiring.

When Frank Holly told Peppy he would have to retire early, he was initially shocked, but this soon gave way to anger and defiance. Even when he was told

This case was written by John W. Lewis, III.

that no other division had a place for him, he refused to accept being eased out, threatening to go directly to the president if Holly could not do something for him in the company. Frank knew his bluff had been called and that unless he could find a place for Morgan, he could expect a personal call from the president.

In recent months, Frank Holly had had to face a growing number of long-term employees who were no longer considered useful in their jobs. In earlier years, when business was booming, managers had not been too concerned about the problem, but the long recession had caused many younger people to be laid off, and the performance of veteran employees was being scrutinized more carefully.

Frank had a few alternatives when these cases reached his office. First, he would try to place the employee in a job opening, or even try to create an opening for the individual. Due to the tightness of operations in all divisions, however, this alternative was becoming less and less feasible. Second, he would try to talk the individual into taking an early retirement, if he was past 60, and had developed an added inducement that came to be known as "Holly's Retirement Plan." This plan provided a company-paid supplement to the worker's regular pension until he reached age 65. Holly's only other alternative was to terminate the employee and try to help him secure a job elsewhere.

PART 2

Frank knew that none of these alternatives would satisfy Peppy Morgan. Therefore, he decided to try a new approach to the problem. As far as he could tell, most of Peppy's years had been productive ones, and he hoped that there was a solution that could take advantage of the talents and experience which Peppy had in the drafting area. There were a number of hurdles in the way of such a solution, however. Morgan's salary was far above even the top drafting jobs, and this would create intolerable inequities if he were continued at such a high salary. Second, there were no openings available in these areas, and in fact several draftsmen had been laid off recently. Third, it was by no means certain that Peppy would even consider such a proposal, but Frank was counting on the fact that Peppy wanted to remain in the company until his retirement and that he would be happy to be doing something useful again.

First, Frank located a drafting manager who had been hired several years earlier by Peppy and who had a personal interest in helping solve the problem. The manager agreed that he would create an opening for Peppy as a senior drawing checker, and he was sure that Peppy was well qualified to do the job needed, if he were interested. He said, however, that he could not afford to take Peppy on at his present rate of salary, but would have to bring him in at the going rate for the checker's position.

With a job possibility now available, Frank met with the plant salary administrator to work out a plan for adjusting Peppy's salary downward. It was determined that a salary reduction of $4000 annually would have to be made in order to accomplish the job change. Together, they worked out a formula for reducing Peppy's salary to the lower level over an 18-month period by deducting approximately $50 per month at the start of each quarter. This would enable Morgan to adjust his standard of living gradually to the new level, and hopefully, would make the adjustment less painful. It was decided that the company personnel department would pay the reducing supplement so that the drafting supervisor would not have to assume the extra payroll burden. Frank felt that this arrangement would lead to a situation more conducive to a successful transition.

Finally, Holly met with Peppy to explore the proposal with him. By and large, the discussion went well until the issue of a major pay reduction was discussed. Peppy felt hurt and could not understand why his present level should be reduced. Frank reviewed what had happened to Morgan over the past several years when his pay was disproportionately high. Gradually, Peppy was able to see the positive side of going back to work again and was willing to accept the cut in pay. After discussing the plan with his wife, Peppy decided to try the new arrangement. Things worked out very well, and he developed a new interest in his work. Only when a further reduction in pay was made did Peppy feel the burden of his reduced standard of living.

THE HOWARD COMPANY

This is a role-playing case with three parts. Do not read past the introduction until your instructor has assigned you the role you are to take, and then read *only* that role.

INTRODUCTION

The Howard Company is a large conglomerate which manufactures a variety of products in about 30 plants scattered across the country. Purchasing has always been done locally by individual plants. However, the company has been steadily growing, and the president of Howard has recently employed an experienced new man as vice-president of purchasing. The president felt that closer coordination of purchasing would result in substantial savings.

After several weeks on the job, the new man, Mr. Leavitt, decided that one of the best ways to bring about substantial economy was to have all contracts or purchases of $10,000 or more coordinated and approved by company headquarters. The idea was presented to the president, who in turn got the approval of the board of directors. Mr. Leavitt then sent out a memo to the plant purchasing agents informing them that from then on they were to notify the vice-president at least a week before any contract exceeding $10,000 was signed.

During the next months almost every plant acknowledged receipt of the memo and promised to cooperate. But although the company was in the beginning of its peak buying season, Mr. Leavitt received no notices that any large contracts were being negotiated.

MR. LEAVITT, VICE-PRESIDENT OF PURCHASING

You are competent in your field, with a Ph.D. in economics, a number of publications (including two books) to your credit, and 15 years of experience in a number of different organizations. Since you have always been successful in making substantial savings in purchasing wherever you have worked, you are confident that the new policy will work at Howard, even though you expect a lot of resistance. You know that local managers are usually jealous of their rights and prerogatives and that the new policy will lessen their autonomy. In addition, although you got polite answers to your memo, you feel certain that it is being disregarded; you have received no notices of contracts or purchases in the six weeks since it went out, and the peak buying season is here.

You have decided that the best way to implement the new policy is to personally visit each of the plants and discuss the new policy and its implementation with the plant purchasing agents. After all, since the board of directors approved the policy, the purchasing agents report to you, at least indirectly, on all purchases or contracts over $10,000. By coordinating and pooling these purchases, you can realize substantial savings for the company, for you are one of the few persons in the company who sees the "big picture," and you are not going to get sidetracked with minor problems and objections. Today, you have scheduled a meeting with Mr. Jones, chief purchasing agent for the Reading plant, which makes electronic instruments for hospital use.

MR. JONES, CHIEF PURCHASING AGENT

You have an M.A. in business administration and a major in purchasing. You have been with Howard's Reading plant for five years, during which you have substantially reduced costs through improved purchasing methods. Prior to coming to Reading, you held purchasing jobs with several other companies.

You feel that the Reading plant's purchasing problems are unique; your plant builds medical electronics equipment which requires frequent engineering changes or the introduction of new products. Most of the other plants, by contrast, have more stable product lines. Your special problem, therefore, is to walk a tightrope between buying too soon (with the possibility of the parts becoming obsolete) and waiting too long for the parts lists to become more stabilized (with the risk of parts shortages caused by late delivery times). In the past five years, you have worked hard at selecting good, reliable vendors who understand your situation and are flexible enough to "give and take" with you.

When you received the memo a few weeks ago, you showed it to your boss, the plant manager, whose only comment was that "they are always trying something new at Corporate. These fads come and go. I've seen a lot of them in my time." However, you don't really feel that the memo applies to you, since a large percentage of the materials you buy are unique to your plant, although you would have no problem with such minor items as office furniture, toilet paper, and paper towels. Indeed centralizing these purchases makes a lot of sense, but to centralize the purchase of special materials would be a major disaster that would increase delays and paper work and disrupt the vendor relationships you have worked so hard to build up. Mr. Leavitt is arriving today, and you want to make these points *strongly*. You told your boss about the meeting, and he may drop in. Although he has not said so directly, you know he feels as strongly about it as you do.

MR. BROWN, GENERAL MANAGER, READING PLANT

You are the general manager of one of Howard's largest plants. Since the plant opened ten years ago, you have steadily progressed from foreman in manufacturing, through purchasing and marketing, until you took over as general manager six years ago. Since that time, you have carefully selected and developed an outstanding management team. One of your best decisions was to fire the existing chief purchasing agent and bring in Mr. Jones, who has made a major impact by reducing parts shortages, reducing material costs, and developing excellent vendor relationships. Additional "red tape" and delay in clearing through Corporate would only result in parts shortages or excessively high inventories and parts obsolescence. The other managers now reporting to you have also improved the operation. In fact, when you took over six years ago, the plant was barely breaking even, and last year, the plant's profits were the highest in the organization, and you received a company award for your accomplishment.

Your plant makes electronic instruments for hospital and similar uses and is the only one of its kind in the Howard Company. You saw the memo from Leavitt about the $10,000 limitation on purchases and were opposed to it. No plant managers were involved with the decision, and when you checked with some of them, they, too, saw it as a "power grab" by the new man. If the new policy is fully implemented, Jones will be reporting to Leavitt. This first step toward centralization could result in the loss of power and authority by all the general managers.

You have decided to attend the meeting and make your views known quickly and definitely. Leavitt's power grab needs to be stopped before it begins. After all, Howard is *not* a chain of grocery stores.

INTERNATIONAL SYSTEMS CORPORATION— AJAX PLANT

You are Robert Bedford, the new plant manager of Ajax Plant, part of the International Systems Corporation. Prior to this, you had been manager for research and development for another of International's plants in a different part of the country. You spent a week at Ajax in Central City getting acquainted with the plant and the people. Then, you had to spend a week at your old plant to finish up some business there. You arrived back in Central City late Sunday night. You came to the plant an hour early Monday morning, March 9, to catch up on your work and to review what had happened since you left.

The Ajax plant had been growing steadily under the management of Kenneth Chandler, the previous manager, who left the company for a better job. The plant now has a capital investment in excess of $24,000,000 and produces a variety of electronic and electromechanical testing and analyzing equipment for both military and civilian markets. The plant staff, excluding top management, now includes 55 engineers and 35 technicians; there are approximately 1100 production employees who work in two shifts.

The department manager in charge of production is William Silva. He has been with the company about 15 years, but has been in his current job for less than a year. The department manager in charge of marketing is Joseph Fleming, who has been in the job approximately two years. Before then, he had been a regional sales manager. His present functions include sales promotion, merchandising, market research and development, and sales. Eighty-five employees are under his supervision.

Al Mumford, the section manager in research and development, is an electronics engineer. Prior to his promotion less than a year ago, he headed up the electrical engineering subsection in the engineering department. His functions are shown on the organization chart. He had 38 engineers and 15 technicians and draftsmen working for him. Because of Chandler's strong interest in research and development, close to seven percent of the plant's profits are allocated to this function.

The finance manager is James Cardinal, who has held this job for about three years. His functions include general and cost accounting, accounts receivable and payable, payroll, and the computer unit. He has a staff of about 25 people.

Charles Gray, the employee and community relations manager, has a staff of approximately 18 people. He transferred from the corporate staff a little over six months ago.

On the following pages are some memos and other correspondence. On a separate sheet of paper, outline and briefly describe what action you would take on each item. *Everything you decide or do must be in writing.* You might write on the items themselves or make memos to yourself about things you want to do later. Draft letters, if appropriate, for your secretary to type. Outline plans or draw up the agenda of meetings you want to call. Sign papers, if necessary. Actually write out memos to your subordinates or to others or make notes of anything you plan to say to them at some future time. (Do not, however, assume what they may say to you in return.) Enter any planned interviews, confirming letters or memos, telephone calls, meeting agenda, notes to yourself or others, and whatever thoughts you may have in connection with each item on the calendar pad. *Each time you make a decision, record fully the reasons behind your actions.*

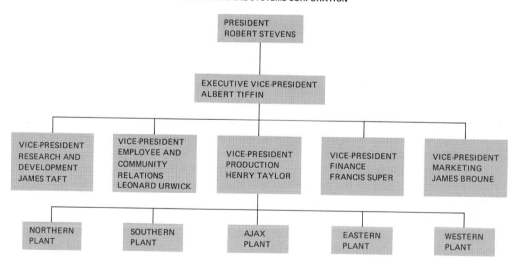

INTERNATIONAL SYSTEMS CORPORATION

PRESIDENT
ROBERT STEVENS

EXECUTIVE VICE-PRESIDENT
ALBERT TIFFIN

VICE-PRESIDENT RESEARCH AND DEVELOPMENT JAMES TAFT

VICE-PRESIDENT EMPLOYEE AND COMMUNITY RELATIONS LEONARD URWICK

VICE-PRESIDENT PRODUCTION HENRY TAYLOR

VICE-PRESIDENT FINANCE FRANCIS SUPER

VICE-PRESIDENT MARKETING JAMES BROUNE

NORTHERN PLANT

SOUTHERN PLANT

AJAX PLANT

EASTERN PLANT

WESTERN PLANT

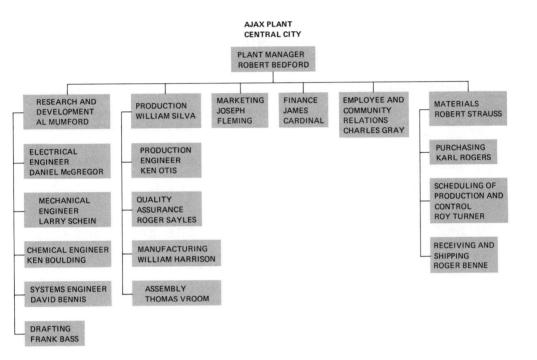

AJAX PLANT
CENTRAL CITY

PLANT MANAGER
ROBERT BEDFORD

RESEARCH AND DEVELOPMENT AL MUMFORD

PRODUCTION WILLIAM SILVA

MARKETING JOSEPH FLEMING

FINANCE JAMES CARDINAL

EMPLOYEE AND COMMUNITY RELATIONS CHARLES GRAY

MATERIALS ROBERT STRAUSS

ELECTRICAL ENGINEER DANIEL McGREGOR

PRODUCTION ENGINEER KEN OTIS

PURCHASING KARL ROGERS

MECHANICAL ENGINEER LARRY SCHEIN

QUALITY ASSURANCE ROGER SAYLES

SCHEDULING OF PRODUCTION AND CONTROL ROY TURNER

CHEMICAL ENGINEER KEN BOULDING

MANUFACTURING WILLIAM HARRISON

RECEIVING AND SHIPPING ROGER BENNE

SYSTEMS ENGINEER DAVID BENNIS

ASSEMBLY THOMAS VROOM

DRAFTING FRANK BASS

Calendar Pad—March 1969

Sunday	Monday	Tuesday	Wednesday	Thursday	Friday	Saturday
						1
2	3	4	5	6	7	8
	Out	of plant all	week			
9	10	11	12	13	14	15
16	17	18	19	20	21	22
23	24	25	26	27	28	29
30	31					

AJAX PLANT
CENTRAL CITY

OFFICE MEMORANDUM

March 6

TO: Mr. Robert Bedford, Plant Manager
FROM: Charles Gray, E. & C.R.
SUBJECT: Employment of the Disadvantaged

According to information I received at a personnel meeting last night, both the State and
Federal Equal Opportunity people will shortly be
giving a hard look at industrial plants in this
area. Currently, our ratio of disadvantaged to
white employees is extremely low, and we may be
in serious trouble.
    I would recommend that we put on a crash
program to recruit and employ at least 70 - 80
nonwhites, in all areas of the plant. I would
further recommend that we not use our normal
testing program for these new employees, since
the use of our regular intellectual and aptitude
tests can also open us to charges of discrimination. We should continue to use the tests for
our normal employment of whites.
    I realize that a crash program may involve,
for the short-run, increased training and labor
costs, but this is preferable to losing our
defense contracts or the bad publicity coming
from an investigation. Besides, I think that
this is the <u>right</u> thing to do.

```
BR   XCL    292  RQ - WVX              March 7

NY   NY                                4:30 PM
```

MR. ROBERT BEDFORD, PLANT MANAGER

MR. JOSEPH FLEMING, MARKETING MANAGER

GOOD NEWS STOP HAVE JUST LEARNED THAT ED BAKER
OF BAKER & BAKER READY TO PURCHASE LARGE NUMBER
OF MODEL 80 SYSTEMS AND RELATED ACCESSORIES STOP
CONTRACT APPEARS LIKELY IF WE CAN PROMISE EARLY
DELIVERY ON GUARANTEED BASIS STOP ADVISE ME OF
ACTION STOP

                                   JIM BROUNE

AJAX PLANT
CENTRAL CITY

OFFICE MEMORANDUM   March 5

TO: Bob Bedford
FROM: Robert Strauss
SUBJECT: Increased Materials Costs

As you know, I've been concerned for quite a
while about parts shortages, high inventory, and
the steadily increasing materials costs. This
is particularly true since more than half of our
direct costs come from purchased materials, due
to the nature of our business.
     My people are working hard to reduce costs
and establish decent manufacturing schedules,
but we can't do it by ourselves. We are
continually having to revise our production
schedules because of manufacturing problems,
particularly with the new models. As a result,
my purchasing people don't get the word early
enough on what we need to buy, and everything
needs to be on rush order and expedited. About
the time we get it into the plant, there is
another design change, and sometimes the parts
we have just rush-ordered are then obsoleted.
As a result, our materials costs are
skyrocketing.
     We need to get designs locked in so that
we can establish decent manufacturing and
purchasing schedules. For example, the Model 95
is supposed to go into manufacturing shortly,
but as yet we have been unable to get a parts
listing that we can rely on.

AJAX PLANT
CENTRAL CITY

OFFICE MEMORANDUM   March 6

TO: Plant Manager
FROM: Jim Cardinal, Finance Operation
SUBJECT: Integrated Management Information System

Two months ago, we completed and debugged our computer-based integrated management information system at a cost of $80,000. This system is aimed at providing us with much more timely and accurate information about sales figures, production and assembly scheduling, vendor order status, and the like. I have been particularly concerned with the fact that the new System would provide me with considerably better cost-accounting data.

However, the new system is not working well. Its effectiveness has been considerably reduced by the fact that many managers do not use it, but instead maintain duplicate records and do not update the computer files regularly. Further, they appear reluctant to give me the cost-accounting figures that I need and do not fully adhere to the new policies and procedures necessary to make the new system work.

Any and all assistance in this matter would be greatly appreciated.

INTERNATIONAL SYSTEMS CORPORATION
CHICAGO, ILLINOIS

INTRACOMPANY MEMORANDUM   March 4

TO: Mr. Robert Bedford
FROM: Henry Taylor, Vice-President
SUBJECT: Meeting   Production Division

I plan to come to Central City on March 25 to
meet with you now that you have had a chance to
become acquainted with the plant. In addition
to the routine general review, I would like to
take enough time for us to discuss the problem
of increasing our rate of new product introduction. We need to increase our research and
development emphasis in both personnel and
facilities, especially since the rate of product
obsolescence is being considerably affected by
our competitors. I would like to have you
prepare a special report on this subject for me.
     In addition, the latest budget reports
indicate that the plant is running well above
the projected operating expenses for both the
last quarter and the year to date. Furthermore,
does the current slight decrease in sales
constitute a signal of a downward trend? We
will want to look at this for both near- and
long-term implications.
     You may ask any members of your staff to
meet with us should you feel it is appropriate.

                              Henry Taylor

HT:hs

AJAX PLANT
CENTRAL CITY

OFFICE MEMORANDUM   March 6

TO: Bob Bedford
FROM: William Silva
SUBJECT: Model 80 retrofit

Although we had a discussion about the Model 80 last week, I thought it wise to drop you a note on the subject. It does not appear possible to make the schedule for the Model 80 retrofit and at the same time make the schedule for the new Model 80s coming out. My production engineering people are going flat out trying to make the necessary production design changes and at the same time help the production people with the retrofit program. I would recommend stopping production on both the retrofit and new production until we get the design problems cleaned up once and for all.

The mistake that I made was accepting the Model 80 for production when I knew that there were a lot of design bugs in it. I won't make that mistake again.

By the way, can you get the finance people off my back for a while? They are trying to put in the computer system. It still hasn't been fully debugged, and I'll be glad to help them out in a month or so when I've had a chance to get caught up with production problems.

AJAX PLANT
CENTRAL CITY

OFFICE MEMORANDUM   March 7

TO: Robert Bedford, Plant Manager
FROM: Joseph Fleming, Marketing Manager
SUBJECT: Slippage of the Model 95

The latest word that I have is that the Model 95
will not go into production for another month.
As you know, we have had repeated delays on
introducing this system. Originally, it was
supposed to go into production last August. Our
sales for this year were forecast on the firm
promise from R&D that the Model 95 would be ready
for production by January 1 of this year.
Apparently, the earliest date now is April 15.
     Our sales forecasts are based on the
expectation that new products will come into the
plant and go into production on specific dates.
Any further delays in the introduction of the
Model 95 will seriously reduce sales for the
year, particularly since delays on the 95 will
also affect other models in the series,
especially the 96 and 97.

AJAX PLANT
CENTRAL CITY

OFFICE MEMORANDUM   March 4

TO: Mr. Robert Bedford
FROM: Al Mumford
SUBJECT: Project Status Report

This is a brief status report with some
accompanying recommendations.
     1. Model 95. Although there have been some
slippages, the Model 95 is close to coming into
production. We have had one brief hangup due to
the failure of the system to pass the packaging
tests, but we anticipate no further difficulty,
and the project should be ready to hand over
completely to production in the next few weeks.
     2. Models 96 and 97. As you know, the
Model 96 is a simplified and less complex
version of the 95. The 97, as an ancillary
system, adds considerably to the capability of
the 95. Both are progressing and should be
ready to be put into production within the next
two months.
     3. We would like to begin design on a
completely new and original system for hospital-
laboratory analysis. What we have in mind is a
multichannel digital system which can conduct as
many as ten different blood analyses almost
simultaneously. However, we are having
difficulties, since Jim Cardinal tells us that
funds cannot be made available within the current
year.
     Recommendations:
     1. We recommend that you seriously consider
hiring some really capable people in production
engineering. We don't want to repeat the Model
80 problem again. We gave those people a good
design, and they were unable to follow it through.
     2. We recommend that you talk to Cardinal
about considerably increasing funding for the
purpose of going into the digital blood system.

THE JANITORS

Since this case is in three parts, it is recommended that you not read ahead to parts 2 and 3 until your instructor suggests that you do so.

PART 1

An instructor was serving as one of several trainers for a first-level supervisory training course. His topic was organizational psychology, and the instructors were covering such areas as labor/management relations, accounting, and safety. The instructor in question was conducting one meeting a month for a six-month program.

Early in the sessions, an overview of motivational theory was given, including the theories of Herzberg and Maslow. Incidental to this, the instructor described the basic concepts of job enrichment, explaining that this meant the "whole man on the whole job" and that the "whole job" consisted of the three basic elements: planning the job, doing the job, and reviewing the results of the work.

One of the foremen objected that the material being presented was too theoretical and raised a question that was, to him, extremely serious. He pointed out that as maintenance supervisor, motivational theory had little to do with one of his biggest problems—the janitorial work force. He felt that the janitors were at the bottom of the pay scale, could not find better jobs elsewhere, were uninterested in their jobs, and some were alcoholics. The other members of the group generally agreed that the janitorial force was not doing a good job.

Discussion Question

1. If you were the instructor, how would you deal with the situation?

PART 2

The instructor felt that this was an important issue, since the maintenance foreman was sincere in his feeling that "motivational theory" was of no use to him in working with janitors. As a result, he stopped his prepared discussion and began to deal with the janitorial problem directly.

He placed three words on the blackboard: "plan," "do," and "evaluate," the major elements of job enrichment. He then asked the maintenance foreman and the other foremen to list duties and activities associated with these three words. Some aspects of the "planning" part of the job were: establishing schedules for maintenance, selection and purchase of waxes and polishes, and determining which janitor covered which areas of the plant. During the discussion the maintenance foreman said that he was about to purchase several new floor polishing and scrubbing machines. All of these planning activities were carried out by the maintenance foreman.

Listed under the "doing" section were the normal activities of janitors—sweeping, scrubbing, waxing, and removing rubbish and refuse. The "evaluating" part of the job included such activities as routine daily checks on the cleanliness of the plant by the maintenance foreman, evaluation of the effectiveness of different soaps, waxes, and polishes, and ensuring that the cleaning schedules were maintained. In addition to these activities, the maintenance foreman also contacted vendors to determine the type of new machines he could purchase.

When the various activities had been listed, the instructor asked, "Which of these activities can be done by the janitors? For example, why do you, Mr. Foreman, determine which soaps to buy? Why not let your janitors decide? How about having the salesmen give the demonstration of the new machine to the janitors and let them decide which of the machines is best?" (In the actual situation, the wording was not quite so blunt, and the entire group of foremen got involved in the discussion about what additional areas of planning and evaluating could be given to the janitors.)

PART 3

Over the next five months, the case of the janitors was discussed, at least briefly, in every session held by the instructor. Meanwhile, the maintenance supervisor was steadily giving more responsibility to the janitors for the planning, doing, and evaluating of their work. They tested out the new machines and made the final recommendations for purchase. They experimented with different waxes to determine which wax stood up the best under normal usage. They began examining the cleaning schedule to determine how much attention should be given to each area. For example, one area which had been wetmopped daily was mopped only as needed after a visual inspection. The janitors developed their own criteria for determining plant cleanliness and began to exert peer pressure on janitors who did not meet the norms. As a result, the maintenance manager was able to report that he had a "turned on" group of janitors. Absenteeism and turnover steadily decreased.

Perhaps more importantly, other foremen began thinking about how they could apply the same principles in their own areas, especially since they could begin to see for themselves the results of the maintenance foreman's work with the janitors. There was a considerable improvement in both plant cleanliness and the janitors' attitudes.

NASA MOON SURVIVAL TASK

OBJECTIVES AND INSTRUCTIONS

Contrary to what many people believe, there is nothing inherently good or bad about groups as such. Groups (and this term is meant to include all human assemblies from committees and social clubs to project teams and departments) have certain unique properties, it is true; but from a performance standpoint, groups function as their members make them function.

The objective of this exercise is one of exploring the performance characteristics of the decision-making group—both its pitfalls and potentials—and the significance of member contributions for the quality of group production. Much is known from basic research about the conditions of effective group functioning. The present exercise attempts to incorporate these conditions in such a way that group performance may be approached in a more systematic cause-and-effect fashion, allowing the individual group member to isolate for himself those functions which either hinder or facilitate group productivity.

Instructions. As much as possible, the design of this exercise parallels the typical group decision-making situation in which an individual (1) forms his own private opinions regarding a decision issue, (2) joins with other individuals—each of whom has his own preconceptions on the issue—for purposes of discussion and decision, (3) commits himself publicly to some group position, and (4) reformulates a private individual decision which may or may not coincide fully with the group position. You will be asked to undertake the following decision steps in the order they are presented below:

1. Working alone and unaided, complete the NASA Moon Survival Task. Be sure that all items have been ranked and that your group designation has been given in the space provided.

2. When asked to do so, turn to the "Decision Process Instructions." Read these comments thoroughly; they serve as guidelines to effective group process. Adhere as closely as you can to their provisions.

3. When all have completed their individual decision and read the Decision Process Instructions, you will be asked to join with your group for purposes of reaching a group consensus on the NASA task.

The guidelines provided on remaining pages are optional; use the forms as you see fit.

DECISION PROCESS INSTRUCTIONS

Research in group dynamics has revealed that the manner in which groups utilize their member resources is a critical determinant of how they perform. In this exercise you are asked to use the technique of *group consensus.* This means that the ranking for each of the 15 survival items must be agreed upon by each member before it becomes a part of the group decision. Consensus is difficult to reach. Therefore, not every ranking will meet with everyone's complete approval. Unanimity, however, is not a goal (although it may be achieved unintentionally), and it is not necessary, for example, that every person be as satisfied as he might be if he had complete control over what the group decides.

What should be stressed is the individual's ability to accept a given ranking on the basis of logic—whatever his level of satisfaction—and his willingness to entertain such a judgment as feasible. When the point is reached at which all group members feel this way as a minimal criterion, you may assume that you have reached a consensus as it is defined here and the judgment may be entered as a group decision. This means, in effect, that a single person can block the group if he thinks it necessary; at the same time, it is assumed that this option will be employed in the best sense of reciprocity. Here are some guidelines to use in achieving consensus:

1. Avoid arguing for your own rankings. Present your position as lucidly and logically as possible, but consider seriously the reactions of the group in any subsequent presentations of the same point.

2. Avoid "win-lose" stalemates in the discussion of rankings. Discard the notion that someone must win and someone must lose in the discussion; when impasses occur, look for the next most acceptable alternative for both parties.

3. Avoid changing your mind only in order to avoid conflict and to reach agreement and harmony. Withstand pressures to yield which have no objective or logically sound foundation. Strive for enlightened flexibility; avoid outright capitulation.

4. Avoid conflict-reducing techniques such as the majority vote, averaging, bargaining, coin-flipping, and the like. Treat differences of opinion as indicative of an incomplete sharing of relevant information on someone's part and press for additional sharing, either about task or emotional data, where it seems in order.

5. View differences of opinion as both natural and helpful rather than as a hindrance in decision making. Generally, the more ideas expressed, the greater the likelihood of conflict will be; but the richer the array of resources will be as well.

6. View initial agreement as suspect. Explore the reasons underlying apparent agreements; make sure that people have arrived at similar solutions for either the same basic reasons or for complementary reasons before incorporating such solutions in the group decision.

7. Avoid subtle forms of influence and decision modification; e.g. when a dissenting member finally agrees, don't feel that he must be "rewarded" by having his own way on some later point.

8. Be willing to entertain the possibility that your group can excel at its decision task; avoid doom-saying and negative thinking.

NASA MOON SURVIVAL TASK

Background Information: Think of yourself as a member of a space crew whose mission is one of rendezvousing with a Mother Ship on the lighted surface of the moon. Due to mechanical difficulties, your ship has crashlanded some 200 miles from the rendezvous site. All equipment, with the exception of 15 items, was destroyed in the crash. Since survival depends upon reaching the Mother Ship, you and your fellow crew members must determine which among the 15 items of equipment left intact are most crucial for survival.

Instructions: The 15 items left intact after the crash are listed below. You are asked to rank these in order of their importance for insuring survival. Place the number "1" in the space by the item you feel is most critical; the number "2" by the second most important item; and so on through number "15" by the least important item.

Rank	Items
—	Box of matches
—	Food concentrate
—	50 feet of nylon rope
—	Parachute silk
—	Portable heating unit
—	Two .45 calibre pistols
—	One case dehydrated Pet milk
—	Two hundred-pound tanks of oxygen
—	Stellar map (of the moon's constellation)
—	Life raft

— Magnetic compass
— Five gallons of water
— Signal flares
— First aid kit containing injection needles
— Solar-powered FM receiver-transmitter

GROUP SUMMARY SHEET

You may find it helpful to begin your discussion by recording each member's rank order on the following chart. This will afford each of you an overview of where the group stands on the decision items.

Items	Individual Predictions												Group Prediction
	1	2	3	4	5	6	7	8	9	10	11	12	
Box of matches													
Food concentrate													
50 feet of nylon rope													
Parachute silk													
Portable heating unit													
Two .45 calibre pistols													
One case dehydrated Pet milk													
Two hundred-pound tanks of oxygen													
Stellar map (of the moon's constellation)													
Life raft													
Magnetic compass													
Five gallons of water													
Signal flares													
First aid kit containing injection needles													
Solar-powered FM receiver-transmitter													

Note: Once you have completed your group decision, you may want to complete the individual (private) ranking on the next page.

NASA MOON SURVIVAL TASK

Post-discussion Ranks

Instructions; Having now had an opportunity to hear what others think, your own thinking may have changed regarding the appropriate ranking of items. On the other hand, you may be more firmly convinced than ever of your initial position. Based on what has transpired in your group (and without referring back to your original ranking of the 15 items) re-rank the items *as you now feel they should be evaluated.*

Re-rank	Items
__	Box of matches
__	Food concentrate
__	50 feet of nylon rope
__	Parachute silk
__	Portable heating unit
__	Two .45 calibre pistols
__	One case dehydrated Pet milk
__	Two hundred-pound tanks of oxygen
__	Stellar map (of the moon's constellation)
__	Life raft
__	Magnetic compass
__	Five gallons of water
__	Signal flares
__	First aid kit containing injection needles
__	Solar-powered FM receiver-transmitter

SCORING YOUR DECISION
Group and NASA Comparisons

On the forms below you may (1) score your individual decision for accuracy by comparing it with the NASA solution, (2) compare your initial decision with that finally produced by your group, and if you made a post-discussion ranking (3) determine the effect on accuracy of group discussion by comparing pre-error scores with post-error scores, and (4) determine the amount your group influenced your thinking by comparing the pre- and post-rankings you made with that produced by your group. All these data may serve to enhance discussion of your group's performance and its impact on you and, in turn, your impact on the group.

Degree of Group Influence

A Difference (C–B)	B Pre-rank	C Group Rank	D Post-rank	E Difference (C–D)
	TOTAL		TOTAL	

Influence Score
(A–E)

Changes in Decision Quality

A Error (C–B)	B Pre-rank	C NASA rank	D Post-rank	E Error (C–D)
	TOTAL		TOTAL	

Gain-Loss Index
(A–E)

GROUP DATA SUMMARY

Sample Scoring:	NASA rank	Predicted rank	Error score
	1	3	2
	2	2	0
	3	9	6
	/	/	/
	/	/	/
	/	/	/
	/	/	/
	/	/	/
	15	10	5
			13 Total

Group Performance

	BEFORE		AFTER GROUP DISCUSSION				
Group	(a) Average resource	(b) Most accurate resource	(c) Group score	(d) Gain/Loss (a vs. c)	(e) % +/−	(f) No. ind. sup.	(g) Creativity index (b vs. c)
					%	/	
					%	/	
					%	/	
					%	/	
					%	/	
					%	/	
					%	/	
					%	/	
					%	/	
					%	/	
					%	/	
					%	/	

For an in-depth discussion of group effectiveness, see the related material prepared for this exercise: Jay Hall, *The Utilization of Group Resources*, (1970), Houston, Texas: Teleometrics, Inc.

THE NEW PRODUCT MEETING

A product manager (PM) had arranged a meeting with representatives of manufacturing and accounting in order to present certain information and to ask them questions about a new product scheduled to go into a test market in several weeks. The meeting took place in a conference room located in the product department office area. The manufacturing and accounting personnel were already present when the PM came into the room carrying a note pad and a dummy model of the package to be used for the new product.

As he walked toward the head of the table, he tossed the package dummy onto the table and said, "Here's the box." As the package was passed around from person to person, the manufacturing and accounting managers asked about its specifications. The PM answered with precise facts and figures and told how these had been determined.

One of the manufacturing representatives asked about the brand's shelf location. The PM replied that shelf location had also been decided on, adding that an alternative location had been considered, but that:

PM: If we go into that section of the store that is an area our competitors' salesmen visit every day, they will simply throw us into the back room.

The manufacturing man nodded. The group continued by discussing topics on the order in which the PM presented them: schedule, direct mail sample promotion, carton size, etc. In each of these areas the PM presented his plans and the reasons for them. There were no disagreements.

Things began going less smoothly, however, when the PM asked the manufacturing people about quality control. In asking the questions, the PM made reference to his superiors:

PM: I've been asked what we are going to do to assure the taste. This is crucial on this brand, and I've got to have something specific to say about it. How would you like to answer this?

The manufacturing representatives replied that taste was important on all brands and that they would, of course, use the same procedures that were always

---

This case was written by Dalmar Fisher.

used to assure quality. A lengthy discussion followed, during which the PM asked the manufacturing representatives to write a special quality-control procedure for the new product, a step the manufacturing managers felt was unnecessary. With minor variations, the parties repeated the following statements:

PM: I'm expected to know exactly what you are going to do on this product.

Manufacturing: But we *know* how to do quality control. What's the matter, don't you trust us? We will use the same statistical techniques on this product that we do on other products having similar ingredients.

PM: I understand that this is your responsibility, but it's our concern as well. Would it be too much to ask you to send us a note saying that the quality will be what is supposed to be?

Manufacturing: You're going to have to accept that we do the job and have faith that we're going to do the same thing that we do on the other products.

PM: It's a bigger problem on this product.

Manufacturing: Well, I wish we had a little black box that we could put the product into and it would flash a light "good" or "bad." You've got to trust us.

Finally, the PM reluctantly replied: "OK, OK, so I trust you," and changed the subject by saying, "OK, what about costs?" Another lengthy discussion resulted when the PM discovered that the cost estimates for the product were now considerably higher than those the accountants had made a few months earlier. The PM expressed a feeling that perhaps the costs had been overstated, since they seemed to be based on start-up, rather than full-scale production.

PM: Now, the way we're starting producing is not the real-world basis, is it? A lot can happen in six months—cartoning improvements, a lot of things. Can't we stay with the old numbers? See, I'm confronted with a situation where a pricing decision has already been made, so if contribution is less than we thought, I'm faced with having to raise price or reduce marketing expenditures, and I have to have an annual program on Friday on this. If people start seeing a lower contribution, I lose all we've fought for. We'll get drilled.

Accounting: If you stay with the old numbers, you'll defeat our whole structure. As we've said, right *here,* on these sheets, are the costs, and as you can see, there is a solid reason behind each of them. We are being as optimistic as we can. After all, how can you quote costs when you haven't even produced a unit of product yet?

PM: Well, that's just it. So you must be saying you're quoting the most conservative costs you can. What if we produced it at the other plant?

Accounting: Well, that would save you some money, but we can't go all the way back to the beginning on costs. You can see from these sheets how much is involved in putting these figures together.

The issue was not resolved. The PM concluded the meeting by saying that he would arrange another meeting with his superior and the controller present. The accounting managers agreed. As the participants were preparing to leave, the PM noticed his superior walking by the door. The PM went into the corridor and quickly briefed his boss on the cost problem:

PM: Look, these guys are coming in with an increase that affects the pricing structure and the marketing budget, so it's getting to be a top-management problem. They're still in there. How about coming in and letting them expose you to it?

Superior: (Frowning and taking two steps backward, away from the direction of the conference room.) What's the probability their numbers are correct?

PM: I'd say 50–50.

Superior: Now wait. Why don't you lay out the numbers on paper, and we will talk about them in the morning. Meanwhile, I'll talk to the controller and get his feel for the reliability of these numbers. See, the company has a history of coming down from these estimates. That makes them a hero. They've "saved" money.

PM: OK, I'll lay out the numbers and then see you again in the morning.

Superior:	OK. See, you have to get tough with these guys. They want to make the estimates very conservative so they will look good later.
PM:	Yeah.

DISCUSSION QUESTIONS

1. Why was agreement reached in the meeting about shelf location? Why did the cost problem remain unresolved? Was the quality control issue resolved? How and why?

2. What did the product manager expect and want from the manufacturing and accounting representatives and from his superior? What did they expect and want from him? Why do you suppose these expectations were what they were?

3. What are the requirements for effective performance in the integrator (in this case, the product manager's) role? How effectively did the product manager in this case perform as an integrator?

4. Do you agree or disagree with the superior's statement that "You have to get tough with these guys"?

NEWCASTLE COAL

PART 1

Prior to World War II, men worked the British coal mines by hand in small groups in relatively small areas. Each group consisted of two colliers (extractors) and an assistant. Frequently, several groups worked a mine seam together. These groups were very cohesive, and there was a good deal of interpersonal interaction. Each group was self-selected, that is, the men chose persons with whom they wished to work. As might be expected, the workers became good friends, and if one was injured or killed, the others generally looked after the survivors in the family.

The miners' work pace was flexible, and there was no continuous supervision. When the work became especially difficult, the coal extraction proceeded unevenly, but when conditions were better, the group could set its own production goals, which were adjusted to men's physical capacity.

Shortly after World War II, coal-extraction technology changed. Mechanical diggers and conveyors were now used but this depended on the workers being spread across a large area of the mine. The artisan and his helper who had worked within the confines of the former small-group extraction procedure were now deemed inefficient and were disbanded. Now, workers were spread across 180–200 yards. In a medium-sized longwall digging, 12–15 lengthy coal seam faces could be dug simultaneously.

Discussion Questions

1. How would you expect the work to be reorganized to include preparing the seam, getting the coal out, and removing the coal?

2. What types of problems and/or advantages would emerge from the production change?

PART 2

After the technological changes were introduced, the work was organized in 7½-hour shifts, with 40 men per work group. Ten of the workers did the cutting;

Modified from E. L. Trist and K. Bamforth, "Some Social and Psychological Consequences of the Longwall Method of Coal-Getting," *Human Relations,* 4, 1 (1951): 1-38.

ten did the extracting, or "ripping"; and approximately 20 were involved with such conveyor-belt activities as filling, moving, and breaking down and reconstructing the conveyer belt. With the new method, there were seven job categories: borer, cutter, gummer (he scooped coal out of a preliminary cut), belt breaker, (he tore down the conveyer belt and helped move it to a new location), belt builder, (he reconstructed the belt at the new site), ripper, and (belt) filler. Each person was paid according to a different standard—time, weight of coal extracted and job performance.

Four groups were involved in the coal-extraction process. The first group prepared the wall for the shot; the second group moved the conveyer belt closer to the seam to be worked on; the third group ripped out the coal; and the fourth group loaded the coal onto the conveyer belt. The four groups worked in three semiautonomous shifts. During the first shift, holes were bored so that explosives could be repositioned, a horizontal cut was made in the bottom of the seam, and a small amount of coal at the bottom of the seam was removed so that when the shot was fired, the coal seam would collapse. Finally, small supports were placed where this coal had been removed so that the wall of coal would not collapse prematurely.

The tasks of the second shift were even more highly interdependent than those on the first shift, and all depended on the success of the first-stage tasks. For example, if the holes bored during the first shift were too low in a seam, coal remained stuck to the roof, and holes that were not deep enough reduced the amount that could be got out with one shot. If the cutter "rode up" in his floor cut, there was less room for the filler to move about and extract the coal, and therefore he earned lower wages, which were based on tonnage. If coal was left from the undercutting (the gummings), then the shot blew upward, leaving the coal intact. If the supports in the undercut were not put in, the coal sagged, thus wasting the shot firing.

During the third stage, the roof of the coal seam was ripped up. If this was not done properly, the roof caved in. Once all of these things were done properly, the shots were fired, and the filling team came in and extracted the coal.

In addition to scheduling, there were other factors to consider. The fillers were highly dependent on the cutting team (a cutter and four gummers), but the cutting team did not really exist as a team, as the gummers (the least skilled and worst paid) were responsible to a deputy foreman. The cutters were responsible only for making the cut. The borers were independent, and half of the conveyer-belt workers (those who took it apart) were on one shift, whereas the other half (those who put it together in a new place) were on another shift. Rippers, on the other hand, were a well-organized, cohesive group and were most similar to the groups working by the original, hand-extraction method. The filler's task, similar to one in the hand-extraction method, was basically manual and un-mechanized. Under the mechanized situation, the filler was isolated from the other workers. Additionally, he was one of an amorphous group served by those preparing the seam. Clearly, the job of the filler depended on those in earlier shifts performing their jobs well.

The bulk of the problems occurred on the filling shift. Since problems were cumulative from shift to shift, the difficulty was compounded unless it was solved immediately. For each stoppage in a filling cycle, 200 tons of coal were lost. The deputy shot firer was responsible for keeping things moving, but because of the darkness and the extensive work area, close supervision was impossible.

The long seams produced physical problems which were difficult to solve. The ceilings frequently sagged, and the floors rose. In addition, there were such other conditions as dampness, heat, coal dust, and gas. Discontinuous seams with cracks, rolls, and faults also caused difficulties.

Discussion Questions

1. What would you expect the workers' reactions to be with the new method of coal extraction?

2. Do you see this as more or less stressful than the situation in Part 1?

3. How efficient was this new technique?

PART 3

When conditions were particularly bad, people had to work overtime, a hardship for older workers, and a situation conducive to sloppy work. Since seams with irregularities could be anticipated, the advent of poorer working conditions created anxieties which were predictable, but hard to cope with.

Workers reacted to the stressful working conditions in four fairly predict-able ways. First, shaky informal groups were formed—when one person needed help, others *might* be willing to help him. These groups were protective and likely to be quickly disbanded. Second, fillers developed a "loner" pattern, the ethic of which was "every man for himself." This led to bribing people who could give out easier assignments. Third, there was a good deal of mutual scapegoating and buckpassing. Fourth, absenteeism was much greater than it had been previously.

The new longwall method of extracting coal had lower norms of productiv-ity than before—well below the capabilities of the workers. In short, the changes did not result in greater output, even though there was a much higher capital investment per man.

Discussion Question

1. What changes would you make to solve the problems and make mechanization compatible with the needs of the workers?

PARTICIPATIVE DECISION-MAKING

Ned Wicker is the manager of the systems proposal department in the electronics division of a large company. This department was organized a year ago to improve the division's efforts to gain new systems business. The department's specific functions are: (1) to review bid specifications for new electronic systems required by aerospace users of such equipment; (2) to evaluate which bids are attractive and within the technical capability of the company; and (3) to prepare the necessary business proposals to win contracts from potential customers.

Ned had been a senior proposal analyst with another company when he was hired to set up the new department. It was his first managerial position, and he wanted to be successful from the start. He recruited and hired seven highly qualified engineers, most of whom had prior experience with customer requirements in the industry. The division manager was enthusiastic about the new group and Ned's aggressive approach to getting things launched.

Since generating technical proposals is costly and time-consuming, Wicker felt the key to success would be the careful screening and selection of bids on which proposals were to be prepared by the group. It was largely for this reason that he had developed both an elite group to work with him and a procedure for full participation by the group in the RFP selection (request for proposal) process.

The procedure was for incoming RFPs to be given a preliminary evaluation by individual analysts in the group, who gave their informal, written recommendations to Ned on Friday each week. Over the weekend, Ned would carefully review all RFPs and recommendations and arrive at his own tentative conclusions and priorities for bid-no bid decisions. Final decisions on proposals were made on Mondays at a full morning review meeting by the entire group. At these sessions Ned explained each RFP in detail, after which the group discussed it. During these discussions Ned was careful not to disclose his own tentative conclusions. After all the RFPs had been reviewed in this way, final selections for making proposals were reached by group consensus. Occasionally, Ned would find it necessary to overrule the group when he felt he had a better understanding of a particular situation. This was not done high-handedly, however, and usually the group could be led to see the wisdom in his final decision.

This case was written by John W. Lewis, III.

The RFP selection procedure seemed to work effectively for the first three or four months, and two proposals submitted by the group resulted in major new contracts for the company. During the next several months, however, the batting average started to decline. Over this period, Ned became disturbed by an apparent change in the Monday morning review meetings. Initially, discussions about the RFPs were lively and included the entire group. Frequently, the sessions ran over into the afternoon. Gradually, however, discussion became more formal, and sometimes Ned and the analyst who had done the preliminary evaluation were the only participants in the discussion. The final blow came one morning when the session lasted merely 45 minutes, and Ned had done most of the talking. Since he considered the review meeting to be the heart of the RFP selection process, Ned became alarmed. Although he still had complete confidence in the men he had selected, he felt more and more that they were holding back their ideas and technical judgment, both of which were crucial for arriving at the soundest bid-no bid decisions.

PRISONERS' DILEMMA

INSTRUCTIONS

In real life, suspects are often separated for questioning at the police station. The district attorney believes that the two suspects have committed a crime, but he does not have sufficient proof to convict either one. The usual technique is to place the suspects in different rooms. They are then told that they have two alternatives—to confess or to deny the accusation. If both hold out and neither confesses, they cannot be convicted for the major crime, but the prosecutor tells them they will be convicted of minor crimes and will receive minor punishments. If both confess, they are promised leniency. But if only one of the suspects confesses, the one who confesses will be freed because he has helped the state, whereas the other gets the maximum penalty. The prisoners' dilemma is that they may confess when they should not, or they may fail to confess when they really should.

Your instructor will give you the specifics for this exercise. In general, however, you are supposed to score as many points as you can.

Prisoners' Dilemma Worksheet
Schedule of Payoffs

Blue team
X   Y

Red team

			A	+4	+8
				+4	-8
			B	-8	-4
				+8	-4

Round	Minutes	Choices		Point cumulation	
		Red	Blue	Red	Blue
1	3				
2	3				
3	3				
4*	3-reps 3-teams				
5	3				
6	3				
7	3				
8	3				
9**	3-reps 4-team				
10**	3-reps 4-team				

*Payoff points are tripled for this round.
**Payoff points are squared for this round.

THE SELECTION DILEMMA

Since this case has two parts, you should not read ahead to Part 2 until your instructor suggests that you do so.

PART 1

A large corporation wanted to improve its selection of college graduates for a financial-management development program. Each year about 30 to 40 graduates were employed to go on a two-year training program, which consisted of two parts—a series of three-month assignments throughout the company on specific jobs, usually under relatively low-level supervisors, and classroom work, i.e., lectures, to give an overall picture of the company and the way that accounting and finance policy and procedures were carried out in the different divisions of the organization.

The company psychologist was asked to help improve the selection process. After discussion, it was agreed that all applicants would take a short test battery for verbal aptitude, numerical aptitude, abstract intelligence, and clerical speed and accuracy. It was also agreed that the tests would not be scored or used until after a year, when they would be validated against supervisors' ratings. These ratings consisted of seven-point graphic scales ranging from high to low on such variables as ambition, attitude, promotability, and job effectiveness.

At the end of the year, the tests were scored, and the results were compared with applicants who had and had not been hired. In addition, the test scores were compared to college grades and supervisory ratings. These analyses showed that the brighter students were more likely to be hired and that they tended to have had higher grades in college.

There was no such correlation, however, when the test scores were compared with the ratings of first-level supervisors. For the first three tests—verbal potential, numerical potential, and abstract intelligence—there was a clear negative relationship between test scores and supervisory ratings. In other words, the higher his test scores, the more likely the trainee was to get a lower supervisory rating. For only one test—perceptual speed and accuracy—was there a positive relationship between test score and supervisory rating.

Discussion Questions

1. What is your evaluation of the validation program?
2. How do you explain the results?

PART 2

The test results were a complete surprise to both the company psychologist and those in charge of the financial-management development program. It did not seem logical for the brighter student trainees to receive low supervisory ratings. Therefore, it was decided to interview some of the trainees and the supervisors.

These nondirective interviews brought out some interesting data. To a large degree, the older first-line accounting and finance supervisors resented the trainees and regarded them as a potential threat to their own job security and potential for advancement. The supervisors' attitudes were apparent from such comments as "These kids come in here and think that they know everything" or "They want to use some 'theory' they learned in college to change things around here."

The trainees, in turn, reacted negatively to the supervisors' hostility. "I was put on a routine, repetitive job and wasn't learning anything that I hadn't had in my first accounting course." "Every time I make a suggestion that might improve the way we do things, my boss tells me that he doesn't need help and that the way we are doing it now is just great and let's not rock the boat."

Discussion Question

1. What does this indicate about supervisory ratings as criteria? About testing for selection purposes? About training?

THE SUPERVISORS AND THE HANDBOOK

Most organizations have a special handbook which is given to new employees. On one occasion, an instructor was giving a training program for lower-level managers. He had planned to use a film, but the projector was not available when the session started. Instead, the instructor went through the employee handbook with the supervisors. In 18 different places, descriptions of policies and practices ended by referring the reader to his supervisor for additional information. The supervisors in the training group, however, were able to give additional information about only one such topic.

DISCUSSION QUESTIONS

1. What implications does this have for supervisory training? For communications between those who wrote the handbook and the supervisors?
2. What can this tell us about the organization as an overall system?
3. What does the organization expect from the handbook, and what do they see as its use?

SURVIVAL TRAINING

A bomber crew, in the last stages of their training, had generally worked well together. One of the reasons for this was that the pilot, the leader of the crew, was liked and respected both personally and professionally. Another reason was that all but one of the crew members came from the New York City area and had much in common. During off-duty hours, they sometimes went to local bars, had a few beers, and interacted well as a social group. However, one of the crew members, an enlisted man, was a social isolate. He came from the mountains of West Virginia, was unacquainted with urban life, and was prevented by his religious training from participating in such social activities as playing cards, dancing and drinking. When the crew got together socially, therefore, this man was usually absent. He spent much of his off-duty time writing letters to his girl and to his parents and reading the Bible.

As part of their training, the crew had to go on survival training, which consisted of being dropped by helicopter into a remote area of the American Rockies with a minimum of equipment and being asked to find their way back to "civilization." In this situation, the mountaineer was in his element. The weather was cold and rainy, and he was the only person who could find dry moss and bark with which to start fires. He knew how to wade in mountain streams and reach down to feel for trout with his bare hands and flip trout out onto the bank of the stream. Gradually, he became the "leader" of the group. The other crew members followed his suggestions and as a result, passed their survival test with flying colors.

DISCUSSION QUESTIONS

1. Why did the mountaineer become the "leader"?
2. What does this tell us about leadership?
3. What effect might this have on his future relations with the rest of the crew?

TECHNOLOGY-INCORPORATED

ENGINEERING MANAGER (FRANK DOWNEY)

You are the engineering manager for a small technology company which you helped John Upton, the president, build from scratch. Most years have been good ones, but several months ago sales began to dip sharply, and the picture is now grim. You have already cut departmental expenses substantially, but unless business picks up shortly, you will have to lay off Mark Bright, your youngest, but most promising, engineer.

Several weeks ago, a potential customer in Chicago expressed interest in buying some new equipment from your company. The prospect is especially attractive to you because: (1) there is substantial engineering involved in the product, and (2) gaining the business will make it possible to retain Mark, whose special talents will be needed on the project. After concluding that this could be a breakthrough for the company, you got Upton's agreement to go ahead, but he stipulated that expenses were to be kept as low as possible.

At this point, you have made three trips to the customer's plant in Chicago, two of them in the last ten days. Although progress toward a signed contract has been slower and more painful than you anticipated, you are still optimistic about getting the business. Even though so much traveling is wearing you down and is causing problems here and at home, you have planned one final trip this weekend. Hopefully, this trip will bring you a firm order.

PRESIDENT (JOHN UPTON)

With the help of Frank Downey, the engineering manager, and a few others, you have built this company from scratch. When business began to turn down sharply a few months ago, the company's picture became bleak, and you fear that the company may not survive unless new production business is brought into the plant soon. Of course, you can't share such a fear, even with Frank. To avert disaster, you have been shaving expenses to the bone in all areas.

A few months ago, Frank made an enthusiastic pitch about some possible engineering contracts from a potential customer in Chicago. Though you strongly doubt his 80/20 odds on the chances for the business, you have given him the go-ahead to pursue it further with the customer. You are not overly

This case was written by John W. Lewis, III.

excited about the project—although it will provide needed work in the engineering department, it will do little in the short term to increase production volume, which is your major problem.

After three expensive trips to Chicago (averaging $560 per trip) by Frank with little noticeable progress, your "gut" tells you that the effort to go after the business should be stopped. To do so would hurt Frank deeply, and this bothers you, but you would rather spend what little resources you have to cultivate new business in more fruitful areas. You'd like to convince him tactfully, yet forcefully, to give up the project.

YOUNG ENGINEER (MARK BRIGHT)

It is hard to believe this is the same company you joined two years ago. Then, the place was humming with work, and because it was small, you have had an unusual opportunity to take on major responsibility for engineering projects. In fact, this prospect was the deciding factor in your accepting this job over the more attractive offers of larger organizations. Now, you wonder whether it was the right move.

Your boss is trying to get a new order from some outfit in Chicago, and the engineering involved on the product is right up your alley. Frank has said that if and when the contract comes through, you will have full responsibility for the project. After the idling you've been doing lately, almost anything to do would make you feel good.

At first, it looked like a shoo-in for getting the business, but Frank has visited the customer three times already, and nothing seems to be happening. Since the technology is not Frank's specialty, you feel sure he is not using a winning approach. Now he is going out there again tomorrow, and you are convinced you should go along to make the technical pitch and that this would clinch the order. There is a lot riding on that trip for you. If that (or some other) order is not obtained soon, you will not have a job.

ENGINEERING MANAGER'S SON (CHIP DOWNEY)

You are seventeen and were just elected captain of the varsity basketball team, an achievement of which you are proud. During basketball season, your dad has been a regular fan at the games except when he had to make an occasional trip or became involved at the plant. Recently, however, things have changed. Two weeks ago, he missed the game and a half-time ceremony in your honor cooked up by the Boosters Club. No big deal, but it would have felt good to have him there. He was also out of town for last week's game, in which you scored 43 points, establishing a new varsity record at the school. This Saturday will be the toughest game of the season, and you were angered and hurt when your mom said he would have to be out of town again.

INDEXES

AUTHOR INDEX

SUBJECT INDEX